"All real living is meeting"

MARTIN BUBER

PRAISE FOR *Taking Our Places*

"Remarkably profound, moving, and far-ranging...Every word is an occasion to align yourself in the most practical of ways with what it might mean for you to be your best self and follow a path of wise action, compassion, and integrity."

—Jon Kabat-Zinn, author of *Wherever You Go, There You Are*

"This book is a beautiful expression of a deep spiritual maturity, which we come to understand as a process rather than a destination. A refreshing and inspiring new work by a teacher and practitioner whose wisdom shines brightly on every page."

—Sharon Salzberg, author of *Faith: Trusting Your Own Deepest Experience*

"This book beautifully illustrates that true maturity is more than a physical endeavor, that it is a lifetime process. Fischer's deep spiritual understanding and kind heart will inspire a new way of seeing the always mysterious and often painful transition that is called growing up."

—Noah Levine, author of *Dharma Punx*

"Crystal clear, highly readable, warm and endlessly wise, this is the work of a truly mature spiritual leader, and offers indispensable answers to the only question worth asking: What do we do with this life?"

—Rabbi Alan Lew, author of *One God Clapping*

"Thoughtful, wise, considered, beautiful. Helps you ask the questions of the heart."

—Jack Kornfield, author of *A Path With Heart*

"Zen-like in its elegant simplicity, this wonderfully wise presentation of maturity as the commitment to live 'truthfully, deeply, and beautifully' is inspirational. Norman Fischer is a poet, and his prose sings!"

—Sylvia Boorstein, author of *Pay Attention, For Goodness' Sake*

TAKING
OUR PLACES

The Buddhist Path
to Truly
Growing Up

NORMAN FISCHER

HarperOne
An Imprint of HarperCollins Publishers

HarperOne

HarperCollins books may be purchased for educational, business, or sales promotional use. For information, please e-mail the Special Markets Department at SPsales@harpercollins.com .

HarperCollins Web site: http://www.harpercollins.com

HarperCollins®, 🏠®, and HarperOne™ are trademarks of HarperCollins Publishers.

FIRST HARPERCOLLINS PAPERBACK EDITION PUBLISHED IN 2004

Designed by Jessica Shatan

Library of Congress Cataloging-in-Publication Data is available upon request.
ISBN 978–0–06–058719–2

HB 11.07.2022

This book is dedicated to
DANIEL, DANIEL, SHONN-MICHEL AND KIERAN,

TO THEIR PARENTS,

AND TO THE SAN FRANCISCO ZEN CENTER COMMUNITY

WHO PROVIDED US WITH

THE PLACE AND OCCASION TO MEET.

—ıxı—

Contents

Contents

RYOKAN'S

TEARS

Dogen, a thirteenth-century Japanese Zen master, asks, "What is it that appears?"

This is also my question. What is it that appears? Who is it who is alive, in this body, in this world?

Time is strange. We live within it, depend on it, take it for granted, yet it relentlessly passes, and our lives slip through our fingers moment by moment. Where does time come from, and where does it go? How is it that every moment we are different, we grow, we develop, we are born, we die? What are we supposed to be doing with this life?

After many years of grappling with these questions during the course of my long spiritual practice, I have come to have a feeling for their answers. We don't really know what appears, what time is, where it goes. But we are here to try to understand. And we all have our own way of understanding, and of expressing that understanding through the living of our lives.

1

Each of us has a place in this world. Taking that place, I have come to feel, is our real job as human beings. We are not generic people, we are individuals, and when we appreciate that fact completely and allow ourselves to embrace it and grow into it fully, we see that taking our unique place in this world is the one thing that gives us a sense of ultimate fulfillment.

Bantu tribesmen, it is said, sneak into the rooms of their children as they sleep and whisper in their ears, "Become what you are."

To take our place is to mature, to grow into what we are. Mostly we take maturity for granted, as if it were something that comes quite naturally and completely as our bodies grow and our minds and hearts fill up with life experience. In fact, however, few of us are truly mature individuals; few of us really occupy our places. We are merely living out a dream of maturity, a set of received notions and images that passes for adulthood. What does it really mean to grow up? How do we do the work that will nurture a truly mature heart from which can flow healing words and deeds? Each of our lives depends on our undertaking the exploration that these questions urge us toward. And the mystery is that the whole world depends on each of us to take this human journey.

Taking our places as mature individuals in this world is not work we can do alone. We need others to help us, and we need to help others. For true maturity can never exist self-contained; it is relational, for we are relational beings, co-created each moment with what we come in contact with. Because we change, because we are open to and affected by the world, maturity must involve our capacity to know and love others.

The words of the epigraph to this book, "All real living is meeting," are those of the German Jewish philosopher Martin Buber. He was making the profound observation that when we truly meet one another—beyond our defenses, beyond our preconceptions, beyond our needs and desires—and open ourselves to each other with the courage to step toward one another, then and only then can we be said to be completely alive.

Real maturity is always meeting what's in front of you in this way. Although true maturity may be rare, we are all capable of it and can recognize it when we see it. When our lives are touched by a mature person, we feel it.

The Japanese Zen monk-poet Ryokan had a teenage nephew who was given to misbehavior. The boy's mother didn't know what to do with him, so she asked her brother for help. "You are a priest and a very good person. Maybe if you talk with him it will have some effect."

Ryokan came to the house for dinner. The mother kept waiting for Ryokan to broach the subject of her son's conduct, but the old monk just sat sadly eating. The meal finished, the dishes cleared, Ryokan made to leave. The boy helped the old man on with his sandals. As he was at work with the sandal straps he felt a warm drop fall onto his head. He looked up and saw Ryokan crying silently. After that night the boy no longer misbehaved.

We are all struggling with our own maturity; none of us can claim the job is finished to satisfaction. But we feel for each other, and that feeling softens and opens us, providing more room for us to grow. Although the process of maturing is endless, and all of us are in the midst of it, we can help each other through our human feeling, which is always wiser than we are.

Some years ago I undertook a project to mentor four adolescent boys in our Zen community. The time I spent with these boys became a deep exploration for me. I had already been teaching Zen for many years and had had many fruitful and close relationships with students. Practicing Zen together had been a good method for us to grow as human beings as we worked to understand and preserve an ancient religious tradition. But as I reflected on my Zen teaching in the light of the mentoring relationship I was undertaking with these four boys, a deeper sense of spiritual practice began to appear to me.

Spiritual practice, I gradually came to feel, is in essence the practice of maturity. The spiritual path leads us to the places we are meant to occupy in this world. Robes, chanting, ceremony, meditation, text study, and all the rest may be valuable in their own right, but their real purpose lies in the service of the path toward maturity. In spiritual practice we use these traditional techniques and practices as vehicles to warmly connect us so that we can help each other to find the true, lasting, and ongoing maturity that each of our lives requires.

Since I have come to feel this way about the spiritual path, I find my view corroborated everywhere in the religious literature I study. Truly growing up and into the fullness of our humanity is the great underlying theme of all religious teaching.

Buddhism, along with many other religious traditions, speaks of the possibility of a lasting and truly satisfying happiness that can endure even when times are tough. Such happiness can't come from possessions or accomplishments, for these are transitory and will not suffice at the end of the day when life's questions and contingencies loom large. In the end, secure happiness comes only with the solid feeling we have when we know that we have become the person we were meant to be in this lifetime—that we have matured and used the life we have been given in the best way we could.

When I think about the world of the future, with so many difficult choices ahead, I know that only mature people will be able to deal with what arises. I am heartened by the many people I know—young and old alike—who are concerned with their own maturity and willing to work toward it with full courage and energy. The development of human maturity does take much work and effort. But I am sure we are all capable of doing the work and enjoying its fruits. Maturity can't be hurried or produced on schedule. Growth takes time. We have to steep ourselves for a while, like a good cup of tea. We need to go through what's necessary for us to endure. We need time and commitment. Probably we also need some luck. But most of all we need encouragement and vision and mentors, grownups in our lives who can help.

Our particular lineage of Zen, founded by Shunryu Suzuki Roshi, puts little emphasis on enlightenment. It's not that we are unconcerned about enlightenment or that we are opposed to it. Enlightenment is certainly important. Personally seeing the truth of the teachings, breaking through the habit of self-centeredness, opening out to something much wider, and having some clarity and flexibility—all of this is crucial. But just as important, or more important, as a sign of readiness to teach Zen is a person's simple human maturity. Maybe someone is not very enlightened, or not enlightened at all. But if he or she is mature, it is good enough, for as Suzuki Roshi taught us, it is the ongoing practice, carried out with balance, faith, perseverance, kindness, and willingness to reach out to others, that is the most important thing. To practice like this takes a quiet and stable maturity.

It is humbling to realize what an immense job it is to truly accept the task of being human. There is so much room for growth and improvement, and the journey is endless. When you consider the lives of exemplary human beings—those who, like Jesus or Buddha, gave themselves totally to their paths—you begin to get a feeling for the depth and breadth that is not only possible but called for in each of us. It's a challenge, maybe even an impossible challenge, but one that all of us have to undertake, for our humanness demands it of us and won't let us settle for less.

Really growing up, becoming truly yourself—this takes openness and receptivity, inspiration, a loving heart, stability and persistence, trust in the world and in yourself. It takes a peaceful mind, but also an active, decisive, and courageous mind. It takes knowing how to live, knowing how to choose, and knowing how to share those choices with others.

What I have to say about all of this comes from my practice and experience through the years, but it is certainly not the last word. There is no last word. Maturity must be contemplated by each of us thoughtfully, and through action, as our lives unfold.

One

MEETING

I THINK MOST OF US ARE TERRIFIED BY THE IDEA OF GROWING up—or would be if we ever considered the idea seriously. Mostly we don't. We usually take maturity for granted, as one of life's givens. You reach a certain age, you get out of school, you get a job, maybe you marry or settle down, maybe not, but time goes by and you're a grown-up. You get a diploma, a credit card, a job, a car, a house or apartment. After you acquire these emblematic prizes, each of which feels like a milestone, you are there. You are an adult. What more is there to it than that? We think growing up, becoming a mature human being, is natural, almost biological, something we all do automatically simply by virtue of the passage of years and the natural course of things. Life happens to us and we go along with it, and there we are, grown up, developed, wise people.

But like so many other commonplace notions that people in the past did not particularly feel a need to examine (like getting married and having children, choosing a profession and staying with it your whole life), what it means to be a grown-up is something that we today, for better or worse, are being forced to take a fresh look at as the confusion and dissatisfaction of our culture and of our personal lives becomes ever more apparent.

And when we do contemplate the question of what it really means to be an adult, fear sets in. We recognize that despite our social position or accomplishments, despite our relationships, our education, and our psychological astuteness, we really don't know what we are doing with our lives. Where is our life going? What is the purpose for which we were born, the fulfillment we deeply seek? We look like grown-ups, we talk like grown-ups, maybe we have grown-up bank accounts and grown-up responsibilities—but do we really have any idea what we are about?

And if, after much struggle, we think we know the answers to such questions, we are forced to ask another, more agonizing question: Are we living those answers? Or do our lives, in the light of those answers, seem like afterthoughts, like still unformed story lines?

Questions like these about the real meaning of growing up were on the minds of four couples in our Zen community. They all had sons about the same age, from eleven to thirteen, and they were concerned about the rocky transition into young adulthood the boys would soon be facing as they entered their teenage years and began to move through high school. So the parents began a series of conversations. They started by discussing their own adolescence, which had been rough for all of them. Thirty years ago society was slower and saner, they reflected. There were neighborhoods and churches that more or less worked, or were only just starting not to work. Today, despite school, despite sports, despite a myriad of activities for young people, society lacks the social supports of the past, and so, these parents observed, it is tougher to be an adolescent now than it was then. In a culture that is rushed and fragmented, the influence of movies, music, television, computer games, the online culture, and shopping, becomes pervasive and unchallenged. Home life, with everyone so busy and stressed, can be a struggle. How can young people keep their balance, they wondered, with no role models, and with public morality so ambiguous?

They concluded after many discussions that their sons needed an adult in their lives who could help them work out what it means to be getting ready to grow up. This adult needed to be someone who represented the possibility of growing up in a graceful and meaningful way, and had to be willing to relate to them over time. They felt confident as parents, and they were good parents. But they saw that at this crucial moment in their sons' lives their parenting would not be enough.

These parents asked to meet with me, to explain all this and make their intentions clear. They wanted me to take on the job of mentoring their sons.

It was a compelling request. I had taught high school English a few years before and loved the work, the engagement with the students, but I had had to give it up when I was elected co-abbot of the Zen Center. Here was a chance to get involved with young people again.

But more than this, I had thought deeply and critically about the Zen practice that I had been doing for so many years, particularly about the Zen enlightenment stories. Once I got beyond the intriguing foreignness of the Chinese literary style, I realized with some astonishment that most of the stories turn on the warm relationship between master and disciple. They are less about solitary visionary experience than the saving possibility of human relationship. Yes, in Zen we sit long hours on the meditation cushion. But Zen practice is communal, not solitary. Enlightenment is the fruit not of isolation but of connection. Zen is the practice of compassionate and warmhearted relationship. The parents were asking me to share this practice with their sons, to test its limits.

I thought it over for a week or so. Was there a way I could engage with these four boys, using the question of what it means to grow up as the foundation for a relationship in which we might discover something together?

Of course I said yes. But three important conditions seemed necessary if we were to succeed. First, it was important that the boys choose for themselves to commit to the group. Although the parents were enthusiastic, it wasn't their enthusiasm that mattered. It was reasonable for them to require their sons to attend two or three exploratory meetings. But no ongoing group could be formed unless the boys themselves genuinely wanted it.

Second, the boys would have to have ownership and creative control of the group—not me, and not the parents. I would give the best guidance I could, but if the effort was really about fostering genuine maturity, then we would have to trust that the boys were capable of maturity and would grow into it as the group went on. I knew that virtually all of the activities that young people participate in are set up by adults for the good of the young and I felt that this group should be different.

Finally, the group would have a rule of confidentiality. The boys needed to know that they could think and say what they were really feeling without any fear that I'd communicate it to their parents or that the boys themselves would tell other friends. (For this book I have changed the boys' names and the details of their stories.)

With these conditions agreed to, we were ready to begin. We got started one spring afternoon in my austere office at the Zen Center. There was a Buddha on the altar, Japanese scrolls on the walls, and no chairs. We sat on meditation cushions on the spotless tatami floor. Very quietly.

The boys were nervous. They seemed not to know what to expect or how to behave. Sam seemed especially bewildered. The youngest in the group, he had a round, soft face and body and still looked very much like a child. Sam was shy even in the easiest of circumstances, but in such unfamiliar and intimidating surroundings, he was nearly paralyzed. James, the next oldest boy, tried to look confident, but he was at a loss in this situation, where the social cues that he had come to be very sensitive to in school were not obvious. Rashid, much taller than the other two and a year older, kept glancing around the room, flipping a shock of dyed red hair back from his eyes and shifting around on his seat as if there were ants on it. I don't think the situation made him nervous, though—he was always that way, a little oblivious, constantly in motion. Tony was the oldest member of the group. At thirteen, he already looked like a teenager, and like a teenager, he sat sullen on his cushion, his face smothered in a black look. The four boys had known each other a long time. Tony and Rashid were close friends. Sam and James lived in the same building, although they didn't hang out together much. Although three of the boys had known me all their lives—James had moved to San Francisco only a few years before—none of them had ever really said more than a few words to me.

Tony began the conversation—not in the most helpful way. "I'm only here because my parents made me, but I don't see the point," he began, somewhat testily. "I am way too busy, and it's too far to come. There's traffic this time of day. Besides, if you want to know what I think, I think it's stupid. My parents are always coming up with stuff like this. Especially my mother. She doesn't seem to know how to leave well enough alone."

I had to admire his nerve. And his honesty. Better that than polite acquiescence.

The effect of Tony's words on the other boys was unclear. I couldn't tell whether they disagreed, or agreed but were too polite to say or even nod their heads in assent. So I asked them. One by one they all echoed Tony: they all had busy schedules and were only here because their parents had made them come. They didn't get what this was supposed to be about.

If there was one thing I had learned as a high school teacher it was to give up all preconceptions about any young person's response in a given situation. You never know what that response is going to be, or whether the response you seem to be hearing is actually the response that is meant. And then a day later it might be something else anyway. So I took in what they said without dismay or disappointment. I could understand how they felt, I told them. I was busy, too. As to the point—what we were supposed to be doing together—that was for us to figure out. The question was: What does it mean to grow up? Is that an interesting question, an important question?

It was hard to tell. The boys were indulging in the most common form of adolescent male communication: noncommunication. Then Sam said, pointing to the statue on the altar, "What kind of a Buddha is that?"

Before I could respond, Rashid burst out laughing, nearly falling off his cushion, as though what Sam had just said were the stupidest thing in the world. James laughed explosively, too, and Tony started in with loud exaggerated guffaws. Sam turned bright red and looked as if he were about to cry.

Then, oddly, the laughter died as suddenly as it had begun,

as if in midlaugh they had all simultaneously thought of something deadly serious. The room was perfectly silent for a minute or two.

"That's the Buddha of listening," I said. "It's also the Buddha of kindness."

More silence. I could hear the boys breathing, their faces relaxing, losing their I-am-almost-a-teenager persona, settling into a childlike vulnerability. I felt very tenderly toward them at that moment. Somehow the sudden laughter that had torn a hole in our conversation, and the silence that followed it, had made the air seem thicker. Time seemed to pass more slowly, and the boys seemed different from the way they were when they'd first come in. They were softer, less guarded.

"If we did do this thing," Sam finally said after a very long pause, "what would we actually do?"

Well, I didn't really know. And that was the point—as of that moment, none of us did. There was no program, no plan. We would have to discover it. We would have to try to be like that Buddha—listening to each other, being kind, trying to figure out together what to do. That would probably take a few meetings. Then once we had an idea of what could be done, we could see whether we actually wanted to commit to doing it.

The boys considered this for a moment. My vagueness seemed to throw them off. They weren't used to an adult without a plan. Because their parents were coming on pretty strong about this group, they said, they would be willing to meet a few more times, to see what developed. But they were making no long-term promises.

"The point of all this," I went on, "is to try to explore, to try to understand, what it means to be a grown-up. You might think that I know, or someone else knows, or that it is obvious, but it is not obvious. It's something I hope we can discover. I am not talking about the received notions of adulthood, the magazine or TV ideas of it, or your parents' ideas of it. What do *we*, what do *you*, actually think about it? Have you ever really thought about it before? How would you define growing up? And how does it come about? Just by time going by? What's the difference between being a grown-up and being a child? Are all the adults you know really grown-ups? If not, how can you tell those who are from those who aren't? Is growing up automatic? If not, how do you go about it?

"Do you want to grow up? How will it change you? What will you get out of it and what will you give up? How do you feel about these questions? Are they serious questions? Are you ready for them? Are they questions worth spending time on? Could you take them seriously, not just fool around with them, but somehow engage them with all your heart?"

As the boys sat on their cushions in the quiet room considering all this, I could feel their ambivalence and confusion. They were becoming excited, interested in what I was saying. It awakened something in them to hear all this and to begin to think about it. These questions seemed to be so important and so timely, yet the boys hadn't ever considered them before. But as much as they were enthusiastic about addressing these questions, they also hung back. They seemed gripped by the kind of dread you feel when something you have anticipated or hoped for without thinking about it much is finally, suddenly, about to come to pass.

Like everyone at this age, these four boys had undoubtedly contemplated, each in his own vague and private way, the thought of growing up, but never as though it were something real that would actually take place. And soon. Beginning to seriously explore their thoughts and feelings about it was both exhilarating and terrifying.

14

Two

MATURITY

ONE OF MY EARLIEST MEMORIES IS OF LISTENING TO AN OLD 45rpm record of Bible stories when I was three or four years old. The record terrified and thrilled me, especially in those climactic moments when God entered the story as a resonant, booming, authoritative male voice. At those moments I'd run to a safe hiding place beneath the dining room table. Despite my terror, I loved the God parts of the record and would play them again and again.

I lived in a small town in northeastern Pennsylvania, on the Susquehanna River, with my parents, my grandparents, and my brother. Our family life was ordinary, quiet, stable, and uneventful, except for my grandfather, who was miserably ill and quite vocal about his pain and frustration. Only this experience of God's voice on the record (magnified by the darkness and wonder of a child's imagination) tipped me off to the fact that there were things in this universe that were more compelling and more mysterious than I knew of.

We lived on Main Street in an apartment over my grandparents' tailor shop, far from where other children lived, so I didn't play much with friends. I was a brooding child, full of questions about life and death and given to vague, dark feelings. My main companion was my grandmother, a tiny woman with a peasant build who had been born in an indefinite place in Europe she referred to only as "the old country." She had come to America as a child, was married by arrangement, learned her husband's trade, and eventually ran the business while raising four girls and caring for my ailing grandfather until he died, when I was seven. Spunky and full of humor (she knew the words to hundreds of dance hall songs, which she sang in a variety of ethnic accents), she was a good friend for me. We had long conversations almost every day. Often she would bring up her own death, which she felt would be coming soon, although her health was perfect. "Soon I will be pushing up daisies, you'll see," she would say, and then chuckle. Although it was forbidden (either by the doctor's orders or by the social customs she'd grown up with), she smoked cigarettes—"on the sly," as she put it—and her smoking as we talked together in her room created a conspiratorial air.

When I was in grade school, the musical version of *Peter Pan* appeared on television. The story presents two clearly opposed worlds: Peter's world is full of adventure, danger, drama, and conflict, and the grown-up world (exemplified by Wendy's parents, benign but shadowy figures to whom Wendy eventually returns at the end of the story) is safe but boring, reassuring but banal. I was impressed with Peter's powerful vow in the striking musical number "I Won't Grow Up." Somehow this anthem struck a chord with me, resonating perfectly with the sense that I was beginning to develop, as I watched the grown-ups around me, that adulthood was a distinctly disappointing proposition. Although you might gain power in achieving it, you lost imagination and nerve—not a very good trade-off it seemed to me. I felt instinctively the huge gap between adult and childhood life, and I was loyal to the latter, especially since, as in the story of Peter Pan, the adults always won out in the end.

A romantic, I loved lost causes. Peter's vow became mine, and I repeated it to myself frequently. *I won't grow up. I won't change. I will never abandon the feelings and thoughts that I have now.* Of course I soon forgot about this vow, but later on, during the turmoil of my adolescence, I remembered the vow, and it seemed more compelling and more serious then than ever before.

Some might well argue that this impossible vow not to grow up is a pathetic cry of fear and avoidance. I suppose this is possible, but that wasn't what it felt like. To me, the vow to never grow up was a commitment to a quest for truth and courage in living. I was determined not to let practical considerations deter me from this quest.

Conscious of my own budding personhood—what I came to feel was the challenge, the problem, of being myself—I began to develop a critical eye toward the world. I looked at my parents, at their friends, at my relatives, and found them all seriously lacking. I began to feel that none of the adults I knew had any interest in what naturally interested me: excitement, growth, development. They seemed to have given up on life's dynamic challenges long ago, and were now just trying to survive, raise their families, earn a living, get by. Their bearing and conduct seemed to express timidity and reluctance, a fearfulness about life. They seemed resigned rather than engaged, and safety seemed to be their crucial and overriding concern.

Although I now participate in and have a great respect for the Jewish tradition in which I was raised, at the time it never occurred to me that religion had any answers for me. Judaism, as I saw it then, was just something Jewish people did as a matter of course. If anything, it seemed only to contribute to the dullness of the adult world.

I went away to college and found the world outside my small town to be exotic, full of ideas I knew nothing about. I was soon devouring books on literature, religion, and philosophy and gravitating toward people whom I could discuss them with. Reading the existentialist philosophers, who were popular then, led me to a book on Zen by the Japanese scholar D. T. Suzuki, who had recently made such a big impact when he taught at Columbia University. Suzuki's book confirmed for me that, yes, just as I was beginning to feel, the world was indeed a wreck, and the people in it fundamentally confused. No one, not even God, was going to fix it. The optimistic American worldview that I had grown up with was definitely naive. Things were not getting better, they were getting worse, and not only did no one know what to do about it, very few even recognized what was happening! And now we had nuclear weapons in our hands, and we were locked in a conflict to the death with the Soviet Union. It seemed we were headed for certain disaster.

On the other hand, we didn't have to succumb to despair. Instead, Suzuki's Zen message seemed to offer a radically new vision of existence, an opening beyond logic and expectation. The world might look rootless and out of control, but the fault was in our own eye, not in the world, his words implied. If only we could see the world as it truly was, if we could open the inner eye, we'd see that beyond our confusion and the world's suffering was a deeper acceptance and perfection, a profound and dynamic peacefulness even in the midst of trouble that made energetic and imaginative engagement with the world possible. This was Zen enlightenment, a sudden and transformative opening to the truth.

I was an instant convert. Enlightenment was surely the answer to this impossible situation. I assumed, as Suzuki's books seemed to imply, that once I was enlightened everything would be clear and simple. I would be cured. I would find a way to live in the world happily and effectively. Little did I suspect that enlightenment would be the challenge of each and every moment of my life and that I was embarking, without knowing what I was doing, on the path of Zen practice, an everyday affair that I would be engaged in meticulously and with heart for a lifetime.

In Mahayana Buddhism, of which Zen is a school, the ideal practitioner is called a *bodhisattva*, literally an "awakening" or "enlightening" being. A bodhisattva is a Buddha in process, someone who is eagerly working on enlightenment, practicing acts of goodness and devotion, studying the teachings, and always aspiring to fully develop all good qualities. The bodhisattva path includes the diligent practice of six virtues: generosity, ethical conduct, enthusiastic energy, patient endurance, meditation, and transcendent wisdom.

But the defining characteristic of bodhisattvas is altruism. Bodhisattvas are awakening beings not only because they themselves are aiming toward awakening, but because their aim is to awaken other beings. This compassionate wish is their primary motivation, and forming, developing, nurturing, and strengthening this wish until it takes on the force of a vow is the essence of a bodhisattva's path.

Bodhisattvas understand the hidden secret of awakening: there can be no self-awakening without the awakening of others. The practice of the Way and the realization of its truth can be accomplished only with the help of others, through helping others. It is only by aiding others with a warm hand

and a warm heart that the bodhisattvas can accomplish their own spiritual work. So the word *bodhisattva* always implies compassion and altruism. Bodhisattvas can't be self-centered. Always concerned for others, they try to help bring others further along on the path.

I have always been struck by the language the sutras use to describe bodhisattvic altruistic activity: the bodhisattva *matures beings*, the sutras say. The work of the bodhisattva is, in other words, to become mature and in doing so to work for the maturity of others.

In doing this work, bodhisattvas must be supremely practical. They must understand the infinite variety of human circumstances and how to harmonize with and master those circumstances for the sake of maturing others. This is called the "skillful means" of the bodhisattvas. If someone needs house repairs, the bodhisattva appears as a carpenter; if someone has a clogged toilet, the bodhisattva appears as a plumber; if someone is sick, the bodhisattva appears as a doctor or as medicine. If a person is hungry, the bodhisattva provides food. If a person is cold, the bodhisattva brings a blanket, a fire, or a space heater.

Studying the implications of these teachings over the years, I came to appreciate that there is a way of becoming truly mature—spiritually, psychologically, and emotionally—without closing down, without resignation, without a loss of delight, and without ever giving up devotion to the pursuit of truth. In fact, I came to feel that the pursuit of truth with rigor, determination, courage, commitment, discipline, joy, and kindness must be what real maturity is all about. How could it be otherwise? And I saw that the maturity of the bodhisattva isn't opposed to a practical everyday life. In fact, such maturity requires a practical everyday life—one lived with energy, kindness, and responsibility—as the training ground for developing the skillful means necessary to complete the endless task of enlightening all beings.

And this is how I eventually came to see that, paradoxically, my vow never to grow up and my vow as a Zen practitioner to become mature myself and to work to mature others were quite compatible. In fact, in true Zen dialectical fashion, these two vows were necessary mirrors for each other. *Not to grow up,* not to drop the endless search for truth because it is too difficult or too risky or too impractical or too costly, really meant *to grow up,* to become a person capable of true responsibility and real love because true responsibility and real love depend on a constant involvement with the truth.

Still in my twenties, I married and had children. At first I found being a husband and a father quite difficult, but soon I saw that the daily challenges of loving someone and backing up that love with loving conduct were worthy of my truth-seeking spirit. Like most of us, I had to work at this. I was shocked, as new fathers usually are, to discover how demanding it is to care for a child, and how much cooperation it requires. Resting comfortably at the end of the day while my wife had everything under control was not in the cards. She was more tired than I was and needed my help as soon as I came home from work. This relentless activity took some getting used to for both of us and produced a certain amount of panic and resentment in me, but it got easier once I decided to see the responsibilities of daily life as a challenge to my bodhisattva practice (I could work on developing enthusiastic energy and patience) rather than as an unmitigated burden. My skillful means was to use the time walking from my car up the steps to our apartment as meditation time, time to refresh myself and get ready to help. I never really mastered this, but it was my daily effort, and as time went on I got better at it.

Thinking about Martin Buber's wonderful statement that "all real living is meeting," we can appreciate that life is nothing but a series of encounters, and that we are always provided, whether we know it or not and whether we like it or not, with a clear choice: Do I move into this moment of meeting, or do I shrink away from it because it may require too much of me? Responsibility is a cornerstone of maturity, but it need not appear as a heavy weight. For a bodhisattva, responsibility appears as a willingness to move into what occurs with full attention, to move into each person, each event, each moment, good or bad, like it or not, and to take on each encounter as a challenge. Recognizing this (with much help from my Zen teachers and my wife and sons), I began to grow up.

It's important to note that the sort of growing up that was beginning to take place in my life at that time, and that I wanted to share later with the four boys in our mentoring group, goes against the grain of our culture. For bodhisattvas, maturity is waking up to what's real even if it doesn't meet our desires and expectations. But America isn't about waking up; on the contrary, it has always been a place for dreaming. We say so pretty clearly when we say that we believe in the American dream. We speak of this dream positively, and politicians run for office on the strength of it.

From our beginnings as a nation, the dream has been central. The earliest settlers, devoted readers of the Bible, saw the New World as the promised land. Their faith was that America was the new Jerusalem, a fresh start, God's country, a place where things that had been impossible elsewhere would become possible. This founding sense of America's supernatural promise became legendary: generations of immigrants saw America as a place of boundless opportunity, a land where there was always room, where wealth, success, and fame could be achieved at any time regardless of who you were or where you came from, where if you failed you could always try again until you succeeded. You could depart from another country where there was suffering and difficulty (as my grandparents had done), arrive here, and escape all the misery of the old country, simply leave it behind forever. The "old country" would become the past, something hardly worth thinking about anymore. (The American dream was not available to those peoples who did not come here seeking it: African Americans, who were forcibly brought here, and Native Americans, who were forcibly displaced. The experience of these peoples has always provided a sobering dose of reality that stands in sharp counterpoint to the dream.)

We live in a child's fairy tale when we deny difficulty and fantasize that trouble will simply dissolve behind us when we leave it and believe that from now on things will always—*should* always—work out just fine. With such a vision, we suffer deeply when things go wrong. Adversity is unthinkable, unacceptable. Should it come, it must be our fault, our personal failing, and we don't want to admit this. It's too painful to fail when everyone else is succeeding so brilliantly (or so we are told). Instead, we pretend that everything is fine, everything is only getting better, this temporary setback is no problem at all, we'll have things right in no time.

Denying difficulty, we never learn that difficulty can be creative and fruitful. This national habit of denial of difficulty does not foster a climate in which maturity can grow. It encourages us all to be children for our whole lives, to be self-deceitful and surface-oriented, skimming along on the slick bubble of the dream, which is terribly fragile exactly because it leaves out the realistic acceptance of life's often drastic actualities. It is no wonder that there is so much suffering in our culture, despite our wealth and power. So many of us seem not to know how to face life as it really is. And therefore we find it very difficult to grow up.

That's the downside of the American dream, and it is a very serious one. But the American dream is also wonderful. The dream keeps us innocent, flexible, and energetic, qualities that have produced our immense national success. Because of the dream, we believe that freedom, democracy, and fair-mindedness are always possible, and we are willing to sacrifice to protect them. Because of the dream, we are inspired by wild and immense spaces untouched by human hands, and we want to preserve such spaces—our forests, mountains, and skies. This hopeful, energetic, almost naive American spirit provides a wonderful basis for a marvelous and open sort of maturity, which is the potential we have. But we haven't realized it yet.

I suppose that most of us think of maturity as simply a matter of timing. Seeds grow into seedlings, seedlings into plants, and plants bear fruit. All living things develop naturally, and people do, too, coming to a stage of possibility, competence, or ripeness when they are ready to. Of course we grow up. Time passes, the body changes, the mind changes, the emotions change. We become adults.

But this natural maturity, though basic and important, doesn't really make us grown-ups. It is only a beginning, a necessary foundation. Beyond this there must also be emotional maturity, spiritual maturity, and maturity of character. This deeper sort of maturity doesn't come naturally. Many of us never develop it, for it takes a particular kind of thoughtfulness and care beyond what is natural and socially established as a minimal standard for adulthood.

This deeper and more subtle growth requires a fuller vision of maturity, a firm and clear commitment to move toward that vision, and a context and a vehicle for getting there. Here was where the boys and I had work to do, if we could figure out how to do it. We had to find a way to discover and evoke this deeper sense of maturity so that it could become real to us. It couldn't be something that I was presumed to have in me and could therefore pass on to them, like liquid that can be poured from one bottle into another. I could make speeches at them if I wanted to, but what good would that do? They had heard enough speeches in their lives already. And what good would it do me to repeat to them things I thought I knew about life? No, mutual discovery was the only pathway, for them and for me. We would have to enter exploratory ground together, traveling fresh, without assuming anything. The vital question, for me as much as for them, became: What is true maturity, anyway?

It's a good question, one that needs to be pondered for a long time. There are answers to life's most important questions, but they are never final; they change as we change. Maybe true maturity is finding a way of keeping such questions alive throughout our lifetime. For when there are no more questions, we stop maturing and begin merely to age.

To explore this question of maturity, the boys and I thought of people we knew who we felt were truly grown up, and tried to discover what it was about those people that made them seem grown up to us. Out of these discussions we began to develop a working list of qualities that we felt were present in most people whose emotional and spiritual lives were deeply mature. Most of these people, we found, seemed to be responsible without being boring, experienced without being closed-minded, self-accepting without being shut off to change and improvement, loving without being corny, stable without being inert, and strong without being brittle. We discussed all of these qualities at length, being as concrete and personal as possible. Out of our conversations came, eventually, a rough list of qualities that we felt marked a mature person—qualities we felt we wanted to study and point toward in our efforts to truly become grown-ups. The first of these qualities was responsibility.

When the topic of responsibility comes up, I find myself suddenly seized with an attack of scruples and am inspired to speak in a deep, archetypal, stentorian voice (like the voice of God on those childhood records) that trails off into vague distances. I suppose this is how most of us view the notion of responsibility—as the opposite of creativity, spontaneity, and growth. No wonder we resist growing up, and no wonder we become boring when it finally seems we must admit that we are adults and had better start acting like it.

But responsibility doesn't have to be like that. In its truest and most literal sense, responsibility is simply the capacity to respond. Being responsible is an inherently lively quality. It is the capacity to react completely and freely to conditions. Being responsible has nothing to do with control and conformity. Quite the contrary, responsibility is the willingness to confront nakedly and clearly what's in front of you on its own terms and to be called forth fresh by what occurs. The Greek root of the word *response* means to offer, to pledge. To be responsible is to offer yourself to what happens to you, to pledge yourself to your life.

Being responsible in this sense isn't easy. Because it is so active and creative, responsibility is the enemy of all forms of laziness. It requires discovery and self-transcendence. To respond with authenticity, to really be present with what your life is, you have to let go of self-concern and preconception as much as possible and be true to your situation. You must have the courage to let yourself be overcome by what happens to you.

This reminds me of the story of one of our Zen Center priests, who arrived at the center in an odd way. Riding his motorcycle in the mountains one day and coming across a dirt road, he decided to see where it led. The road ended up at our monastery, Tassajara, which was just then opening. The young man came in to look around and was so intrigued by what he saw that he decided to stay for a few days, which became a few months, and then a few years. Eventually he ordained, studied traditional carpentry in Japan, and came back to America to help build the Zen Center's finest temple buildings. He had driven down a mountain road only to see what was there, but because he was willing to respond fully to what he encountered and give himself to it completely, his life turned into a life of benefit.

A mature person is someone who is willing to hear the call, no matter how faint or unexpected it may be, and respond. It is not necessary, however, to look around for things to be responsible for if nothing appears. But when something does appear, you are ready to respond with all of your attention and loving care, and with no excuses, no avoidance, no fanfare. You just roll up your sleeves and do it.

In his well-known text *Instructions to the Head Cook*, the Japanese Zen master Dogen recounts the story of a seminal encounter he had with an old Chinese monk who was serving his monastery as head cook. Although Dogen wanted the old monk to stay with him and engage in conversation about religious matters, the old man said he could not. Since he was head cook, it was his duty to go out in the hot sun to dry mushrooms, a job that had to be done immediately so that the mushrooms would be ready for the evening meal. When Dogen implored him to stay and to get an underling to take care of the mushrooms instead, the old man said, "You do not understand. I am head cook. If I do not do this job, who will do it? And if I do not do it now, when will I do it?"

There is a deep simplicity in taking responsibility in this way. The head cook wasn't trying to prove anything, to get credit for anything, or even to accomplish anything. He was simply occupying his place, fulfilling his role. Although we might not be alert enough to notice it, being responsible in this way has reverberations beyond what we can predict or control. For life's endless possibilities arise in response to our passion to give ourselves fully to what we are doing wherever we are. Our tomorrows can neither be saved up nor created out of our heads; they flow out of our present engagement. Responsibility, far from limiting or shutting down our lives, provides the potential for opening. Even if responsibility seems to keep us in one place for a very long time (as with the young priest who rode his motorcycle) or to press our nose to the grindstone (as with the head cook), we don't feel this as restriction. When we give ourselves to our situation we're letting go of preferences and habits and trusting what's in front of us, with faith that it will provide the wisdom we need. To truly be responsible is to recognize that reality is smarter than we are.

Another clear characteristic of maturity—one that any of us would mention—is experience. A grown-up is someone who is experienced and, through having lived long enough to have seen many things, has a point of view and a measure of savvy about how life works. There is certainly no substitute for the experience that accumulates as the years go by, but it is also possible to be alive for a long time and not really experience our living, not really see our life. The human capacity for self-deception and blindness runs deep. We may be alive, but we have not necessarily lived. If we accumulate experiences without really engaging with them, then our experience tends to make us stodgy and boring. As we catalog and define our experiences, possessing them without ever really being possessed by them, we begin to expect that new situations will just be repetitions of old ones. Soon we feel as if we've seen it all before. We know what to expect. Our point of view gradually becomes a set of blinders rather than a searching flashlight.

But if we pay close and open attention to our experiences, life's larger patterns begin to come into view. We see that all things are transitory and unique. Nothing repeats. We understand that, though always instructive, the past can never tell us what the future will be. Within the larger pattern that experience reveals, there are endless variations. Insofar as we see this, our experience increases our wonder at and appreciation of all that happens. With little life experience, we might be naively excited by the novelty of a person we meet or an event that occurs. But when we truly appreciate our experience, we respond to that newness with a deeper understanding of its meaning and wonder as we relate it to what we have seen before. Far from dampening our sense of wonder, real experience refreshes and mellows it.

Some years ago I attended a peace conference in Belfast, Northern Ireland, with His Holiness the Dalai Lama. We were sitting in a large auditorium listening to the stories of people who had been victims of what is called in Ireland "the troubles," the long, violent conflict between Protestants and Catholics. One person was blind. One was wheelchair-bound. Another was emotionally scarred from having seen his father shot down before his own eyes when he was a child. When I glanced over at His Holiness, I saw that he was weeping like a baby, leaning his head on his assistant's shoulder. A few moments later he was being photographed with two Irish religious leaders, one a Catholic priest, the other a Protestant minister. It happened that both men had bushy white beards. For some reason His Holiness thought this was very funny, so he reached up and gave their beards a tug. I remember that he almost fell off the podium with laughter. The next day the *Irish Times* carried a front-page color picture of the Dalai Lama laughing hysterically while "bearding" the two shocked clergymen. It seemed amazing to me that His Holiness could be so shattered with sadness one moment, and then so freely—almost inappropriately!—merry the next. A man who has seen and felt so much, and who carries a great burden of responsibility, the Dalai Lama nevertheless seems to hold his experience lightly.

We often think of growing up as a slow and inevitable process of dying to life, something to be avoided for as long as possible. We contrast maturity with childhood or youth, which we see as full of excitement and promise. Certainly we encounter a lot of sadness as life goes on. The older we get, the more trouble we've seen, and there's no doubt that life will show us the face of loss. Time passes, youth fades, and people disappear from our lives. And time will also introduce us to bitterness, disappointment, and defeat.

But it is exactly in digesting and accepting the profundity of our difficulties that life opens up to us. The truly experienced person knows and feels the preciousness, fragility, and impermanence of life. Certainly the Dalai Lama has known his share of suffering and has taken it in with all seriousness. But the experience of suffering hasn't dampened his enjoyment of life.

In Japanese culture the appreciation of life—of the beauty of a flower, the peacefulness of a shrine, the purity of a mountaintop scene—seems to be tied to a recognition of impermanence. Often life's most moving moments are found right in the middle of sadness and loss. The twelfth-century Japanese Buddhist poet Saigyo penned this verse:

Winter has withered
Everything in this mountain place:
Dignity is in
Its desolation now, and beauty
In the cold clarity of its moon

Self-acceptance is another key quality of the mature person. Someone who lives long enough, and with enough heart, to truly understand his or her experience, will gradually come to self-acceptance. Observing accurately and without shame our thoughts, deeds, and feelings over time, we begin to see a clearer picture of our character. We let go of our expectations and illusions about ourselves and settle with confidence, into who we really are. As we become familiar with our weaknesses and all the trouble they have caused us, we are less dismayed at them and do not run away from them as often; this new response, in turn, brings us a calmness that helps us stop indulging our weaknesses.

We also come to appreciate our strengths enough to see that we don't have to make a big deal out of them. We don't need to keep reminding ourselves and everyone else about our strengths. Instead we can simply enjoy and make use of them. As time goes on and our self-acceptance deepens, the very idea of strengths and weaknesses seems off the mark because the closer we look, the harder it is to distinguish between the two. All human qualities have a flip side: we're loving, but we meddle; we're fearful, but we're helpfully prudent; we're critical, but we are very perceptive. It's all a dance. As we realize this, it seems increasingly silly to judge ourselves one way or the other.

Still, no matter how well we know ourselves and how much we achieve a steadiness of character, we are never immune to mistakes. With self-acceptance we know this, and we try to make use of our mistakes, learning from them as best we can. Over time we see how often our worst mistakes and most ig-nominious failures have turned out to be our greatest teachers. Some of our greatest disasters turn out to have powerfully positive consequences for our lives, even though it may take a long time for us to recognize it. Given all of this, we become less worried about making mistakes, although we are regretful when we make them, especially when others are hurt in the process. Zen Master Dogen famously referred to his long life of spiritual endeavor as "one continuous mistake."

Sometimes our mistakes can be helpful to others: if we show that there can be dignity in making mistakes, others can learn from us that they don't have to live in constant fear of error. Many times in my life I have witnessed mistakes that my teachers made—being headstrong or stubborn, being angry when it was inappropriate, being nervous when I wanted them to be clearheaded and cool. Sometimes they said or did things impulsively, or even deliberately, that they shouldn't have said or done. Most of the time I appreciated these mistakes, for they made me see my teacher's humanness and vulnerability. Far from seeing the mistake-making as a flaw that lowered the estimation of my teacher in my eyes, I saw it as a wonderful badge of his or her humanity, which helped me to accept my own imperfection more easily.

I remember the one-hundredth birthday party of my friend and teacher Charlotte Selver, who has been teaching and practicing sensory awareness, a powerful mindfulness training, for more than seventy-five years. After birthday cake and a champagne toast, people gathered around to recount stories from Charlotte's life, incidents that revealed her wisdom. After many tales were told of the wonderful and perceptive things that Charlotte had said or done in the presence of her students, one man said that what he cherished the most were the stupid arguments that Charlotte and Charles, her husband of many years, used to have, often right in the middle of a workshop session. "It was the way you did it," the man said. "So wholeheartedly, without embarrassment or justification. Somehow it gave me permission to be myself without feeling there was some ideal I was supposed to be living up to."

Self-acceptance is paradoxical: we see and accept our essential character, the personality that seems to define us, but at the same time we know that that character is actually in constant flux. When we feel this dynamic interplay between change and constancy and accept the paradox of human character, we see how we can avoid being trapped by ourselves, as so many people are. Since we accept who we are, and are no longer driven to improve, we're not constantly self-critical and off-balance. On the other hand, since we know that who we are isn't fixed but rather is always subtly being reinvented by conditions, we know that we can and will grow and improve if only we pay attention and stay present for what happens to us. With self-acceptance we are confident that we can trust what happens. We begin to realize how much power and subtlety there is in simply seeing ourselves without distortion, without shame, without guilt or desire.

A short and instructive Zen dialogue I am very fond of evokes this profound sense of self-acceptance. A monk named Hui Chao asks his teacher, "What is Buddha?" The teacher replies, "You are Hui Chao." A mature person appreciates the simple fact of being himself or herself, knowing that in the entire cosmos there is now and will only ever be one temporary occurrence of this person. He or she also knows that something deeply unique and necessary is being expressed through his or her life.

Such profound self-acceptance tenderizes the heart, and opens our empathy for others, for we recognize that the precious and unique person we are has been formed and is being formed through our relations with others. We are always creating each other—our moods, our personalities, and our attitudes are always connected to the moods, personalities, and attitudes of others. Experiencing our own suffering without excuse or attempt to escape, we know that others have suffered as we have. Deeply reflecting on all this, we become open to and capable of love. We come to understand the profound truth that there is nothing but love and therefore nothing is more worthwhile, more pervasive, or more necessary.

We think of love as a big enthusiastic feeling. Certainly emotion is part of what love is, but it's not limited to that. Our society's focus on romantic relationships seems natural and delightful, at least if you are in a relationship yourself that is reasonably happy. But love is a much larger container than romance. A person can be loving whether or not he or she is in love with someone. I have many friends who are monks and nuns, among whom are the most loving and mature individuals I know. They are living proof that the power of love, and of loving connection that is deep and satisfying, is a mark of maturity for all of us, regardless of the nature of our relationships.

Love is practical and down-to-earth. It exists in the rough and tumble of real human relationship, with all its problems and misunderstandings. Love requires human warmth and contact. It also requires all the other qualities of maturity I have already discussed—responsibility, experience, and self-acceptance—insofar as we have developed them. Love evokes the healing power of simple human kindness. Mature people are not aloof, coolly distant, or stuck within themselves. They might not all be jolly extroverts, but they all have the capacity to meet others with some degree of warmth and interest.

In my own work with Zen students over the years, I have felt the awesome power of love. Although it may seem extravagant to say so, the truth is that I love the people with whom I practice Zen. I get to know many of them over time and to see their lives unfold, with all the inevitable triumph and tragedy. Sharing all this with them, admiring their courage and sincerity in facing what they face and their determination to keep on devotedly with the practice, how can I not love them? If there is any benefit in our practicing together, all of it comes from this loving relationship, which has a healing power no one can measure or truly understand.

In Zen literature the word *intimacy* is often used as a synonym for enlightenment. In the classical Zen enlightenment stories, a monk or a nun is reduced simultaneously to tears and laughter as he or she suddenly recognizes that nothing in this world is separate, that each and every thing, including one's own self, is nothing but the whole, and that the whole is nothing but the self. What are such stories telling us if not that love is much wider and deeper than an emotion? Love is the fruition of, the true shape of, one's self and all that is.

THE BOYS AND I DISCUSSED THESE AND OTHER QUALITIES that we felt are demonstrated by mature people, but certainly mature people are all different. Some are calm and quiet, others are talky and jumpy. Some are decisive and stubborn, others more thoughtful and softer. Still, it seems that maturity brings stability into a person's life, no matter what that life looks like. When you have lived long enough to find a way of being that suits you, you do become calmer and more stable. When you've learned how to be confident enough to give yourself willingly and completely to what's in front of you, life holds you in place, for you are not off-balance, grabbing for something other than what arises in front of you. You are willing to stand where you are, looking straight ahead without glancing off in a million directions. Some might call this strength of character, but to me it seems more like inspiration. We are inspired by what happens, and what happens deepens us. Life becomes more interesting. Rather than feeling that we have to seek new or exotic experience, we become fascinated with whatever our situation happens to be. We love wherever we are, we love whatever our life provides. Living, just as it is, is enough for us. There's tremendous steadiness and reliability in this acceptance, whatever our personal style of expressing it may be.

I think of my own teacher, Roshi Sojun Weitsman, longtime abbot of the Zen Center in Berkeley, where I began my practice long ago. Sojun is a straightforward and down-to-earth person who, as long as I have known him, has maintained stability in all circumstances. His virtue as a teacher comes from his steadiness. He has been true to the practice for many years and has remained in his seat, so to speak, patiently practicing, no matter what happens, through many changes. He came to Berkeley as a new priest almost forty years ago and simply began to sit meditation, welcoming anyone who wanted to join him. He was there every day, day in and day out, no matter what.

When I was young and having a difficult time in my life, his stability was crucial for me. I was able to sit meditation next to Sojun in the early mornings, and though he said little to me, just seeing him sitting there quietly, and then later in the day steadily going about his business, helped my life. Years went by, and he kept on meditating, kept on being there, kept on taking care of things in a simple way. More and more students came, and now the Zen Center is a thriving community with many seasoned practitioners and teachers. Sojun never calculated about anything or made special efforts to build up the group. He just stayed stably with his practice and continued to give his whole heart to it quietly over the years. And that was enough.

The quality of mature people that is most difficult to understand is strength, because we usually think of strength as toughness or roughness, power or assertiveness. We think of some tough superhero. But mature strength is not like this; it is strength of resolve, the sometimes quiet and sometimes not so quiet courage it takes to stick with what you feel is right and with the course you have decided to take.

Many years ago the meditation hall at Tassajara, our mountain monastery, burned down. It was a rather spectacular event, since the entire community was in the hall doing a ceremony when the fire broke out. We evacuated the building as quickly as possible, without even taking the time to save the precious Buddha statue on the altar. Once outside, we turned back in astonishment to see the old redwood structure completely engulfed in flames. The whole thing happened in the space of a few minutes.

Our community was still young at the time, and losing the meditation hall was the greatest disaster we had ever experienced. The terrible event occurred just as we were making preparations for our most ambitious project, the establishment in San Francisco of Greens, our well-known vegetarian restaurant. This was an enormous undertaking, one that we probably had no right to think we could manage, but our abbot at that time, Richard Baker, felt sure we could do it, and had to do it, not only for the financial support it would provide us but also as an offering to the world. When the meditation hall at Tassajara burned down, we all naturally assumed that the Greens project was off. How could we possibly raise enough money and come up with enough personnel to take on that project as well as the rebuilding of the meditation hall? Clearly it was out of the question. Yet within hours after the fire was put out, Roshi Baker was putting the finishing touches to the architectural plans for Greens, talking to funders and contractors on the telephone, and assuring us that the project would definitely go ahead as scheduled.

When we heard this, many of us thought that the Roshi had gone a bit crazy. Maybe the fire had rattled him so much that he'd lost his judgment. While it might have looked crazy at the time, Roshi Baker's decision turned out to be the right one. Always true to his vision and willing to pay the price to see it through, Roshi Baker had a strength of purpose that was probably the single most important ingredient in the establishing of Greens' success.

Strength of resolve is, however, a tricky thing. It too easily shades off into stubbornness and a pernicious quality of being unyielding. Later on Roshi Baker had many problems at the Zen Center. Things did not turn out well, and it may be that his resolve and strength of purpose contributed to his problems. Real strength is not unyielding. Like a tree that can bend but never break, the strength of a mature person includes flexibility. A mature person has learned through experience that life requires us to be flexible. There is no use insisting that you are right about something. Even if you are, the next minute things may change and you may be wrong. I think of Master Zhaozho, a simple monk who kept his position of leadership not by rigid self-assertion or stubbornness but by quiet and flexibility of word and deed. His strength sometimes appeared as weakness, and there are stories about him that turn on this point. Once a monk came to see him, thinking he was visiting an impressive Zen master. When he saw the unimpressive old master standing before him, the monk rose up to his full height and said, "I came expecting a stone bridge and I only see this rickety wooden one." The master simply replied, "Yes, you see the wooden bridge; you don't see the stone one." No need to shout or contradict. Real strength is like that. It is an inner conviction that transcends external positions or appearances. When you have confidence in your own decisiveness, you can change your mind and not worry about it. When you know your own power, you can be soft without worrying about it. When you know how to stand firm, you can yield when that's the right thing to do.

In Zen there's a dichotomy between two teaching styles called "the grasping way" and "the granting way." The grasping way is tough: it always brings up emptiness and impermanence, never gives the student anything to go on, and withholds for the purpose of fostering the student's independence. The granting way, on the other hand, emphasizes the other side: connection, unity, and warmth. The granting way affirms and encourages the student, helping him or her with constant kindness. These opposing styles are actually not as different as they seem. One depends on the other, and neither can stand without the other. Teachers have always used them both, depending on the student and the situation. To be capable of understanding and manifesting only one side is to misunderstand its nature. To define the granting way as the opposite of the grasping way, or vice versa, and not to see the relationship and interdependence between them, is to make of each teaching style a limitation and a trap. Strength that doesn't know softness and flexibility becomes too brittle and eventually breaks.

In fact, all the qualities of maturity discussed in this chapter can become traps—brittle and limited when we define them too strictly, without subtlety and acuity. When we start to see ourselves as mature in a certain way—as responsible, stable, strong, or experienced, for example—and to judge and order our experience according to one of these prearranged and static concepts, we are already starting to harden and stiffen our experience. As soon as we have a fixed concept of responsibility, true responsibility disappears and we are just trying to be good. As soon as we establish for ourselves a fixed concept of experience and think about how experienced and wise we are, we become dull and incapable of receptivity. Self-acceptance reduced to a fixed concept becomes excessive self-consciousness and self-congratulation. When we reduce love to an idea of love, it dissolves into sentiment. And when we begin to receive awards for our wonderful stability—for doing this for twenty years and that for fifteen years—our stability becomes stodginess and we lose the capacity to change when it is time to.

In a very real and practical sense, then, the important thing is to realize that notions of responsibility, experience, self-acceptance, love, stability, and strength are merely reminders and guideposts to help us keep track of our lives, to encourage us to pay attention and be active by continuing the inner work that we need to do to keep our life lively. Maturity is a matter of making the effort, over time, to be open and sensitive to life. In Zen we call this effort "practice." The most important word in this book, practice is what we do when we foster in our lives a sense of ongoing effort and exploration that isn't just conceptual, but that also involves concrete processes we can work with—and are committed to continue working with—our whole life through. In the rest of this book, I want to discuss some of the practices that can help us achieve maturity.

Three

LISTENING

I STEPPED INTO MY OFFICE FIVE MINUTES LATE FOR OUR meeting. Three of the boys were already there. They were in the midst of an argument.

"You owe me one dollar," James was saying to Tony, with some heat.

"No way," Tony said dismissively.

"You do," Sam said.

Tony slowly turned to face Sam and gave him a withering look. Sam shrank back.

James, his chin trembling, was about to say something else when Rashid burst into the room, disheveled. He looked at the other three boys with a sense of utter disconnection, as if he had never seen them before. They looked at him like an invading force.

Watching all this, I felt invisible, as I often did in the boys' presence. They had a way of being together that was so all-encompassing that anything not within its sphere seemed nonexistent. I resisted the temptation either to ignore them by drifting off or, in schoolteacher fashion, to dispel what was going on and call the meeting to order.

Instead, I listened. I paid close attention to what was going on. I watched the boys' faces, heard their words, observed their body language. As often occurs, my bearing witness in this way served to settle things down. The argument over the dollar, which seemed somehow to be more than an argument over a dollar, dissolved.

Listening with full presence, and with as few preconceptions, notions, or desires as possible, to what was said and to what was not said was crucial to our meetings. And I was not the only one listening—eventually the boys were listening this way as well. Because we were able to do this, the boys began to speak and open up to each other and to me.

Listening is magic: it turns a person from an object outside, opaque or dimly threatening, into an intimate experience, and therefore into a friend. In this way, listening softens and transforms the listener.

Listening is basic and crucial because it is the soil out of which all the fruits of our human relationships grow. Listening takes radical openness to another, and radical openness requires surrender. This is why listening is frightening, although we don't usually think of it that way. It requires a kind of fearless self-confidence that most of us have never developed.

Self-confidence isn't egotism. Egotism is being stuck on yourself, insisting, perhaps quite unconsciously, on seeing everything through the lens of your own interests, your own intelligence, and your own views, capacities, and opinions. With too much egotism, listening is impossible. True self-confidence is different; it isn't confidence in your own superficial self, in your cover story, your views, capabilities, and résumé. It is, on the contrary, the willingness to suspend all of that for a while, in favor of a faith in yourself that goes beyond the surface of who you are. When you are truly self-confident, you are flexible with regard to ego: you can pick up ego when necessary, but you can also put it down when necessary in order to learn something completely new through listening. And if you find that you can't put ego down, at least you know that this is so. You can admit it to yourself. It takes profound self-confidence to be humble enough to recognize your own limitations without self-blame. If you can do that, very soon you will be able to listen.

The next time you are in a conversation pay attention to your listening. Don't just go on automatic pilot. Instead, reflect on what is actually going on. Chances are you will notice that more often than not, when another person is talking, you are not listening. You may be more or less hearing what the person is saying, getting the general drift, but you are probably also preparing or anticipating the remark you will soon be making in rejection of or agreement with what you are hearing. Maybe you interrupt, maybe you lose attention or think about something else, or maybe your mind simply wanders gently off to no place in particular. Daydreaming is a habit so unconscious that it is much more prevalent than any of us realize. Since you are so often not actually listening but rather are absorbed in your own mental habits, you are probably missing out on something, some piece of information, some discovery about yourself or the other person or the world, some *news*.

What's usually in our minds isn't really news. It's the residue of what we've learned, or hoped for, or feared, or been hurt by. Whether we are conscious of it or not, we are almost always strategizing when we engage in conversation with others—trying to find the advantage or to protect ourselves from something foreign or unknown. We aren't listening at all. If we want to survive with some happiness, however, in this world of difference—a world in which we are constantly confronted with one utterly different and unknown person after another (even those we know and live with for many years are sometimes utterly unknown to us)—we had better study the art of listening.

To truly listen is to shed, as much as possible, all of your protective mechanisms, at least for the time of listening. To listen is to be willing to simply be present with what you hear without trying to figure it out or control it. To listen is to be radically receptive to what occurs. To do that, you have to be honest with yourself. You have to be aware of and accepting of your preconceptions, desires, and delusions—all that prevents you from listening. But you also have to be willing to put these preconceptions, desires, and delusions aside so that you can hear what the speaker is saying for what it is. Because truly listening requires that you do this, listening is dangerous. It might cause you to hear something you don't like, to consider its validity, and therefore to think something you never thought before—or to feel something you never felt before, and perhaps never wanted to feel. This feeling might make something happen within you that never happened before. This is the risk of listening, and this is why it is automatic for us not to want to listen.

But listening, however dangerous, is a necessity. If you want to stay open to life and to change, you have to listen. To listen, really listen, is to accord *respect*. Without respect, no human relationship can function normally, for the pain and hurt that inevitably arise from disrespect eventually pervert it. When your mind is occupied (usually quite unconsciously) with your own thoughts and plans and strategies and defenses, you are not listening. And when you are not listening, you are not according respect. The speaker knows this and reacts accordingly.

It doesn't take a psychic to know that someone is not really listening. We all know whether or not we are being listened to. But we are so accustomed to not being listened to that we take it for granted and even see it as normal. This is why it is so startling, and so powerful, almost magical, when we are actually heard by another person within the openness of true listening.

Perhaps the most common and pernicious form of nonlistening is our nonlistening to ourselves. So much of what we actually feel and think is unacceptable to us. We have been conditioned over a lifetime to simply not hear all of our own self-pity, anger, desire, jealousy, wonder. Most of what we take to be our adult response is no more than our unconscious decision not to listen to what goes on inside us. And as with any human relationship, not listening to ourselves damages our self-respect. It occludes the free flow of love from ourselves to ourselves. To allow ourselves to feel what we actually do feel—not to be afraid or dismayed but to open up a space inside our hearts large enough to safely contain what we feel, with the faith that whatever comes up is workable and even necessary—this is what any healthy, mature human being needs to do and what we so often fail to do.

The practice of listening has many depths and many dimensions. In *Zen Mind, Beginner's Mind*, Suzuki Roshi speaks of true listening as emerging from what he calls "beginner's mind"— the mind that is willing to remain receptive and open to surprise. Such a mind is always ready and alert, willing to receive what comes. It has few preconceptions. Unlike the expert's mind, which filters everything through its expertise, beginner's mind is innocent and fertile.

Listening requires beginner's mind, for no one can be an expert on what has never before been heard, in exactly this way, at this precise moment. Listening is being ready to live this moment and willing to confront what's truly new, unhindered by what has happened before. "If your mind is empty, it is always ready for anything; it is open to everything," Suzuki Roshi writes. "In the beginner's mind there are many possibilities; in the expert's mind there are few."

Another expression in Zen for this fertile, empty, listening mind is "I don't know mind." The statement "I don't know" doesn't signify ignorance or stupidity or even humility; rather, it points to this kind of ready, fertile, receptive mind that has no preconceptions and no identities that need to be held as barriers against what wants to come in.

When an old Zen master was asked about this "I don't know mind," he said, "Not knowing is most intimate." Since knowing gives us definition and control, it enables us to keep the world at arm's length. Having established our ideas and preferences about what is, we no longer have to bother to pay attention. Not knowing, on the other hand, leaves us vulnerable and free. It brings us very close to experience, unprotected and fully engaged. Not knowing, we merge with what confronts us. We let go of identity and evaluation and allow ourselves to surrender to amazement.

In retreats and especially in our mountain monastery, where it is so very quiet, I am often able to practice listening in this radical way. When the mind becomes quiet and free of schemes and strategies, it is a real pleasure—an astonishment—to hear the peep of a bird, the roar of the creek, the crunching of feet on the gravel path, or the clattering of dry leaves in the windswept branches. *Intimate*, with all its connotations of warmth and ease and pleasure and coziness and no need to prove or accomplish, is a good word for this experience. Sometimes in meditation I practice—and instruct others to practice—simply listening: sitting still, letting go of everything in the mind, and focusing intently on sound. Sometimes you hear the sound of your own heartbeat. And sometimes you hear the sound of your heartbeat and the sound of the wind or the stream as the same sound. Su Shih, the Song Dynasty Chinese poet, wrote soon after his enlightenment experience: "All night long I hear a hundred thousand scriptures in the sound of the mountain stream."

We all instinctively know how to listen in this way, and we don't have to be deep in the mountains to do it. There is no trick to simple listening. We just shut up, stop what we are doing, cock our ears, and listen. "*Shhh . . . ,*" we say, and then, with a hush in our voice, ". . . *listen.*" The only problem is that we forget to do it, and the only way to remember is to keep coming back to this kind of listening over and over again, so that we begin to develop the habit.

So practice listening: turn off the radio, turn off the television, and just listen once in a while. Listen to traffic or work sounds. Listen to your own thoughts. And of course, listen to others. Start with people in your own family and set up special times, and special exercises, for listening. Make it a priority.

I think this profound kind of listening is the source of all inspiration and creativity. I imagine that sages of old—biblical prophets, shamans, poets, musicians, and artists—all tapped into this listening as the wellspring of their visions and insights. I know as a poet that my practice is almost entirely the practice of listening. I practice receptivity to the poem, to its shape and to its impulses. I don't write the poem. I let it write me.

There's a wonderful passage in the Surangama Sutra, an old Chinese Buddhist text, that describes the magical listening of Kuan Yin, the bodhisattva of compassion, whose representation sits on my office altar. Kuan Yin's practice is deep listening to the heart of the world. Through this practice, she "turns the mind around," and saves it from the suffering of outward grasping, allowing the stillness to emerge that understands that nothing is outside or inside and that nothing is incomplete or lacking. Through this profound practice of listening, Kuan Yin acquires various miraculous powers and grounds of self-confidence. She is able to hear all the cries of the world and to respond to each and every one of them with appropriate help. With her many hands and eyes she becomes a protector for the world—the world's helper and lover.

All of these wonderful consequences, however, derive from only one side of the practice of listening—the inspiring, beautiful side. It is also the easy side. Flowers and trees listen with this kind of purity, and we have to try to listen purely, too.

But in the human world there are complications. For better or worse, we have the capacity and the responsibility to exercise choice and action, to evaluate and to respond to what we hear. Although we need to be able to practice total receptivity in listening, we also have to do more than this. We cannot only be passive listeners. In the end, listening's completion is *negotiation*.

Conversation is a give-and-take. If we don't listen, we don't hear anything, and real conversation is over before it begins. We haven't taken anything in, and so we are just beaming our message at the other person.

But if we do take in what the other person is saying, this is just the beginning. Next we have to give something back—we have to respond. The key is to be willing to hold what you give and what you receive in balance, to be aware of and interested in both sides of the conversation, so that something dynamic occurs.

In our Zen community we have often set aside special times to work on listening and responding. After all, we have been living together fairly intimately, some of us for many years, and misunderstandings that harden into conflicts could be (and have been!) disastrous for us. So it is very practical and very necessary for us to learn to listen to each other. We have an annual listening retreat at our temples (separate from our meditation retreats) and we also offer occasional workshops or trainings in listening.

Gary Friedman, a longtime friend and neighbor, has helped our community enormously over the years to improve our capacity for listening. He is himself an exceptional listener and mediator who has trained thousands of attorneys in North America and in Europe in the fine art of listening. Gary teaches two key listening techniques that over the years have become part of our community process. They are simple and commonsensical, and once you learn them and experience their effectiveness, you will be amazed to realize that you have for so long failed to do something so obvious and so useful. He calls these techniques "looping" and "dipping."

"Looping" is shorthand for "closing the loop of communication." Communication is an exchange, a transfer of something from one mind to another. You have something in your mind, you put it into words that you address to me, and I receive your words and form in my mind an impression of what those words were meant to convey. Presumably, I now know what was in your mind. The loop of communication is closed once I really do have in my mind the impression you wanted to convey. In order for the loop of communication to be completed, however, it is necessary that I actually listen. If I don't actually hear what you have been trying to tell me (which is what usually happens) but instead have leapt to a conclusion or an assumption based on my own preconceptions, misunderstanding will snowball if the conversation proceeds along in this way. It is entirely possible that I will become quite upset with you for something you did not mean and did not say. And if I do, and if I react out of that upset, then it is likely that you *will* say or do something very shortly that really will upset me. And on it goes.

Looping is the technique of checking to making sure that the loop of communication has been completed. When I loop, I am making sure I really heard what you said. Looping slows down the conversation and gives us both the chance to see whether we are listening to each other accurately as we go along. Then, if we are going to disagree and get upset with each other (and of course we well might), at least we will be upset accurately, based on real differences of opinion rather than imagined or projected ones.

An exercise in looping works this way: you speak, I listen carefully. I do not interrupt or occupy myself with my own thoughts. I listen 100 percent. When you finish speaking, I repeat to you as closely and carefully as possible what I have just heard you say. I try to leave out all my interpretations, judgments, and reactions to what you have said and simply repeat it as straight as I can, as if I were a tape recorder. You then listen closely to my repeating your words (they need not and will not be exact, of course, but all the parts of what has been said, even the digressions, must be included), and you let me know whether what I have repeated is accurate and complete. If it is not, you don't complain. You simply fill in what I left out or correct my misapprehensions. Then I repeat back to you what you have just told me. When you are satisfied that I have heard you, then the loop of communication is closed and I can go on to reply to you. As Gary often tells us, a successful looping is your ticket to speak. In the communication exercise, you can't speak until you have demonstrated that you have really listened.

The practice of "dipping," Gary's second technique, has to do with listening to ourselves. The chief reason we don't listen to other people is that we're distracted. We're listening with only half our mind. With the other half we are busy talking to ourselves. As a result of this divided listening, we hear neither ourselves nor the other person. With looping, as we have just seen, we carefully listen to (and demonstrate that we have listened to) the other person. With dipping we listen just as carefully to ourselves.

To practice dipping in a conversation, take the time to *intentionally* stop listening to the other person (as opposed to distractedly forgetting to listen) and check in with yourself. Do you have a feeling, positive or negative, about what you are hearing? Do you have a feeling that is unrelated to what you are hearing, something that just popped into your mind for no reason, or that popped in as a result of what you have been hearing?

Of course, things are always popping into our minds during conversations and at other times. Generally we don't notice them, although they may exercise an enormous influence over what we say and how we react in conversation. If, for instance, I am upset about a conversation I had a short while ago with another person and am not quite aware of it, then certainly when you approach me with a problem you have with me, I am not going to be able to hear you too well. If I react with irritation and anger, you will think my reaction is entirely about you, and we will have a bad time of it. Or if your words have in fact upset me quite a bit and a powerful anger or fear or sorrow is arising in me, it is good for me to know this clearly and to realize that it will certainly be conditioning my own words in response to you. So I need to take a short time out to dip—to recognize that I am upset, perhaps to see why, and to take that into account.

In ordinary conversation you have to be able to dip from time to time without losing track of what is going on with the other person's words; this is not so easy, but it is possible to do once you get used to it. But when you are communicating explicitly using these techniques (which you can do, say, in an intentional group process, agreeing to use them all the time, or once in a while, when communication seems particularly problematic), you can say out loud that you want take a moment to check out how you are feeling.

Dipping may involve saying out loud how you feel. This can be very helpful. It can be extremely educational if the other person understands how his or her words have affected you or if he or she learns that something strong is going on in you that has nothing to do with his or her words. Most people imagine that their words are inconsequential, and it can be a shock to realize that their words can be effective and powerful, even if negatively so. But it is not always necessary for you to say out loud what you feel. It is only necessary that you yourself know.

When our community works with Gary in the context of a workshop, or when he comes to do a sort of "intervention" to help with communication between specific individuals who are having a hard time together, he often stops the conversation and asks one participant or the other to dip. Everyone just waits for a moment. Then Gary asks whether the person who has dipped would like to say what he or she is feeling. That person is free to say yes or no.

One of the most impressive demonstrations of these techniques I have ever experienced occurred during a nasty argument that my wife and I had. It was a rainy night after a long workweek, and we were on the highway in a huge traffic jam. We were en route to a friend's cabin where we were to spend the weekend discussing an important family decision. Neither one of us was quite sure how the other felt about the issue at hand, though of course we both had our preconceptions and fears. Ahead we could see an endless line of red taillights in front of us, and an endless line of yellow headlights coming toward us. The rain was steady and chilly, the road was unfamiliar, and we felt pressure to reach our destination before it got too late. All in all a fairly aggravating situation. In the midst of it we began talking about our impending decision. Immediately we got into a terrible fight. We are not particularly an arguing couple, but this time we really got into a mess together, our voices rising, our hearts thumping, the emotional pace inside the car picking up as the physical pace on the highway slowed. Finally I said, "Wait a minute, time out. Let's do some looping and dipping."

So we slowed down the conversation and began carefully looping each other. It was astonishing. The simple decision to loop—almost even before doing it—changed everything in my mind. When I began to repeat to my wife what I had just heard her say, I could hear in my mind the words I was so strongly reacting against. They were not the words she was saying—they were words I was projecting onto what she was saying, out of my own fears and desires and bad habit of assuming attitudes on her part that weren't necessarily there. It was all so clearly and strongly off-base—obviously not what she had been saying at all. Slowing down enough to see this, I began to listen to her, and then I could hear what she was saying. I could repeat her actual words back to her.

We did manage to work out our decision that weekend, and it wasn't easy. In fact, it was agonizing and took a great many hours of discussion. But I am certain that had we not taken the time to make sure we were really understanding each other accurately so that we could get down to what we actually did disagree about—rather than what we thought we disagreed about—making our decision would have been far more difficult, if not impossible.

Careful listening can produce harmony and agreement out of apparent disharmony and disagreement. But sometimes, as in this case, real listening, though it helps to calm things down and therefore to make things clearer, doesn't eliminate disagreement. It may simply clarify the disagreement.

I suppose that on an absolute level there is no such thing as disagreement. If my listening is total and deep, if I have entirely let go of myself and the whole world, if my receptive beginner's mind is perfect, then nothing I hear is ever too great a problem. Everything and anything is workable. I think it is good to appreciate things at this level. We seldom do, and it would be liberating to be able to do it, even if only for a moment.

But in the everyday world of negotiation and opposing interests, there will forever be disagreements involving emotions, principles, and contention over the distribution of love, power, or goods. The truth is that most of our disagreements are trivial. We would all be capable of seeing this if we could only listen to ourselves and others long enough to evaluate our disagreements—and especially to consider their cost to us. Some rational reflection would usually lead us to simply let go of a small disagreement that is causing a large grief. If we gave ourselves the chance, we would quickly realize that it just isn't worth it.

On the other hand, some disagreements are not trivial, and even on reflection we would not want to let go of them because they are important to us. We have no choice but to work them out. In such cases we need to clarify the disagreement so that we can separate its real root from the attendant overlay of emotion. Disagreements need to be negotiated, and successful negotiation certainly depends on clarity and calmness. Sometimes even with clarity and calmness solutions cannot be found, disagreements go on for a long time, and we have to bear with them and suffer through them until at last they have run their course. But even then we don't sit back and simply wait for the storms to clear (though there may be a time and a place for that, too). We keep on trying to negotiate, to listen, to understand, to consider our own views and the views of others, to work toward change, compromise, accommodation. It might take quite a while, sometimes even a lifetime or more, but we have to be willing to keep on doing these things, because listening is the road to eventual peace.

I am thinking of the deep and old conflicts between nations and peoples that are now—and seemingly always have been—rife throughout the world. There are also intractable conflicts in workplaces, in families, and among friends and lovers whose pain and sorrow can influence us for many years. Although it may take a long time to work out these conflicts, we can never afford not to try. It won't do to set them aside and just go on with things. We can never give up making an effort to listen.

Conversation is the culmination of listening. It includes everything I have been talking about—self-confidence, receptivity, give-and-take, even disagreement and conflict. Conversation is dialogue, real communication and communion through our words and our presence. Founded on deep listening, deep speech, and an honest self-awareness without too much fear or judgment, conversation is a way to connect with ourselves and with each other, to enter each other's lives and help each other heal.

What primarily keeps us feeling lonely and misunderstood—and fuels our hatreds and prejudices—is simply a lack of conversation. We all talk most of the day. We talk at work, at school, at home. But how much do we really say, and how often do our words get at what really matters to us?

Rabbi Nachman of Braslav, an eighteenth-century Hasidic rabbi, had a practice of holding conversation with God. He'd concentrate his mind and heart, grow quiet within himself, and then pour out his honest words to God, telling his troubles, his hopes, his fears, his aspirations. He considered this conversation to be the highest form of meditation and prayer. It healed him and gave him a way to go on. Other people pray in this way as well, bringing forth words from their souls out into the world in order to clear and release their hearts. Conversation between two people, if carried on with that amount of sincerity and confidence in themselves and in each other, can also be a form of prayer.

A crucially important element of my own spiritual practice is "practice interviews." Called in our tradition *dokusan* (literally, to meet yourself), these intimate meetings between teacher and student take place within a formal setting, often during meditation retreats, when both the student and I have had a chance to practice receptive deep listening on our meditation cushions. Out of the quiet and mindfulness that this provides, we come to meet each other, and in doing this each of us meets himself or herself—and everything else.

The English word *interview* describes it quite well: we "interview" each other, sharing our views together, mixing them until they merge, with a mutuality inspired by trust and openness. Since all of us are inevitably a mass of intersecting and conditioned viewpoints that come from our upbringing, our education, our experiences, our wounds, our desires, our joys, and our sorrows, we are communing with each other on an intimate basis when we interview each other, and thus freeing ourselves from the blindness that our views can so easily foster. Over the years I have come to appreciate these interviews and the range of what happens in them, and I feel fortunate to have such a practice in my life. I hold *dokusan* frequently, and I always look forward to it. No matter what kind of mood I have been in beforehand, I always leave the interview room with a sense of reverence and hope for the human condition. I have a great admiration for the wisdom of the ancients, who in creating this practice of interview, saw the transformative possibility of simple human communication.

Practice interviews take place in most Zen retreats, but for each student they represent only a small part of the retreat, which mainly takes place in silence. Interviews take place only between teacher and student—they do not take place between students. Thinking about this, and about the power and importance of conversation for spiritual practice, I began some years ago to experiment with a new kind of Zen retreat, one that isn't entirely silent. In these retreats we do much silent sitting practice, but there is also time to engage in conversation. With our ears cleared out by the sitting practice, and with some careful structures, we find that we are able to speak and listen to one another more deeply than is usually possible.

Our structure is this: in groups of three or four, each person is given the chance to speak uninterrupted for six or seven minutes. During this time the nonspeakers practice listening intently—not thinking about what they are going to say when it is their turn to speak, not evaluating what they are hearing, not allowing their minds to wander to other concerns, but simply listening as precisely and attentively as possible. After each person has had a chance to hold the floor in the surrounding space of the others' listening, dialogue and discussion begin.

Most of the retreats I do this way are for people who work in the world of business, which I don't know a thing about. I got into doing these retreats some years ago when I had a chance to attend a meeting of businesspeople. This was in the early 1990s, when many businesses were downsizing for the first time. Many employees were laid off, afraid of being laid off, or in a state of grief over all their coworkers who had just been laid off and the resulting extra work for them. I was dismayed as I listened to people speak of the heaviness and pain of their feelings—and of the fact that there was no place for them to go to discuss it. They couldn't discuss their feelings at work, and it was too difficult to do so at home, where families might be destabilized and upset by such talk. They were relieved to be able to commiserate at the meeting. Hearing all of this, I wondered out loud whether it would be of any benefit to hold a retreat at our temple for the purpose of sitting together in silence and then conversing about these things. Everyone was very enthusiastic, and the "Company Time" retreats began.

We have been doing these retreats now for some years, and they have moved beyond support group status. In an ongoing conversation about the possibility for spiritual practice in the workplace, we come together several times a year to sit silently and to talk. Through our conversations we are sharing and developing a vision and a community built on the notion that it is possible to be a fully feeling and aware individual at work, and that it is okay to admit this and to share it with our coworkers.

I offered one of my sitting-talking-listening retreats at the peace conference in Belfast, Northern Ireland, which I mentioned earlier. We practiced sitting, and then we practiced listening, this time using the techniques of looping and dipping. People's reactions to this practice were startling. They were genuinely shocked by several things. First, they exclaimed how wonderful it was to listen, and to be able to speak when someone else was actually listening. Many of them noted that although we were several days into the conference, which consisted of almost nothing but listening and speaking, this was the first time they had felt they had actually heard someone, and had been heard. Second, people noticed how difficult it was to listen with accuracy. Almost everyone found, after they had looped the speakers, that they had made numerous mistakes and misapprehensions and that they had left out or distorted whole sections of what had been said. People remarked that it was no wonder that the Protestants and the Catholics of Northern Ireland had such an impossible time getting along. How could they even begin to make peace if they literally couldn't hear what the other party was saying?

Another time I did the same exercise of listening and speaking at a short retreat I gave for employees of Yale University in New Haven, Connecticut. The various pairs of speakers went to different rooms to speak, and I roamed around to listen so that I could get a sense of what kind of experience the participants were having. In one group a man was speaking about how the exercise had gone for him. "I am a manager," he was saying, "and am fairly high up in the pecking order. So people listen when I talk. For years this has been the case: I talk, they listen. But today I discovered that even though they look as if they are listening, they actually aren't listening. I am not sure if, before today, I have ever actually been listened to by anyone. It feels great!"

Being heard does feel great. We all want to be listened to—we all need it. Many of us suffer terribly for lack of it. When you consider the problems of sexism, racism, ageism, classism, or homophobia, which have had tragic effects throughout the world, they really stem in large measure from the fact that people are not recognized and are not heard. Everyone wants and needs to be included in the human family, and being included means more than being equal under the law, more than having equal economic and social opportunity. It means being heard, truly heard.

During the time I spent in conversation with the four boys, I came to feel that adolescents, too, desperately need to be heard and seldom are. Their hearts full of the uncertainty that comes with shifting identity, they find it almost impossible to listen to themselves and to each other. They desperately need to be heard by adults, but they almost never are because adults are prejudiced against them. The truth is that adolescents have a bad reputation with adults, most of whom view them in their unruly awkwardness, moodiness, and exuberance, as alien, absolutely "other."

Think about how you feel when you see a group of adolescents approaching you on the street. Do you look at them with curiosity and interest? Do you move a bit closer to hear what they might be saying, to experience a little bit of their atmosphere? Or do you find yourself tensing up, bracing yourself for their approach, and trying to avoid them? Because what they have to say so often seems challenging, angry, or unclear, adolescents are the last people we want to listen to, and yet they are the ones who need our listening most. And since they represent the future for all of us, it is in our best interests to do that listening.

During my time with the four boys, in our many meetings that sometimes seemed fruitless and sometimes were delightful, I found that listening to adolescents is also listening to ourselves. Talking to them month after month about what it really means to grow up and joining them in their struggles with all the questions about living in our difficult time as an independent, responsible human being, I found that I was reliving these questions for myself, making them fresh, bringing them to life.

When I really did *listen*—which is to say, when I could overcome the temptation to advise them and share my wisdom and experience and instead could be with them in all their doubt and uncertainty—my own life was affected. Little by little it became impossible for me to coast along on the an-

swers I had found out for myself in my own youth. They were
fine answers and had stood me in good stead. But they were
old answers, products of a person who no longer was and a
world that no longer existed. Gradually I saw all of my old answers called into question. It was almost as if all those often la-
borious meetings with these four boys were waking me up in
ways I needed to be waked up. It was providing me with the
ground of doubt and questioning I needed at that time in my
life to really grow up myself.

The practice of listening will always raise more questions
than it answers. In this it is fertile soil for the development of
true human maturity.

Four

PERSISTENCE

THESE FIRST SIX OR SEVEN MONTHS MEETING WITH THE BOYS were dramatic, with plenty of highs and lows. In the beginning there was the excitement of embarking on something brand-new. On their own, the boys had made a commitment to do something that felt special, even unique. But naturally the novelty of meeting with the Zen priest in his Zen room wore off after a few months. Still, there was enough genuineness in our being together, in the way that we spoke and listened to one another, to keep the meetings something that we all looked forward to and enjoyed. We had many great conversations that left a warm afterglow. But that, too, wore off as time went by and the boys seemed to return to more habitual ways of relating to me and to each other. After about six months we hit a bumpy patch.

Something was going on with the boys—with them as a group, and with each of them separately. I couldn't tell what it was. The dynamics between them were changing. Tony and Rashid, who had come into the group as close friends, seemed not to be so close any longer. Rashid was upset about something, and this distracted him so much that he seemed incapable of relating reasonably to anyone. Tony, for his part, was growing more sullen by the week. Sam continued to be diffident. His body language was eloquent: he shrank back from the others, literally leaning away from them, and he almost never spoke. Some meetings it seemed that he hardly even lifted his head to look at anyone. Meanwhile, James seemed more and more uncomfortable with something, maybe mostly with himself. Whenever he said anything—and he said a lot—you could hear him second-guessing himself. He seemed perpetually flustered and embarrassed. In short, all four of the boys were becoming normal adolescents.

One day Rashid came to our meeting in an extremely agitated state. He spent the first half of the time acting out disruptively. This was disturbing to all of us, and it was the first and only time I'd ever had to engage in a disciplinary conversation, taking him out of the room into the hallway to speak with him in private for a moment. Because of our practice of listening, and because, despite the ups and downs we had been experiencing, we'd hung in there with each other, a sense of trust had developed between us. I'm not sure we knew that until this day when, out there in the hallway, Rashid started to cry as he told me what was on his mind. We came back into the room and he told the others, too—about the marital troubles his parents were having, about the tension he felt in the household, about how that tension tied his stomach into knots so that he was having trouble sleeping at night and staying interested in school.

It was a relief finally to hear Rashid come out with all this. I had asked him repeatedly over the last month or so what was up with him, but he would never say. It was obvious that something was going on, and it was difficult to get through meeting after meeting with Rashid acting out the way he had been. But I kept my patience, for I knew that I couldn't force anything. I knew that we would hear about it when Rashid was ready to speak.

Persistence—the ability to hang in there with something difficult without turning away, to be willing to simply wait when waiting is what's called for—is not a throwaway virtue, and it is not simply a form of passivity. Persistence is a powerful and positive virtue that can be cultivated and developed. It's a key practice for nurturing all the qualities of maturity that we value: stability, responsibility, self-acceptance, a loving heart—all require that we persist with what we are up to, that we stick with it steadfastly, without glancing off or running away.

I have had a lot of experience with the practice of persistence, and I have needed it. I am naturally an impatient person, and when I was young I was given to great bouts of unbridled frustration at the way the world so often insisted on not cooperating with my needs and desires. The power of my anger was quite frightening, I think, to my parents, who were mild-mannered people. When I began Zen practice, I felt a good deal of frustration because the practice was so difficult. It was physically difficult to wake up early and sit long hours in meditation, especially during weeklong retreats and monastic training periods, which went on for months at a time without relief. But more than this, it was emotionally difficult, because it was impossible to be successful at it. The harder you tried, the worse it got, the further the goal receded from you. There's a koan about this. When the master is asked, "What is the Way?" he replies, "Everyday mind is the Way." The student says, "If everyday mind is already the Way, how can I aim for it?" The master replies, "If you aim for it, you will be going in exactly the opposite direction."

Patience wasn't my problem alone. Compared to most kinds of training and study, Zen practice really is frustrating. But this is part of the method: pressured by frustration, you have no choice but to develop persistence if you are going to continue. This is how it was for me. Besides being impatient, I am also quite stubborn, so far from discouraging me, the difficulty and frustration of Zen practice only made me more determined to go on.

Stubbornness and persistence are not the same thing. Stubbornness has a meanness to it, like a pit bull hanging on to a pants leg. It's reactive and often self-destructive (as it was in my case). Persistence, on the other hand, is not reactive or mean. It has a quality of faith and determination to continue, whether results are apparent or not. Persistence bears you up and helps you to move forward against the odds. In fact, with the practice of persistence, odds don't matter much one way or the other. Persistence doesn't wear you out by forcing you into a tight corner, as stubbornness does. Persistence provides some calmness in the face of adversity. It has been my job through the years of my Zen practice to massage my stubbornness, little by little, into persistence. I am still working on this.

In the shaping of our lives, we pay a fair amount of attention to skill and effort, to intelligence, talent, good looks, technique, training, education, and so on. But it seems to me that a primary virtue is the simple ability to be persistent with what you do, to not look for quick fixes or miracle cures, to be able to go on with a good feeling come what may.

The real beauty of persistence—and its true power, as the boys and I discovered in our time together—is that it eventually blossoms into trust. And trust is the secret ingredient, the

magic of our lives. It's what makes all our relationships, including our relationship to ourselves, satisfying and in the end
fruitful. Trust is always lovely and always touches us deeply,
and its healing effects can last a lifetime.

A person who chooses to walk the path of maturity is a
trusting and trustworthy person. He or she has learned,
through clear observation over time, that there is no alternative to trusting what is, for to mistrust what is, is to reject our
life experience, which is all we've got to build on, no matter
how hard it may be. To take our places in this world we need
to trust the world, ourselves, and each other this much.

The word *trust* comes from a Germanic and Old English
complex of words that suggest firmness, reliability, steadfastness. The word *tree* comes from the same root words, and
trees are the very image of solidity, faithfulness, and dignity.
Cognate words include *truth* and *truce* and *pledge*. According to
legend, Buddha's mother gave birth to him as she leaned
against a tree. Buddha meditated under a tree, was enlightened under a tree, and died lying down between two trees.
Buddhist meditators throughout the generations have been
instructed to "sit at the foot of a tree" for meditation or to do
walking meditation near trees. Simply to look at a tree mindfully, to stand under a tree with appreciation, or to stroll in
the woods with a quiet heart can be wonderful spiritual practices. We need trees as trees for their own sake, of course, but
also for ours: trees stand for the possibility of steadfastness
and trust in our lives.

For most of us trust is difficult. We have experienced the
unreliability of people and of the world at one time or another, in small and sometimes large ways. We know that there
are no guarantees in life and that it is foolish to trust naively. If
we do, we think, we will probably be betrayed, taken advantage of, made a fool of, lose out. Because we want to avoid and

are quite frightened of those possibilities, we find trust risky. It seems much safer and more rational to be wary.

But the practice of persistence can shift this attitude. When you dedicate yourself to showing up, to coming back over and over again to a situation or relationship regardless of how it seems to be going, when you seem to be strengthened by frustration rather than frightened off by it, a serenity begins to set in. You see that producing or avoiding any particular outcome isn't really the point. Simply being there is the point. Trust is the point. If you keep on showing up long enough, trust will dawn in you—not trust that things will turn out a particular way, or that a person will give you what you want, but a bigger, wider trust, a calm feeling inside. A trust in what is. And a trust in yourself, confident that whatever happens, you will be able to make use of it somehow.

This special kind of trust born of persistence is truly remarkable when manifested in human relationships. Showing up, as the boys and I did at our mentoring meetings, week after week, month after month, making a practice of persistance, began to create the atmosphere of trust that gave Rashid enough confidence to begin finally to speak his mind, and his doing so, in that trusting atmosphere, was healing for us as well as for him. *Dedication, devotion, diligence*—these words could all be synonyms for the persistence I am talking about. Although they may seem like fairly prosaic virtues, they produce a power that is hard to match. Mature people know the sheer power of simply showing up.

A lot of what I have discovered about the transforming effects of persistence and how it leads to trust comes from my time as a high school teacher. I came to the profession later in life than most, and I did my student teaching at the local high school, in the town near the Zen Center where I lived. The school's demographics reflected the white, middle-class community in which it was located. But the school also served a smaller outlying African American community. The youngsters from that community were, on the whole, a fairly alienated population within the school.

Entering high school is a shock for any student. The social situation (you have only a few friends in a sea of new faces), the academic demands (chemistry?!), the knowledge that after high school you are going to be leaving home to go off to who knows where—all conspire to make the transition quite stressful. This ordinary difficulty was greatly compounded for the African American students, who had come from a predominantly black middle school.

The white school community—students, faculty, and administration—was liberal, fair-minded, and certainly not intentionally racist. But the community had very little understanding of and appreciation for what the African American students felt and how they saw the world. So it was easy to see why the African American students felt misunderstood and unseen. They kept to themselves and did their best just to get through. In fact, most of them didn't. Although the school targeted the African American students with good special programs of all sorts, the programs were always a bit off-putting to the students, and so were by and large ineffective.

I wanted to get to know the African American students better, so I decided to start a writing group, which I ran on a volunteer basis once a week. I recruited several students who said they were interested. But when the time came, only one or two students showed up—and many times no one came at all. It was disappointing. I would stand there in the empty classroom waiting (occasionally someone did come, maybe half an hour late for the forty-five-minute session) and digesting my feelings, trying to let go of my affront and disappointment—feelings that, of course, weren't helping. On days when no one at all showed up, I'd go out into the school yard. Often I'd see one or several of the writing group members hanging around there. When I'd ask them why they hadn't shown up, they would cheerfully give me some far-fetched excuse about what had happened. Yes, they'd be there next time. For sure. No problem. And they never were. I was fairly certain they were putting me on.

Still, I kept showing up. This was my practice of persistence. Maybe I was being foolish, but it's what I did. When no one showed up, I'd go out into the school yard and look for the students. They'd offer me yet another bizarre excuse, with assurances that they'd be there next time, and then we'd have a conversation.

After a while I realized that these conversations *were* the writing group. The truth is, they were pretty interesting, much more interesting than whatever writing exercise I'd have been able to cook up. I think the students also began to be impressed with my sheer doggedness and good humor. I knew perfectly well that their excuses were jokes at my expense and that their promises to come to the group next time were intentionally off-putting. But I never complained, and I really didn't mind. I just kept showing up.

One day the topic came around to racism. What about it? I was astonished at the sudden shift in mood: casual bantering turned to passionate, sharp, highly intelligent social criticism. The students eloquently analyzed American government, social mores, arts, culture, the school system, black culture and arts, black history and its implications. I got caught up in their enthusiasm. "Suppose we write about this," I said. "Suppose we write about racism. This stuff you're saying here, the way you're saying it, your experiences as black teenagers, not being actors or rap stars, not making it dramatic or special, but just the way it really is, in your own words. People need to hear from you. Suppose we write it up, tell the truth about how you see things. We could get a grant and publish a book about it so everyone can hear what you guys have to say."

This struck the students as exactly the thing to do.

It would be nice to say that after this my writing group was full at every meeting. But life is not so neat. The following week I think one or two, or maybe no one, showed up. We did start writing about racism. I had a method: we'd have a short conversation, develop a question about racism that we could write about, then sit around a round table together and all write about the question. (I wrote, too.) The practice was timed writing: don't lift your pencil until I say stop. There was some enthusiasm. But still, we poked along—until things turned around in the end because of one young man named Isaiah Howard.

Isaiah was a quiet but very impressive person. He was a star on the football team, a respected person among his peers. He had obvious integrity and real moral force. One day he showed up at the group, did the writing, wrote something that he thought was pretty good, and got the idea. He knew, I think, from my record of persistence above and beyond the call of duty—and even good sense—that I was trustworthy. He could see that I was not trying to impose anything on him or the others. He also saw that the project could be worthwhile, even important and useful. Then and there he committed himself to it and began to show up every week. He took on the practice of persistence. And because he showed up, three other kids showed up, and they practiced persistence, too, being as loyal and steady in the group as Isaiah was. One of the students, D'Ron, had a white mother. For him the group became a way of working out his racial identity.

Each week our times of writing, though short, were powerful and pleasurable. Sitting pretty close around the table, we could feel each other's concentration and energy. One of the group members, Ronnie Hughes, was always in trouble. He came from a family enmeshed in the drug culture and had a history of drug use and expulsion himself. He was incurably defiant and funny, with an uncontrollable big mouth. One week in the writing group Ronnie got inspired and wrote an elegant and energetic rap poem about how terrific it was to be black. We determined that we'd put the poem at the beginning of our book, as a kind of introduction.

Ronnie's poem was a high moment for all of us: it encouraged us to write more and better material. After many sessions we had quite a stack of it. Each week we'd add to it and admire the growing pile of pages. We were getting excited. As it turned out, we did receive a grant to self-publish the book. To get the grant the students had to make a personal presentation to the granting committee at its offices in the local civic center. They handled it masterfully.

To do the final edit of our book we went on a three-day retreat at the Zen Center and worked hard to pare down and streamline what we had. Within a few weeks production was complete, and our book entered the local bookstores under the title *Racism: What About It?*, with a wonderful photograph of the students on the cover. It was a smash success. For a long time I had to keep ordering more copies from the printer because it kept selling out. The youngsters were really proud of themselves and became famous in their community. Ronnie Hughes became a local celebrity and would stride around the school full of pride. One night we gave a reading at a local bookstore. The place was packed. There was one deranged lady heckler whom Ronnie handled with kindness, firmness, and consummate cool, managing to get us all out of what could have been a very difficult and embarrassing situation. I had never seen anything quite like it before.

To practice persistence you have to have a long-range view. If you expect to see results in a week or a month or a year, it's easy to get impatient. *I expected that something would happen by now,* you may think, *and it didn't. Why not, and who's to blame? And shouldn't I stop what I am doing now and go on to the next thing, which will surely bring me the rewards I am seeking?* When you expect a lot in a hurry, however, disappointment is guaranteed.

In our world short-term thinking is the norm. Our economy, our educational system, our social lives, even our personal goals are driven by short-term thinking. Sports teams rise and fall with this week's scores, businesses with the last quarter's profits or losses, and schools, influenced by business models, offer outcome-based education: by such and such a time such and such a student will be able to demonstrate such and such skills. If one looks at things exclusively through a short-term lens, it becomes impossible to consider questions of value and questions of maturity and inner ripeness, upon which, in the end, all lasting and worthwhile results depend. Such questions do not even compute on the short-term scale.

It's not that we shouldn't make immediate plans or try to achieve immediate goals. There is no way to live in a human world without doing this. We make appointments we plan to keep. We embark on projects we expect to complete. We set short-term goals we try to achieve. But we are relaxed and open-minded about the realization of our plans and the achievement of our goals. We recognize that there is always a very good chance that what we are aiming for will not come about. Despite all our good efforts, outcomes are never really predictable. They are simply not within our control. The appointment is canceled, or it turns out quite differently from what we expected. The project runs into an unforeseen snag. The goal can't be met, or it is met but has far different consequences than we had anticipated; sometimes there are no discernible consequences at all. Something that may have seemed initially to be bad turns out later to have good effects, or the good consequences we worked for turn out to have disastrous implications down the line.

As we come to see by careful observation over time, it is impossible to know what kind of results are being produced in the long run by our actions. Of course we try our best to plan and shape our actions. But we know that too intense a focus on short-term effects usually leads to disappointment and ineffective action in the end. The more flexible and open we are to what occurs, the better things will go in the long run.

The view of the bodhisattva—the enlightenment being who is working on his or her own maturity and whose goal is to aid others toward their maturity—is essentially a long-term view. The bodhisattva knows that short-term, results-driven planning doesn't work very well; instead, he remembers the "I don't know mind" that is open, flexible, and sensitive, moving easily with changing conditions. Paying attention to results, both long- and short-term, is practical and cannot be ignored. But results come and go—good results suddenly turn bad, or bad results suddenly turn good. Results don't measure anything. They are just rough indicators of what might be going on.

I have always lived my life trusting more to values and commitments than to results. Having faith in your values and commitments and remaining true to them, being courageous enough to act on them no matter what—being, in a word, persistent—will always lead you where you want to go. You come to trust this after a while.

The traditional Buddhist concept of karma has a lot of implications for thinking about short-term results and the long-term view. Although the analysis of karma is fairly complicated in Buddhist thought, its basic thrust is fairly simple: actions have consequences. Good actions have good consequences, bad actions have bad consequences. In any given moment of your life you are presented with a situation whose roots are in the past. This situation is a given. You cannot change it. But in the middle of this given situation you face a choice: What will you do? Will you be discouraged and impatient, emphasizing the worst of the situation, or will you, with persistence, make the effort to turn that situation toward the good for others and yourself?

No matter what your situation is, no matter how fortunate or dire it seems, this choice is always there, always staring you in the face in each moment of your life. It's inescapable. And each moment, whether you intend it or not, whether you make an effort or not, you always do inevitably make your choice. Consciously or unconsciously, every moment you are choosing your life, and that choice is always decisive, never trivial. Your choices always have important consequences for the future, whether you can see them immediately or not.

Recognizing the importance of your choices helps you to cultivate the attitude necessary for the practice of persistence. Yes, there is much in your life that you simply cannot change and need to accept, without complaint. What has happened really has happened, and it can't be undone. The person you are, the social and intellectual forces that have shaped your attitudes—these are what they are. And yet, given the situation you find yourself in, at any moment you have the power, and the obligation, to choose how you will act. You can choose to act for the good or not, and your action one way or the other will definitely be effective in the long run, even though you may not yet be able to see how. If you look at things like this, you will quite naturally persist in your wise action because you are certain that what you are doing is for the good, regardless of the short-term results.

You don't need to take anyone's word on this claim. If you study your intimate experience carefully, you will see for yourself that it is true. For example, when you indulge your natural impulse to be angry or blaming, you become agitated and unhappy, and those with whom you are angry become enemies, making your life uncomfortable. If, on the other hand, you try your best to let go of anger or blaming, then your heart is more at ease and the person who was the object of your anger is either neutral to you or even friendly. It is true that in the short term your anger may help you to win your point. But in the long term, if you persist in letting go of anger and blaming, your happiness will increase and your relationships will become more positive. Winning your point will give you only short-term satisfaction, to be followed later by more battles, more anxiety, and more chances to lose.

If you test this out repeatedly, you will become convinced—as I have through much bitter and sweet experience—that long-term confidence in the power of goodness is never misplaced. With that confidence you won't focus so much on short-term gains because you will know for certain that a long-range commitment to the good produces much stronger gains in the end.

Human conduct in this world is often very discouraging and it would make sense that any of us would feel impotent and dismayed by it. After all, what can any one person do? If even the leaders of nations, who supposedly have their hands on the world's tiller, seem to be powerless to make things better, what are we ordinary people to do? But when you see the power of persistence and the certainty of long-term good results flowing inevitably from good actions, no matter how small and personal those actions may be, you do feel that what you do matters and makes a difference in this world. Drops make brooks that flow on eventually as rivers and oceans—and this is the only way rivers and oceans are made.

If you reflect on any personal quality you might be trying to cultivate, you begin to realize that developing that quality depends on working with its opposite. If you want to cultivate love, you have to work to overcome hatred and indifference; if you want to be strong, you have to work with what is weak within yourself in order to become stronger. And so it makes sense that the cultivation of the practice of persistence mostly has to do with studying and working with frustration, because frustration is the main obstacle to persistence.

Frustration isn't entirely bad, of course. If you are stubborn like me, frustration can spur you on. And even if you aren't stubborn, frustration is useful because it can motivate you to change a situation that should be changed. When you get frustrated enough, you look at conditions, discover what can be adjusted and fixed, and then roll up your sleeves and do what it takes to improve things.

It's nice when it's possible to improve things, but unfortunately it sometimes isn't. Often we are frustrated by conditions that can't be changed, or can be changed only at tremendous cost. We're frustrated with other people whose behavior is impervious to our correction, with illnesses that can't be cured, with losses that can't be prevented, with terrible social conditions that persist, or with emotions that arise in us that are just going to be there no matter what we try to do about them. Such frustration can be overwhelming and may easily escalate into anger, despair, or some other form of acute anxiety or shutting down—insomnia, compulsive behavior, addiction.

There's nothing good about being overcome with frustration; it is entirely counterproductive. There is much wisdom in the serenity prayer of Alcoholics Anonymous: "God grant me the serenity to accept the things I cannot change, the courage to change the things I can, and the wisdom to know the difference." No matter how justified our anger over our frustrations seems to be, no matter how convincing our despair, it is obvious that anger and despair do us no good at all.

Persistence, on the other hand, is always helpful. Persistence is not gritting your teeth and toughing it out. It's not brute endurance, or stubbornness. Persistence—which could also be called endurance, forbearance, patience—is the positive quality of calmly and steadily sticking to your goal for as long as you see that you can. If your initial commitment to your goal was good, then being able to follow through is good, too. Even if you never reach your goal, a calm and persistent effort will have made your experience much more pleasant and worthwhile than frustration. Persistence is its own reward. Even if you give up your goal in midstream, it is better to make that decision with the calm mind of persistence than with the confused mind that is overcome with frustration and quits in disgust, weakened for the next thing that comes along. If you have to change course, it is better to do so with the feeling that you have learned something you can build on, even if you have been defeated in what you tried to accomplish.

In the Zen tradition there's a story that's often told about this kind of persistence, this calm and peaceful abiding with an impossible situation until something shifts. The story is usually attributed to Hakuin, an eighteenth-century Japanese Zen master. Once a young girl of the village became pregnant out of wedlock. When her parents asked her who the culprit was, she said it was Hakuin, the old priest on the hilltop. The parents were outraged, and when the child was born, they whisked it off to the temple in a huff, demanding that Hakuin take the child in. "Here is your doing," they told him. "Now you deal with it." And off they went. "Oh, is that so?" Hakuin said, accepting the warm bundle.

A year or so later the girl, overcome with remorse, finally admitted to her parents that she had lied. The father was not Hakuin at all, but a young man of the village whose parents were very strict and who would surely disown their son if they knew the truth. The girl's parents, on hearing this, were mortified and again raced up the hill to the temple in a panic of shame and guilt. Bringing gifts and offerings, they bowed deeply to Hakuin in apology and took the child back. "You are such a good priest not to have said anything, to have accepted our terrible words with such composure." "Oh, is that so?" the old priest replied. Hakuin's practice of persistence, his forbearance with conditions no matter what they brought, was so strong that he was affected by neither praise nor blame.

One very effective way to practice with frustration is to make a detailed study of it just at the moment when you find yourself in its grip. Trying not to be frustrated when you are is just piling more frustration on top of your frustration. So why not instead look at it close up? When you do, you will notice that when frustration arises, the first thing you naturally do is look for someone or something to blame—even if that someone is yourself. But as soon as you do that, you are actually increasing your frustration, because you are leaping over your actual experience of frustration—futilely trying to avoid it, in effect—by focusing your energies on the object of your blame. The pile of frustration is always too high, however, to leap over. You only fall back in, over and over again.

Blaming is useless. It is a smokescreen, a blind, a weight that drags you down and doesn't get you anywhere. It is important to notice this as soon as you are frustrated and start blaming. Catch yourself. (This takes practice—you have to be quick.) Then focus instead on observing the actual feeling of frustration.

What does frustration feel like? Does your breathing tighten? Do your shoulders tense up, or does your face get red and hot? Do you clench your teeth? Your fists? What thoughts fly into your mind? Are there memories that come up? Visual images? What is frustration really like?

Oddly, if you accept frustration as frustration and study it without trying to relieve it by blaming or becoming angry, it will not overcome you. Instead, it will dissipate fairly quickly, or at least more quickly. You will simply digest it naturally.

Every human being already has a degree of persistence: we need some persistence just to stay alive, to hold down a job, to keep a human relationship functioning. All of us show up for our lives to some extent. We are all more patient and forbearing than we know, and we should recognize this and congratulate ourselves for it. We don't need to create the quality of persistence out of nothing. Rather, we need to expand and strengthen the persistence that is already there. Cultivating persistence takes persistence.

Let's say that now you have studied frustration and you are clear that you can indeed work with it. You have seen that by not indulging frustration as you have previously done you can replace it little by little with calmness and persistence. At this point, when frustration arises, you may no longer be seeing it as something to be avoided at all costs but as a challenge, an opportunity, almost as something to look forward to! You can immediately turn toward it, stop what you are doing, and start consciously breathing. It might help to smile on purpose or to relax the muscles in your face or shoulders. One Zen master I studied with told me that when he was frustrated and didn't know what to do, he would close his eyes and imagine the waves breaking gently on the beach on the Japan Sea where he grew up. Let the frustration wash through you and fall away like those waves, then feel the calmness arise. This is really not so different from the old saw about counting to ten when you are angry. If you have the presence of mind to start counting with one, you will have a lot more presence of mind by the time you get to ten.

You have to work on this with very small things until you get better at it. View every little frustration, every little daily setback, as another chance to reduce your bondage to frustration and strengthen your persistence muscle. Pick one: getting cut off in traffic, forgetting where you put your keys, walking out of the grocery store and realizing that you forgot to get the one important item you went in for. If you can develop your skill with small things, after a while it becomes possible to use it with major frustrations. The more you practice, the better you get at it. You catch your frustration sooner and turn it into persistence more easily and more frequently, all the way up to the point at which frustration hardly arises at all. Instead, a general spirit of persistence comes up fairly consistently with whatever you do.

Don't think about progress or results, though. To stay with the practice of persistence you can't be occupied with progress or results. That would be counterproductive. If you do see results, wonderful, but it is good not to be too confident about them. The truth is that it is very difficult to have a positive attitude of persistence with the fundamental frustrations of life: everything we set up will fall down, and we eventually lose our family and friends, our bodies and minds, to death. Zen practice focuses on persistence at this level. Zen practice is mostly the practice of failure.

Practicing failure, total failure, is the ultimate practice of persistence. In Zen practice we come back over and over again to this point: right now, just the way we are, with all our problems, with all the built-in frustrations that come from loss and impermanence and the final vanity of everything human, we are also perfect and everything in the world is complete. The only thing necessary is to embrace this point.

Of course we can't do it. We always fall to one side or the other, either crying over our problems or, stupidly, thinking in a moment of transcendence that we are beyond all problems. Many of the Zen stories turn on this point: how to see any failure as *absolute* failure, beyond any idea of success or failure. An old Zen master used to say, "Whether you're right or wrong, still I'll give you thirty blows!"

Contemporary Zen is generally more gentle than this, at least in the West, but practitioners nevertheless go through a psychological impasse with failure. If the practice group and the teacher treat this impasse with kindness and respect, it can be very useful, and ultimately very strengthening. You have the inner experience so many times of being wrong, of failing to grasp life's fundamental point, of getting (metaphorically at least) those thirty blows whichever way you turn. But finally you see: it's so simple! It's just myself as I am, letting go of all ideas of gaining or losing. There are no mistakes, no mistakes at all, there's only what happens—what has happened, what is happening, and what will happen. Life is only life. It's always a little messy. But that's fine. That's what being human is all about. It's trusting your life in an ultimate way, trusting your own ultimate goodness and the goodness of the world that surrounds you, the world that is you and you are it.

Finding this sort of trust in yourself is not a solo endeavor. While it may be true that all of us have to find wholeness within ourselves, without expecting someone else to give it to us or to complete us in some way, nevertheless I have found—and much spiritual literature corroborates—that it takes another person, or probably several others, to help us to find this out. Human relationships provide the magic, the catalyst, we need to come to a true self-trusting that will water the seed of true maturity in our lives. This is what I found in the years I spent with the boys' mentoring group, and it's what I found with my Zen teachers and students, with my parents, with my family, and with friends. We touch and awaken each other, not so much in conscious ways—in ways we can figure out and produce at will—but just by persisting with each other, just by hanging in and being together.

Zen literature often uses the metaphor of a chick breaking out of an egg to describe the way in which trust nurtures and aids our maturing process. When the chick intuitively senses that the time is right, she begins to peck on the shell from the inside, gently at first, then with more and more force. This pecking is necessary, but it is not sufficient. Outside the shell the mother hen, seeing the chick pecking from inside, also begins to peck. With perfect trust and sensitivity their pecking is perfectly timed; the shell breaks and the chick emerges. In the emerging of the chick there is only blossoming, only life reaching its proper fullness. Although there is pecking from the outside and pecking from the inside, the experience is just one pecking, without boundary. A Zen master wrote a poem about it:

The chick breaks out, the mother hen breaks in.

When the chick awakens there's no shell.

Chick and hen both forgotten,

Response to circumstances is unerring.

On the same path, chanting in harmony,

Through the marvelous mystery, walking alone.

Five

CONNECTION

ONE DAY RASHID WALKED INTO MY STUDY FOR OUR MEETING with a completely different attitude. It was unmistakable. He carried himself differently—he walked slowly, and with dignity. Instead of hurling himself down on his seat, as he usually did, he sat down with gravity. As soon as we were all assembled and settled, he announced, "My parents separated over the weekend. My mom moved to an apartment downtown." He seemed relieved. The worst had finally happened.

Rashid wanted to talk about it, and he did, without pause, for over an hour. He talked about how the fear that had covered the unspoken feelings in his household had been like a hot iron rod in his body all through this time; about how much pressure he'd felt in everything he did, as though his words and deeds could bring his parents closer together or drive them further apart; about how angry this made him with his parents, with himself, with the world; about how crazy he had felt, about how much he had not realized what was going on, and then when he did, how much he didn't understand about how bad it was; about how trying not to think about it or talk about it had made it much worse; and about how now that what he had feared most had finally happened, as it had happened to so many of his friends and classmates, he knew he'd be able to deal with it.

For a long time, he said, he'd held a grudge against his parents for what they were unknowingly doing to him and to each other. Their problems were simple. They just had to stop being so stubborn, so headstrong, so oblivious to each other. He could see it—why couldn't they? Why did they have to make such a mess and then spread the mess to him and his brother? But now that it had finally happened and he could see their suffering, their confusion, their grief, he could understand that they couldn't help it. They were caught in their own traps and couldn't get out of them. Now that he saw how hard it was for them, he could forgive them. Now that he knew it wasn't really their fault, he could support his mother in her anger and frustration and his father in his bewilderment and sorrow. Now he knew that what happened wasn't his fault, but also that he could make it better, easier, because he could forgive. Rashid told us how much it meant to him that our meetings had continued, and that he had a place where he could say all that he was saying today, and that others would listen without trying to give him advice.

As I sat taking in Rashid's torrent of eloquence and wisdom, I began to appreciate again the power of human pain. So much of what motivates us in our lives is the avoidance of pain, at any cost. How often we distract ourselves, run away, strategize solutions that never work out, or just decide without really deciding not to take notice. But as I was now hearing from Rashid plainly, pain can never really be ignored or avoided. And when pain is confronted, it has the power to open us up—if it doesn't break us apart. It has the power to inspire us, as it had Rashid, to wisdom, forgiveness, and compassion. Nothing connects us more to life, to ourselves, and to each other than our unavoidable human suffering. This connection to the reality of our own lives that we make only through our own pain is the seed of our maturity. Although we can prepare the ground for growth through listening and persistence, it is only when we meet the suffering that inevitably arises in our lives that we are finally able to begin the real work of growing up.

In early Buddhism the focus on suffering was very clear. "I teach suffering and the end of suffering," Buddha often said in the earliest scriptures when asked to describe the essence of his doctrine. The whole of the Buddhist path was designed with this in mind—to see suffering for what it is, and then to live in such a way that suffering is not only reduced but entirely put aside. Nirvana, the path's goal, was said to be "cool," "extinguished," like a candle flame blown out. Buddhas were beings who had so completely quelled the restless energy of their desire and longing that they were now living their final life. After this present life, they would find total peace and would not return, as the rest of us do, to this world of strife and confusion again and again.

But with the emergence of the bodhisattva path in Mahayana Buddhism some centuries after the Buddha's lifetime, the passion for saving others through compassion became so strong that the path's goal changed drastically. Rather than working to end suffering once and for all so that there would be no more coming back into life through future rebirths, the bodhisattva worked to develop a compassion so powerful that it would cause him or her to return to life again and again—not to suffer fruitlessly and repeatedly but to suffer gladly and purposefully in order to benefit others. Rather than trying to end suffering, the bodhisattva made heroic efforts to absorb his or her own suffering and that of others and through that suffering to connect to life at the deepest possible level. In the Western Judeo-Christian tradition there is also this sense of the nobility and power of accepting suffering as the way to connect with our lives. The story of the Jewish people's enslavement in and liberation from Egypt is a story of redemption through suffering, as is the passion of Jesus, who suffers for and with all creatures.

Rashid had been suffering for some time, silently and without much awareness of what was going on. But now, his crisis coming to a head, his very suffering had suddenly become his path through it. Connecting to his own pain, he could see his parents' pain, and this enabled him to know them as he had never known them before. Before his parents' marital problems had happened—before the tension, the uncertainty, and now the separation—Rashid had simply taken his parents for granted. They were just there. Mom and Dad. As they had always been. Parental archetypes perhaps, problems for him in many ways, part of his story, but not really people on their own, in their own right. But now, with all that had been happening and all that he had been feeling, he began to notice what his parents were really like. They were both stubborn, each in a different way. His mother was quiet, and yet indomitable. His father was aggressive, and yet passive. Rashid didn't describe them this way, but he saw them quite astutely (and much more accurately than I could have despite the fact that I had known them for many years). And unlikely as this is, he saw them in their fullness—what was good about them as well as what was bad—and he saw them widely, with compassion and forgiveness.

Because of Rashid's experience, the other boys also began to take stock of their parents. They, too, had had the normal teenage view of their parents as overly protective, a little dense, a little dim. But beyond this, they also gradually came to see, through our discussions (which at this point I directed, quite naturally, toward the issue of parents), that their parents were both good people and limited people, as all people are. And like Rashid, they began to have a feeling of forgiveness toward them.

Forgiving our parents is an important step in the direction of maturity. It is astonishing how many people fail to take this step, choosing to remain, in effect, adolescents throughout their lives. Even into old age, many people maintain the same wounded, angry, or disappointed relationships with their parents that they formed when they were young. People I know who are like this say that they can't help it. Their parents are extremely difficult people, they say, and getting worse with age. They are certain that it is impossible to make peace with their parents and overcome the old hurts because their parents have constantly reopened the old wounds with each new encounter over the years.

I am sure my friends know what they are talking about. I have no doubt that these parents are just as impossible as their children say they are. (I have met some of these parents and can corroborate this!) And yet, although my friends may be quite right in their assessments, I disagree with their conclusions. Peacemaking never depends on the other person. Peace is made in our own hearts, and nowhere else. If negotiations and changes are to be made outside ourselves, these proceed (at least ideally) only after we have made peace within ourselves. If we are fortunate enough to have our parents' cooperation in the peacemaking effort, so much the better. But if not, the work goes on anyway.

Throughout the years of my spiritual practice I have met many people who thought that a serious engagement with spiritual practice could be a substitute for all this messy work. Taking up a lifestyle radically different from the one they grew up with and spending many long hours in meditation or prayer, they thought, would help them transcend the family wounds that had brought them to their practice in the first place. But eventually their spiritual practice, when they actually paid attention to it (and not everyone does—it is possible to be half-asleep in our practice), and whether they liked it or not, brought them back to their family wounds vividly enough that they had to deal with them. Sometimes they did this through psychotherapy, sometimes through dialogue with their families, sometimes through relationships with their spiritual teachers, and sometimes simply on the meditation cushion. Although we all have a tremendous capacity for self-deception and avoidance, the meditation cushion generally works against it. Sitting peacefully in a retreat one day, you may well be blindsided by a rush of feelings about your parents you never expected or knew were there.

The truth is that no matter what kind of upbringing we have had, whether we were raised by saintly parents full of loving kindness and wise in the ways of child-rearing or by parents who were just the opposite, all of us were hurt in our early years to some extent, and so all of us have some forgiveness work to do with our parents. Beyond the inevitable mistakes they made, there is the hurt and humiliation that life itself brings to all of us. Every child has been thwarted, every child has been terrified, every child has been turned back sometime when he desperately wanted to plunge ahead. Growing up always involves much humiliation and disappointment as those early feelings of omnipotence and promise gradually yield to the reality that the world is full of insurmountable obstacles, many in the shape of other people who may be stronger, smarter, better-looking, better educated, and more skillful than we are. Although from a rational point of view this reality may have nothing to do with our parents, from the child's imaginative and symbolic perspective all of life seems to be connected to them, to swirl around our memory of them or our relationship to them, like a troubling nimbus. The vulnerable child we all have been both absolutely loves and absolutely fears the all-powerful, all-wise parent who inevitably betrays the child's trust sometimes with an angry look, a cross word, or a threatening gesture, whether real or imagined.

I am sure that we all reach adulthood with a need to forgive our parents simply for being who they are or were. Many of us never do forgive them. Although our adolescent anger may subside, we go on for a long time harboring a heavy weight of guilt and occlusion in relation to our parents, a weight that we feel in our own living as a blockage of energy or love. So whether or not we are interested in making peace with our parents for their sake, we need to do it for our own.

I have a friend who is a geriatric psychotherapist. She runs groups for people who are over eighty years old. She tells me that the number-one topic in most of her groups is parents. Amazingly, the octogenarians are still chewing on childhood stuff, so many decades after their parents have left this world.

These knotty feelings focused on our parents apparently are much more powerful within the Western psyche than in the psyches of people from traditional Eastern cultures. There is a commonplace imaginative practice in Tibetan Buddhism that is used to help students generate compassion: they are asked to imagine that all beings are their mother—as if, in some distant past life, all beings actually had been their mother. The idea is that since all people naturally feel that there is nothing in this world more pure and more wonderful than a mother's love, imagining beings as our mothers will make us feel a strong and positive connection to them. But I have never attended any sort of meeting in the West in which this practice was given without hearing a few people in the audience say (what probably many more are also feeling), "Regard all beings as my mother to generate loving kindness! You must be joking! You have never met my mother. She is controlling and needy and absolutely impossible!"

Because I know how strong and pivotal our need is to forgive our parents, I created my own version of a traditional Buddhist loving kindness meditation. In one part of the practice, students visualize each of their parents in turn, and then repeat these phrases, as sincerely as they can: "May he (or she) be happy. May he (or she) be content with himself (herself). May his (or her) heart be open." This turns out to be a fairly tough practice. Most people find that when they try to send out these loving wishes for their parents, much ambivalence comes up. They often, though certainly not always, have a reservoir of love and positive feeling to bring to this practice, but just as often negative feelings arise, sometimes in relation to the parents but quite often in relation to themselves. It seems as if buried deep below our hurt feelings about our parents are hurt feelings about ourselves—such as guilt for having had so much antipathy toward those we are supposed to love, or self-hate derived from an unconscious identification with a parent we have rejected. Such feelings are complicated and differ from person to person. But observing people do this practice over the years has convinced me of the deep significance of our feelings for our parents.

Another practice that I have taught and often done myself is the practice of imagining our parents as children. I see my father as a skinny little boy. I see my mother as a frightened little girl. I imagine the clothes they are wearing, the places they are growing up in. It is likely that this little boy and this little girl have often been hurt, confused, upset, or utterly despairing. I see my father and mother as adolescents. Probably they looked at their parents with the same mixture of love and dismay, guilt and confusion, bitterness and respect, that I felt as an adolescent when I looked at them. Just as I struggled with them, they struggled with their parents. Certainly the way they related to me as a child had a lot to do with the way their parents related to them. And their parents had learned from their own parents, on and on into the distant past. There isn't anything I can do to change all that, but simply by appreciating it, vividly and visually in my mind's eye, I can forgive my parents for who they were and what they did. Maybe I have made the same mistakes with my own children that they did with me. Or maybe I have made other mistakes.

I have found that if people stay with this kind of practice without avoiding the complexities of the feelings that inevitably arise, but just allowing those complexities to come without trying to fix them and without giving in to resistance and avoidance, they eventually experience a moment of forgiveness, a moment of liberation from old feelings. And even, finally, some gratitude.

In the end our maturity demands that in accepting our parents we find a way to be grateful to them, no matter how terrible a job they may have done with us. To come to this acceptance and gratitude for our parents is to accept and be grateful for the lives we have lived. Although it may take a lifetime's work, and although even then we may not complete the job, to accept our parents with gratitude is to accept the world as it actually is and to understand its suffering and confusion with a wide wisdom. If we can forgive our parents for being who they are and understand the conditions that caused them to be the way they were, we will have a measure of peace in our own lives.

Although I have been arguing that we need to spend a long time working with our feelings about our parents—until we eventually reach the point of appreciation—in the end our growth demands that in some deep, inner sense we leave our parents behind. The myth of the Buddha's life has something to tell us about this aspect of working with our feelings about our parents. The prince Siddhartha (Buddha's name before his awakening experience) was a talented and skillful young man who enjoyed a happy life in the palace. He got along well with his family and was destined to succeed his father as king. Siddhartha's father was quite protective of his son. Hoping somehow, as all good parents do, to accomplish the impossible feat of shielding his son from the world's harshness, he tried to keep Siddhartha always near the palace, where life was pleasant and things went well. Of course this restriction could not hold. Siddhartha was after all a young man—he would naturally go exploring. He sneaked out of the palace grounds several times to see what the world was really like and was dismayed to discover the shocking truth about the human condition: suffering, old age, sickness, and death were inevitable for all.

In those days in India it was quite common to become a religious seeker in the face of such hard facts, and Siddhartha decided to undertake that life. Since this intention went counter to the wishes of his parents, he had to leave his family secretly in the middle of the night, without warning and without looking back. Later, as an enlightened sage, he began a new religious order of "homeless ones" who were required to leave their families entirely behind. When he eventually returned to his home territory on one of his many journeys, he was reunited with his parents, not as their son but as the

Awakened One, the World Honored One, the Buddha. Deeply moved, Buddha's father became a devoted lay follower, and his stepmother, who had raised him after his mother died in childbirth, became, poignantly and after much struggle, the first Buddhist nun.

Whether we like it or not, our parents play an integral part in our path toward maturity. They loom large in our psychic lives, giving us all the trouble and resistance we need, whether they intend to or not. Insofar as they have caused us suffering and we can connect to that suffering as part of our life's wounds and forgive them, they have also helped us. And yet, once we have connected to our own pain and the unique reality of our own lives—and thus truly begun our journey toward maturity—there is almost nothing our parents can do for us. The work of taking our places is our own work, never theirs. Like the Buddha, we must leave, spiritually if not physically, in the middle of the night. Our parents, good or bad, alive or dead, are going to do whatever they do and be whoever they are. We can't help that or change it one way or the other. But no matter what they do or don't do, what they are or are not, our path lies ahead, and it must go through and beyond our parents. Somehow we have to engage in a transformative struggle with our parents—or at least with the archetypal parents that exist in our minds. The struggle may be (though it need not be) painful and difficult and full of bitterness and misunderstanding. In fact, if we are aware of what is going on and understand the struggle as our own inner process that includes our parents, not as a political battle with our parents for control (as we may have viewed it in our adolescence), we can minimize the difficulty and the damage. Buddha's break with his parents was decisive, drastic, dramatic, and total. Ours is probably more gradual and internal. But either way, we, too, must be home leavers—and then, like

Buddha, we can eventually become returners, giving our parents good teachings for their own journeys toward the end of their lives.

These days I have many friends whose children are going off to college. There is a mixture of sadness and relief for them as they watch their children leave. I remember when I went off to college. I was one of the few in my high school graduating class who went to school out of state, and I viewed it as a tremendous adventure. My parents took me there and dropped me off at my dorm on a sunny fall day with all my bags. I couldn't wait for them to leave, and I do not remember experiencing anything more than a brief moment of sadness when they did go. By contrast, the day our first twin left home for college was one of the saddest days of my life—about as emotionally powerful for me as the day he was born. He was leaving to attend a very tiny college in the high California desert, and all four of us drove him there. The trip was absolutely terrible: driving there, depositing him in his room, camping out overnight, leaving the next morning. I will never forget the feeling of that day, especially waving good-bye to him and driving down that narrow dirt road away from the campus, watching him standing there getting smaller and smaller in the rearview mirror, continuously waving.

That's how it always goes. The Buddha once said, pointing out the obvious (as religious sages so often do), that all meeting ends in parting. If you can accept the truth of this and digest it, you will begin to realize that all your relationships are precious, for each one has taught you something unique that you could not have learned in any other way. Each of our relationships ought to be handled like a delicate gem, with full respect for its particular beauty.

Martin Buber tells a Hasidic tale that beautifully expresses this poignancy of human relationships. It is in the form of a commentary, given by Rabbi Barukh on a line in the 119th Psalm: "I am a sojourner on the earth; hide not thy commandments from me." Concerning this verse the great rabbi said: "He whom life drives into exile and who comes to a land alien to him has nothing in common with the people there and not a soul he can talk to. But if a second stranger appears, even though he may come from quite a different place, the two can confide in each other, and live together henceforth, and cherish each other. And had they not both been strangers, they would never have known such close companionship."

As close as we are to our parents, for good and ill they are strangers to us, like everyone we encounter in this world. For at the deepest levels of the heart none of us really understands other people or the world. We are all strangers here, gathered from other realms to make our destiny together. Each of us struggles to belong, to feel comfortable, to claim our own place. Such struggles are the journey of a lifetime. In this alien situation, as the rabbi says, it is a great comfort to meet and recognize another stranger, someone who knows our struggle, who appreciates our pain, because he or she is going through the same thing. Our parents are the first such strangers we encounter in this world.

Working to forgive our parents for being who they are usually brings into view the fact that we also need to forgive ourselves for being ourselves. It is truly staggering to recognize the extent to which most of us harbor serious grievances against ourselves. We are annoyed with ourselves in a million ways—we don't like our looks, our talents, our skills, our attitudes. As difficult as it may be to forgive our parents, it is even more difficult to forgive ourselves. Probably the latter depends on the former, or at least goes hand in hand with it. Our grievances against ourselves—our disappointment, anger, frustration, and dismay at our limitations and character flaws—are so deeply ingrained that most of the time we aren't even aware of them. They seem simply to *be* us, the wound that is our self. I have always considered it the pinnacle of the spiritual life when we can simply allow ourselves to be who we are, forgiving ourselves for all our failures to live up to our ideals and expectations. To see that who we are is a gift and a path forward, not a mistake.

Unlike the Buddha, who is depicted in the texts as a perfect human being, the Zen masters of old were rough, pungent characters with many foibles. Paintings of them show scraggly beards, scowls, and stooped shoulders, not glowing, smiling beatific countenances. Despite their many imperfections, the Zen masters didn't rail against themselves, trying desperately to become someone else. Instead, they embraced the way they were, taking on joyfully the task of being themselves and acting spontaneously and confidently. They seemed to celebrate themselves. Their long practice on their meditation cushions showed them the shape of essential human suffering as it had manifested in their own lives, and they came to accept that, affirm it, and make use of it. To really take our places in this world we need to forgive ourselves and accept ourselves. Without self-forgiveness and self-acceptance we are always at best slightly embarrassed about who we are, and at worst tortured.

If the key to forgiveness of self and others is connecting to our own suffering, you might be thinking, *I have been aware of my suffering for a long time, and it hasn't made me forgive myself or others. Aren't we all acutely aware of our own suffering most of the time, even to the point of obsession? What good does it do us?* Complaining and obsessing about our suffering is not what I mean by "connecting" to it. As long as I see my suffering as "mine," as unfair, as tragic, as something that should not have happened or should be removed, I am not really connecting to it. Quite the contrary, by thinking of the suffering as mine, as a mistake, and as something to be eliminated, I have reduced it to something manageable and at the same time distanced myself from it. To see my pain as "mine" and then to complain that it shouldn't be is to distract myself from it, to disconnect from it. I connect with my pain when I realize that it's not merely *my* pain—it is *the* pain, *the* human suffering, everyone's suffering.

This realization is what we are trying to avoid when we complain and wish that things were otherwise. Really connecting to our suffering seems so immense that we think it's unbearable. But we are quite wrong. To accept the immensity of our suffering is to find comfort in the heart of it. To connect this deeply with our own suffering is to open ourselves to the suffering of others and to be met in our own pain.

Once a woman came to the Buddha holding the corpse of her dead child, wailing in her anguish and pleading with the Buddha to bring the child back to life. The Buddha said that to do this he would need a rare ingredient: a mustard seed from the household of a family that had never known death. He sent the woman out to find such a mustard seed. But her desperate search yielded no such seed—only many stories of grief as great as and greater than her own. In the end these stories connected her deeply and truly to her own suffering, and so she was healed from her anguish.

It's easy to sympathize with the woman's feeling at the beginning of the story. The human desire to remove pain from our lives is strong. It is tough to connect to our pain so deeply that we see everyone's pain in it. We are so afraid of this that we do all that we can to avoid our pain, to run away from it if we can, to change or fix it somehow, or, if possible, to ignore it.

The most compelling form of pain avoidance is blaming. If you can occupy yourself enough with blaming your suffering on something or someone—even yourself—you don't have to notice the horrifying weight of your suffering. To feel that weight is to feel disempowered and weak. But when you blame, especially when you have some justification for blaming, you can replace the feeling of powerlessness with something much more energizing: anger and hatred. Now you are powerful, and you can do something to act out your power. Blaming brings a measure of satisfaction, even if it is yourself you are angry with, rail against, and sabotage, odd as that may seem. Knowing the culprit and going after him or her, you can safely avoid your sorrow and grief.

In my lifetime I have seen many instances of harbored anger and long-term grudges. Even when the parties involved have had sincere hearts and wanted very much to forgive each other, it was sometimes impossible for them to do so. In each and every case of forgiveness I have known, it occurred only when one of the parties, sometimes after years of denial, was finally able to fully connect to his or her own suffering and hurt. Then and only then could the heart soften toward the other person.

Forgiveness, then, isn't a special and unusual practice; it is the ongoing practice of accepting responsibility for your own difficulty. It is inner work. Reconciliation—reaching out to those who have wronged you or whom you have wronged—is another step. It comes out of our practice of forgiveness. Reconciliation requires us to understand the pain of the other person, without losing sight of our own pain, so that eventually we can express all the pain of the situation. In reconciliation we seek to make peace based on this recognition of the mutuality of pain. To reconcile is to balance appropriately one side with the other, until both sides of the scale come to rest.

We can't expect too much. The truth is that it is very difficult to communicate with someone when there is pain between you. There is a tremendous risk that the pain that caused the distance between you will so occlude communication that any effort to talk will lead to renewed pain. Sometimes reconciliation is impossible—at least for the moment. Maybe a lot of time has to go by before any effort to reconcile is even thinkable. Maybe it would be best to agree that nothing can be said without causing more trouble and to part company for a while with, if possible, a commitment to try again later.

Our personal lives are full of irreconcilable conflicts. Once two of my mother's sisters had a bitter argument over which of them was going to inherit a vase that my grandmother had owned. The vase was not particularly valuable or attractive, but the battle over it was intense and lasted for the rest of their lives—the sisters died without reconciling. Watching this conflict unfold over the course of many years, I eventually saw quite clearly that it was not about a vase at all (though this was not at all apparent to some other members of my family, who became fiercely partisan). The conflict was not even about my grandmother's death and the sisters' inability to digest and understand it. It was about a lifetime of unacknowledged conflict and suffering that hurt so badly that there would never be a way to overcome it, let alone recognize it for what it was. The sisters had hurt each other many times since childhood and had never been able to express that hurt until it erupted into open and permanent warfare over a vase. Such stories are not rare in families. And when they involve not only families but whole communities that have hurt each other over the generations, the scale of the tragedy becomes immense.

Many years ago our community suffered its most bitter crisis when our second abbot, Roshi Baker, resigned under fire. Many people left the community at that time, and the depth of hurt in those who left, as well as in those who remained, was immense. So many had felt betrayed—by Roshi Baker, by their friends in the community, by themselves for believing in what they now felt to be a foolish dream. The emotions were far too strong to deal with for many years. We simply had to wait them out. But after about fifteen years we were able to organize a retreat to try to open up and heal.

With Gary Friedman's help, we brought together about forty people who had been involved with the community in the days when all the trouble had happened, including Roshi Baker. We spent a weekend together practicing some meditation but mostly talking in the style of our reconciliation meetings. It was the most difficult and emotional weekend of my life. For hour after hour we listened to each other's stories, learning things about each other's inner lives we had never imagined. Although the meeting did not effect miraculous reconciliation, it did significantly change the hearts of many people. When you have a chance to hear another's sorrow, honestly told without blame or resistance, you see more clearly the large pattern of human hurting, and even if your pain remains so strong that you can't reconcile and make a new relationship, perhaps you can let go of some of the bitterness of the past.

In 1991 I led a Zen training period at our temple. The Gulf War had recently begun, and each day we would hear news of the killing. One of the women students had a son in the army who was stationed in the Persian Gulf. As is always the case in a war, the situation in the area was constantly changing, and the news was never complete or accurate. Every day this student feared that this would be the day her son went into combat, to kill or be killed. Her tension and fear became a major concern in all of our minds.

The theme of my talks was the Buddha's noble truth of suffering—accepting and understanding that all conditioned existence is of the nature of suffering, and that suffering is therefore unavoidable and fundamental. When we accept and digest this fact, connecting to our own pain and through our pain to the suffering of others, we can find some peace, just as the woman looking for a mustard seed discovered. Although I encouraged the efforts of our many students and supporters at the time who were protesting the Gulf War in an effort to stop it or slow it down, I also knew that humans have always been—and probably always will be—aggressive and violent, and that a true and deep vision of life requires us to know and accept this. Time and time again the woman whose son was in the army would cry out when I said this. She refused to hear it, to sit still for it. She could not even begin to accept the fact that her son might any day be put in the midst of such jeopardy.

And I knew that she was right. Suffering is inevitable and must be accepted. And yet, suffering is also unacceptable. The world is what it is; all we have to do is read the newspaper to see how full of pain the world is. Our anguish is only increased when our hope that the world will be different turns once again to disappointment: things haven't improved, civilization hasn't made us more humane. We despair that there will always be wars and famines, injustice and trouble. And yet, I also know that as human beings we must keep wanting the world and ourselves to be better than we are. So we have to hold both things in our minds and hearts at the same time: accepting what is, just as it is, and working to make it better some day. Accepting the war completely at the same time that we are trying to stop it.

Connection to our own suffering is connection to the fullness of life. It brings us to a profound compassion for ourselves and others. The journey of maturity is long, sensitive, and essentially spiritual. It involves responding truly and faithfully to conditions, owning our own experience honestly without being limited by it, and developing the strength and stability to bear life's troubles and the self-acceptance necessary to be able truly to love others. None of this is possible if we ignore or avoid our suffering. Connecting to our pain is connecting to our life as bodhisattvas do—in identity and solidarity with the world, sharing its joys and its sorrows even though we know they are endless.

Six

MEDITATION

WHEN I WRITE ABOUT RELATIONSHIPS—ABOUT LISTENING, persistence, trust, connection, forgiveness, and all the other associated practices that build maturity—I seem to be assuming an abnormal human capacity for serious and deep attention. On the surface at least, it seems as if most of us are incapable of paying this much attention to our lives. We're all so harried, running around to take care of work, family, social engagements, entertainment, housekeeping, and so on. We are barely able to keep body and soul together, let alone be thoughtful and reflective about it all. Do any of us really have the time, let alone the psychic space, to nurture ourselves sufficiently so that we can grow and mellow into the people we most fundamentally are?

I see the problem, but I am not discouraged by it. I am sure that everyone has the capacity to develop profound attentiveness—and moreover, I know that everyone longs and needs to develop it. Our lives cry out for attentiveness, our hearts yearn for it.

Developing attentiveness doesn't take extra time. It's not an additional item on our already full "to do" lists. Rather, attentiveness is the spirit, the style, the attitude, and the skill with we approach those lists. In fact, attentiveness saves time. It eliminates automatically the many extra items that are on our lists because we lacked attentiveness in the first place. With attentiveness we don't complicate things so much—we don't mindlessly create messes that require more activity to sort out. With attentiveness we naturally review and reorient priorities, and our lists slowly change character, becoming simpler. Although it makes no sense to say that we are too busy to be attentive, it is true that attentiveness must be cultivated. The best way to cultivate attention is through meditation practice.

Soon after Rashid's impassioned outburst about his parents' separation, the boys and I decided to practice meditation in our meetings. We experimented with different forms of meditation and eventually found the practices that became our own. We began our meetings with an offering practice, traditional in Buddhism, but almost universal in spiritual traditions: mindfully making symbolic gestures of gratitude for our lives, accompanied by words or silent intentions of aspiration for spiritual growth. We offered incense before the Buddha image on an altar that also included a lit candle and fresh flowers.

Many kinds of altars are possible. Your altar could be built around a picture of Jesus or Mary, a copy of the Koran or the Bible, a picture of a mountain or a sunset, or simply a stone or a pinecone. And the offering can be anything—an apple, clear water, a treat. It is not the details that are important but the feeling the altar represents or evokes of peacefulness, reverence, gratitude, and spiritual aspiration.

The boys and I made our offerings in silence. Carefully,

each boy would take his turn placing the lit incense in the pot. Sometimes we spoke words of dedication as we made the offering gesture ("With this incense offering may we find the way to a true maturity that benefits all humankind"), and sometimes we were silent with our own feelings.

After the incense offering, we moved silently into a meditation practice in which we chanted the Japanese syllables *namu dai bo sa* ("I identify with the great bodhisattva"). I had learned this chant from the late Maurine Stuart, one of my Zen teachers, and whenever I chant it I think of her belting it out in her strong, clear alto voice. I taught it to the boys, and they liked it, so we chanted it at each meeting, rhythmically over and over to the accompaniment of a small Korean drum. At first the chanting would be a little ragged, and we were self-conscious about it, but as we persisted our voices gradually began to blend, until we made one sound together that seemed to go deep inside. After the chanting, the silence in the room was strong. We sat in its midst for a few minutes, paying attention to breathing in and out. We chanted a Japanese Zen phrase, but other phrases can be used. The practice of chanting or singing, like offering, is also common to most spiritual traditions.

Our third practice was the bell meditation. I had a good, small Japanese meditation bell with a clear, reverberating sound. One of us would strike the bell (we took turns), and then we sat quietly listening as closely as we could to the rising, swelling, and disappearing of the sound, to the silence that succeeded the sound, to the ambient noises that then filled the silence, and then to the sound coming back when the bell was struck another time. The boys' imaginations were captured by the notion of trying to find that elusive place where the sound of the bell disappears into silence. We struck the bell six times, with lots of space in between each striking. After the sixth time, we again sat quietly in meditation for a few minutes, breathing and paying attention to the feeling of our bodies. This three-practice routine at the beginning and end of each meeting became our custom and made a difference in the kind of conversation we were able to have together.

When I first began meditation practice more than thirty years ago, most people thought of it as something inherently Asian and therefore unnatural for Westerners to do. D. T. Suzuki, the early Zen pioneer in America whose books I had read as a college student, felt that Western people would never be able to do classical meditation practice and that they would come to spiritual insight through books, reflection, and conversation with adepts like himself. But Suzuki was quite wrong. Meditation practice isn't Asian—it isn't even Buddhist or Hindu. It is human. Anyone can do it, and today, in the West, millions do.

Meditation practice does calm us down—and this is important—but it is much more than a tranquilizing technique. Meditation practice is a powerful way of getting deeply in touch with your life at its most essential level. As you become more in touch with your life at this level, you naturally become more attentive, awake, and attuned to your thoughts, emotions, and inner currents. Meditation practice is a spiritual process that unfolds with your life. It requires no doctrine or belief system, and it can be adapted to many purposes and systems of thought. In its broadest sense, meditation practice is an approach to life that promotes self-awareness, self-kindness, and self-forgiveness and brings us the clarity to see what we need to do in our lives and the forbearance to stay the course. Meditation practice fosters the calmness and balance that enable us to be honest with our emotions and needs without being limited and trapped by them. Meditation practice makes it more possible for us to act out of our deepest, calmest, most accurate selves.

In short, meditation practice helps us to firmly set the cornerstone of the most important relationship of our lives: our relationship with our self. As this relationship develops, our meditation opens up to include others, and as our relationships soften and deepen, loving kindness and openness become more natural to us. Meditation practice nourishes our maturity.

While I am convinced of the efficacy of meditation practice and know that ordinary people can do it in the context of ordinary lives, I don't want to underestimate the difficulty. Although anyone can meditate for ten or twenty minutes once in a while, the real fruits of meditation practice require some commitment, some discipline, and some courage.

In Asia over the generations meditation practice has been the province of monastics. By and large meditation has not been practiced by ordinary people, who have imagined that it requires a level of truth-seeking and determination far beyond what they could muster. "Maybe next lifetime," the faithful would typically say. In the West, too, contemplative life has been largely monastic, requiring total commitment and great self-sacrifice. Zen, too, is essentially monastic, and has a reputation as a fairly rigorous discipline. Certainly the stories of the tough old Chinese Zen masters, who sat without moving for days at a time and shouted at their students when they weren't whacking them with sticks, make Zen meditation practice seem pretty daunting.

It is true that meditation practice is not for the fainthearted. I have always felt, however, that a life inspired by disciplined meditation practice (or some other form of spiritual endeavor) is easy compared to the alternative: the rigors and travails of ordinary life. Especially these days, with traffic snarls, media blizzards, the dizzying upturns and downturns of the economy, and the consequent twin epidemics of busyness and stress, just getting through an average day takes a great deal of fortitude. It seems to me that no form of austere monasticism is more difficult than this. During all the years I spent living in Zen temples, rising early in the morning to meditate and chant, and then working all day, I always felt that what I was doing was quite easy compared to nonmonastic life.

But ordinary life has always been difficult and rigorous. There's an old story about the "bird's nest Roshi," a Zen teacher of the T'ang dynasty who practiced meditation in a bird's nest up in a tree branch. The branch was high up in a tall tree, which was exactly the point: the Roshi sat up there to force himself to stay awake and alert. If he dozed off, he'd surely fall and kill himself. The Chinese poet Po Chu I, who was a government official, came to visit and called up to the Roshi: "Why do you meditate up there? It's so dangerous." The bird's nest Roshi replied: "It may look dangerous to you, but to me, being down there is far more dangerous."

In its simplest and most basic forms, meditation is stopping your complicated activity for a while and taking time to focus your mind steadily on one thing. The more useless that thing is the better, because if it is something useful—a task or a problem, for instance—your mind is likely to become too interested in it. When the mind is too interested in something, it wants to do something with it, and desire activates the mind, causing it to search for solutions, run through possibilities, project into the future, review the past. With meditation you want the mind to be bright and alert but calm, so the meditation object should be something definite enough to hold on to but not so thrilling that you get excited about it. It's good to use something like the breath, or the posture, or simple physical sensations.

After trying and failing to anchor the mind on one or more of these things, you might well get a bit frustrated. And frustration, as we've seen, is very useful because it promotes the practice of persistence. The more you practice meditation, the more you appreciate that it is less a matter of actual meditation on the object than it is a matter of persisting in coming back over and over again to the object when you have lost track of it. As any meditator knows, the mind's tendency to distraction is prodigious. The mind won't stay put! So you gently persist in your efforts to train the mind as you would persist in training a small child or an animal—with patience and much repetition.

Trying to focus the mind on an object but being unable to do it for very long, despite all our efforts, is a humbling experience, and that in itself is something quite useful. With practice over time, however, it does become easier to settle the mind, slow it down, calm it, sharpen it, stabilize it. With this stabilization come many physical changes. The heartbeat, breath, and brain activity all slow down. The whole body enters a state of restfulness and calm. It is the production of these physical changes that makes meditation so useful for our health and well-being.

When the body is calm and the breath comes strongly into focus, thoughts are less compelling, and less deceptive. We feel emotions strongly, but they do not have as much power over us as they usually do. Our emotions are less seductive, less obsessive. We see and experience what's going on inside us with much more accuracy.

It is this capacity to clearly see our attitudes, thoughts, and emotions that makes meditation practice so important for the development of maturity. Once the mind slows down and is relieved of its various jobs and projects, it becomes simply present, alert but not anxious, and things get interesting. We begin to notice and experience things we never noticed or experienced before. We see the subtle patterns of thought and feeling that ceaselessly arise and pass away in our minds—patterns, we realize, that were probably present all along but that we never noticed before. For most of us it is initially quite a shock to see close-up how often we are petty, greedy, jealous, lazy, stupid, dull, or confused, how often we repeat ourselves, daydream, gripe, or speculate wildly, how radically dissatisfied and restless we are so much of the time.

As you continue to meditate and to notice these patterns you may well begin wondering whether it was a good idea to begin meditation practice in the first place. Before meditation practice none of the patterns you're noticing were a problem, because you didn't notice them. Or perhaps the meditation practice is producing more of these troubling mental states than you would otherwise have been experiencing. Maybe you were better off before. Maybe meditation practice is making your life worse! I have heard such doubts expressed by many students over the years, but they are always expressed with a certain bemused humor, as if the meditation practice they have done has given them a sense of well-being that is somewhat in advance of their capacity to think about it.

Of course, meditation practice doesn't make your life worse, it makes it better. But it makes your life better the way most things that are lasting and important do—by a long and circuitous route. Meditation practice improves your life by showing you, first of all, with some difficult clarity, the mess you are in. Indeed, you see that you've been in this mess all along but never noticed it before. Most of us do not like to think we are in a mess. We are well conditioned to put the best face on things, to be cheerful, to look the other way if something unpleasant comes up. It is ordinary common sense: to hope for the best and act as if everything were for the best. Often we behave like those three monkeys who cover up eyes, ears, and mouth to see no evil, hear no evil, and speak no evil. Who wants to look at unpleasantness, to dredge it up, to dwell on it? And besides, none of us wants to see ourselves as someone with problems, someone who needs help, someone who is not doing terribly well. So we don't see our true condition, and we don't particularly want to see it. Even if once in a while we do get a glimpse of how things really are with us, we dismiss it as an aberration, just a bad day or week, and try our best to distract ourselves, to stay busy, to go on to other things.

If you were someone who doesn't like to see difficulty and strongly prefers to deny or ignore it, you probably wouldn't be interested in meditation in the first place. Meditation would seem threatening at worst and boring at best. Why waste time sitting around doing nothing when there's so much to do, especially if the sitting around doing nothing is going to make you brood on how much you are failing as a human being! Where's the advantage in that?

Anyone who's interested in meditation in the first place probably already senses that we are all in a mess, the human mess, and that we have no choice but to clean it up. People who are ill—with heart conditions or cancer or stress-related illnesses or simply greater-than-average unhappiness—or people who have been deeply affected by profound experiences of death or loss are strongly motivated meditators. They have been forced to recognize the inescapable truth that life isn't easy and smooth, that it inevitably brings problems, that going along with business as usual as if none of this were so is simply not sustainable. Such people have realized that life is always in crisis, not only for them but for everyone. Meditation practice helps us to face this crisis as it really is and nourishes our process for working on it.

When you begin to admit that there is a mess, and then to view the mess with calmness and accuracy, the mess becomes less threatening. It becomes interesting. You appreciate the beauty of its shape and pattern. You gradually come to see that the mess isn't so bad really. It's just that you have been adding a mess on top of your mess, making matters worse in your life by not paying attention to the way you have been living or to your thoughts and emotions. Without knowing what you were doing, you set in motion habits of mind that emphasize trouble and make it worse and that deemphasize— or sometimes miss altogether—wholesome and helpful states of mind and heart. Sitting on your meditation chair or cushion, you begin to see more and more clearly how this is so. And once you begin to see more clearly, you begin to change, even without trying to. Naturally, without any special effort, the awareness that meditation promotes inspires you to gradually let go of your strong habit of making matters worse. Seeing your life more clearly helps you to do what comes naturally to all of us: encourage what makes us happy and let go of what makes us suffer.

As you continue meditating, other fundamental insights begin to come into view. You see that your sense of self is not as fixed as you once believed it was. Rather than being some essence of "me-ness" that is somehow inside you or enclosing you, you see that your sense of self is a fluid series of experiences, impressions, feelings, attitudes. You begin to see how much of a burden it has been to try to shore all of that up into a concept of "me" that you have spent your life defending, justifying, building up, and sometimes self-destructively and painfully tearing down without realizing you were doing this. You can feel how much pain this burden of "me" has caused you, in small ways every day and in large and tragic ways through the major crises of your life. You realize that much of that wasn't necessary, that your "me" never needed defending in the first place. Within the wider space of your meditation practice your "me" seems to come and go with flexibility and ease. Even when your concept of self is painful, you see how the very painfulness has within it a path toward release, for you come to know that your pain has come not from the "me" itself, but from your clutching it so tightly, and that once you relax your hold you find peace. And sometimes, when your mind is very quiet, the sense of self isn't even there at all. There's only the feeling of being, without any particular boundaries or issues.

As you sit in your meditation place trying to quiet your mind, day after day, year after year, you realize that the fundamental basis of your life is not, as you had always imagined, "me." The primary fact of your life, and of all life, is that everything changes ceaselessly. Sounds, images, sensations, thoughts, feelings, memories—all come and go. The body isn't a thing, it's a process. Your breathing circulates endlessly. Your heart beats. Sitting there, your body doesn't feel like an object, it feels like a living world, always in flux, always new. Moments waft by like smoke. Life is fleeting, ever-changing, tragic, joyous, precious, precise. When we appreciate all of this as the fruit of our meditation practice, we no longer hang on so hard to the mundane "me" aspect of things. We don't get so tangled up in our own lives. We don't create so much trouble for ourselves or others.

Meditation practice shows us the power of presence in our lives. We are alive only in the present: the past is memory and the future is speculation. But this present has no boundary. You feel this on your meditation cushion, where with each silent moment of full awareness, past, present, and future meet. Every present moment carries with it the past's conditioning and the future's seed, so every present moment freshly offers the possibility of redemption from what has been and the healing into what will be. Meditation practice doesn't cause this to be so. It simply is so and has always been so. Meditation practice only helps us to appreciate it.

A Zen koan makes this point in a few words. Damei asks Mazu, "What is Buddha?" Mazu answers, "This very mind is Buddha!"

To simply be present with our lives at the depth that meditation practice can take us to is a profound accomplishment. To inhabit our lives in this way is to meet and become the Buddha, to be touched by and to touch the divine. Cutting through our entanglements without denying them, we reach the ultimate, not by an act of transcendence, but simply by living with full awareness.

How exactly do we practice meditation? First, remember that the essence of meditation practice is focusing the mind calmly. This is the fundamental thing. You don't have to twist your legs up into a pretzel and sit rigidly upright. Still, the yogic posture called the full lotus, in which you fold your right leg on top of your left thigh and your left leg on top of your right thigh so that you are sitting with your feet in your lap, was not a creation of masochists or fools. In fact, this posture (or one of its many variations) is very stable and helps you keep your back fairly straight, which is important. But you don't need to assume the lotus posture in order to meditate.

For basic mediation, take a seat, either on a meditation cushion or on a chair. This could be a straight-backed chair or a comfortable chair or couch. You want to be comfortable, but remember, though meditation may be deeply relaxing, the point is not relaxation in and of itself. The purpose of meditation is seeing our lives as they really are. This accurate seeing takes alertness and awareness, so you do not want to lounge or recline (unless, because of an illness or injury, there is no other way). I usually recommend that meditators sit up straight without leaning on the back of the chair or couch, so that the back supports itself. This is possible for most people; if you have a weak back or a back injury, you might have to use the back of the chair for support.

Sit on the chair, couch, or cushion squarely and evenly. Check out your rear end to make sure that the sitting bones are firmly on the seat. (If you are on a cushion, you'll want to sit at the edge of it, not squarely in the center, so that the cushion is just a wedge supporting you.) Stretch the back top of your head up toward the ceiling. Tuck your chin in. Lift up your chest and pull your shoulders back a little, but don't tense them. Let your shoulders drop. Rotate your pelvis forward and arch the lower back slightly inward: this movement will naturally lift up the upper body, stretching the spine so that you are sitting up straight, without constriction. Posture is important and something to work with; though sitting up straight may feel unnatural at first, it will feel more natural as you continue to practice. Fold your hands in your lap or place them on your knees palms down or up, whichever way is comfortable for you.

Once you have settled into your posture, bring your attention to your lower belly and see how it moves with your breathing. Without manipulating your breathing in any way, just pay attention to the rising and falling of the belly that happens with each breath in and out. Keep your eyes half open, gazing out in front of you. If you can sit facing a blank wall, which is preferable, lower your gaze and look at the wall, without focusing your eyes too much. Keep your mouth closed, but don't clench your jaw. Let your tongue rest on the roof of your mouth and touch the back of your front teeth, as it naturally will. Wear comfortable, nonconstricting clothing so that the abdomen area can be as open as possible. Count exhales silently, beginning with one and going up to ten. If you lose count, go back to one without blame or worry. This is not a contest. If you get to ten, go back to one again.

After a while, you can leave off counting if you like and just sit peacefully but alertly following each breath, in and out, in the lower belly. If you feel sensations in the body (like ache, warmth, or release), or if you notice thoughts or emotions arising (which you no doubt will), treat them all the same way: pay attention, but do not get too interested or complain too much. As soon as you notice your preoccupation with a thought, emotion, or physical sensation, use that very thing as a cue to come back to awareness of posture and breathing in the belly.

If you need to move your posture or take a rest, allow yourself to explore your discomfort for a few breaths before you relieve it. This can be extremely instructive and helpful. If you find you are getting drowsy because you are too relaxed, try to sit up a little straighter or open your eyes wider to try to rouse yourself. Pay attention to whatever light there is in the room. (You don't want to meditate in a room that's too dark, but a glaring light is no good either.) If you are really sleepy, then stand up and continue the practice in the same way standing with your hands at your sides. I usually recommend that people meditate for twenty to thirty minutes a day—long enough to begin to settle the mind, but not so long that it gets tiresome or too tough. It is good to sit regularly, with a firm commitment. Meditating now and then when you feel like it, or when you feel you need to, is not as good. Remember the practice of persistence!

This basic technique of Zen meditation is done in many other schools of Buddhism as well. Catholic monks and lay-people practice it in monasteries and retreat centers, rabbis and their congregants practice it in synagogues, people in clinics, jails, workplaces, and in homes practice it. There is nothing particularly Zen about this technique. I think of it as basic human meditation.

Note the sheer physicality of the practice. In Japanese it is called, literally, "just sitting"—in other words, simply being present with the fact of being alive, breathing, in the body. It is such a simple thing, and yet so profound, to appreciate directly that we are living, breathing bodies. Mostly we take this for granted and occupy ourselves with what seem like more significant concerns. But in fact, there is nothing more significant than being our bodies. Meditation practice is a physical practice. In the West many centuries of philosophical thought have produced a deeply embedded belief that the mind and body are split off from each other. We assume that our essential selves reside in our minds, in our personalities, in our wills, or in our intellects. The Western mind-body split leads us to assume that spiritual practice, of all things, is not physically determined.

One of the most important of all early Buddhist texts, the Mindfulness Sutra, says that awareness practice is the only way to spiritual opening, and that awareness practice begins with awareness of the body in all its dimensions, from the simplest (awareness of standing or sitting, awareness of breathing) to the most complex (awareness of the composite and impermanent nature of the body). The sutra goes on to show that the practice of awareness of the body is a foundation for the practices of awareness of the mind and its states, which are in turn supports for awareness of the deepest spiritual truths. The path begins with, and is grounded in, awareness of the body.

Most of us, however, have very confused relationships with our own bodies. We objectify them and see them as a presentation of ourselves—one that most of us are ashamed of, or at the very least are alienated from. We look in the mirror and think that what we see there is us. We judge the body critically and are forever imagining ways it could be improved. But in fact what we see in the mirror is not the body. The real body, as meditation practice shows us, is not an image. It is a set of experiences and sensations, a complex of inside and outside, a vast and nearly unknown plethora of activity. The heartbeat, the workings of the organs, the breath—these activities are also the body. Alternating sensations of cold and heat, hardness and softness, heaviness and lightness; thoughts associated with aches or pains; emotions that tense or relax the limbs or organs; wishes, dreams, and fleshly desires—all of this, too, is the body. Who can encompass the body's dimension? Who can explain its functioning?

We don't know the body, and we don't know the mind either. We cover our thoughts with "shoulds" and "oughts," or with dullness and distraction. Most of the time we really don't know how we feel, what we love, what we fear, what we desire. We aren't even all that clear about what we see, hear, taste, touch, and smell. Meditation practice serves little by little to introduce us to the complicated and not easily categorized person we call our self. Little by little, if we persist in our practice, we find ourselves establishing a warm and realistic relationship with this person, and that will be the basis for forging warm and realistic relationships with others and with the world.

In one of his many commentaries on Hasidic teachings, Martin Buber cites one old rabbi who taught that everything depends on oneself. "When a man has made peace within himself," Buber writes, "he will be able to make peace in the whole world." Buber speaks of the necessity of our "decision" to "straighten ourselves out" so that we can straighten out the world. We do this, he says, by aligning ourselves with our-selves, so that our deep inner conflicts can be healed.

Buber is telling us that so long as our relationship with our-selves is awry, the whole world remains awry. How can this be so? How can making friends with ourselves affect the world? Am I so self-centered as to think that I am the center of the universe, and that somehow when I am happy the whole world is going to stand up and rejoice? Here we come to the deepest aspect of meditation practice. The paradox is that when we enter into true friendship with ourselves, we see that we are not atomized individuals separate from and opposed to the world. Being aware of the body and the mind as acutely, alertly, and peacefully as possible, I become aware of that which is larger than myself, which holds me in its embrace, and which is what I truly am, was before I was born, and will be after I leave this life.

This is what I have appreciated in my meditation practice over the years. It is why as time goes on I have been seeing less and less difference between the silent meditation I prac-tice and the many other forms of spiritual practice that exist in this world. To me sitting in open silence is a prayer. It is the prayer of the body, the wordless prayer of the world. And when I do engage in formal prayer, as I sometimes do, it feels the same to me. Sitting in open silence is also a ritual: it is the ritual of the body, of the breath.

Yet meditation practice isn't something special. Fundamen-tally, it is just life, life in its fullness and depth. Can we experi-ence life at this level without the aid of technique, without prayer, without meditation practice, without ritual? We can, and sometimes we do. But meditation practice helps to remind us of what our life really is. It inspires us and makes it more possible for us to develop the many personal qualities we need to go on with the real work of growing up.

ABOUT A MONTH AFTER RASHID'S OUTBURST, SAM'S ELDERLY grandfather fell ill, and Sam and his parents traveled back east to see him. While they were there, his grandfather died. After Sam returned to, he was eager to talk about it. He said, "When Grandpa died a space opened up in the room. You could feel the space glowing around him just when he was nearest to dying. Then after he died, it glowed even stronger until the nurse took him out.

"Afterward I felt very quiet. I went outside into the woods past the hospital grounds. The leaves were beginning to turn. I saw one leaf twist off its stem and float down. Then it blew up again. When it finally landed it disappeared into all the other leaves. My father said this is like meditation practice. The big space, I mean. I think we should do meditation practice at our meetings."

That was how our mentoring group began to meditate.

Seven

VOWING

WHEN I HAD ORIGINALLY THOUGHT ABOUT WHAT IT MIGHT be like to engage in a discussion about life with four teenage boys, I was skeptical. How would I keep a conversation going? I tried my best to come up with techniques and tricks and ways of presenting things that would keep their interest alive. But I had not figured on the eruption of dramatic life events into the process. Now it seemed obvious that such things were bound to happen.

The death of Sam's grandfather and his subsequent grieving and questioning; the separation of Rashid's parents and his forgiving them through confronting his own pain—these happenings were like stones dropped into the pond of our conversation: they made initial splashes, and then many ripples radiating outward. As the weeks went by we found ourselves talking, quite personally and passionately, about many things—suffering, parents, romantic relationships, death, spirituality.

Whenever you go on with something long enough—whether it is a group like ours, a relationship, a task, or a discipline—inevitably things happen that will shape events beyond anyone's ability to foresee them. If you are open to what occurs and welcome it even if it is something difficult, as Sam and Rashid did, things usually turn out all right. Whatever happens can be grist for the mill.

The group was becoming lively and engaging. I looked forward to the meetings, and I think the boys did, too. The meditation practices we were now doing only increased the range and depth of what we talked about. But not all the boys were equally engaged. Of the four of them, Tony still remained somewhat aloof. Although there were moments when he seemed as enthusiastic as the others, his initial sullenness hadn't changed all that much. So I was quite surprised when one day he announced to us all that he intended to take Zen lay vows, committing himself in a formal ceremony to the Zen ethical precepts.

The other boys didn't know what to make of this, and Tony's explanations about his decision were abstract and hard to follow. When I had a chance to talk to him about it later, he was reluctant to speak at first. But finally he said that what was bothering him, and had been bothering him for a long time, was that he was bored. He wasn't interested in school, he wasn't interested in social life, he wasn't interested in sports, he wasn't interested in anything.

"That was okay before," he said, "when I was ten or twelve. Then I could just stay in my room and play or watch TV. But now I need something to go on, some kind of an idea." And since he could find no such idea anywhere in the world he saw around him, he decided that he would make his own idea, out of a vow. Although he didn't have much sense of what the Zen vows actually meant, he had seen the impressive ceremony performed when he was a child and was quite sure that this was the answer to his problems. I felt as though he needed to think about this step further, so from then on vowing and ethical conduct became new topics for our group discussions. At last Tony's interest was piqued.

I BELIEVE WE ARE BORN WITH VOWS. AS CHILDREN WE KNOW this. We feel instinctively the power of our vowing, of the deep intentions inside us we know we must live out somehow. This vowing power is what makes childhood so rich and mysterious. Childhood's world is full of magic and story, and each event is a contributory detail in the tale of our inner journey toward the fulfillment of our heart's desire. All children hold vows to learn, to grow, to create, to love, to experience, to plunge forward into the endless and unknowable future. Although as they grow older children forget these vows—and the many other vows they find inside themselves—they do not forget entirely. Vowing remains a latent force in our lives, no matter how hidden it may seem.

Earlier I spoke about my childhood vow not to grow up, a vow that conditioned my life in many ways. I am sure that following it and allowing it to transform into something clearer and deeper was responsible for my decision to choose the spiritual life. But I had other vows as well. I can remember sitting in a Sunday school classroom one day and hearing the sad and inspiring stories of the Jewish martyrs, stories that frightened and impressed me. I felt myself sitting in my seat at that moment as though it were an eternal moment, and I thought, *I will be like that, too: I will never give up what I am, never give up what I know to be so, because someone tries to force me to.* I felt that because of what people before me had endured in being true to their deepest identities and commitments, I, too, would endure and remain steadfast, in their honor and in their name. As a Jewish child listening to a Jewish tale, I felt a vow come upon me to hold fast to being a Jew no matter what, a vow I have always kept in my heart, despite the fact that I have practiced Buddhism for so long.

I am sure that all of us, if we remember our lives deeply enough, could uncover vows that spontaneously arose in our earlier days. Those vows reenter our conscious minds and willing hearts when we are ready for them, when we really need them, when our sufferings, our disappointments, our life's trials, bring them to the surface. Sometimes it's our joys that do this: our love and devotion to another person causes us to remember our vow to keep a tender heart, to remain open to love. Awakened anew to these old vows, we make a new, adult vow to share our life with another person. And sometimes, without any particular provocation but simply through our living, our deepest vows float back into our consciousness: the vow to be a good person, to live as truthfully, deeply, and beautifully as the heroes who strode through the stories we heard when we were young.

Earlier I described connection to our own pain as the beginning, the seed, of our maturity. We can't attain true maturity until we see life as it really is, with all its difficult realities and our own limitations. Meditation practice is the nutrient that this seed of maturity needs for its sustained development. Meditation—the practice of fundamental awareness—promotes engagement with our whole life, inner as well as outer, and enables us to grow into the human beings we were made to be. Vowing is the next step. A seed that has been planted and nurtured must be watered so that its roots will go deep. By our vow we deepen and anchor our lives.

When you vow, you get in touch with and give yourself completely to what matters most: the experience of receiving an inner calling and answering that calling with your whole life. The vowing life begins intimately and personally but expands outward, bringing the passion of the personal, through discipline and commitment over time, to deeper and wider realms.

There are many ways to live a life of vowing. I have known people who live their vow through art or work or service; others do it simply by remaining for a long time in a particular place that they have come to know well and to love. Perhaps most movingly, I have also known people for whom the need to overcome great suffering—personal tragedies like abuse or loss, social forces like sexism, racism, or homophobia, a physical or mental illness, the long tragic course of an addiction— has been a vital and courageous path of vowing.

Vows are energies. Vows are aspirations. They are larger than life. Endless sources of inspiration, vows differ from goals, which are limited in scope. Goals can be met. Vows can be practiced but never exactly completed, for they are essentially unfulfillable, and it is their very inexhaustibility that propels us forward, opens us up, shapes our desires and actions.

One of my Zen teachers, Roshi Bernie Glassman, once vowed to end homelessness, an absolutely preposterous idea. How could one person, even with many helpers, end homelessness? And this was a religious person—a meditation master—without connections, resources, or skills suited to the task. And yet, through the power of his vow, Bernie established the Greyston Foundation, a network of social service agencies in Yonkers, New York, that house the homeless, educate their children, and offer them jobs, job training, counseling, and other services. I visited Greyston recently and was astonished to see how much had come from one person's devotion to an impossible vow. Did Bernie actually end homelessness? No, not at all. Are there fewer homeless people today than there were when Bernie began to practice his vow? I don't know and neither does he. But it makes no difference. Bernie goes on practicing his vow.

If vows are unfulfillable, why undertake them? Why frustrate ourselves trying to do the impossible? Because this is how we are: making vows is what we seem to need to do to find a deep sense of satisfaction. Unlike all other beings, who live entirely in the world of actuality, human beings live in two worlds: one that is, and one that isn't. We can imagine and long for a world that doesn't exist and might never exist. A world without homelessness or war. A world with more love than hate. Such a world can be as real to us as the earth we walk on. We can contemplate it and yearn for it even if it is utterly impossible. Vows are the vehicles for that contemplation. They transform contemplation from mere abstract musing into the driving force of a lifetime.

The power and immensity of vowing began to dawn on the boys and me as our discussions continued. The idea surfaced that we might all want to take vows—not just Tony—as part of the process of our group. This idea terrified James, and he said so. It was too heavy, too serious, too stark a possibility. But James couldn't simply say no. A very competitive boy, he felt challenged by Tony's unwavering decision to take the Zen vows. If Tony was determined to do this, James thought, maybe he should be doing it, too. Why would he not do it? Because he was afraid? Because he was too immature?

Although at this point the other boys didn't see themselves taking vows, the conversation challenged them, too. It made them realize that they were getting older and coming to the time in their lives when they would be faced with consequential choices—inescapable and decisive choices that would shape them forever. Only Tony seemed undaunted by this prospect. He seemed to thrive on the idea of making vows and binding choices. It was as if he wanted to plunge as quickly as possibly into the problems of adult life, if only to present himself with a challenge that would be exciting and dangerous. His resolve to take Zen vows remained firm. Something about vowing appealed to that part of him that had played endless superhero games when he was a child.

Indeed, vowing is risky. Even as benign and ordinary a vow as the wedding vow commits us to "plight our troth" (put our personal truth at risk) in our commitment to our marriage partner and to "love, honor, and cherish" him or her, regardless of what the future brings. Insofar as vowing sets us on a course of action beyond what we may desire or can control, it is always challenging. The dictates of our vow may well run counter to our wishes and apparent self-interest. Being true to our vow may force us into difficult decisions or heroic actions. Vowing opens us up to self-transcendence and destiny. It is a path that could easily involve hardship.

One of the most drastic and problematic stories of vowing in all of world literature is the story of Abraham and Isaac, one of the tales on the Bible stories record I listened to as a child. As many times as I heard it, it never failed to raise the hair on my neck. The faithful Abraham, God's devoted servant, prays for many years for a child with his wife, Sarah, until finally (when they are both in their nineties!) God preposterously proposes to give them a son. Husband and wife both laugh at the idea, but the son is born and grows up healthy. Of course they adore him. Then God commands the sacrifice of that very son, "Isaac, your favored son, the one you love." Abraham and Isaac slowly and silently walk together up to the top of Mount Moriah, the mountain of sacrifice. The servant boy has been told to stay behind. Isaac carries firewood. Abraham carries a knife and the fire to be used for the offering pyre. Isaac asks, "But what shall we sacrifice?" "Don't worry, son," Abraham replies. "God will provide."

Any child of any parent—if he or she has any imagination at all—is going to be affected by this story. Fear is probably the first and foremost reaction. Betrayal. Confusion. Shock. The irrationality and cruelty of God's request. The monstrosity of it. And the obedience of Abraham, the blind trust he has in his God. Although there are passages in the Bible where characters protest mightily against God's commands (as Abraham himself does when God becomes angry and wants to destroy the cities of Sodom and Gommorah), here there is no such reaction. Abraham goes along silently with God's order. He rises early in the morning to carry it out, diligently and methodically. Nothing is said about how he feels or what goes through his mind as he walks up that steep trail side by side with his unsuspecting son.

Probably no story in world literature has been discussed and commented on as frequently as this one. My own feeling for it has changed over the years. When I was young, I considered the story a scandal and an affront. How ridiculous of God to craft such a test, how sinister, how bullying. And Abraham—where is his nerve? Why doesn't he scream and curse? Job does. Why doesn't he simply refuse? Jonah does. What's the worst that can happen to Abraham? If God kills him, so what? Who wouldn't choose to die in place of his own son, to die rather than carry out such a hideous request? Is Abraham merely a coward? Is his fear stronger than his love? Does his fanatical blind faith cause him to lose sight of all human decency, not to say nobility? Or is he simply too stupid to conceive of the idea of disobedience?

Later I came to feel that it is neither fear nor stupidity nor fanaticism that motivates Abraham, but devotion. Not devotion to a person, to a sense of duty, or even to an idea or creed, and not to his own integrity. Devotion rather to the vow he made to God, who I now knew not as the stern and bullying father represented by the booming male voice on my childhood record, but as the vast all-inclusiveness, the universally connected immensity of reality we all share. Not everyone may be comfortable with this or any other idea of God, but most people can feel that there is a powerful mystery at the heart of being. It is this mystery that is the ultimate ground of vowing. And this is why vowing seems so frightening.

Most of us don't think much about this immense and mysterious aspect of our lives. Most of the time we are too busy or engaged to think about it. This mystery seems quite irrelevant to our many problems and concerns.. What does it have to do with our work, our friendships and family, our effort to simply get through the day? And yet, where would we be without it, this immense and ineffable spaciousness out of which we have come and to which we return?

Abraham knows this mystery and takes it personally. Somehow it is as palpable to him as dirt, as real as his own heartbeat. Impassioned by it, he trudges up that trail. The sacrifice he is prepared to offer makes no sense in any ordinary terms. Sacrificing his son is simply wrong, even insane. But Abraham's vow to remain true to the mystery, dangerous as it might be, takes him beyond himself. He lives not by his own lights but by the vow. He trusts that what is right and good for his life will transpire, even though he cannot see it. He gives up control, but he does not give up choice: he chooses trust.

In the end Abraham is not required to sacrifice Isaac. His faithfulness to his vow proves to be stronger than the harshness of God's test. Perhaps Abraham knows all along that this will be the outcome. Perhaps he walks up that mountain with serenity and confidence, knowing that as long as he holds to his ultimate vow of trusting the mystery, no evil can possibly occur, that God must be, in the end, good. Or perhaps, being human and therefore subject always to doubt, he still feels a powerful fear despite his perfect faith.

Vowing is never an easy path, but life isn't easy. We have all been brought up to deny this. Like the Buddha's parents, our own parents tried to protect us from the harsh side of life so that we would grow up with a sense that the world is fair, pleasant, and manageable. Maybe they wished this were really so and hoped that they could actually make it so for us. But they did not succeed, for life's troubles cannot be eliminated. Only something as thoroughgoing as vowing is strong enough to overcome our deep underlying disappointment and dismay about how life really is.

I've used as a theme for this book the Buddhist notion of the bodhisattva, the enthusiastic "enlightening" being who is dedicated to the work of maturing others. In their dedication to the ultimate welfare of all beings, bodhisattvas make heroic efforts over many lifetimes. They also make heroic vows. In Zen temples all over the world the four great bodhisattva vows are chanted daily: to benefit an infinite number of beings; to clarify an infinite amount of delusion; to do an infinite amount of good; and to completely become this infinite vow.

Like Roshi Bernie's vow to end homelessness, the four great bodhisattva vows are impossible to fulfill. One can benefit many beings, but not an infinite number; one can clarify a certain amount of delusion, perhaps even a great deal, but not an infinite amount. The four great bodhisattva vows are impossibly idealistic on purpose, for such idealism is a necessity for human beings, who are creatures capable of imagining infinite worlds that might be and are not. Because of the inexhaustibility of our imaginations and conceptualizations, we humans are insatiable creatures. No sooner is one of our desires satisfied than we conceive of another desire—or a better way of satisfying the first desire. Because of human imagination and conceptualization, human desires are endless, and so human dissatisfaction is also without end. What other than an endless, impossible heroic effort could possibly be equal to the protean immensity of our conceptual minds?

We need the impossible idealism of the bodhisattva vows, but we also need to balance that idealism with realism, lest we are overcome with fantasy and fanaticism, as we so easily can be. Realism is the opposite of idealism: devotion to what is rather than to what should or might be. Without impossible idealism we would always be selling ourselves short and so would never be able to find satisfaction. But if we were only impossibly idealistic, we would soar off into the heavens, losing our place on earth, and become feckless dreamers or, worse, ruthless tyrants for whom the end of pursuing our vow justifies all means. So we need to balance idealism with realism, giving our best attention not only to what could or should be but also, with a gentle honesty, to what actually is.

Suppose our vow is a personal one: for instance, to live with integrity and kindness. We aim for that in everything we do, we take our vow seriously, and we make efforts in that direction and are willing to keep up these efforts no matter how difficult it may be. But we also see clearly how we actually are now—we are not always so kind, not always so straightforward, and in fact we often forget our vow entirely! But that's all right. We can be patient with ourselves. Our realism about how we are is no cause for despair. Naturally we are not yet where we want to be. Naturally we have all sorts of doubts and imperfections. We probably always will. The journey is long, but there's no rush. Each day's progress starts from where we are—where else could it start from? There is no use wishing it were otherwise. There's an old saying in Zen: if you fall down on the ground, it is the ground you use to get yourself up. The vow uses the ground of our present imperfection and doubt as purchase to establish itself ever more firmly. Each time we acknowledge our limitation and affirm our vow anyway, we strengthen it. It is fine and normal to fall short of our aspirations. How could it be otherwise?

We need to learn what it takes to pursue our vow and how to take care of ourselves in the process so that we don't eat ourselves up with obsession or burnout. Bernie certainly did this. He remained faithful to his spiritual practice as a way of keeping his own balance. In establishing Greyston he had to learn how to fund-raise, set up a large social service organization, work with poor people whose culture was quite different from his own, and master local politics. Staying aware of his impossible vow with constant faith, was certainly important, but not enough. He also had to figure out, as all of us need to, what it really takes in practical terms to fulfill our vow as best we can. And he had to be flexible enough to deal with failure and adjust his plans when they didn't work and change direction when circumstances called for it.

So idealism and realism are not incompatible. In fact, they depend on each other. How can we hold the vow to be better—as good as we can possibly and impossibly be—without being patient with how we are now? How can we vow to change the world unless we know the world, know how to work in it as it actually is, and can take care of ourselves in the process?

To live with complete dedication to our vows doesn't require that we give up all personal enjoyment or self-interest, or that we live grimly and desperately, devoted solely to our cause, with no sense of play. The vowing life has plenty of enjoyment in it. But when we practice vowing, we aren't seeking pleasure or joy for its own sake—that's not our goal or motivation. Like Abraham, we trust that we will find all that we really need through following our vow.

I know many monastics who have taken solemn vows of poverty, stability, obedience, and chastity. To most of us such vows seem forbiddingly austere. Although we might respect them, we certainly don't see them as the path to a joyful life. And yet, many of the monastics I know are joyful people, and both interesting and interested. One of them, the Benedictine monk Brother David Steindl-Rast, has spent most of his life traveling all over the world, sharing his spiritual life not only with Catholic lay and monastic practitioners in the West, but also with people of different faiths and cultural backgrounds. He has practiced in many different spiritual centers, even spending time living in our Zen monastery, Tassajara. His long life has been full of diverse adventures and friendships. Brother David took his monastic vows more than fifty years ago; I am sure that at the time he never imagined that his life would turn out as it did. It seems quite counterintuitive that vows of stability, chastity, obedience, and poverty would lead to such a life, but Brother David, always true to his vow, found it quite unexpectedly to be so.

Although most of us will never take monastic vows or other formal religious vows (other than, perhaps, marriage vows), we respect the values of faithfulness and commitment that lie at the heart of vowing. Most of us hold these values in our relationships and in our personal lives. Every commitment, every act of faithfulness, and certainly every vow is an act of restraint: whatever I choose wholeheartedly (and vowing is nothing if not wholehearted) will necessarily entail letting go of that which I haven't chosen. This requirement seems like a limitation, and indeed in this era of choice and possibility people seem unwilling or unable to make commitments because of it. Many of us imagine that our limitless potential will be diminished by any committed choice we may make.

This is true of all of us, but perhaps especially of young people. When you're young, you feel the immense expansiveness of the unlived life yet ahead, the imaginary, limitless, undefined, and undisclosed possible life. But I sometimes wonder whether any of us, at any age, have really given up our youthful dreams of a colorful and exciting life. Maybe we've just stored them away in the deep drawers of our heart's attic and bring them out now and then in our quiet daydream hours. Maybe, holding on to these possibilities, we have always held ourselves in reserve, not giving ourselves fully to what our lives have become. To live a life of vowing is to offer ourselves completely to our lives, with nothing held back.

Philip Whalen, one of the original Beat poets, was one of the most important mentors and friends in my life. A large bearded man and a voracious reader, he made a vow to poetry early in his life. Specifically, he vowed to carry on with writing as his sole and full-time occupation no matter what it cost him. Outwardly this vow cost him quite a bit. He was often poor to the point of being destitute, and sometimes he was lonely, lost, and in despair. I am sure that many of his friends criticized him for not having a career or livelihood. Eventually the passion of his vow to poetry met his faith in the practice of Buddhism, and he came to the Zen Center, where he ordained as a priest, and this is how I got to know him.

Externally Philip's life was quite plain, poor, and uneventful. He had few possessions, hardly ever traveled, and became more and more quiet as he got older. In the end, when his eyesight failed him, he even gave up poetry—or at least the writing and reading of it. But his inner life remained full, extravagant and imaginative. This anyone could see from reading his poems. Even after he stopped writing, I saw it in his conversation, in the style and attitude he kept at the heart of all aspects of his living. When he died recently, his many friends from all over the country and the world paid tribute to him. His vow, even accounting for all the limitations it put on his life, turned out in the end to have given him a life that was expansive and full of love.

There is a discipline at the heart of Philip's life and Brother David's life. Philip's discipline was his ongoing writing of poetry as well as his Zen meditation practice, to which he was completely faithful. For Brother David, the life of prayer and contemplation remains a discipline still. Vowing requires some form of discipline if it is to be sustained. Discipline is a way of reinforcing our intention and passion to live a wider life. If we don't back up these vows with concrete and regular practice, they grow stale and eventually fade away.

It also helps to do such practice in the midst of a community so that we can find encouragement and support to carry on with what we know is the right thing to do, even though sometimes our energy or commitment may flag. When that happens, the others in our community pick us up and help us along—and we do the same for them. This is why religious practice over the millennia in all traditions has been communal and includes observances to be carried out at appointed times of the day, week, month, and year.

Although religious traditions are by no means the only examples we have of the vowing life, it is certainly true that vowing and the establishment of a life that supports vowing have been religion's central offerings. The world's great religious traditions are alive and well, and they are still capable of supporting us in our vows. But it may be that these traditions, in and of themselves, no longer provide enough support. We have become habituated to them by long cultural tradition; for many people, religious tradition has become time-worn and less useful in the effort to awaken and sustain their true vows. This is not to say that the great traditions can't wake us up, but rather that to do so they need to be constantly renewed.

For the last several years I have been practicing Zen beyond the San Francisco Zen Center temples, where I lived for so long and served as abbot. As a way of testing and extending my vows, I founded, with some friends, an organization called the Everyday Zen Foundation. It was our idea to see whether it is possible for the powerful sense of vow as practice to be effective for ordinary people in the everyday world. We can't all be Roshi Bernies or Brother Davids. We can't all take religious orders and live in monasteries or Zen centers where our vows are reinforced on a daily basis. Is there a way to live our vowing in our ordinary worldly lives as we find them?

So far we have been finding that there is a way. Most of the students of Everyday Zen find tremendous fulfillment in their spouses and children, and many are pursuing important and useful careers. But they come seeking, in addition to satisfying careers and family lives, a sense of vowing. Many of them have been able to find it by engaging in daily meditation practice at home, attending weekly and monthly meetings with others to share practice and teachings, and most important of all, using all these things to find and sustain within themselves the vow that has always been there.

The students of Everyday Zen aspire to be bodhisattvas—saving all beings, ending all confusion, mastering all wisdoms. I think they are succeeding in this, impossible though it may sound. One person does it by working for the United Nations Health Organization and traveling all over the world training doctors in the treatment of AIDS. One person does it through medical research to find cures for rheumatism and Parkinson's disease. Another does it through her psychotherapy work with children who have suffered serious illness, as she did herself when she was a child. Someone else teaches meditation to the prisoners of San Quentin, still another takes care of dying people as a hospice nurse. Another devotes herself to the care of her severely disabled son. Not all manifest the bodhisattva spirit in ways that appear so overtly altruistic—financial advisors, business executives, ordinary blue- and white-collar workers of every kind also find ways to express their practice through their work. One student of Everyday Zen has a unique approach: he has undertaken to get the world dancing by renting and installing dance floors all over the West Coast and as far away as Texas! Together we encourage each other to see that these and other methods—in combination with our meditation practice and the cultivation of our inner feeling of kindness and honesty—can be skillful means of serving and strengthening our path of vowing, which is endlessly and gloriously unfulfillable and crucially necessary.

Making our vows explicit and clear helps us to strengthen them. This can be done through ceremonies of vowing (as Tony wanted to do, and as many students of Zen do) or in a more personal way by reflecting on your own vows for a long time until they become formed into words within your heart. I have often advised students to write down these words and carefully compose phrases that express their feeling and sound like intentions they can live by. Some students aspire to have a profound effect on the world. But most find their vows to be about inner work, about ways of living or feeling. Some may write words like, "I vow to live in kindness," or, "I vow to listen, to let go of self-interest, to be the kind of parent to my children my parents could not be to me." Such a vow could be the product of many hours of tearful reflection and gathering determination. You can place written vows like these on a personal home altar so that they become a daily inspiration and reminder for your practice. You can also repeat them during your meditation or prayer, or even as you take a moment for reflection during any part of your day.

Sometimes sharing our vows with others helps to strengthen them. In our Everyday Zen meetings we have sometimes given up the formal question-and-answer periods that are customary in Zen practice in favor of intimate small group discussion periods in which we share with each other our deepest explorations and commitments. In this way we hear other people's vows in the making, and their struggles and successes can inspire our own, giving us increased confidence that it really is possible to live a life of vowing.

Vowing is like walking toward the horizon: you know where you are headed, you can see the destination brightly up ahead, and you keep on going toward it with enthusiasm even though you never arrive there. As the Talmud says, "It is not for you to complete the task. But neither are you to ignore it."

Eight

CONDUCT

In classical Buddhism, as in all religious traditions, the spiritual life is seen as all-encompassing, embracing the whole of a person's life. All our conduct, all our thought and feeling, all our relationships, encounters, and decisions are part of the path. If we take the spiritual life to be the fullness of human maturity, as I believe it is, then spiritual practice can't be something merely private and personal, limited only to a separate and special part of life.

In Buddhism spiritual practice is likened to a tripod whose three balanced legs hold a bowl steady and firm. These legs are the three practices of ethical conduct, meditation, and wisdom. They work together, each one helping to support the other two. Although it is easy enough to sit down on a cushion, you can't really practice meditation without practicing right conduct. If your actions are thoughtless and crooked, your meditation will reflect this, and calm concentration will be hard to achieve. But if you go on with meditation anyway, you'll begin to see the shadows that your conduct is casting on your mind and heart. You'll feel these shadows as unpleasant and undesirable, and you'll want to change your way of life. When you do, your meditation will deepen, becoming calmer, and some insight will come. You'll have fewer illusions about yourself and will be able to appreciate yourself as you really are. Accepting yourself realistically, in turn, will give you more energy for your meditation practice. It will become clear to you that practicing ethical conduct is necessary because it directly affects every thought and action, small and large. In this way meditation, ethical conduct, and wisdom refine, deepen, and balance each other, until little by little the vessel of your life stands strong.

In Zen the practice of ethical conduct is both beginning and advanced practice. While new students are encouraged to conduct themselves straightforwardly in order to learn the practice, experienced students know that their conduct is the expression of their practice in the world—the most difficult accomplishment of all. In some schools of Zen the koans that come at the very end of the long course of study involve a thorough penetration of the ethical precepts, which are seen now not as simple moral rules but as profound spiritual truths. In our school of Zen, which does not have a systematic curriculum of koan study, precept study that includes the deepest insights of our teaching lineage is offered at the very end of formal training. (Precepts are studied at the beginning and middle of practice as well.)

Zen practice has two parts—sitting down and getting up. When we sit down, we calm, clear, and illuminate the mind. When we get up, we live our life in this world as an extension and expression of the beauty of our sitting. Sitting down and getting up together comprise a full and mature human being, one who is receptive and open but also responsible and committed.

Although we recognize the importance of ethical conduct and believe we know the difference between right and wrong, how much thought have we really given to what right and wrong mean in this complicated world? Living an ethical life is not a simple matter. In addition to some understanding of the foundations of morality, living ethically takes a degree of courage and awareness that few of us have taken the time to develop. Have we considered ethical conduct as an active, thoughtful, challenging, and ongoing practice?

It would be comforting to think that ethical conduct can be clearly codified, that it is founded on certainties, and that to do good is simply to conform to these certainties. Unfortunately, this isn't so. Life is full of gray areas, and we are full of unexamined motivations and self-deceptions. We are much better off when we admit this and are willing to look at our conduct honestly, with as much awareness as possible of our real motivations and the consequences of our actions. The practice of ethical conduct requires that much honesty and awareness, for it is an ongoing exploration, a constant steering of a moral course that depends on accurate information, not theory and bluster. Fixed moral codes are always theoretical. They are vastly subject to interpretation, since no ethical norm can ever take into account all of life's subtlety and complexity. Instead of focusing our effort on such norms, we need to pay more attention to what we feel, what others feel, and what actually happens.

Given this indeterminacy (and it is already a mark of maturity to accept it, for only the immature hold fast to certainties), it makes sense that in practicing ethical conduct we are going to make mistakes, and plenty of them. We steer our boat by paying attention to the rocks and shoals. We know that once in a while, because the rocks are hidden, or because we weren't watching, we are going to hit one, and that sometimes this is the only way to find out that it is there. Mistakes are not tragedies. Without them there's no learning or growth. It is precisely our moral mistakes, much more than our moral victories, that deepen our sense of what ethical conduct is. Our mistakes mature us and temper us; they fire us like strong pottery.

Of course, this does not mean that we are casual about our mistakes, or that we don't try to avoid them. A mistake that we don't care about is a mistake we haven't noticed, a mistake we haven't learned from yet. We need to care deeply about our mistakes and to have sincerely terrible feelings about them—remorse, embarrassment, shame.

If the powerful negativity of a really bad mistake doesn't come home to you, if it never sears your soul, then that mistake has been useless to you; it will not serve to temper and tenderize your heart. Once you fully feel remorse for your mistake, you are ready to confess it, and then to forgive yourself. This process might take a good deal of time. Some really terrible mistakes may need to stay buried for many years, since feeling them might be too painful, at least for a while. But most of the time we eventually do come to feel the effects of our mistakes, and we find a way to forgive ourselves and move on—a little wiser and clearer about where we are going and what we need to watch out for.

Our mistakes are painful not only because they make us feel bad, but because they have consequences. As responsible people, we want to accept those consequences and not try to escape them. When we make a mistake, we admit it not only to ourselves but to others. We pay the price for it by apologizing to whomever we might have hurt and making all possible amends. We also resolve not to make the same mistake again, and we take steps in our lives to make sure we are able to stand by that resolve. If we make the same mistake over and over again we haven't really owned the mistake, been truly aware of it, forgiven ourselves for it, and so been changed by it. We have just been playing out the terrible consequences of our continuing blindness—and in fact reinforcing it.

For some of us the practice of ethical conduct takes us through some pretty rough and narrow passages, and we crash and founder disastrously for some time. We may have to nearly drown before we are ready to be aware enough to forgive ourselves. We may have to hit bottom before we can float up. The Talmud tells the story of Eliezar ben Durdia, an awful sinner who sinned constantly and paid no attention to what he was doing. His favorite sin was fornication. One day a prostitute he was with turned to him, looked him in the eye, and said, "You will never be forgiven for this!" Ben Durdia was deeply affected. He leapt up, ran outside, and threw himself down on the ground, tearing his clothes, throwing ashes on himself, and weeping uncontrollably. He cried out to the earth to help him, but the earth would not help him. He cried out to the sky to help him, but the sky would not help him. He cried out to the planets and the stars, but they were totally indifferent. So he just sat there wailing for a very long time. Finally a voice out of the heavens said to him, "You have won life everlasting." When the rabbis heard about this, they were furious: they had never heard a voice come out of the heavens promising *them* life everlasting. They who had worked so hard to be good, and were so good, had never received the reward that this miserable sinner received.

Forgiveness for our mistakes is always possible once we start to pay attention to what we have been doing, no matter how long it takes us. And sometimes, as this story shows, a person who has been unaware for a long time and finally comes to suffer horribly for it finds a deeper, more sudden, and more moving redemption than the rest of us.

If there are no fixed moral standards we can refer to in all circumstances, and if mistakes are not only inevitable but even useful, is there no moral compass? Is ethical conduct a matter of trial and error—with the emphasis on error? Is our own eventual guilt and remorse following wrong actions the only way we have of steering our conduct?

I believe there is indeed a moral compass, one that all religious traditions recognize. The needle of that compass is kindness, simple human kindness. I am in agreement with the Dalai Lama who says, "My religion is kindness."

Bodhisattvas build their practice of ethical conduct on a vision of the world's interconnectedness. They see with their wisdom eye of meditative insight that the world is empty of separation, boundary, and cramped limitation and that it is full of connection, merging, warmth, and embrace. The clear consequence of this profound spiritual experience is a feeling of kindness. Since we are all so closely related, all of us articulations of one body, one soul, how could we not have affection for each other? More than a warm fuzzy sentiment, kindness is the natural and powerful urge that wells up inside us when our vision of reality is deep and clear.

We all recognize kindness when we see it or feel it, and we all honor it and are moved by it. We don't need to be convinced. The fact that we are capable of kindness, of a pure and unselfconscious concern for others, is the center of our practice of right conduct. We can rely on kindness and on our good heart to show us how to act in the world. Although we may not always know whether a particular action is good or bad, whether it will lead to well-being or suffering, we can pay attention to our motivation, moving it in the direction of our natural kindness whenever possible. When this is not possible—when we find that we can't shake our jealousy, anger, fear, greed, or aggression—we can at least admit this and recognize that these feelings are not what we affirm, not what we want to use as a basis for our actions.

In one of the many sutras in which he speaks of right conduct, the Maha Assapura Sutra, the Buddha says, "We will not praise ourselves and disparage others on account of our purified conduct." A crucial aspect of our practice of ethical conduct is that we refrain from cheering about our moral successes and grumbling about others' moral failures.

The Rule of Saint Benedict, the fifth-century monastic code that still governs all Christian monasteries, makes much of the virtue of humility, which is considered the cornerstone of the religious life. To be humble is to be willing to make efforts toward right conduct without measuring our success. The point isn't to see ourselves as good or bad, worthy or unworthy. The point is to go on doing our best to be kind in our actions and clear about our intentions.

Hui Neng, the Sixth Ancestor of Zen, says, "I see and I don't see." When someone asked him what he meant by this, he said, "I see my own faults, but I don't see the faults of others." We are most thoroughly humble when we literally do not see the faults of others. This doesn't mean that we are fools who don't recognize wrong action when we see it—and if necessary, try to prevent it—but rather that we do this with passion for the good, not with a sense of judging or criticizing others. Even when circumstances dictate that we criticize others, we try to do so with a generous, nonblaming spirit.

In particle physics the search for the irreducible core of matter yields only a seemingly endless proliferation of parts. The more closely you look at the parts, the less easily they can be found—they seem to be indeterminate and relative to the very act of your looking. While on a gross level we can distinguish one thing from another, on a refined level no thing is actually findable. Similarly, the more closely you look into your own conduct and the conduct of others, the less you will find a "me" to be right or a "you" to be wrong, and the less you will find a "right" or a "wrong," a "good" or a "bad." There is only the wide, true, and deep effort to be effectively kind beyond moral judgment or discrimination.

Humility and kindness are good flashlights for illuminating the path of ethical conduct. But even if we are genuinely humble and perfectly kind, we don't necessarily know what to do in a given situation. We also need practical path-finding skills to help us see which way to go. Bodhisattvas are always working to develop this capacity to know what is needed in any given situation. Each situation is unique. What is right one moment may be entirely wrong the next. Ethical conduct is a wonderfully complex dance; in addition to a kind and humble heart, it takes intelligence, experience, feeling, common sense, and a willingness to start fresh each time.

When Suzuki Roshi, the founder of our Zen lineage in America, was a young disciple, he had the job of bringing tea to his master. The first time he did this he filled the cup half full, as is usually done with handleless Japanese teacups (so that the cup won't be too hot to hold). But his master scolded him harshly: regardless of custom, he wanted the teacup filled to the brim. So Suzuki learned to pour tea in this way. One day a guest came to the temple, and Suzuki served the tea as he had been taught. Again he was scolded bitterly—a teacup should be filled only half full, he was told. Do you want our guest to burn her fingers?

Sometimes full, sometimes half full, depending on the circumstances. Skill is the sensitivity and readiness to discern what's right in the circumstances that are arising just now.

Ethical conduct requires such skill, as well as kindness, flexibility, humility, and a powerful appreciation of life's complexity and fullness. Because of this, the practice of ethical conduct can be seen as the pinnacle of the spiritual life. Through it we express and live what we have learned and become. The practice of ethical conduct is both a tool for the development of our maturity and the very expression of that maturity, which is neither a state of mind nor an accomplishment, but an ongoing path toward understanding that is reflective as well as active. To be truly mature is to always make the effort to conduct and express ourselves with kindness, clarity, wisdom, and beauty. In this sense, the practice of ethical conduct is fundamental to our maturity. All the other practices that we have discussed support, deepen, and strengthen it.

THE SIXTEEN BODHISATTVA PRECEPTS

In Zen the practice of ethical conduct is summarized in the sixteen bodhisattva precepts. Though these precepts are said to describe most profoundly—and also quite practically—the way a mature person conducts himself or herself, they are not understood as a fixed code of conduct. Instead, they are approached as koans—as objects for contemplation and clarification through the lessons of our lives. Students work on the precepts one or several at a time—or sometimes all at once— using them as points of illumination to shed light on aspects of conduct. Precepts are understood as practices.

The sixteen precepts constitute the vows that Tony had decided to take, and they formed the basis of the discussion of ethical conduct that went on for some time in our group meetings.

The sixteen precepts begin with the ancient Buddhist formula of taking refuge in what's traditionally called the Triple Treasure of Buddha, Dharma, and Sangha:

149

1. I take refuge in Buddha (the principle of enlightenment within).

2. I take refuge in dharma (the enlightened way of understanding and living).

3. I take refuge in sangha (the community of all beings).

After these come the three "pure" precepts:

1. I vow to avoid all action that creates suffering.

2. I vow to do all action that creates true happiness.

3. I vow to act with others always in mind.

Next come the ten "grave" precepts of conduct, which can be stated in both negative and positive form—as what to do and what not to do:

1. Not to kill but to nurture life.

2. Not to steal but to receive what is offered as a gift.

3. Not to misuse sexuality but to be caring and faithful in intimate relationships.

4. Not to lie but to be truthful.

5. Not to intoxicate with substances or doctrines but to promote clarity and awareness.

6. Not to speak of others' faults but to speak out of loving-kindness.

7. Not to praise self at the expense of others but to be modest.

8. Not to be possessive of anything but to be generous.

9. Not to harbor anger but to forgive.

10. Not to do anything to diminish the Triple Treasure but to support and nurture it.

(There are many ways of stating the precepts. The above is my favorite version.)

The sixteen precepts evoke the depth and power of human responsibility. The more thoughtful we are about our life, and the more we deepen our thoughtfulness through our spiritual practice, the more we see that the scope of our life is wider than we ever imagined. All our actions have effects that spread subtly throughout the world. This means that all of our actions, even the seemingly inconsequential ones, have huge implications. We practice the sixteen precepts with the understanding that we are responsible for the whole world and capable of redeeming the whole world through our acts. In Zen there's an old saying that expresses this: "When you pick up one piece of dust, the entire world comes with it." All our actions, however small they may seem, can have wondrous effects, if only we are wholehearted enough in our practice of ethical conduct.

This same point is made in Judaism's Hasidic teachings (and, I am sure, in the mystical teachings of all religious traditions). It seems that the Baal Shem Tov, the eighteenth-century founder of the Hasidic movement, was unmatched in the fervor of his prayer. He sometimes prayed with such passion that he would fall ill, and it was only the encouragement of his disciples, who loved him dearly and feared for his well-being, that kept him in this world. The Baal Shem loved God very much, but the real reason for his passionate prayer was that he felt personally responsible for the whole world. He felt as if his prayers, and his alone, were all that kept the evil and confusion of the world from inundating humankind.

I am sure that the Baal Shem realized that the world would not fall apart if he forgot to pray for one day, and yet, at the same time his feeling of ultimate responsibility was quite real to him, and it must have given his prayer a power that helped him to live a life of depth and seriousness. We are all like the Baal Shem: the whole world really does depend on the awareness and good conduct of each one of us.

The Triple Treasure

The first three of the sixteen precepts are the Triple Treasure— taking refuge in Buddha, dharma, and sangha. The word *refuge* means, literally, to fly back, to return, as a bird flies home to her nest. To take refuge in the Triple Treasure is to return to our own real nature as conscious human beings who were born with, and have never ceased to possess (however much we may have forgotten it) open minds and tender hearts.

Returning to Buddha is acknowledging that our inmost nature is the nature of awareness, of awakening—that awareness is the root of our consciousness and awakening is the birthright of our life. Returning to dharma is acknowledging that we have always longed to understand life in accord with our open mind and tender heart, and that we have always wanted to live lives based on that understanding. Returning to sangha is acknowledging that we have always been a part of the interconnected network of all beings—who cannot be separated from one another any more than water can be separated from water or sky from sky—and that we want to embrace that fabric of connection fully, and be embraced by it, living in concert with all that is.

If we could fully and completely take refuge in the Triple Treasure, if these acknowledgments could be entirely incorporated into our understanding and living, then the spiritual path would be complete, and we would surely take our places immediately as mature and awakened human beings. There would be no need to take up the study and practice of the other precepts—we would already be them, and our conduct would naturally flow from our being.

But none of us has fully and completely taken refuge; none of us has completely returned to the fullness of our human potential. The first three precepts are expressions of our intention and our commitment to a way of life and action. They are always, for any of us, a work in progress, a path, a hope, the endless effort we want to make.

The Pure Precepts

The next three precepts, the "pure" precepts, are less poetic and less metaphysical than the Triple Treasure. Coming down from the lofty heights of the purity of the awakened open heart, we practice these precepts to affirm that on the human plane on which we are born and die there are wholesome and unwholesome actions, and wholesome and unwholesome consequences. There is good and bad, as we would say in plain English.

The first pure precept commits us to avoiding unwholesome action that will increase suffering; we restrain ourselves from doing or saying—even, as much as possible, from thinking—things that will cause harm. The second pure precept comes at conduct from the opposite angle: we pledge ourselves not only to practice restraint and neutrality but beyond this to discover and do that which is wholesome and promotes not a superficial but a lasting happiness. The third pure precept considers our motivation for following the first two: it commits us to act to avoid suffering and to promote happiness unselfishly in order to benefit others, not only ourselves. This is not conventional altruism. The Triple Treasure shows us that when we return to our own true nature, the benefit and happiness of others is none other than our own benefit and happiness.

The Grave Precepts

The final ten precepts are called the "grave" precepts, for they are the most gravity-laden, the most embedded within the weightiness of the relative world. Although the ten precepts are also light and joyful, just as the ordinary world is light and joyful when seen with the spiritual eye, they represent the issues we must grapple with as we get down to the real business of manifesting our maturity in the world. The ten precepts take us beyond the soaring insight of the Triple Treasure and the high good intentions of the pure precepts to what we do and don't do in the daily course of living.

The First Grave Precept: Not to Kill but to Nurture Life

On the surface, this precept seems quite simple to keep. The murderers among us are vastly in the minority; for most of us it is fairly easy to restrain ourselves from acting on the violent impulses that now and then arise. But as we will see with all ten of the grave precepts, looking a bit deeper always raises many doubts. Maybe we find it easy to refrain from killing our coworkers, spouse, or children when they upset us, but what about killing animals? Do we do that for sport? Maybe not, but do we eat meat or fish? If so, are we participating in killing? Even if we are vegetarians, killing is still involved in our consuming. Maybe we don't think a vegetable minds being harvested, but what about the insects and animals that are inevitably killed in the process of growing food, no matter how carefully we do it?

I remember a Zen talk given at our temple by the priest who at the time was in charge of our fifteen-acre farm. Speaking about this precept of nonkilling, he told us about all the killing that he had done that very day as he drove his mower through a thick field of cover crop—the birds' nests, snakes, and field mice that he had unintentionally sliced in half, all in the service of producing our good organic produce. No matter how pure we are trying to be, we certainly participate in some killing if we eat to satisfy our appetites and preserve our lives.

Beyond this, do we pay our taxes and enjoy the benefits of living under a government that might kill people in war or, through neglect or ignorance in its policies, kill the poor and homeless? I know that in San Francisco scores of people die on the streets each year for lack of housing and medical care because the local, state, and national governments have decided to spend funds that might have helped them on other projects.

Beyond literal, physical killing, what about killing the spirit, killing the heart—forms of violence that might be just as bad, if not sometimes worse? Not killing means affirming life, nurturing and respecting life. Do we really practice that? Or are we often thoughtless about how we talk to and view others, treating them dismissively or disrespectfully because we are too cranky or tired to do otherwise? Or perhaps because we view them as enemies or rivals and feel the need to cut them down to size? Or simply because they have hurt our feelings and we want to retaliate?

To nurture life requires that we cultivate an attitude of respect for other living beings, not because there is anything special about them, but simply because they *are* living beings and therefore part of the network of life. For many of us, affection for plants and animals and for the earth comes easily enough. But when it comes to nurturing other people, we are not so sanguine.

In classical Buddhism there is a wonderful practice for cultivating the nurturing heart called sympathetic joy: imagine that the success or benefit that someone else is enjoying is also your own success or benefit. When someone wins, even if they have defeated you in the process, rather than saying, "What about me?" you train yourself to say, "How wonderful; this joy is mine also." Look for opportunities to replace your habitual way of thinking with the discipline of thinking in this new way. If you take on the practice of sympathetic joy with diligence, a sense of participation with people will replace your former feeling of wariness. You will become much more capable of nurturing life, and less apt to want to diminish it.

The Second Grave Precept: Not to Steal but to Receive What Is Offered As a Gift

Again, this precept seems easy. You haven't robbed a store lately, and you have no plans to do so. Neither have you embezzled, committed credit card fraud, or shoplifted. If you don't go to an office every day, you can't steal paper clips and legal pads. But even if you do lift something once in a while—well, isn't that just something minor, hardly even worth mentioning?

When it comes to stealing, where do we draw the line? If you use more than your share of this world's resources, is that stealing? If you profit from a stock that goes up owing to shady dealing or unfair advantage, is that stealing? Suppose you simply waste too much of your wealth or live too high off the hog instead of giving your money to causes that support the needy. Are you stealing from them? What about tax avoidance? You can do your best not to steal in any way that you can see, but you may be stealing in unseen ways. How much responsibility do you bear for that?

There are also many harmful forms of stealing that have nothing to do with material things. What about stealing our own or others' precious time with trivial or harmful pursuits? When we spend too much time fooling around with our computer when we could be helping out someone, or even doing something to preserve and enhance our own lives, maybe we are stealing from them or from ourselves. What about our human relationships—do we give as much as we get? If people pursue friendships with us because they are after our business or our money or our ability to introduce them to someone we know whom they want to meet, we usually have the feeling that they are stealing something from us. Do they feel this, too?

The root cause of stealing is probably the feeling that we are not getting enough, that others are getting more than we are, or that we are afraid somehow that unless we look out for ourselves aggressively no one else will. If we steal, however unconsciously, it must be because we feel separate from the world and beset by it. The practice of generosity is a good way to counteract whatever tendency to stealing we might have. To practice generosity is to make a conscious effort to give away whatever we can—money, time, food, feeling—as a way of realizing that generosity is perfectly safe and it's even a relief to give things away. Giving to others doesn't diminish us, it expands us—our hearts and minds open more widely, and we relax.

For some, generosity comes naturally, but others have to work hard at it. Even the naturally generous can practice generosity further, however, for generosity can be expanded without limit. There is no limit to how much you can give inside.

Generosity is a factor in all human encounters. There is always the choice: Am I going to share myself with this person, or will I hold back? Holding back may seem less bothersome, but it will have a shrinking effect on the spirit, making you a smaller and more isolated person.

Generosity also extends to our willingness to share power. Having lived for many years in a Zen community full of good and well-intentioned people, I know that even the best of us can have trouble sharing power honestly. There is probably no way to avoid clashing over power issues, for in the end our struggles over power are struggles about identity. We identify with a position, person, or view and so feel that an opposing position, person, or view threatens us to the very core of who we are. It's difficult to be generous with someone who opposes your view or is at odds with someone you like. And yet, not being generous at times like these only increases the potential for trouble and conflict.

A Greenpeace worker once told me about her efforts to negotiate a coastal protection agreement with a large logging company in the Pacific Northwest. As the negotiations proceeded, the increasing intransigence of the logging company spokespeople made the Greenpeace negotiators feel more and more entrenched in their own views. Finally, the Greenpeace people realized that this total lack of mutual regard was going to kill off the discussions—and therefore the chance to improve the condition of the coastline. So they decided to employ what they called "the love strategy." They worked at developing generous feelings for the logging negotiators and at creating expansiveness in their feelings and views instead of the smallness and stinginess they had been experiencing. In the end this strategy worked: the Greenpeace negotiators reached an agreement that they felt good about.

The positive side of nonstealing is accepting whatever we

receive as a gift. Rather than thinking we deserve what we get, or have earned it, we let go of any feeling of entitlement and are grateful for what comes to us, as if it were freely given to us by a beneficent universe. This feeling of gratitude for everything may be the fullest expression of the understanding of this precept.

It's not easy to cultivate gratitude in the world we live in: everything seems to be tagged to a bottom line, and even intangibles are viewed in terms of exchange, as income balanced by expense. It is possible, however, to overcome the prevalent attitude. Years ago when I worked as a plant nurseryman and received a monthly check for my services, I remember thinking one month that I was being paid very little. Could my time really be worth such a small number of dollars? I decided to consider how much I thought my time was really worth. It didn't take me long to see that my rate of compensation was very far below the value that I placed on my own time. I thought about the per-hour dollar value of my time: it seemed to me that my time was a rare and extremely valuable commodity, precious almost beyond measure considering that each moment of my life, once gone, could never be recouped. I realized that no one could afford to pay me what my time was actually worth. So I decided to consider myself a wealthy person, and to imagine that I was working for free, simply donating my labor. When my check came at the end of the month, I regarded it as a donation, a gift freely given. Since then I have always applied this practice of working for nothing, receiving my compensation as if it were a gift.

The Third Grave Precept: Not to Misuse Sexuality but to Be Caring and Faithful in Intimate Relationships

This is a difficult precept, for when it comes to sexuality, very few of us are completely clear. Our sexuality is deeply rooted in our hearts, and there is always more to it than meets the eye. As a spiritual teacher, I have often been asked to bear witness to the private lives of others and so have seen many people fall prey to their hidden sexual needs and desires in ways that have caused great suffering. Certainly we want the maturing of our spiritual lives to open us to love. But how do we distinguish between the wholesome love between spiritual friends, and the neediness and inner pressure that can lead to self-deception and sexual disaster?

I am amazed at sexuality's power, and at our fascination with it—both far out of proportion to the amount of time we actually spend directly indulging in sexual activity. The realm of sexuality can have disturbing inner reverberations at times: it awakens not only our need for pleasure and fulfillment but also our senses of shame, inadequacy, identity, fear, aggression, obsession. Sexuality is also a way to transcend the desert island of the isolated self and join in some profound way with the life of another. Sexuality holds the promise of self-transcendence, of self-surrender. Are we ready for this? Are we whole enough to endure it? For some the sexual quest is a spiritual journey that can be deeply satisfying as almost nothing else in our life is.

Sexuality also has the power to hurt us as almost nothing else can. Our stability and tranquillity can suddenly be upset—much to our shock and utter surprise—by the strength of sexual feelings that rise up fiercely out of nowhere, compelling us to deeds we never thought we'd do. We have all seen this happen to others if not to ourselves, and certainly we are made aware of it almost constantly in the movies, on television, in magazines, and in books. Even more disturbing is the rape, incest, child abuse, and sexual debasement of all kinds that we now know, after generations of cover-up, to be commonplace. No human tragedy evokes as emotional a response as sexual crimes, which occur everywhere, even within our churches, schools, professions, and civic organizations. And then there are the less dramatic but almost countless ways in which we hurt each other every day with our sexual advances and suggestions—a boss's inappropriate joke or touch, a boyfriend's intimidating sexual need, a wife's rejection of an amorous husband, or vice versa, the wolf whistle on the street, the gesture, the stare.

In the face of sexuality's power and complexity, we try to practice this precept as well as we can, making the effort to be caring and faithful in our sexual relationships. Sexual styles and appetites are vastly different within different societies and individuals, and within the same societies or individuals at different times in their development. So it is impossible to say which sexual acts are hurtful or not hurtful—it depends on the people involved. One thing is certain: we must build our intimate relationships on a fierce honesty about our own sexual needs and feelings. Fooling ourselves about them only opens us to confusion that might lead us to commit harmful actions without knowing what we're doing. Being honest about our own sexual vulnerabilities, we know that others must have their vulnerabilities, too. Just as we know that we can be hurt, so we know that others can be hurt, and we're clear that it can't be right to satisfy our sexual needs without considering the needs and feelings of others as much as we consider our own. To do that we need to take on the responsibility of knowing our partner as deeply as we can.

It seems to me that the more we do know and care for the person we are intimate with, the more satisfying and meaningful our sexual relationship will be. While a long-term committed relationship may not be everyone's goal, this ideal does exist in the hearts of many of us, and it is a worthy one. I myself have been happily married for many years, and I have seen the ideal realized in others. For married people, or people who are otherwise explicitly committed to one another, this precept implies a degree of faithfulness and honesty about sexual conduct that both partners agree to and support.

Whether or not a committed sexual relationship is part of our life path, probably no one has gotten very far into adult life without stumbling onto a few sexual side roads and detours. I don't know of anyone who hasn't had some sexual disasters in his or her lifetime—encounters, whether short or long in duration, that in hindsight have evoked feelings of shame or guilt or anger, or that perhaps evoked those feelings even at the time. If we have hurt someone, been hurt by someone, or stupidly allowed ourselves to go on being hurt by someone when we could have or should have prevented it, we need to acknowledge that and heal it if we can. We try to forgive not only the other person but ourselves; that involves stopping the sexual patterns of aggression or passivity or confusion that got us into trouble in the first place. In severe situations, like rape or abuse, it may be the right thing for us to accuse and prosecute the perpetrator and to be moved to do so by our anger and hurt. Still, in the end we need to find a way to forgive, if only to cleanse our own heart.

Buddha and many other religious people throughout the ages have understood this precept about sexual misconduct in a very clear-cut way: engage in no sexual activity at all. The point of this understanding, I believe, is not to label sexuality as inherently evil or antispiritual, but to acknowledge that it is so powerful and difficult to manage that it interferes with a full commitment to the spiritual life. This may be true for some people, but celibacy certainly doesn't solve all sexual problems; it doesn't eliminate sexuality, no matter how much a celibate person might wish this were so. As Freud pointed out long ago, sexuality is everywhere, coloring almost all areas of our lives, whether we are sexually active or not. The monastic commitment to abstain from overt sexuality is not meant to create an asexual or cold lifestyle, but rather to widen sexuality, taking it beyond genital activity with selected partners to warm-hearted relationship with all.

Most of us are not committed celibate monastics. And yet, the fact is that most of us are celibate most of the time. Even if we are sexually active, we spend much of our time interacting with people who are not our sexual partners—and even with our sexual partners we are most of the time not being overtly sexual. If we are sexually inactive, not by choice but by circumstances, then we certainly are celibate in a literal sense. So rather than either being always on the prowl sexually or blocking out our sexuality because it has proven unsuccessful in our lives, why not affirm our temporary celibacy as an opportunity rather than a deprivation and use it to develop a greater warmth and connection to ourselves and the world?

The Fourth Grave Precept: Not to Lie but to Be Truthful

Lying is an unwholesome action that leads to trouble and unhappiness. Internally, lying makes you nervous. With the first lie you begin to spin a web of untruth around yourself, for soon you need a second lie to support the first, and then further lies, until you are confused about what your story is supposed to be. Sooner or later you will feel the sinking feeling of being so bound up in the web of lies that you can't move. Externally, your lies will hurt others, confusing them and diminishing their capacity to trust.

Few of us consider ourselves to be liars, but probably most of us lie inadvertently, through laziness, inattentiveness, exaggeration, or too much attachment to our own point of view. This kind of subtle lying can ruin a relationship—acting like a slow poison, it gradually robs the relationship of its vitality.

Reflecting on this, we may recognize our laxity and try to improve. We find, however, that it's not so simple. The more scrupulously we try to tell the truth, the more we see that truth isn't always such a clear path. As we look more closely at our words, our hearts, our thoughts, our feelings, and our motivations, we become less and less clear about what's true. There's an old Zen saying: "Everything's true, everything's false." The truth (and falsity!) of this statement begins to impress itself on us as we intensify our efforts to be truthful with our words.

It is nearly impossible most of the time to know what's true. Reality is so multifaceted that the truth seems to shift and skip and slide around. In the famous Akira Kurosawa film *Rashomon*, a story is told over and over again, each time from the point of view of a different character. Each telling is quite different from the others, and each seems true. Like a fun house full of mirrors each of which shows a different distortion of the same reality, the film leaves the viewer dazzled and disturbed. Life is like this, too—the more versions of your story you consider, the harder it becomes to find a single truth.

But even supposing you could discover the one view that is true above all others, you'd still have to put that truth into words and communicate it somehow. This raises the question of *how* we speak the truth—skillfully or unskillfully, thoroughly or with only a few details, kindly or not so kindly, at the right time or at the wrong time. In what style and at what pace do we communicate this version of the truth? With what attitude and tone of voice? All of these factors make more of a difference than you might think, not just in style but in substance.

This uncertainty about truth is even more pronounced in the emotional realm. The truth is that we are aware of our feelings only selectively—so much of what motivates us and disturbs or pleases us remains below the surface. The way others see and experience us is often vastly different from the way we see and experience ourselves. Anyone who has ever been immersed in an emotional conversation about feelings and attitudes with an intimate friend knows that emotional truth can be very elusive.

Truth is no easier to find in the public arena, where we are supposed to be dealing with objective facts. Politicians, attorneys, and businesspeople are constantly accusing one another of subverting or obscuring the truth, and it is difficult to evaluate who is right and who is wrong. Facts do not seem to be facts—they are endlessly subject to spin and interpretation. We might well wonder whether there is any such thing as a public truth. And yet, when we hear truth spoken publicly, we feel its power. Speeches by Abraham Lincoln, Martin Luther King Jr., Nelson Mandela, Mahatma Gandhi, Frederick Douglass, or Cesar Chavez still stir us with their truth power.

Public or private, truth-telling does have magical power. Despite the difficulty of finding and proving truth, we all know truth when we hear it because it resonates with our own deep sense of what's right. Like a Mandela or a Gandhi, we, too, through reflection and the courage of our convictions, can go beyond the confusion of our biases to discover what we feel is true and speak it.

Someone who habitually exaggerates and speaks untruthfully out of selfishness, anger, or impetuousness will be known for that. Losing value day by day, his or her words will eventually be discounted. But the person who tries to remain aware of his or her own motivations and desires, and speaks what's true, not to win a point but simply out of concern for what's right, will be heard and respected. This person's words will be healing and effective.

I am fortunate to know many people who practice telling the truth. They are not saints or great leaders but ordinary human beings who have recognized how satisfying it can be to tell the truth. They know that the heart and mind are relieved when we tell the truth rather than speak only out of a guarded self-interest. They practice this precept in both their work lives and their private lives, committing themselves to saying what's true as they honestly see it and feel it, with sensitivity and understanding. One person I know manages to do this in his work as a financial adviser for a large brokerage firm. When he first took on the practice of truth-telling with his clients and coworkers, he feared that it would cost him many accounts, his investment performance would go down, or his coworkers would disapprove. But the opposite has been the case. While his success at work has not increased dramatically, neither has it fallen off, and he has a lot more peace and happiness with what he is doing.

The Fifth Grave Precept: Not to Intoxicate with Substances or Doctrines but to Promote Clarity and Awareness

This precept is usually understood to be about the use of substances like drugs or alcohol, but its practice actually goes much deeper. This precept strikes at the heart of our relationship to what's difficult and unpleasant in our lives. A mature person is patient and steady enough to be able to face what is. He or she knows that trying to escape or avoid unpleasant realities simply doesn't work, for a problem avoided is a problem compounded. Intoxication is an act of avoidance—refusing to face what is by covering it over with something else we hope will be more pleasant. In this sense, almost anything can be an intoxicant—television, music, games, reading, shopping, even relationships, doctrines, or ideologies. Whatever functions in our lives to blunt the force of our awareness, preventing us from experiencing our life as it really is, is an intoxicant.

Intoxication that masks strong, unacknowledged pain in our lives is the most virulent kind, for it easily snowballs, and we find ourselves the victims of a strong compulsion to go on and on with our practice of intoxication until we become dysfunctional. This is the realm of addiction, which is all too common in our time. In Buddhist mythology a being called a hungry ghost dwells in hell and is constantly seeking food and drink. His quest for food is especially desperate and pathetic because his belly is huge and his throat is the size of a needle. No matter how much he stuffs into his mouth, he can never get enough through his throat to satisfy his hunger. Hungry ghosts, constantly ravenous, howl and moan their way through their lives. This painful image fits very well the tragedy of human compulsive desire, which truly is a hell realm. No one would ever enter it consciously.

Intoxication is also a confused attempt to cope with our deep-seated and unlimited human desires. We want so much, consciously and unconsciously: inner qualities like happiness, love, and satisfaction, and outer acquisitions like money, property, power, beauty, and youthfulness. Most of us find the pressure of these desires too much to bear, so we try not to notice them. We may drink a bit too much alcohol every evening—it is so much simpler than making the effort to find the peace we seek. Instead of admitting our loneliness and trying to do something about it, we may watch a lot of television or shop more than we need to or can afford. Rather than confronting the energies inside us, which might liven us up if only we could find a way to deal with them, we dull ourselves with intoxicants.

We all understand the tragedy of addiction, and most of us avoid the more serious forms. But how many of us depend on one form of intoxication or another just to get through the unhappiness and confusion of our days? Do we know the difference between relaxation and running away?

How can we work with our desire and our pain? The positive side of this precept gives us a way—the practice of awareness. Leaving off distraction and avoidance, we try to face what really is: our disappointments, our stresses, our pain, our desire. Everything we feel and experience in our lives is our gift and our responsibility. We have to find a way to meet it, live with it, and give it room to transform. Rather than using distraction to leap over our feelings, we practice staying with them, turning toward them, facing them, until they change, as all things do if we allow them to. When we practice this way, we find that even our worst problems can be useful. We can learn from them, bringing depth and liberation to our lives. Even our wild desires can be tamed and give us pleasure in ways that don't hurt us or anyone else. Doing this work of transformation does take some kind of spiritual discipline, like meditation or prayer and the support of others who are committed to doing the same work. But discipline can be developed and support can be found; the work can be done.

The Sixth Grave Precept: Not to Speak of Other's Faults but to Speak out of Loving-Kindness

Talk is cheap, as the saying goes, because words are plentiful. We won't run out. But talk is also precious: what we say to and about others matters a great deal, and whether or not they say so or even know it, people are hurt by our careless words, just as they are helped by our inspired or kind words.

Because we have critical intelligence, we can't help but evaluate others—our minds simply function this way—and then naturally we speak about the mistakes and shortcomings we see. It seems that this is unavoidable, that if we took a pledge never to speak about the faults of others, we'd fall silent in almost all conversations! Everyone loves to gossip. It is so effortless and seems so innocent, and the opportunities for it are practically endless. Gossip is especially compelling when we are with friends who we know will agree with our critical assessments of others outside our circle—especially when our assessments are humorous and entertaining.

The practice of this precept of not speaking of the faults of others gives us pause and reminds us that gossip isn't as harmless as it may seem. When we run another person down in his or her absence, we color our feeling about that person, so that the next time we see him or her a pall is cast in our minds. This pall, subtle as it may be, makes it hard for us to face the person with openness and we don't feel clean and honest in the encounter.

The pall extends still further: if you and I gossip about a third party, I can't help but suspect that you may gossip about me with someone else. Maybe you have been doing this already. How can I trust you, knowing that you are capable of speaking this way about someone? (Even though I'm doing it, too!) If that's so, can I trust myself? Do I turn my critical eye and satirical tongue inward as well as outward, diminishing my self-regard? Like a corrosive liquid that slowly seeps through many layers of fabric, gossip's negativity has a way of saturating our hearts and our relationships.

Suppose we took seriously the universal religious teaching that all human beings are potentially loving, kind, and worthwhile. Suppose we realized that our not seeing them like that is as much the fault of our own vision as of their imperfection. How then would we speak about them? And suppose we recognized and respected the power of our own speech, knowing that, as Zen master Dogen says, kind speech "can turn the destiny of a nation." If we recognized this power, would we ever speak poorly of anyone—even people who richly deserve our reproaches? Wouldn't we rather recognize that everyone—especially those about whom the most terrible things can truly be said!—needs our kind speech and can benefit from it?

In the course of real life as we know it, this seems a tall order. Surely it is not always possible to speak kindly and nicely about everyone. How can you practice kind speech if you are a supervisor needing to give feedback to an employee, or even needing to fire him or her for malfeasance or incompetence? What if you have been forced by circumstances to take on an adversary or defend a position? Aren't these special cases in which this precept might not apply?

I think not. In fact, no matter what you need to say to or about someone in whatever circumstances, it is always possible, and even necessary in the long run, to speak from a heart of kindness and understanding. Even if you need to be critical or speak defensively, there is always a way to do it honestly and in a way that does not express dislike, denigrate the other side, or engage in personal attack. For just as your speech conditions the experience of another person, it also conditions your own experience. If your speech depicts a world populated by bad, incompetent, thoughtless, nasty people, then that's the world you live in, and you will suffer the consequences of it. Truly the world we most intimately inhabit is the world created by our thought and by our speech, which is both the result of and the cause of our thought. As the first verse of the ancient Buddhist text, the Dhammapada, says, "What we are today comes from our thoughts of yesterday, and our present thoughts build our life of tomorrow; our life is the creation of our mind. If a person speaks or acts with an impure mind, suffering will follow as the wheels of a cart follow the beast that pulls it."

Gossip and fault-finding speech can be avoided. There is always a way to speak that communicates what needs to be said without diminishing the mind that sees the potential for good in others. Making the effort to speak like this is one of the best ways to transform our lives.

The Seventh Grave Precept: Not to Praise Self at the Expense of Others but to Be Modest

This is another precept about speech and its power. Not to praise self at the expense of others is to speak about ourselves with modesty, not favoring ourselves too much in what we say. Practicing this precept helps us cultivate a heart that is as concerned about others as it is about itself. Self-centered speech is quite normal—we don't have to be raging egotists for our speech to regularly favor ourselves. In ordinary conversation, how often do we ask about others in anything more than a polite way? And when we do want to hear about others, isn't it often for the purpose of comparing or relating their experience to our own?

When our speaking is habitually focused on ourselves, we are creating a world separate from others. The world in which I occupy the center is a small world indeed. On the other hand, the world in which others' lives are just as important as my own is a world large and various enough for me to grow in. To practice not praising self at the expense of others slowly extends the world in which we live, making it more and more inclusive and less and less in need of defending.

It is easy to see why we so strongly favor ourselves in our speech practice. Because we feel instinctively that our situation is shaky, that we are not as wonderful or as talented as we ought to be—or as someone else is—we are in constant need of praise and confidence-building. Since our experience has been that very few will give us this boost, we feel we need to take matters into our own hands. So much of our posturing and self-promotional speaking has its root in our lack of feeling self-worth. The person who speaks modestly, not favoring self and praising others, is someone who is secure enough not to need extra praise. To practice this precept is to gradually become such a person.

As with all the speech practices, not praising self at the expense of others requires the discipline of paying attention to what comes out of our mouths and honestly observing how our words make ourselves and others feel. The hardest part of the practice is remembering to do it—unconscious speech, we quickly see, is natural and pervasive. But we do get better at this practice. We train ourselves to notice when we are interrupting or monopolizing a conversation, we make the effort to catch ourselves and stop. We train ourselves to ask about how someone else is doing, and then to actually listen to what they say. Can we respond with something truly supportive? Can we be imaginative enough to see the other person's joys, sorrows, and accomplishments as if they were just as real and important to us as our own? And when it is time for us to speak about ourselves, can we do that in a balanced way, without excessive and exaggerated (though probably subtly masked) self-praise?

As we go on with this practice, less self-consciousness and restraint is required. As with all the precepts, the effort eventually becomes quite natural and spontaneous. It begins to seem dull to go on and on about ourselves and never notice others. Self-praise begins to seem foolish. How can we take credit for things—our accomplishments are achieved only thanks to the help of many others. All things depend on each other. Without the food he had for breakfast (produced by the farmer with the aid of rain, soil, and seed and delivered by truck), the highway he drove into town on (paved by workers with the help of machinery manufacturers, administrators, and taxpayers), the clothes he is wearing (made abroad by women working in factories), and many other things requiring cooperation and aid that comes from all over the world, the salesman would not have made the sale that won him the achievement award. This is true of anything anyone has ever done. We can accept credit for our accomplishments, but we must always recognize that we have had countless collaborators.

On the other hand, true modesty doesn't require us to denigrate ourselves. In fact, when we denigrate ourselves and underestimate our skills and talents, we are not keeping this precept but breaking it. The habit of self-denigration is the sneakiest form of self-centeredness. Feeling miserably sorry for ourselves gives us full permission to dwell on ourselves constantly and to seek support from others all the time without having to give back any support in return. Though on the surface they might feel and look different, self-denigration and self-inflation are two sides of the same coin, two ways of putting ourselves at the center of things. These habits of thought and speech may not be easy to break. But when we practice this precept, we begin to recognize them for what they are and see exactly how they create suffering. Then we can begin little by little to break them.

The Eighth Grave Precept: Not to Be Possessive of Anything but to Be Generous

Possessiveness seems like the most natural thing in the world. At a certain age children learn to say "mine" quite emphatically as they yank on a toy that another child is holding. Who doesn't need and want many things? Throughout human history people have been fighting over territory, property, and precious objects. Even the Bible is a tale of getting and fighting to keep. Is it possible—and is it even desirable?—to practice nonpossessiveness? I think it is. As strong as our will toward possessiveness is, just as strong is the knowledge that possessiveness is ultimately tragic, for in the end we cannot keep what we have, and trying to do so makes us anxious, narrow, and mean-spirited.

I have a friend who made a good deal of money a few years ago when the stock market was booming. He became quite obsessive about his holdings and had several television monitors installed in his home so that he could keep close tabs on the fluctuations of the market. When I visited him in his quiet house high up on a hilltop overlooking town, I found it difficult to carry on a normal conversation with him because he was always looking over my shoulder at one of the monitors on the wall and occasionally excusing himself to make an important phone call. As more and more money came pouring in, my friend, who is quite creative, found more and more ways to spend it. When he became interested in thoroughbred horses and bought several, he also eventually needed to purchase a stable for them and hire a crew of people to train and groom them. He took an interest in real estate all over the world and purchased several homes in far-flung countries. He bought yachts, a small fleet of cars, and I am sure many other things I had no idea of.

All of these new possessions seemed to be on his mind constantly. He seemed happy enough, even to be thriving, but he was extremely busy and quite distracted. When the stock market fell sharply and the several businesses he had started crashed to earth, he was busier than ever, but much less happy. I ran into him one day at a restaurant, and he told me that he was continuing to lose millions of dollars every day and that keeping the stables going was becoming increasingly difficult. When I suggested that he save himself the trouble and sell his horses, he looked at me with a deep sadness in his eyes and said, "You don't understand. I love these horses. They mean everything to me. I've put millions of dollars into them. I've got to fight to keep them." Although it was hard for me to understand, he did seem truly desperate about the horses. I felt sorry for him, for it seemed as if his rather spectacular possessiveness had made him miserable.

Few of us will live out our practice of possessiveness quite so dramatically. And yet we can all relate to the misery that comes when we don't get something we want, or when we are in danger of losing something we have. Loss is built into the very idea of possession: possessions are precious exactly because they can be lost. Most of us do not recognize this, and when we experience loss, we become frightened and hold on even more tightly. But if we are wise enough to see that it is painful to deny that loss is inevitably a part of possession, we have a lot of incentive to practice nonpossessiveness. We learn to keep a loose enough hold on what we have that we won't be destroyed when we lose it.

The more we focus on our possessions as the substance and measure of what we are, the more vulnerable we are. When we expand our sense of self to include others—as well as the sky and the wind and the darkness of the night—our possessions do not loom so large in our lives that they actually possess us. We don't have to live in a state of deprivation or renunciation to practice nonpossessiveness. It is possible to practice nonpossessiveness even in the midst of great wealth. The practice of nonpossessiveness has less to do with what we have or don't have than it does with how we understand and live with what we have.

Most of us have a great deal of conditioning about possessiveness. To practice the precept of nonpossessiveness is to work with our conditioning and make the effort to expand our understanding, let go of our habitual concepts and feelings, and loosen the stranglehold they have had on us.

Having lived for so long without much money, I always found it difficult to go shopping and pay the high prices the stores always seemed to charge. I decided that I could work on this by recognizing that when I bought something, I was not, as I had always felt, relinquishing too much of my hard-earned money, scarce as it was. Instead, I was giving money to people who needed it—store clerks, factory workers, farmers. Practicing like this over time, I was able to shift my perspective so that I no longer minded or worried as much about the price I paid for things.

Ultimately, to practice nonpossessiveness is to recognize that it is impossible to possess anything. No one actually owns anything. Things own themselves. They are constantly circulating, passing from hand to hand, transforming, changing shape and location. We work so hard to ensure that our possessions will remain securely in our own hands—installing locks and gates, buying insurance policies, hiring armed guards, making contingency plans. But in the end we die, and all that we have worked for and tried so hard to protect ends up in someone else's hands.

If we don't really possess things, how much less do we possess the people in our lives. The very nature of our relationship to them, if it is a truly loving human relationship, is freedom, even though it may include commitment and obligation. To really love someone—a spouse, a child, a colleague, or a friend—is to recognize that they are not us, that they have needs, aspirations, and lives that do not belong to us and that we cannot control. Can we appreciate and give of ourselves to them without fixating on what they will give us in return? Can we allow them their freedom and autonomy? Love like that may be the highest form of the practice of nonpossessiveness.

The closer we look, the more we see that our lives have

arisen as a result of, and always in connection with, so many others. Our thoughts, feelings, and attitudes come and go, produced in large part by our associations with all that we have encountered in our lives. Even our bodies are a flow that is not really our own, maintained by processes that will transform one day into wind and water, liberated from our thoughts, our wishes, and our histories. At its deepest level, to practice nonpossessiveness is to act on the recognition that our life is always sharing. Knowing this is so, we naturally want to be nonpossessive with material things, with our time and energy and presence, with our words, and, especially, with our love. Nonpossessiveness is the practice of bodhisattvas.

The Ninth Grave Precept: Not to Harbor Anger but to Forgive

This precept is subtle and important. Although all spiritual traditions deal with the question of anger, it seems to be a particular specialty of Buddhism to analyze and discuss anger. Buddhist practice affirms that anger is never a good thing and that we should always let go of it once we are aware of its destructive power.

But this is a tricky business. What about justified anger—anger at social ills, or anger that wakes people up out of their stupor and rouses them to necessary action? I suppose these cases beg the question of exactly what we mean by the word *anger*. If anger is, as I would define it, "the powerful blind impulse to do harm," then it is never justified and it never helps. Although the righteous energy to change unjust social conditions or to rouse someone to take action in his or her life might include some degree of annoyance or ill will, it is not really anger if it comes from a positive motivation. Psychologically, someone whose feelings of hurt or loss have been deeply suppressed may need to rouse a great anger in order to overcome the old emotional blockage. But in this case anger is only a stage, a temporary expedient, whose real root is the original hurt or loss, not the motivation to harm. If the anger goes on for too long or is inappropriately encouraged and so hardens into an attitude of revenge, it would not promote healing—it would only perpetuate and strengthen the initial wound.

Anger more commonly arises when we have been crossed or violated in some way and we do not want to admit this or to experience it fully. In this sense anger is an intoxicant, a cover-up for the painful hurt feelings we can't bear to feel. The practice of this precept doesn't require that we never be angry. That would be impossible—when the conditions for anger arise, anger inevitably appears. In practicing this precept, however, we can make the effort to turn toward our anger when it arises, bearing witness to it and experiencing it fully, but not grabbing hold of it, justifying it, or acting on it. Practicing this precept will give us the confidence and the spaciousness to stop supressing our anger—to see that we can feel our anger and honor it without being consumed by it, that we can allow it and *be* it through and through, giving it space inside to fully manifest, without indulging it.

Anger is usually not pleasant. The eyes bulge out, the heart races, the body is full of tension and pulses with uncomfortable energy. All this can be experienced without causing harm, and it may even be beneficial sometimes. It's not the anger itself that is the problem—it is the grabbing hold of the anger and acting on it that causes harm. There is an old Buddhist saying: "Anger is like a pile of shit: in order to throw it on someone else, you have to pick it up first." And when you do, you are the one who ends up smelly. To practice not harboring anger is to allow ourselves to experience anger, to respect and honor it as a raw and basic emotion without becoming victimized by it.

Unpleasant as it may be, anger can also feel very good sometimes. It can make us feel powerful in the face of the impotence we might otherwise feel when we have been wronged by another. The other person has gotten the better of us and robbed us (it always comes down to this) of our sense of autonomy and worth. This is what hurts—the feeling of being diminished, defeated, weakened. But now that we are angry we are no longer weak—we have become fear-inspiring and powerful. People get out of our way. They may even yield to our demands. This seems much better than being a weakling or a doormat.

But this view of anger as power is based on a mistaken sense of what personal power really is. The power to dominate or overcome is a tragic power in the end, for it is always bound to fail. No matter how strong or clever we are, someone else is always stronger and more clever. No matter how loudly we yell, there is someone else who will yell louder. Holding personal sway over others is always temporary—sooner or later the victor becomes the vanquished. The power to embrace conditions and let go is a much stronger power than the power to dominate. The true source of human power lies in recognizing what we truly are—beings with an infinitely wide scope, who can be limited externally but never internally, except by ourselves. By making imaginative use of whatever happens and cooperating with rather than resisting what is, we do not need to indulge our anger in order to feel strong.

Anger is in the end a marker of our weakness, not of our strength, and this is why it is so useful. Our anger will show us, once we have practiced with it long enough to be able to notice, the limits of our power, for anger always flares up precisely in the places where we are most vulnerable, where the boundaries of our sense of self are most easily challenged. The person who doubts her beauty will get angry when someone suggests that she is not beautiful; the person who feels inadequate sexually will get angry when someone else flaunts his sexuality. Studying our anger shows us those places where we are brittle and defended, where we are weakest and most need to grow. As we practice not harboring our anger, with full attentiveness, we come to see ourselves much more accurately and viscerally. Using our anger well, we can pinpoint our weak points, our personal narrowness, and expand there, so that as our practice progresses and the horizons of our personal power expand, anger arises less often and less virulently.

The positive side of this precept is the practice of forgiveness, which is just this expansion. Working with our anger, studying it, and softening into it, we eventually forgive ourselves for our weaknesses, and that very forgiveness transforms those weaknesses. Although they may not go away, they won't hurt us anymore. Forgiving ourselves also helps us to recognize over time that others who have hurt us are themselves victims of their own narrowness and weakness. As we understand this—and see it directly and immediately in our experience—we more easily forgive others for their hurtful actions. As forgiveness and empathy expand, anger lessens. We don't need to get angry to feel powerful anymore. We feel a truer and deeper power in settling into what is, with compassion and understanding.

The Tenth Grave Precept: Not to Do Anything to Diminish the Triple Treasure but to Support and Nurture It

This precept returns us to the beginning. With the commitment to take refuge in the Triple Treasure of Buddha, dharma, and sangha, we began the journey of the practice of ethical conduct by recognizing our real and most fundamental human nature—that we are all, at bottom, awakened, maturing beings who have it in our hearts to make the effort to become what we most deeply are. That initial recognition and commitment has led us to consider step by step how we view ourselves and live in the world. Along the way we have gradually come to see that our conduct does count, that all our acts of body, speech, and mind matter. We have come to see that the more we are aware of our conduct and work toward clarifying it, turning toward openness and sharing with others and away from narrow and frightened self-centeredness, the happier we become, and the happier we are able to make other people in our lives. We come to see that the possibilities for refining our conduct and deepening our view of life are endless.

This final precept affirms and reinforces all that has gone before. It is all sixteen precepts rolled into one. It reconfirms us in our pledge to always make an effort to nurture and sustain our highest and deepest commitments and never to knowingly choose to do anything that would diminish them in any way.

THE TEN GRAVE PRECEPTS SEEM TO COVER DISCRETE AND different topics, but in precept practice—as in almost everything else in life—categories and distinctions are only convenient devices that help us reflect on our life and our conduct. In fact, the precepts are hard to keep separate. They seem to blend into one another from time to time: nonstealing becomes nonpossessiveness, nonlying becomes not praising self at the expense of others, and so on. Although in our daily practice we can focus for a time on one precept or another, in fact throughout our lives we are constantly practicing all of them at once. Some say that in reality there is really only one precept—taking refuge in Buddha, returning to our true capacity and identity as an awakened, caring human being. The precepts offer an infinite variety of ways to practice that fundamental point.

Traditionally it is said that precepts are practiced simultaneously on three different levels: the literal, the compassionate, and the ultimate. On the literal level, we do our best to follow the precepts to the letter. Not killing means not killing—we try our best to kill nothing. The literal level is also quite practical. Knowing we are always living with others in community, we know we need to make an effort to act as peacefully and as harmlessly as possible. We abide by ethical and social codes as straightforwardly as we can—not breaking laws, not offending against custom. We try to reduce our fixation on our desires and satisfactions so that we can promote the greater good.

At the compassionate level of precept practice, we may find it necessary to go beyond rules, laws, or customs, motivated not by willful self-interest but by compassion, which sometimes causes us to transcend the literal level of good conduct for the purpose of helping others. For instance, if telling the truth will hurt someone seriously, we might tell a lie to save that person. If we feel that the world requires us to speak out dramatically against political or social injustice and we need to break a law in the course of doing that, we break the law. Compassion might sometimes require us to act to disturb the peace—to transcend the expected and the approved.

The third level of precept practice is the ultimate level. Through our spiritual endeavors—meditation, prayer, contemplation—we try to penetrate to this level, until we come to appreciate that the precepts are deeper than we have ever imagined: so deep that they can never be completely understood. We come to see that our ordinary, mundane choices and actions are really much more than they seem, reverberating beyond anything we had imagined. On the ultimate level, we appreciate that precepts are beyond breaking and not breaking, distinctions we now see as products of our limited conceptualizing minds. Like the precepts, ultimately we and the world cannot be violated, for we are complete and perfect as we are. At the same time, we and the world are tragically limited—things will always be a little off, and conduct will always fall short. On this ultimate and paradoxical level, it doesn't even make sense to utter the word *precept* or the words *good, bad, self* or *other.* Beyond the dividing narrowness of our limited view, things are connected and complete, and no rules or restraints are required. Appreciating this level (even if only intellectually), we know that we don't need to be hard on ourselves or others for breaking precepts, or congratulate anyone for keeping them. The only important thing is to go on forever making the effort to practice precepts, without measurement or seeking after results. On the other hand, we also see how easy it would be to use the ultimate level as a cover for our self-deception, justifying our willful bad conduct with the thought that "precepts can never be broken anyway, and everything is already perfect." This trap is all too clear. The truth of the ultimate level notwithstanding, we are forever subject to the practical obligations and effects of our actions.

The three levels do not represent a hierarchy of understanding. They are just ways of speaking that help us appreciate the depth and strangeness of life, and to recognize that living ethically is a task that requires our best attention. In the end the long road toward maturity leads us to mystery, the true ground of growing up. Knowing that we don't know doesn't prevent us from trying to know. Knowing that conduct is always ambiguous in an imperfect world doesn't discourage us from trying to conduct ourselves beautifully. The practice of ethical conduct and all the other practices for maturity that we have been discussing bring us to the recognition that truly growing up is more than ordinary, more than natural. It is not a chore, something to be accomplished quickly, so that we can get on with more important things. To walk the road toward maturity is to journey to the center of life's mysterious meaning.

Afterword

BUDDHA'S
SMILE

THERE'S A LINE IN THE LOTUS SUTRA I'VE BEEN THINKING about for more than twenty years. It comes at a crucial moment in the narrative, as the Buddha is revealing the esoteric meaning of his teachings to a vast assembly of astonished practitioners. "In the past," the Buddha tells them, "I taught in a linear and straightforward manner about what's wholesome and what's not, about suffering and the end of suffering, about samsara and nirvana. I taught ethical conduct, meditation, and insight, setting forth a path of practice that was clear and manageable.

"But all of this," Buddha confesses, "was merely skillful means I had to use, knowing that it was as much as you were capable of understanding at that time. Now I am revealing a deeper truth—that the path, the teachings, the practice, is much larger than I indicated before—in fact, it is infinite in scope, limitless, because beings are infinite and limitless. Although I defined it

185

before, in truth the path cannot be defined. No ordinary person could possibly know it, for it is beyond all knowing."

Now comes my line: "Only a Buddha and a Buddha," he says, "can understand it." Even a Buddha by himself can't understand it. Only a Buddha *and* a Buddha can. Only through profound relationship, deep encounter, ineffable meeting, can we ever hope to appreciate the immense dimensions of our human life.

Our life is really nothing more than a series of moment-by-moment meetings. When we meditate, we can see this. Slowing down and focusing the mind, we meet what's inside us. Sitting quietly, paying close attention, we meet thoughts, we meet feelings. We meet our breath, we meet sensations in our body. We meet fear, memory, desire, aversion, the oddly taken-for-granted experience of identity. Every moment brings a new opportunity for meeting; every moment is a challenge to remain awake enough, soft and persistent enough, to be present with what comes forth. As our practice continues we see how often we don't meet what's inside us, how much of our life remains hidden to us because we are not willing to let it in. But as we learn more and more that it is possible to be present, even with difficult meetings, our trust in life grows. We are willing to stop trying to control and shape what happens according to our desires. We are willing to meet what comes forth in our life as completely as we can on each occasion.

When we get up from our meditation seat, we meet a more varied world, a world of color, shape, noise, and complexity. Our eyes meet visual objects, our ears meet sounds, our noses meet smell, our tongues meet taste, our skin meets touch. Our minds put together a world out of all this. We meet that world and try to understand and embrace it—to find our place in it. The world calls us forth and we express ourselves. We make choices, and we stand by those choices. We meet mountains, trees, streams, animals, and other people. Coming to maturity in this complicated world is a matter of meeting each thing, inside and out, with sensitivity, awareness, and persistence, with trust, love, and wisdom. We need these qualities in order to fully meet what's in front of us. When we can do that naturally, we find our place in the world.

Zen practice emphasizes the inclusiveness of each moment of meeting. To meet one thing completely, the Zen masters of old tell us, is to meet everything. When Mazu tells us, "This very mind is Buddha," he means that every moment of mind, every moment of meeting, includes the whole of reality. When Dongshan is asked, "What is Buddha?" and he responds, "Three pounds of flax!" he is pointing to the same thing. In Japanese culture, which was profoundly influenced by the Zen feeling for life, it is natural to create art forms out of simple everyday acts like making a cup of tea or arranging flowers, for in these ordinary domestic gestures all that is profound in life can be discovered. The whole world is in one cup of tea; all beauty is in each flower. Each thought in the mind, truly met, contains all that has ever been thought. Every emotion, deeply encountered, contains all that has ever been felt. Every person we meet evokes all of humanity. In the Zen meditation hall we bow to our meditation cushions with this same spirit, honoring the small place on which we are about to sit, knowing it contains all of space and time.

Recognizing the immensity of each moment of meeting doesn't necessarily make life easier. In a way, it makes it more difficult. But there's satisfaction in such difficulty, for it is always real. So often spiritual practice is presented as ethereal and joyful, full of enlightening moments and peak experiences. Such experiences sometimes do occur—we meet them, too, enjoying them without making too much of them. Like all experiences, they pass. The great thing is not a marvelous spiritual experience but an ongoing way of practice that takes into account all of life—its difficulties as well as its joys—and that includes not only our own personal experience but the feeling we can have for others and the world.

If you see life as only positive, only wonderful, only encouraging, you haven't really been paying enough attention. Life is much more than that. There's a famous picture of Shunryu Suzuki Roshi on the back of his book *Zen Mind, Beginner's Mind.* Suzuki Roshi isn't smiling blissfully, as we might expect of a spiritual master. He is simply staring straight ahead into the camera lens, with a determined but amused look on his face that says, "I am meeting whatever comes with interest and patience. Sometimes it will be good, sometimes it will be not so good. But whatever it is, I will be glad to meet it."

One friend who practices Zen with me studied long ago with Suzuki Roshi. He told me: "I came to the Zen Center just a few months before Suzuki Roshi's illness. But in those few months I made such a strong connection because I felt so completely met by him. No one else in my life, before or since, has ever met me that thoroughly. He seemed to be always ready and waiting for me in every encounter—wide open, yet unassuming and quiet. It touched me deeply." I have heard this same comment from many other people who practiced Zen with Suzuki Roshi. So many of them say they still think of him almost every day and feel as if in some strange way he is continuing to meet them even now.

True maturity is being willing and able to show up for all of life's meetings. This takes listening, but also responding—receiving something deeply, trusting life enough to allow that thing to change you, and then coming forward forthrightly, trusting yourself and your instincts. Maturity is knowing that the world is constantly creating you moment by moment, but also that you are creating the world as you come forward to meet it with your skills, talents, and activity.

When we are young, this process of meeting teaches us about the world and about ourselves. So much of what we meet we have never met before, and like the practitioners in the Lotus Sutra assembly, we are astonished by what transpires. Our response to all this input teaches us what kind of people we are—how we think and feel, what's easy for us to do, and what's difficult. We build new worlds; that is how we explore our hearts and minds when we are young.

When we get older, we have seen and experienced more. We've been excited, but we have also been disappointed. We've had many victories and defeats, and we've had the time to reflect on it all, to evaluate and understand. At this point in our lives we learn from teaching others, from passing on to them, as best we can, the fruits of what we have come to know. This is not to say that we have things figured out. Far from it—life teaches us to be humble, to recognize how much we don't know and probably never will know. But from now on we learn as much from being in the presence of others as we do from our own insights and experiences. This sharing and teaching is an important part of the maturing process. Through it we come to some real accord with others. We feel we can entrust them with our spirit, with our sense of what life is about. The culminating moment of the Lotus Sutra comes when the Buddha hands the teachings down, trusting the bodhisattvas to carry it forth after he is gone.

Zen practice puts great emphasis on this sharing and entrustment. More than many other schools of Buddhism, Zen emphasizes the teacher-disciple relationship as the vehicle for understanding, the container that makes maturity possible for both parties. Zen masters are neither teachers in the ordinary sense (possessing knowledge that can be explained or imparted) nor gurus possessing spiritual powers and virtues. Instead, they are, like Suzuki Roshi, seasoned practitioners who are willing to meet other practitioners, each one on his or her own terms. The magic of this meeting—which is neither the teacher's nor the student's doing but exists at the point of contact between them—produces the awakening suggested by the words of the Lotus Sutra: "Only a Buddha and a Buddha can understand." This "warm hand to warm hand" meeting is said to have begun with Buddha and his first disciple and to have continued through the generations down to the present. It is called "face-to-face transmission."

Here is the Zen story of the first transmission from Buddha to Mahakasyapa. Long ago, when the Buddha was at Vulture Peak giving a talk, he held up a flower before the assembly. At this everyone remained silent. Only Mahakasyapa broke into a smile, and Buddha smiled, too. Buddha then said, "I have the treasury of the eye of truth, the ineffable mind of nirvana. I now entrust it to Mahakasyapa."

This is a story of pure meeting. There's no instruction, no test, no program, no content. There are no words, nothing you could put your finger on other than a smile shared between two people who are appreciating together the profound beauty of the flower that is our life.

OUR COMING-OF-AGE GROUP MET REGULARLY FOR ABOUT two years. After two years, just as we were getting to know and appreciate each other, it seemed time to bring it to a close. We discussed rituals that we might end with, because it seemed impossible, after all that we had meant to each other, to simply disband. We had had a months-long discussion of ethical conduct, and the boys were now starting to pay attention to what they were saying, doing, and thinking, in a com-

pletely new way. Together we decided that our closing ritual
should acknowledge this.

Again, it was Tony who came up with the creative idea. Instead of taking the Zen precepts in the traditional ritual, he
would take them as part of a ritual we would create. As we
talked this over further, devoting several meetings to the discussion, we saw that we needed more than one ritual in order
to reflect the many kinds of relationships that had been developing between us over the two years we had been together.
Each boy had established a new relationship with himself,
meeting himself for the first time as an adult in an intentional
way. Each had also, as a consequence of this, made a new relationship with his parents. (As part of our work, the parents
had met with me and with each other from time to time, and
each set of parents met with their son to talk over what was
going on in the group.) Each boy had also made a relationship
with me, and my relationship with each of them was unique.
Finally, together, the five of us had made a relationship of
deep spiritual friendship that included the limitations of each
one as well as the fullness of each one.

In the end we decided that we would have two rituals. One
would include all of us as a group—the four boys, the parents,
and me. It would be a private ritual to mark the end of our
group meetings. After this I would continue to meet with each
boy individually to create with him (and with the consultation
and participation of his parents) a personal individual ritual
that would express his present understanding and commitment for his life. It was in this ritual that Tony would commit
himself to the sixteen precepts. As it turned out, the others
boys also made similar (though not identical) commitments to
an ethical code that they intended to pledge themselves to
live by. And so we began the process of thinking through and
performing this series of rituals.

All rituals are expressions and transformations. They express a deep feeling we have about our lives, and through that expression they transform us from one state of being into another. If you take religious ordination, you enter the room a postulant, express your intention to devote yourself to your practice, and leave the room an initiate. If you get married, you walk down the aisle as two single people, express your intention to commit yourselves to loving each other, and leave the room transformed into a married couple.

The rituals the boys and I wanted to create were likewise expressions and transformations: they would express our feeling for the work we had done, and they would be rites of passage, the final step through childhood into adulthood. To help us reflect on how to construct the rituals, we studied rites-of-passage ceremonies in different cultures. Such ceremonies usually involve some form of physical ordeal, symbolizing the process of being born into a new life. The ordeal may take days, weeks, or even months to complete. Often there is fasting, sleep deprivation, or other austerities, and there may also be secrecy, danger, or risk. Rites of passage often culminate in the participant receiving a new name to reflect his or her new adult status. Rites of passage, we found, are also renewal rituals, not only for the participants but also for the communities to which they belong. When one more person takes his or her place as a full-fledged adult member of a community, the whole community rejoices, knowing it has a future.

The ritual we settled on took place outdoors, all night long. Beginning at about eleven o'clock on a full-moon night in January, I hiked up the hill overlooking our temple with the four boys. We hiked in silence for about a half hour, gazing around us at the hills and the sea bathed in moonlight. Finally we arrived at our first destination, the particular spot I had picked out for Tony. I told Tony to stay in this spot, to pay attention to his breathing, to quiet his mind, and to watch the dried grass tips waving in the wind, studying them carefully. Then I went on with the other boys. I deposited James in another spot. I also gave him meditation instructions, asking him to pay attention to his body sensation as he looked very closely at the huge boulder in front of him, at all its detail of ridges, cracks, and colors as they dimly appeared in the moonlight. I did the same with the other two boys, giving each one a special spot out of sight of the others and a special meditation practice to stay with all night long. The sky that night was clear, so it was cold and bright. Because of the full moon, fewer stars than usual were visible. The boys were dressed warmly. Each remained in his own place for many hours.

I had asked the fathers weeks before to think about what they wanted to share with their sons on this night. What were the lessons they had learned through their lives, perhaps from their own fathers? What were the stories, the feelings, the failures, the loves or losses, that they would want their sons to hear and to know about as they were preparing to become adults? I hiked once again up the hill in silence with the fathers, bringing each of them to his son. The fathers came with hot chocolate and blankets and sat down with their sons quietly. I left each father-and-son pair alone in their own place. I have no idea what they said to each other, or whether they spoke at all. After a while I returned, and all nine of us hiked silently down the hill in the moonlight.

While all of this was taking place, the mothers had been in one of the large meeting rooms at the temple complex, where there was a good fire going in the woodstove. They talked quietly or meditated, and after a while they began to write letters that I had asked them to compose for their sons, letters that would express their feelings on this occasion. What was it like to give birth to a child, to care for him and to love him, perhaps to center your life and identity around him, and then to give him up, let him enter the wide world alone? As the few stars faded and the dawn came, the nine of us joined the mothers, and we had warm drinks and snacks. We talked on and on for hours about what we had experienced.

After that night I met with each boy individually, starting with Tony, to develop the second ritual, which would be unique for each boy and performed publicly, in the midst of family and friends. Although each of the rituals was slightly different, they all followed a format that seemed right to us. First, the assembled community was led in meditation practice by the boy. We did the practices that had become our own— the bell meditation, the chanting meditation, the incense offering, the quiet breathing. Next I spoke briefly, saying something about my relationship with the boy and something about our group and what it meant to us. Then I turned the floor over to the boy, who spoke of his experience of becoming grown up and of why he had chosen to make the commitments he was about to make, and what they would mean to him in his life.

Then there was precept taking. With Tony I administered the sixteen bodhisattva precepts in the traditional wording. For each of the other boys it was something different, each one coming, through the process of our meeting and deliberating about it, to a particular wording that he felt expressed his understanding and commitment. (For Sam and James, for instance, the idea of "promises" rather than "precepts" or "commitments" seemed right.) After this the parents were called on to speak to this moment in their son's life, and then the floor was opened to all who wanted to speak, beginning with the three other boys, who on each occasion were eloquent in speaking true words about how much they saw and appreciated in their friend. Finally, I gave each boy a new name, following our Zen ritual of ordination names. I calligraphed the name on a scroll in both English and Japanese characters, presenting the scroll and the name at the end of each of the ceremonies.

They were truly wonderful rituals, full of emotion. Each boy on his day felt, I think, something that few of us ever have a chance to feel: completely seen and appreciated, celebrated and revered. The ceremonies were more powerful than I could have hoped. At the receptions that took place afterward, people seemed buoyantly happy, as if all of them had also just committed themselves to a path of adulthood that was firm, clear, and hopeful. In fact our ceremonies impressed people so much that word of our mentoring group spread quickly, and now there are many mentoring groups for both boys and girls being conducted in several Buddhist communities, based on the work we did.

It is now some years since my time with the boys. I no longer see them very much, though I hear about them. After a period of dropping out of high school, Tony went to junior college, where he is studying industrial drawing. Rashid is also in college. I saw James recently at the Green Gulch temple, and we were both very pleased to bump into each other. Mutually amazed, we beamed at one another stupidly for long minutes before either of us could speak. There wasn't much to say, but the feeling was strong. James is also in college now, as is Sam, who is probably the most changed of the four boys. Small and soft when we first started our group, he has turned out to be lanky and quite tall, well over six feet.

Although the time of our closeness is over and probably won't return, I know how precious that time was for the five of us. Our relationships and all that developed from them have had a powerful effect on each of our lives and on the lives of the many other people who appreciated and witnessed what we did together. The other day I saw a bumper sticker that said something like, "Do not doubt that a few committed people, working together, can change the world. Indeed, this is the only way it ever has." Thinking of the four boys and of our time together, I felt the truth of these words.

The journey through adulthood can be lackluster if we only drift, but it can be profoundly valuable if we completely say yes to it and are willing to travel on wholeheartedly—valuable for us, for those around us, and, in some way we cannot really understand, for the whole world. As I came to discover in my time with the boys, and am continually discovering as I go on practicing Zen with others, a necessary part of that journey is communicating the joy of it to others, inspiring them by traveling side by side with them. Like the Buddha stopping and simply twirling a flower, this is the most natural thing in the world. It makes you smile, and it makes others want to smile with you.

Everything we have and enjoy in this lifetime is in our hands only temporarily. It cannot be held for long; it must be passed on. Taking responsibility to see that it is passed on in a good and thoughtful way is the particular joy of the mature person. Every father and mother, every coach or teacher, knows this. When you pass it on, you discover it anew. In the eyes of the other, your own eyes light up.

Selected Mentoring Resources

Stepping Stones Project The Stepping Stones Project is dedicated to bringing Rites of Passage programs into our communities. We recognize the importance and complexity of the transition from childhood toward adulthood and seek to offer guidance and support that facilitates youth forging a new connection to themselves, their community, and the environment. Our programs are for middle school students entering into adolescence and for high school students becoming young adults. We also consult with organizations and schools seeking to create rites of passage within their communities.

> www.steppingstonesproject.org
> (415) 721-9605

San Francisco Zen Center The Coming-of-Age Program inspires, guides, and encourages our children to lifelong spiritual inquiry and engagement, and provides a supportive environment of peer and mentor relationships in which young people ages eleven to thirteen can meet and discuss their views and perceptions of the world around them. This two-year program includes regular meetings, special events, and activities, including a Family Weekend at Tassajara, and culminates in a Coming-of-Age Ceremony. Please contact Barbara Wenger for further details, 415–502–5217 or e-mail bwenger@itsa.ucsf.edu

> San Francisco Zen Center
> 300 Page Street, San Francisco, CA 94102
> www.sfzc.org

Spirit Rock Meditation Center Offers a variety of meditation classes & retreats for families and young people.

> Spirit Rock Meditation Center Teen Program
> c/o Family Program Director
> P.O. Box 169
> Woodacre, CA 94973
> 415–488–0164, x227
> www.spiritrock.org

Check your local Buddhist and yoga centers for similar programs around the country.

Acknowledgments

I'd first like to thank the young people in my life who inspired me to consider what it really means to grow up—my sons Aron and Noah, the four boys in the mentoring group, to whom this book is dedicated, the students in the "Racism, What About It?" writing group, and all my students at Tamalpais High School in Mill Valley, California. All of them have shown me what I was incapable of seeing when I was young: the beauty of youth straining to grow. Much thanks also to Barbara Wenger who, with her usual energy and passion, took the work the boys and I did to the next level in establishing Zen Center's Coming-of-Age Program, and to Noah Levine and Ethan Patchell, the first mentors in that program.

Because maturity is such a difficult subject to be clear about, this has been a difficult book to write. I want to thank my old friend and literary agent, Michael Katz, for his vision, persistence, calmness, and sense of adventure. I would especially like to thank my editor, Anne Connolly (also a Zen student), for her brilliant, cheerful, thorough, and tough-minded work, for her firm belief in this project, and for her unerring ability to see the difference between effective and stupid writing. Thanks also to the many other editors and workers at Harper San Francisco, especially managing editor, Terri Leonard, who made the production aspects of the book delightful.

Praise for Kathleen Tessaro's

"A wonderful fictional landscape."
—*Cleveland Plain Dealer*

"Touching and comical . . .
Tessaro's breezy style and sly irreverence provide
a refreshing counterpart to the oh-so-serious
pronouncements of Madame Dariaux. The combination
of the two makes for highly entertaining reading."
—*Orlando Sentinel*

"The perfect summer read—
as delightfully fruity as a glass of Pimm's and with
a similar kick, one that catches you unawares. . . .
A delicate evocation of the female world written with as
much élan and panache as Madame Dariaux's original."
—*Daily Mail* (London)

"Kathleen Tessaro writes beautifully and with great confidence. I was totally hooked by her unique combination of wit, irony, and darkness."
—Marian Keyes

"Tessaro manages to rise to the upper echelons of the chick-lit genre. . . . She takes a clever, sometimes funny, sometimes mortifying look at familial relationships, the bonds of friendship, sexuality, and self-identity."
—*USA Today*

"An irresistible love story and self-help manual rolled into one."
—*Elle* (UK)

"A brilliant read."
—*New Woman*

"Funny and witty...devilishly fun to read."
—*Romantic Times*

"Tessaro is a skillful writer, and in her capable hands
this subject receives the respect it deserves. . . .
Readers will enjoy following the harrowing
journey of self-discovery, renewal, and reinvention
to its uplifting conclusion."
—*Booklist*

"Witty . . . clever . . . *Elegance* makes the journey in style."
—*Fort Lauderdale Sun-Sentinel*

"Witty… proves that confidence
never goes out of fashion."
—*Glamour*

"A deeply nuanced work."
—*Pittsburgh Tribune*

"Fans of Helen Fielding's *Bridget Jones's Diary* will love
this unique Pygmalion tale, an impressive debut novel."
—*Library Journal* (*Starred Review*)

Elegance

Also by Kathleen Tessaro

Innocence
The Flirt
The Debutante
The Perfume Collector
Rare Objects

Elegance

A Novel

KATHLEEN TESSARO

HARPER

NEW YORK ■ LONDON ■ TORONTO ■ SYDNEY

HARPER

Excerpts from *Elegance: A Complete Guide for Every Woman Who Wants to Be Well and Properly Dressed on All Occasions* © 1964 by Genevieve Antoine Dariaux, reprinted and adapted by kind permission of the author. *Elegance* was first published in the United States by Doubleday & Company, Inc.

A hardcover edition of this book was published in 2003 by William Morrow.

HarperCollins books may be purchased for educational, business, or sales promotional use. For information, please email the Special Markets Department at SPsales@harpercollins.com.

Reissued by Harper Paperbacks in 2019.

Library of Congress Cataloging-in-Publication Data has been applied for.

ISBN 978-00-6-052227-8 (pbk.)

19 20 21 22 23   LSC   20 19 18 17 16

To my beloved friend and mentor,
Jill

Several years ago now, I had the good fortune to stumble across an extraordinary book in a secondhand bookshop entitled *Elegance* by Genevieve Antoine Dariaux. Years later, when I decided to write a book myself, it became the guiding inspiration for this novel.

By generous permission of the original author, I have been allowed to use a selection of the original headings and have adapted them to suit my story. (Only the entry *B* for Beauty remains wholly my own.) However, much of the tone, and certainly the most brilliant gems of advice, belong entirely to Madame Antoine Dariaux herself.

It is with enormous gratitude that I wish to acknowledge her contribution to this book and to thank her for being both my muse and the touchstone of all that is elegant for these past two and a half years. She is, I can assure you, even more gracious and enchanting in person than her wonderful words of wisdom reveal.

It's a freezing cold night in February and my husband and I are standing outside of the National Portrait Gallery in Trafalgar Square.

"Here we are," he says. But neither of us move.

"Look," he bargains with me, "if it's dreadful, we'll just leave. We'll stay for one drink and go. We'll use a code word: potato. When you want to go, just say the word potato in a sentence and then I'll know you want to leave. OK?"

"I could always just *tell* you I want to leave," I point out.

He frowns at me. "Louise, I know you don't want to do this, but you could at least make an effort. She's my mother, for Christ's sake and I promised we'd come. It's not every day that you're part of a major photographic exhibition. Besides, she really likes you. She's always saying how the three of us ought to get together."

The three of us.

I sigh and stare at my feet. I'm dying to say it: potato. Potato, potato, potato.

I know it's a complete cliché to hate your mother-in-law. And I abhor a cliché. But when your mother-in-law is a former model from the 1950s who specializes in reducing you to a blithering pulp each time you see her, then there is really only one word that springs to mind. And that word is potato.

He wraps an arm around me. "This really isn't a big deal, Pumpkin."

I wish he wouldn't call me Pumpkin.

But there are some things you do, if not for love, then at least for a quiet life. Besides, we'd paid for a cab, he'd had a shave, and I was wearing a long gray dress I normally kept in a plastic dry cleaning bag. We'd come too far to turn back now.

I lift my head and force a smile. "All right, let's go." We walk past the two vast security guards and step inside.

I strip off my brown woolly overcoat and hand it to the coat check attendant, discreetly passing my hand over my tummy for a spot check. I can feel the gentle protrusion. Too much pasta tonight. Comfort food. Comfort eating. Why tonight, of all nights? I try to suck it in but it requires too much effort. So I give up.

I hold out my hand. He takes it, and together we walk into the cool, white world of the Twentieth-Century Galleries. The buzz and hum of the crowd engulfs us as we make our way across the pale marble floor. Young men and women, dressed in crisp white shirts, swing by balancing trays of champagne and in an alcove a jazz trio are plucking out the sophisticated rhythms of "Mack the Knife."

Breathe, I remind myself, just breathe.

And then I see them: the photographs. Rows and rows of stunning black and white portraits and fashion shots, a collection of the famous photographer Horst's work from the 1930s through to the late '60s, mounted against the stark white walls, smooth and silvery in their finish. The flawless, aloof faces gaze back at me. I long to linger, to lose myself in the world of the pictures.

However, my husband grips my shoulder and propels me forward, waving to his mother, Mona, who's standing with a group of stylish older women at the bar.

"Hello!" he shouts, suddenly animated, coming over all jolly and larger than life. The tired, silent man in the cab is replaced by a dazzling, gregarious, social raconteur.

Mona spots us and waves back, a little half scooping royal wave, the signal for us to join her. Turning our shoulders sideways, we squeeze through the crowd, negotiating drinks and lit cigarettes. As we come into range I pull a face that I hope passes as a smile.

She is wonderfully, fantastically, superhumanly preserved. Her abundant silver-white hair is swept back from her face in an elaborate chignon, making her cheekbones appear even more prominent and her eyes feline. She holds herself perfectly straight, as if she spent her entire childhood nailed to a board and her black trouser suit betrays the casual elegance of Donna Karan's tailoring. The women around her are all cut from the same expensive cloth and I suspect we're about to join in on a kind of aging models' reunion.

"Darling!" She takes her son's arm and kisses him on both cheeks. "I'm so pleased you could make it!" My husband gives her a little squeeze.

"We wouldn't miss it for the world, would we, Louise?"

"Certainly not!" I sound just that bit too bright to be authentic.

She acknowledges me with a brisk nod of the head, then turns her attention back to her son. "How's the play, darling? You must be exhausted! I saw Gerald and Rita the other day; they said you were the best Constantine they'd ever seen. Did I tell you that?" She turns to her collection of friends. "My son's in *The Seagull* at the National! If you ever want tickets, you must let me know."

He holds his hands up. "It's completely sold out. There's not a thing I can do."

Out comes the lower lip. "Not even for me?"

"Well," he relents, "I can try."

She lights a cigarette. "Good boy. Oh, let me introduce you, this is Carmen, she's the one with the elephants on the far wall over there and this is Dorian, you'll recognize at least her back from the famous corset shot, and Penny, well, you were *the* face of 1959, weren't you!"

We all laugh and Penny sighs wistfully, extracting a packet of Dunhills from her bag. "Those were the days! Lend me a light, Mona?"

Mona passes her a gold, engraved lighter and my husband shakes his head. "Mums, you promised to stop."

"But darling, it's the only way to keep your figure, isn't that right, girls?" Their heads bob up and down in unison behind a thick cloud of smoke.

And then it happens; I'm spotted.

"And this must be your wiiiiiiife!" Penny gasps, turning her attention to me. Spreading her arms wide, she shakes her head in disbelief and for one horrible moment it looks as if I'm expected to walk into them. I dither stupidly and am about to take a step forward when she suddenly contracts in delight. "You are adoooooorable!" she coos, turning to the others for affirmation. "Isn't she just adoooooooooooorable?"

I stand there, grinning idiotically while they stare at me.

My husband comes to the rescue. "Can I get you ladies another drink?" He tries to attract the bartender's attention.

"Oh, you perfect angel!" Mona smoothes down his hair with her hand. "Champagne all around!"

"And you?" he turns to me.

"Oh yes, champagne, why not?"

Mona takes my arm proprietarily. She gives it a little cuddle, the kind of disarming squeeze your best friend used to
give you when you were ten that made your heart leap. My
heart leaps now at this unexpected show of affection and I
half hate myself for it. I've been here before and I know it's
dangerous to allow yourself to be seduced by her, even for a
second.

"Now, Louise," she has a voice of surprising power and
depth, "tell me how you're doing. I want to hear *everything*!"

"Well . . ." My mind races, desperately flicking through
the facts of my life for some worthy gem. The other women
look up at me expectantly. "Things are good, Mona . . . really
good."

"And your parents? How's the weather in Pittsburgh?
Louise is from Pittsburgh," she mouths, *sotto voce*.

"They're well, thank you."

She nods. I feel like a contestant being introduced on an afternoon quiz show and like any good quiz show host, she helps
to jog me along when I dry up.

"And are you working right now?"

She says the word "working" with the kind of subtle significance that all show biz people do; there is, after all, a world of
difference between "working" and having a job when you're in
"the profession."

I know all this but refuse to play along.

"Well, yes. I'm still with the Phoenix Theatre Company."

"Is it an acting job? Our Louise fancies herself as a bit of an
actress," she offers, by way of an explanation.

"Well, I *was* an actress," I blunder. No matter how hard I
try, she always catches me out. "I mean, I haven't really
worked in a while. And no, this isn't an acting job, it's working front of house, in the box office."

"I see," she smiles, as if she can discern a deeper meaning I'm not aware of. And then Dorian asks the most dreaded question of all.

"Have we seen you in anything?"

"Well, of course I've done the odd commercial." I try to sound casual, shrugging my shoulders as if to imply "who hasn't?"

"Really?" She arches an eyebrow in a perfect impersonation of a woman impressed. "What commercials?"

Damn.

"Well . . ." I try to think. "There was the *Reader's Digest* Sweepstakes Campaign. You may have caught me in that one."

She stares at me blankly.

"You know, the one where they're all flying around in a hot-air balloon over England, drinking champagne and searching for the winners. I was the one on the left holding a map and pointing to Luton."

"Ah ha." She's being polite. "Well, that sounds fun."

"And now you're working in the box office." Mona wraps the whole thing up in a clean, little package.

"Yes, well, I've got a couple of things in the pipeline, so to speak . . . but right now that's what I'm doing." I want my arm back quite badly now.

She gives it another little squeeze. "It *is* a difficult profession, darling. Best to know your limitations. I always advise young women to avoid it like the plague. The simple truth is, it takes more discipline and sacrifice than most modern girls are willing to put up with. Have you seen my picture?"

Keep smiling, I tell myself. If you keep smiling, she'll never know that you want her to die. "No, I haven't had much of a chance to look around yet; we've only just got here."

"Here, allow me." And she pulls me over to a large photograph of her from the 1950s.

She's incredibly young, almost unrecognizable, except for the distinctive, almond shape of the eyes and the famous cheekbones, which remain untouched by time. She's leaning with her back pressed against a classical pillar, her face turned slightly to the camera, half in shadow, half in light. Her pale hair falls in artfully styled curls over shoulders and she's wearing a strapless gown of closely fitted layers of flowing silk chiffon. It's labeled "*Vogue*, 1956."

"What do you think?" she asks, eyeing me carefully.

"I think it's beautiful," I say, truthfully.

"You have taste," she smiles.

A press photographer recognizes her and asks if he can take her picture.

"Story of my life!" she laughs and I make my escape while she poses.

I look around the crowded room for my husband. Finally I spot him, laughing with a group of people in the corner. He has two glasses of champagne in his hands and as I make my way over, he looks up and catches my eye.

I smile and he says something, turns, and walks towards me before I can join them.

"Who are they?" I ask as he hands me a glass.

"No one, just some people from one of these theater clubs. They recognized me from the play." He guides me back towards the photographs. "How are you getting on with Mums?"

"Oh, fine," I lie. "Just fine." I turn back and look but they're gone, swallowed by the ever shifting crowd. "Didn't you want to introduce me?"

He laughs and pats my bottom, which I hate and which he only ever seems to do in public. "No, not at all! Don't be so paranoid. To be frank, they're a bit, shall we say, over-enthusiastic. I don't want them boring my charming wife, now do I?"

"And who might that be?" I sound much more acerbic than I'd intended.

He pats my bottom again and ignores me.

We pause in front of a photograph of a woman smoking a cigarette, her eyes hidden by the brim of her hat. She leans, waiting in a doorway on a dark, abandoned street. It must've been taken just after the Second World War. There's something unsettling in the contrast of the shattered surroundings and the pristine perfection of her crisp, tailored suit.

"Now *that's* style," my husband sighs.

Suddenly it's too hot. I feel overwhelmed by the crush of people, the smoke, and the sound of too many, overly animated conversations. Mona's waving to us again but I allow my husband to walk over to her and make my way into a smaller, less crowded room off the main gallery instead. There's a flat, wooden bench in the center. I sit down and close my eyes.

It's foolish to get so tense. In another hour, it will all be over. Mona will have had her moment of glory and we'll be safely on our way back home. The thing to do is relax. Enjoy myself. I open my eyes and take a deep breath.

The walls are lined with portraits—Picasso, Coco Chanel, Katharine Hepburn, Cary Grant—rows and rows of meticulous, glamorous faces. The eyes are darker, more penetrating than normal eyes, the noses straighter, more refined. I allow myself to slip into a sort of meditative state, a spell brought on by witnessing such an excess of beauty.

And then I spot a portrait I don't recognize, a woman with gleaming dark hair, parted in the middle and arranged in a mass of black curls around her face. Her features are distinctive; high cheekbones, a seductive Cupid's bow mouth, and very black, intelligent eyes. Leaning forward, with her cheek lightly resting against her hand, she looks as if we've happened to catch her in the middle of the most engaging conversation of her life. Her dress, a simple bias-cut sheath, is made from a light satin that shimmers against the dull material of the settee and her only jewelry is a single strand of perfectly matched pearls. She's not the most famous face or even the most attractive, but for some reason she's undoubtedly the most compelling. I get up and cross the room. The name reads: Genevieve Dariaux, Paris, 1934.

However, my solitude is brief. "There you are! Mona's sent us to find you." Penny comes strolling in on the arm of my reluctant husband.

Stay calm, I remind myself, taking a much-needed gulp of my champagne. "Hello Penny, just enjoying the exhibition."

She leans forward and waggles a finger in my face.

"You know, Louise, you're very, *very* naughty!" She winks at my husband. "I don't know how you can let her drink! You're both as bad as each other!"

My husband and I exchange looks. Come again?

She leans in further and drops her voice to a stage whisper. "I must say, you look amazing! And this," she continues, feeling the fabric of my dress gingerly between her thumb and forefinger, "this really isn't too bad at all. I mean, most of them look like absolute tents but this one's really quite cute. My daughter's due in May and she's *desperate* for something like this that she can just pad about in."

I feel the blood draining away from my head.

She smiles at both of us. "You must be soooooooooooo pleased!"

I swallow hard. "I'm not pregnant."

She wrinkles her brow in confusion. "I'm sorry?"

"I am not pregnant," I repeat, louder this time.

My husband laughs nervously. "You'll be the first to know when she is, I can assure you!"

"No, I think I will," I say and he laughs again, slightly hysterical now.

Penny continues to gape at me in amazement. "But that dress . . . I'm sorry, I mean, it's just . . ."

I turn to my husband. "Honey?"

He seems to have found a point of fascination on the floor. "Humm?"

"Potato."

I don't know what I thought he'd do, defend me somehow or at least look sympathetic. But instead he continues to stare at his shoes.

"OK."

I turn and walk away. I feel like I'm having an out-of-body experience but somehow manage to gain the safety of the loo. A couple of girls are fixing their makeup as I enter, so I make a beeline for an empty stall and lock the door. I wait, with my back pressed against the cool metal and close my eyes. No one ever died of humiliation, I remind myself. If that were true, I'd have been dead years ago.

Finally, they leave. I unlock the door and stand in front of the mirror. Like any normal woman, I look in the mirror every day, when I brush my teeth or wash my face or comb my hair. It's just I tend to look at myself in pieces and avoid joining them all up together. I don't know why; it just feels safer that way.

But tonight I force myself to look at the whole thing. And suddenly I see how the bits and pieces add up to someone I'm not familiar with, someone I never intended to be.

My hair needs a trim and I should really dye it to get rid of those prematurely gray strands. Incredibly fine and ashen-colored, it drapes listlessly around my head, forced to one side by a faux tortoiseshell clip. My face, always pale, is unnaturally white. Not ivory or alabaster but rather devoid of any color at all, like some deep-sea animal that's never encountered the sun. Against it, the bright red smear of lipstick I've applied seems garish and my mouth far too big—like a gaping, scarlet gash across the bottom third of my face. The heat of the crowd has made me sweat; my nose is glistening, my cheeks shiny and flushed, but I haven't any powder. And my dress, despite being dry cleaned, has gone hopelessly bobbly and is, now that we're being honest, shapeless in a way that was fashionable five years ago, though definitely out of style now. I remember feeling sexy and confident in it when it used to just skim the contours of my figure, suggesting a sylph-like sensuality. Now that I'm ten pounds heavier, the effect is not the same. To finish it all off, my shoes, a pair of practical, flat Mary Janes with Velcro fastenings, make my ankles look like two thick tree trunks. Faded and scuffed, they're everyday shoes, at least two years old, and really too worn to be seen anywhere but inside my own house.

I'm forced to conclude that the whole effect does rather shout, "Pregnant woman." Or, more precisely, "This is the best I can do under the circumstances."

I stare at my reflection in alarm. No, this person isn't really me. It's all just a terrible mistake—a Bermuda Triangle of Bad Hair Day meets Bad Dress Day, meets Hippie Shoes from Hell. I need to calm down, center myself.

I try an experiment.

"Hi, my name's Louise Canova. I'm thirty-two years old, and I'm *not* pregnant."

My voice echoes around the empty loo.

This isn't working. My heart is pounding and I'm starting to panic. I close my eyes and will myself to concentrate, to think positive thoughts but instead the images of a thousand glossy black and white faces crowd my mind. It's like I'm not even of the same species.

Suddenly the door behind me opens and Mona walks in.

Triple fucking potato.

She leans dramatically against the basin. "Louise, I've just heard. Listen, she didn't mean anything I'm sure and besides, she's blind as a bat."

Why does he have to tell her everything?

"Thanks Mona, I appreciate it."

"Still," she comes up behind me and pushes my hair back from my face with two carefully manicured fingers, "if you like, I could give you the name of my hairdresser, he's really *very* reasonable."

My husband is waiting when I come out. He hands me my coat and we leave the party in silence, finding ourselves standing in the same spot in Trafalgar Square less than thirty minutes after we arrived. Scanning the street for any sign of a cab, he takes a pack of cigarettes out of his pocket and lights one.

"What are you doing?" I ask.

"Smoking," he says. (My husband doesn't smoke.)

I leave it.

The yellow light of a cab lurches towards us from a distance and I wave wildly at it. It's misting now. The cab slows down and we get in. My husband throws himself heavily against the backseat then leans forward again to pull down the window.

Suddenly I want to make him laugh, to cuddle him, or rather to be cuddled. After all, what does it matter what I look like or what anyone else thinks? He still loves me. I reach over and put my hand over his.

"Sweetheart? Do you . . . do you *really* think I look OK?"

He takes my hand and gives it a squeeze. "Listen Pumpkin, you look just fine. Exactly the way you always do. Don't pay any attention to her. She's probably just jealous because you're young and married."

"Yes," I agree hollowly, though it's not quite the effusive sea of compliments I'd hoped for.

He squeezes my hand again and kisses my forehead. "Besides, you know I don't care about all that rubbish."

The cab speeds on into the darkness and as I sit there, with the cold wind blowing against my face, a single, violent thought occurs to me.

Yes, but I do.

What is Elegance?

It is a sort of harmony that rather resembles beauty with the difference that the latter is more often a gift of nature and the former a result of art. If I may be permitted to use a high sounding word for such a minor art, I would say that to transform a plain woman into an elegant one is my mission in life.

— *Genevieve Antoine Dariaux*

It was a slim, gray volume entitled *Elegance*. It was buried between a fat, obviously untouched tome on the history of the French monarchy and a dog-eared paperback edition of D. H. Lawrence's *Women in Love*. Longer and thinner than the other books on the shelf, it rose above its modest surroundings with a disdainful authority, the embossed letters of its title sparkling against the silver satin cover like a glittering gold coin just below the surface of a rushing brook.

My husband claims I have an unhealthy obsession with secondhand bookshops. That I spend too much time daydreaming altogether. But either you intrinsically understand the attraction of searching for hidden treasure amongst rows of dusty shelves or you don't; it's a passion, bordering on a spiritual illness, which cannot be explained to the unafflicted.

True, they're not for the faint of heart. Wild and chaotic, capricious and frustrating, there are certain physical laws that govern secondhand bookstores and like gravity, they're pretty much nonnegotiable. Paperback editions of D. H. Lawrence must constitute no less than 55 percent of all stock in any shop. Natural law also dictates that the remaining 45 percent consist of at least two shelves worth of literary criticism on *Paradise Lost* and there should always be an entire room in the basement devoted to military history which, by sheer coincidence, will be haunted by a man in his seventies. (Personal studies prove it's the same man. No matter how quickly you move from one bookshop to the next, he's always there. He's forgotten something about the war that no book can contain, but like a figure in Greek mythology, is doomed to spend his days wandering from basement room to basement room, searching through memoirs of the best/worst days of his life.)

Modern booksellers can't really compete with these eccentric charms. They keep regular hours, have central heating, and are staffed by freshly scrubbed young people in black T-shirts. They're devoid both of basement rooms and fallen Greek heroes in smelly tweeds. You'll find no dogs or cats curled up next to ancient space heaters like familiars nor the intoxicating smell of mold and mildew that could emanate equally from the unevenly stacked volumes or from the owner himself. People visit Waterstone's and leave. But secondhand bookshops have pilgrims. The words "out of print" are a call to arms for those who seek a Holy Grail made of paper and ink.

I reach up and carefully remove the book from its shelf. Sitting down on a stack of military history books (they will migrate if you're not careful), I open to the frontispiece.

Elegance
by Genevieve Antoine Dariaux

it announces in elaborate script and then underneath,

A COMPLETE GUIDE FOR EVERY WOMAN
WHO WANTS TO BE WELL AND PROPERLY
DRESSED ON ALL OCCASIONS.

Dariaux. I know that name. Could it be the same woman I saw in the photo? As I leaf through the book, the faint fragrance of jasmine perfume floats from its yellowed pages. Written in 1964, it appears to be a kind of encyclopedia, with entries for every known fashion dilemma starting with *A* and going through to *Z*. I've never before encountered anything quite like it. I flip through the pages in search of a photo of the author. And there, on the back cover, my efforts are rewarded.

She looks to be in her late fifties, with classic, even features and heavily lacquered white hair—Margaret Thatcher hair before it had a career of its own. But the same black, intelligent eyes gleam back at me; I recognize the distinctive, imperious set of her mouth and there, luminous against the fitted black cardigan she's wearing, is the trademark strand of impeccably matched pearls. *Madame Genevieve Antoine Dariaux,* the caption below the photo reads. She doesn't look directly at the camera with the same beguiling candor of her earlier portrait, but rather beyond it, as if she's too polite to challenge our gaze. Older now, she's naturally more discreet, and discretion is, after all, the cornerstone of elegance.

I turn back eagerly to the preface.

Elegance is rare in the modern world, largely because it requires precision, attention to detail, and the careful development of a delicate taste in all forms of manners and style. In short, it does not come easily to most women and never will.

However, in my thirty-year career as the directress of the Nina Ricci Salon in Paris, my life has been devoted to advising our clients and helping them to select what is most flattering. Some are exquisitely beautiful and really need no assistance from me at all. I enjoy admiring them as one enjoys admiring a work of art, but they are not the clients I cherish the most. No, the ones that I am fondest of are those who have neither the time nor the experience necessary to succeed in the art of being well dressed. For these women, I am willing to turn my imagination inside out.

Now, would you like to play a little game of Pygmalion? If you have a little confidence in me, let me share with you some practical ideas on one of the surest ways of making the most of yourself——through elegance, your own elegance.

At last, I have found my Holy Grail.

∞

It's only 4 P.M., but it's already growing dark when I leave the shop. I weave through the streets, down Bell Street, over Marble Arch, across St. James's, and then into Westminster, clutching my magical parcel.

Big Ben chimes in the background as I push open the door and am greeted by the sound of a Hoover.

My husband is home.

There's something about the persistent, draining, incessancy of domesticity that inspires a deep inner resolve in my husband. (Those who know him only as a rising star of the London stage are, in fact, blind to his most astonishing talents.) Each day finds him bravely battling the enemies of filth, disorder, untidiness, and decay with renewed determination. A resourceful soul, he can transform any sort of disarray into a clean, habitable environment, usually in under half an hour.

He can't hear me as I come in, so I poke my head into the living room where he is furiously forcing the vacuum over the parquet wood floor (he claims to be able to actually *see* the dust settling on it, so remarkable is his sensitivity to that sort of thing) and shout to him.

"Hey!"

Switching off the Hoover, he rests his arms against its handle with the same masculine ease of a television cowboy leaning on a fence. He is a man in his element, setting the world to rights.

"Hey yourself. What've you been up to?"

"Oh, nothing really," I fib, concealing the brown paper parcel behind my back. In the face of my husband's never ending schedule of home improvements, spending an afternoon ferreting around old bookshops seems like a kind of betrayal.

"Did you return that lamp shade?"

"Ah, yes . . . ," I confirm, "but I couldn't find anything better, so they gave me a credit note."

He sighs, and we both look mournfully at the pale marble lamp Mona gave us a month ago.

In every marriage there are certain ties that bind. Much more substantial than the actual marriage vows, these are the real-life, unspoken forces that keep it glued together, day in and day out, year after year, through endless trial and adversity. For some people it's their social ambitions, for others their children. But in our case, the pursuit of the perfect lamp shade will do.

We are bound, my husband and I, by a complete, relentless commitment to the interior decoration of our home. And this lamp is the delinquent, drug-addicted teenager that threatens to destroy our domestic bliss by refusing to coordinate with any ready-made lamp shade from a reasonably priced store. It's incredibly heavy and almost impossible to lift. We are doomed to a Sisyphean fate, forever purchasing lamp shades we will only return the next day.

My husband shakes his head. "We're going to have to go to Harrods," he says gravely.

Harrods is always a last resort. There will be no "reasonable" lamp shades at Harrods.

"But you know what?" he adds, his face brightening, "you can come with me and we'll make a day of it if you like."

"Sure." I smile. Lamp Shade Day—certain to be right up there with the Great Garden Trellis Outing and the Afternoon of a Dozen Shower Hoses. "Wouldn't miss it for the world."

"Great." He forces one of the windows open, relishing the gust of cool air. "Of course, you'll be glad to know I've been considerably more successful here while you were away."

"Really?"

"You know those pigeons that roost on the drainpipe just above the bedroom window?"

"Yeah . . . ," I lie.

"Well, I've attached some barbed wire around the pipe. That's the last we'll see of them!"

I'm still trying to place these pigeons. "Well done you!"

"And that's not all—I've got some fantastic ideas for draining the garden path which I'm going to draw up during the intermission tonight. Maybe I can show them to you later?"

"Sounds brilliant. Listen, I'm just going to do some reading in the other room. Maybe you'll look in on me before you go?"

He nods, surveying the living room contentedly. "It's all coming together, Louie. I mean, the place is really starting to shape up. All we need is that lamp shade."

I watch as he switches the Hoover back on.

There is always one more lamp shade, one more set of authentic looking faux-Georgian fire utensils, one more nonslip natural hessian runner carpet. Like Daisy's green light in *The Great Gatsby*, these things call to us with the promise of a final, lasting happiness yet somehow remain forever out of reach.

Retreating into the bedroom, I close the door, kick off my shoes, and curl up on the bed.

The bed is enormous. It's actually two single beds that are joined in the center. "Zipped and Linked" is what the man at John Lewis called it. We needed a bed that was big enough so that we wouldn't disturb each other in the night: my husband twitches like a dog and I can't bear noise or any sort of movement.

"You are *sure* you want to sleep together?" the salesman had asked when we briefed him of our requirements. But my husband was adamant. "We've only just been married," he informed the offending fellow haughtily, implying a kind of rampant, newlywed sex life that could only just be contained within the confines of a solidly made double bed. So now he twitches away somewhere west of me and I slumber, comatose, half a mile to the east.

Climbing underneath the duvet, I remove the delicate volume from its brown paper bag. I'm on the verge of something very big, very real.

This is it.

I open to Chapter One.

And the next thing I know, I'm asleep.

When I wake up, he's already gone to the theater. There's a note on the kitchen table. "Were snoring, so didn't bother to wake you." My husband is nothing if not concise.

This is bad.

The truth is, I sleep far too much—wake up late, take naps in the afternoon, go to bed early. I live with one foot dangling in a dark, warm pool of unconsciousness, ready at any moment to slide into oblivion. But it's just a little bit antisocial, all this sleeping, so I try to hide it.

I make toast. (I believe that's what's known as cooking for one.) Then climb back on board the bed. Turning to the first letter in the alphabet, I try not to get butter on the pages.

A

❧

Accessories

You can always tell the character of a woman by the care and attention she lavishes upon the details of her dress. The accessories worn with an outfit——gloves, hat, shoes, and handbag——are among the most important elements of an elegant appearance. A modest dress or suit can triple its face value when worn with an elegant hat, bag, gloves, and shoes, while a designer's original can lose much of its prestige if its accessories have been carelessly selected. It is indispensable to own a complete set of accessories in black and, if possible, another in brown, plus a pair of beige shoes and a beige straw handbag for the summer. With this basic minimum, almost any combination is attractive.

Of course, it would be ideal to have each set of accessories in two different versions: one for sport and the other dressy. And in this regard I cannot restrain myself from expressing the dismay I feel when I see a woman carry an alligator handbag with a dressy ensemble merely because she has paid an enormous sum of money for it. Alligator is strictly for sports or travel, shoes as well as bags, and this respected reptile should be permitted to retire every evening at 5 P.M.

And here, as in no other department, quality is essential. Be *strict with yourself. Save. Economise on food if you must (believe me, it will do you good!) but not on your handbags or shoes. Refuse to be seduced by anything that isn't first-rate. The saying, "I cannot afford to buy cheaply," was never so true. Although I am far from rich, I have bought my handbags for years from Hermès, Germaine Guérin, and Roberta. And without exception, I have ended up by giving away all the cheap little novelty bags that I found irresistible at first. The same is true of shoes and gloves.*

I realize that all of this may seem rather austere, and even very expensive. But these efforts are one of the keys, one of the Open Sesames that unlock the door to elegance.

I look down at my own handbag, crumpled in a heap on the floor. It's a navy Gap rucksack—the kind that seems to attract bits of dried crackers to the bottom, even if you haven't eaten a biscuit in months. Needless to say, it could do with a wash.

Or a glass of milk.

I wonder if it qualifies as a sports bag. I can remember purchasing it in the Back to School department several seasons ago and feeling quite elated that I'd managed to resolve all my handbag dilemmas in a single swoop. It would never occur to me to buy more than one bag, in more than one color or style.

The only other one I own is a squashed maroon leather shoulder bag I bought on sale at Hobbs four years ago. The leather has worn away and the framework of the bag is exposed; however, I'm too attached to it to throw it away. I keep pretending that I'm going to have it repaired, even though it's gone out of style.

The more I think of it, the more hard-pressed I am to think of any accessories I own that might be described as even remotely stylish, let alone first-rate. Certainly not the collection of woolly brown and gray berets I live in, so practical because they won't blow off your head during the windy London winters and because they're invaluable for those days (always on the increase) when I haven't washed or even combed my hair. I like to think of them as "emergency hair."

I find myself gazing at my feet, or rather at the pair of well-worn beige Keds that adorn them. It's been raining and they're soaked through. The fabric's worn away above my big toe and I catch a glimpse of the green and red Christmas socks underneath. (My mother sent me those.) I give my big toe a little wiggle.

My nose is running and as I fumble for a tissue in my raincoat pocket, I discover a pair of mismatched black gloves I found on the floor of a movie theater two weeks ago. They seemed like quite a find at the time but suddenly it's clear, even to me, that I've obviously *not* been lavishing enough care and attention on the details of my dress.

Elegance may be in the details but my situation appears to be a little more serious than that. Clearly, drastic action is needed. I resolve, in an unprecedented burst of enthusiasm, to begin my transformation with a thorough cleansing of my closet. Systematically working my way through my wardrobe, I'll weed out the elements that don't flatter me. And then I'll be free to construct a new, improved look around those that do.

Fine, let's get cracking! I fling open my closet door with a dramatic sweep of my arms and nearly pass out from hopelessness.

I possess a rail of items gleaned from secondhand clothing stores all over the country. Everything in front of me symbolizes an element of compromise. Skirts that fit around the waist but flare out like something Maria von Trapp would wear.

Piles of itchy or slightly moth-eaten woolly sweaters—not one of them in my size. Coats in strange fabrics or suit jackets with no matching skirts bought simply because they fit and that in itself is an event.

But that's not the scariest thing. No, the thing that completely stuns me is the color. Or rather the lack of it. When did I decide that brown was the new black, gray, scarlet, navy, and just about any other shade you can name? What would the *Colour Me Beautiful* girls make of that? Or Freud, for that matter?

I stare in fascinated longing at the bold, crimson drawing room of the house across the street but my own walls are magnolia. Matte magnolia, to be precise. And now here it is, the dreadful consequences of playing it safe: I have the wardrobe of an eighty-year-old Irish man. That is, an eighty-year-old Irish man who doesn't care what he looks like.

However, I won't be put off.

I open my underwear drawer.

I dump the entire contents on the floor.

I sift through the piles of runned and not too runned tights (the only kind I own), the baggy knickers, the ones with the elastic showing, and the bras I should never have put in the washing machine which now have bits of deadly underwire poking through them. I diligently make a pile of keeps and nonkeeps.

Done.

I go to the kitchen, grab a black trash bag and begin to fill it. A strange, unfamiliar energy infuses me, and before I know it, I'm working my way through the rest of my closet.

Piles of ugly, vague brown clothes rapidly disappear. I throw away sweaters, jackets, and every last one of the *Sound of Music* skirts. Here's another trash bag: in go the worn out shoes, the natty scarves. Now the maroon leather handbag from Hobbs. I can buy a new one. Beads of perspiration run down my face and in my closet empty hangers clash together like wind chimes. I tie the tops of the bags together and drag them out to the garbage bins in the back of the building. It's dark and I feel like a criminal destroying the evidence of a particularly gory crime.

Finally, I stand in front of my near empty wardrobe and survey the result of all this effort. A pale pink Oxford shirt swings from the rail, a single black skirt, a navy fitted pinafore dress. On the floor in front of me, there's a small pile of just about wearable underwear.

This is it. This is now the basis of my new wardrobe, my new identity, and my new life.

I take a Post-it from the desk in the corner, write on it in bright red marker, and stick it on the corner of the wardrobe mirror. It reminds me:

Never be seduced by anything that isn't first-rate.

No, never again.

I'm on the train headed for Brondesbury Park to see my therapist. It's my husband's idea; he thinks there's something wrong with me.

After we were married, I began to have recurring nightmares. I'd wake up screaming, convinced there was a man at the foot of the bed. The room would be exactly the way it was in waking life and then all of a sudden, he'd be there, leaning over me. I'd chase him away but he'd return every night without fail. After a while, my husband learnt to sleep through these nightly terrors, but when I started to cry during the day and couldn't stop, he put his foot down. He explained to me that I had too many feelings and I'd better do something about it.

When I get to my therapist's house, I ring the bell and am admitted into a waiting room, which is really part of a hallway with a chair and a coffee table. There are three magazines and have been ever since I started therapy two years ago: one *House & Garden* from spring 1997, and two copies of *National Geographic*. I can recite the contents of all of them. However, I pick up the copy of *House & Garden* and look again at the cottage transformed into a treasure trove of Swedish antiques using nothing but Ikea furniture and a few paint effects. I'm falling asleep when the door finally opens, and Mrs. P. asks me to step inside.

I take off my coat and sit on the edge of the daybed that is her version of a couch. The room is muted, sterile. Even the landscapes on the walls have an eerie calmness, like lobotomized Van Gogh's—no wild, swirly, passionate mayhem here. I like to think that behind the glass door that separates her office from the rest of the house, there lies an explosion of primitive, phallic art and dangerous modern furniture in a riot of vivid colors. The chances are slim, but I live in hope.

Mrs. P. is middle-aged and German. Like me, her fashion sense lacks a certain savoir faire. Today she's wearing a cream-colored skirt with a pair of knee-highs and when she sits down, I can see where the elastic pinches her leg, causing a red, swollen roll of flesh just under the knee. The German thing doesn't help. Every time she asks me something, I feel like we're enacting a badly scripted interrogation scene from a World War II film. This may or may not be the root of our communication problems.

I sit there and she stares at me from behind her square-rimmed glasses.

We've come to the impasse: part of our weekly routine.

I grin sheepishly.

"I think I'll sit up today," I say.

Mrs. P. blinks at me, unmoved. "And why would you like to do that?"

"I want to see you."

"And why do you want to do that?" she repeats. They always want to know why; there's not really a lot of difference between a therapist and a four-year-old.

"I don't like to be alone. I feel alone when I'm lying down."

"But you're not alone," she points out. "I'm here."

"Yes, but I can't *see* you." I'm starting to feel really frustrated.

"So," she adjusts her glasses further back on her nose, "you need to '*see*' someone in order not to feel alone?"

She's speaking to me in italics, throwing my words back at me, the way therapists do. I won't be bullied. "No, not always. But if I'm going to talk to you, I'd rather be looking at you." And with that, I push myself back on the daybed so that I'm leaning against the wall.

I start to pick at the bobbles in the white chenille throw that covers the bed. (I'm intimately acquainted with these bobbles.) Three or four minutes drag past in silence.

"You do not trust me," she says at last.

"No, I don't trust you," I agree, not so much because I believe it to be true but because she says it is and after all, she is my therapist.

"I think you need more sessions," she sighs.

Whenever I don't do what she wants me to do, I need more sessions. There were whole months where I had to come every day. This is normally as far as we get; for two years we've been arguing about whether or not I should be allowed to sit up on the daybed. But today I have something to tell her.

"I bought a book yesterday. It's called *Elegance*."

"Is it a novel?"

"No, it's a kind of self-help book, a guide that tells you how you can become elegant."

She raises an eyebrow. "And what does 'becoming elegant' mean to you?"

"Being chic, sophisticated. You know, like Audrey Hepburn or Grace Kelly."

"And why is that important?"

I feel suddenly frivolous and girly—like a female member

of the Communist Party caught reading an issue of *Vogue*. "Well, I don't know that it's important but it's worth striving for, don't you think?" And then I spot her beige, orthopedic sandals.

Maybe not.

I take another tack. "What I mean is, they were always pulled together, never unseemly or disheveled in any way. Every time you saw them, they were perfectly groomed, fault-lessly dressed."

"And is that what you would like, to be 'pulled together, never unseemly or disheveled in any way'?"

I think a moment. "Yes," I say at last. "I'd love to be clean and chic and not such a terrible mess all the time."

"I see," she nods her head. "You are not clean. That makes you dirty. Not chic. That makes you unfashionable. And a ter-rible mess. Not just a mess, but a *terrible* mess. So, you feel you are unattractive."

She makes everything sound so much worse than it is.

Still, she has a point.

"Well, no, I don't feel very attractive," I admit, wincing in-wardly as I say it. "The truth is, I feel the opposite of attrac-tive. Like it doesn't matter what I look like."

She peers at me over the top of her glasses. "And why doesn't it matter what you look like?"

A thick wave of unconsciousness swims up to meet me. "Because . . . I don't know . . . because it just doesn't mat-ter." I try unsuccessfully to stifle a yawn.

"But surely your husband notices," she insists.

I wonder what she means by "notices." Is this some kind of euphemism? Does her husband "notice" her in her knee-highs and skirt?

"No, no he's not that way," I explain, pushing the unwelcome vision of them "noticing" each other from my mind. "He's really not interested in that sort of thing." My eyelids are at half-mast now; it feels like they weigh a ton.

"And what sort of thing is that?"

"I don't know . . . bodies, appearances, clothes."

"And how does that make you feel?" she persists. "That he is not interested in your body, your appearance or your clothes?"

I think for a moment. "Tired," I conclude. "It makes me feel tired. Anyway, why should he be interested in those things? He loves me for who I am, not the way I look." I'm sinking further and further into the daybed like a deflating balloon.

"Yes, but love is not just a feeling," she continues, unde-terred. "Or an idea. It's completely natural that there is a phys-ical side too. You are young. You *are* attractive. You are . . . falling asleep, am I right?"

I pull myself up with a jerk. "No, no I'm fine. Just a little drowsy. Late night last night." I don't know why I bother to lie. Perhaps what she says is true: I don't trust her.

"Well, in any case, time is up for today."

As soon as she says it, I start to revive.

I leave, head straight to the newsstand on the corner and buy two Kit Kats. I eat them in rapid succession, waiting for the train. I'll never get this therapy gig. Can't wait till I'm cured and have been given some sort of certificate I can show my husband.

A disembodied voice comes on over the intercom to an-nounce that, due to signaling problems, the next southbound train will be in twelve minutes. I sit down on a bench in the corner and take the copy of *Elegance* from my bag. A gust of wind rustles through it and the book falls open on a page from the preface.

From my earliest childhood, one of my principal preoccupations was to be well dressed, a somewhat precocious ambition that was encouraged by my mother, who was extremely fashion-conscious herself. Together we would go to the dressmaker and select combinations of fabrics and styles that ensured our outfits were entirely original and impossible to copy.

I think of my own mother and of how she hated shopping, dressing up or looking at herself in mirrors. Not only did she not aspire to elegance, but I believe she suspected it as a pursuit. It was at odds with the aesthetics of her strict Catholic upbringing, belonging as it did to the world of movie stars, debutantes and divorcées.

Pale and bespectacled, with short dark hair she cut herself, she preferred to spend most of her time in Birkenstocks and plain, loose trousers, maybe because in the male-dominated world of science in which she excelled, fashion was of little practical use. However, in textbook Freudian fashion, her unlived dreams and ambitions spilt out onto my sister and me. She longed for us to become professional ballet dancers, paragons of grace and discipline, and we trained for hours every day after school to that end. She indulged us in bizarre shopping trips, made more surreal by the fact that we rarely seemed to buy any actual children's clothes. It was as if she was taking us shopping for her alter ego.

It's a Saturday morning. My mother's just picked me up from ballet class and we're in Kaufmann's department store in Pittsburgh. I'm about twelve, but already I'm sporting a pair of high heels, "wedgies" to be exact, with thick crepe soles, and a denim wraparound skirt, just like my idol, Farrah Fawcett, in *Charlie's Angels*. Like all the girls in ballet school, I want to look like a prima ballerina. We cake on tons of foundation, eyeliner, and mascara and roll our eyes around like silent film stars on acid. We're dying swans with our exaggerated posture, ridiculous turnout, and scraped-back hairdos. It never occurs to us that makeup that's meant to read on stage to the last row of the Metropolitan Opera House might not be suitable for street wear.

My mother and I are shopping in the evening wear section. It's ten-thirty in the morning and we're looking at sequins and taffeta. She's going to a formal Christmas party with my father and we're here to shop for her, but she can't bear to look at herself or try anything on. I carry gown after gown into the changing room, where she's slumped on the stool in her bra and girdle, cradling her head in her hands. "You put them on," she says and I do, preening and posing like a miniature version of Maria Callas. My mother is a ghost, thin and shorn next to my drag act. "You're so slim," she says as I shimmy into a pink sequined sheath dress. "You look good in everything."

We spend hours wading through piles of silk and satin and in the end she buys me a black sequined top and a cream-colored marabou jacket at vast expense, which I wear over my school uniform, despite the fact that it lands me in detention for a month.

My mother buys nothing.

And after we shop, we go to the chocolate counter and buy a pound box of Godiva chocolates, which we eat on our way back home in the car. My mother and I don't do lunch. Lunch is, after all, fattening. So we sit in the front seat of the car, not looking at one another, cramming chocolate into our mouths instead.

By the time we get home, the excitement of shopping is gone. Vanished. Mom is suddenly, furiously angry and I'm filled with fear and shame. She gets out, slams the car door, and strides across the garage into the house, where I can hear her yelling at my brother. She yells for no reason—because a towel is badly folded or because the television is on. She yells because she hates herself; because she's spent $300 on evening clothes for a twelve-year-old; because she's so livid she can't contain it anymore. She throws something but misses.

I hear her storm upstairs and slam her bedroom door. Getting out of the car with my bags, I take the now empty chocolate box with me. It's important that no one should see it. And I walk, or rather waddle the way dancers do, into the house. My brother's there, crying and there's a pile of glass and plastic that used to be a clock around him on the floor. He looks at me with my Kaufmann's bags and the Godiva chocolate box and I know that he hates me. I stick my chin in the air and walk on. I am a bad person. I am a very bad person.

My mother doesn't go to the Christmas party. She has an argument with my father and spends the evening locked in her room instead.

Closing the book, I get up, and walk down to the end of the platform. In the corner, where the cement gives way to rubble and grass, I turn and throw up the two Kit Kat bars.

The light is softly dimming and I notice, as I wipe my fingers on a clean tissue, that the birds are singing, the way they do sometimes at dusk on early spring evenings. They sound impossibly hopeful.

And suddenly it occurs to me that maybe my mother and I have something in common.

Maybe I come from a long line of women who felt like a terrible mess.

B

❧

Beauty

Since time began, women have sought after beauty with all the passion and vigour of Menelaus pursuing Helen into Troy and often with similarly violent results. And why shouldn't they? Being beautiful has always been synonymous with owning the world on a string and what girl would not wish that?

Sadly though, only God and nature can make a beautiful woman and, to be perfectly frank, most of us do not and never will fall into that exclusive category. Perhaps you think I am being a little hard? Maybe I am. But I am of the philosophy that it is best to face the facts about oneself, especially the most unpleasant ones, early on in life and make peace with them rather than to waste years in nervous agitation pursuing goals and expectations far beyond our reach.

Besides which, being beautiful is no guarantee of happiness in this world. I have known many beautiful women whose own inelegance and lack of breeding rendered them so hopelessly unattractive, that it would've been simpler and less painful for them if they had been born plain. A woman must have a very strong character not to become distracted by her own unnatural power to excite attention everywhere she goes. And there is nothing more tragic than the sight of a badly ageing beauty who never had to develop her wit or imagination in order to amuse her companions or who always relied upon the excellence of her figure rather than the elegance of her clothes to make an impression. They are poor company and almost invariably develop "champagne chins."

While beauty, in its purest physical form, is nature's gift alone to bestow, elegance, grace, and style are infinitely more democratic. A little discipline and a discerning eye, along with a generous helping of good humour and effort, are all that's needed to cultivate these admirable qualities. And a plain girl who spends a little time in honest self reflection and who applies herself with diligence to the improvement of her mind and character, will awake soon enough to discover that she has blossomed into a fully fledged swan. The time she spent alone and undistracted by the world will fortify her, the discipline she learnt will carry her into old age with grace and courage, and above all, she will possess compassion, which never fails to make a woman more attractive to those around her.

I reach across to my bedside table and pick up the Post-its and a pen, while taking another sip of my tea. Of all the pleasures in this world, reading in bed in the morning with a fresh, steaming mug of tea has to be the most luxurious. I prod the mountain of pillows behind me into a more yielding shape and lean back.

To be beautiful. There are days when I feel fairly confident that I'm attractive, but am I or could I ever be beautiful? Or am I one of those women who are better off facing up to the "unpleasant facts of life"?

It's not really a question a girl should ponder before nine in

the morning, still suffering from bed head and wearing her favorite Snoopy nightshirt. (I couldn't quite bring myself to
throw it away.) I push it from my thoughts and resolutely peel
off another Post-it. "Beauty is no guarantee of happiness" I
write firmly, "strive instead for elegance, grace, and style,"
and then paste it next to the other one on the wardrobe mirror.
My husband, who's getting dressed to do a radio play at the
BBC, sighs wearily.

"I sincerely hope we're not going to become one of those
'happy-clappy households' with charming little inspirational
signs posted everywhere." He reaches for a pair of navy chinos
and a worn Oxford shirt his mother bought him two Christ-
mases ago. "I don't want our home looking like the Sunday
school meeting room of a church hall."

"And what would you know about Sunday school meeting
rooms?" I parry lightly. "Anyway, when you close the
wardrobe door you can't even see them."

"Still," he persists, slipping his feet into a pair of ancient
loafers, "I think that's enough. I don't want to dress in the
morning faced with a thousand slogans declaring 'I am enough'
and 'This too shall pass' or whatever pop self-help jargon is
being bounced around these days."

"Fine," I say, more to end the conversation than anything.
"I'll keep them to myself."

And it occurs to me that if he's going to be out all day, it's a
perfect opportunity to renew my membership at our local
gym. Bending down, I search underneath the bed until I locate
my old gym bag, covered in dust, complete with a pair of
twisted old trainers still lurking inside.

Perfect.

But my husband hasn't finished yet. He removes the most
recent Post-it and examines it more closely. " 'Beauty is no

guarantee of happiness—strive instead for elegance, grace, and style.' What's all this about, Louie? You're not going all funny, are you? How are things going with your therapist?"

I'm certain I still own a pair of sweatpants somewhere and there must be a matching sock for this one . . . I rummage through the laundry basket.

"No, I'm not going funny," I assure him as I sift through piles of dirty clothes, "and things are fine with my therapist. I'm just trying to make the most of myself, that's all. It's something I'm doing for me."

He looks unconvinced, so I change my tack. "What I mean to say is, I just want you to be proud of me."

His face softens. "But, Pumpkin, I'm already proud of you. You're a very good girl," he says, kissing my forehead and patting me lightly on the head. "You're a very good girl and a very good Pumpkin."

"Yes, thank you," I say, smiling back at him. "Only, would you mind terribly not calling me Pumpkin?"

He looks at me as if I'd just slapped him across the face. "Not call you Pumpkin? What's wrong with Pumpkin?"

"Well, I know you mean it as a term of endearment but it's just so fat sounding. So round and heavy. Couldn't we have another name? What if you called me something like Sweetheart, or Angel or . . . or, I don't know, what about Beauty?"

He frowns at me.

"OK, well what about Pretty? My Pretty? That's nice, isn't it?"

"I've always called you Pumpkin. You *are* my Pumpkin," he says firmly.

"Yes, I know, but we're allowed to change a nickname, aren't we?" I try to pacify him by wrapping my arms around him but he sidesteps me and reaches over to pull his jacket from the back of the bedroom chair.

"You can't just make up a new nickname because you feel like it. After all, I'm the one who has to say it. And 'My Pretty' sounds like a pantomime pirate."

"Yes, fine. But all I'm asking is that perhaps I could have a more attractive nickname . . . I don't know . . . if it has to be a food then what about Sweet Pea? A sweet pea is a lot smaller than a pumpkin."

"I am not some aging southern belle, Louise." And he sighs, pressing his fingers to his forehead and closing his eyes to concentrate. "Right," he says at last, "what about Sausage? It's my final offer."

"Sausage!"

"I'm English. You knew that when you married me. I cannot call my wife Sweet Pea or Sugar or My Little Dumpling or any of the other gourmet, internationally recognized terms of endearment."

"But you can call me Sausage?"

"Well, not just Sausage. My *Little* Sausage." He smiles. "I think it's sweet."

Now it's my turn to look unconvinced.

He shrugs his shoulders. "Beside which, I really don't have time for this right now. I must be going." He strides into the hallway and grabs his script from the small round table by the door. Leaning forward, he plants a quick kiss on my forehead. "I'll see you when I get back tonight, Sausage."

The door slams shut.

I walk back into the bedroom and stare at the dusty gym bag and curly, old trainers. What's the point of going to all this effort if at the end of it, I'm still not beautiful and the most flattering thing my husband can think to call me is Sausage?

The siren song of the duvet begins to call me, luring me back into bed, away from the gym and this pointless pursuit of self-improvement. After all, I have only a few precious hours on my own to spend in a state of complete oblivion before he returns. My breathing begins to slow and my eyelids droop.

And then I see it, the little yellow Post-it my husband was examining earlier, floating like a butterfly near my pillow. "Beauty is no guarantee of happiness—strive instead for elegance, grace, and style." I pick it up and paste it back on the mirror.

"I am not a pumpkin," I say to my reflection. "Or a sausage."

And I pick up my gym bag and leave the bedroom as quickly as possible.

While I still can.

C

Comfort

The idea of comfort has invaded every domain; it is one of the categorical imperatives of modern life. We can no longer bear the thought of the slightest restriction, physical or moral, and many of the details which were considered to be a mark of elegance some years ago are condemned today for reasons of comfort. Down with stiff collars, starched shirts, cumbersome hats, and heavy chignons! Practically the only die-hards to resist are women's shoes.

However, if women continue to seek comfort above all twenty-four hours a day, twelve months a year, they may eventually find that they have allowed themselves to become slaves to the crepe-rubber sole, nylon from head to toe, pre-digested meals, organized travel, functional uniformity, and general stultification. When comfort becomes an end in itself, it is the Public Enemy Number One of elegance.

It's seven-fifteen on Friday morning and I'm getting ready for work. Although part of me still clings to the dream of being an actress, I earn my real money selling tickets in the box office of a small, self-producing playhouse in Charing Cross.

My husband is asleep on the other side of the bed and I get dressed in the dark. There's not a lot left in my closet to choose from so I put on the navy pinafore dress and the pink Oxford shirt. The dress is figure hugging and very tight, which is why I haven't worn it in years. As I zip it up, my spine becomes erect, encased in the rigidly tailored bodice. I try to revert to my normal, semi-slouched posture and nearly asphyxiate myself. Next, I slip into a pair of dark brown stilettos I wore at my wedding. They're the only pair of high heels left after the Great Cull, and suddenly I'm tottering around the flat like a little Marilyn Monroe. After so many days in cheap Keds and baggy chinos, it feels very unusual. I comb my hair into a side part, pin it back with a rhinestone clip and then apply a soft red lipstick. Leaving the flat, I catch a glimpse of my reflection in the hall mirror.

Who is this woman?

I'm going to be late. But what I fail to take on board is the tremendous restriction of movement created by pairing a long, straight skirt with a pair of high, strappy heels. This ensemble is fine for staggering around the flat but obviously not meant for long-haul journeys. The faster I try to walk, the more I look like a windup doll. The only way to move forward at all is to transfer my weight in a slow, rolling motion from one hip to the next. The dress is now in control; it dictates when I arrive at work and how. So, I sashay forth precariously, swaying gently as I go.

There's something about a slow-moving female in the middle of rush hour traffic. Everyone, everything changes. And I discover that moving slowly is one of the most powerful things you can do. It's different from being infirm or depressed. The dress makes sure I'm bolt upright, imbuing me with a look of haughty dignity, as if I'm above petty concerns like being at work on time. I appear to be walking because it amuses me, not because I have to. And in the sea of darting pedestrians around me, I have become majestic.

If you're going to walk that slowly, you might as well smile. And here's where it gets really interesting. Cab drivers slow down, even though their light is green, just to let me cross the road. The policemen in front of the Houses of Parliament say, "Good morning" and tip their hats. And the tourists who cluster so frustratingly in front of Big Ben with their cameras step aside politely, as if they've suddenly found themselves in the middle of a great big living room and they've only just discovered it belongs to me.

Yes, the world is my living room and I'm a gracious hostess passing through, checking to see if everyone's all right.

I have a look around. That's another advantage of moving slowly, plenty of time for browsing. The air is delicate and sharp, the sunlight crisp and wholly benevolent. Breathing deeply, or rather, as deeply as the dress permits, a strange, unfamiliar awareness descends upon me.

Everything's all right. Everything really is all right.

As I saunter into the theater foyer, my heart's pounding and my cheeks are flushed. I notice my hand as it pushes against the brass plate of the box office door; it seems small and delicate and pretty. For a moment, I'm not quite sure it's mine. But it is mine. And it is small and delicate and pretty.

Colin's there, waiting for me. I have the keys to the box office door.

"Well, look at you!" he says, kissing me on each cheek.

I smile archly. "Whatever can you be referring to, Mr. Riley?" I unlock the door and switch on the lights.

"Whatever, indeed! Let's put the kettle on and then I want to hear all about it!"

Something amazing has happened. I'm no longer invisible.

Colin's my best friend. He doesn't know it, but he is. He's always chiding me about how unapproachable and distant I am, but in fact, he knows more about me than my therapist and husband combined. A reformed "West End Wendy," he used to be a dancer in *Cats* until a tendon injury put his span-dex unitard days firmly behind him. He can still do an im-pressive pirouette when he wants to, but now he contents himself with teaching seated aerobics to the over-sixties in his local community center (he loves it because they all call him "The Young Man") and working part-time in the box office with me. We share not only a love of dance and theater, but also a very similar Catholic upbringing, with what sounds like exactly the same sadistic nuns (or their relations) rapping our knuckles on different sides of the Atlantic.

"So you got dressed today! What's this all about? Having an affair?" He automatically examines the inside of the kettle for encroaching lime scale. The office kettle is de-scaled twice weekly and the mugs sanitized with bleach when Colin's bored. We're used to coffee that both fizzes and removes the stains from your teeth.

"Hardly!" I switch on my computer.

He takes a small plastic bag out of his rucksack, removes two well-wrapped plastic containers and pops them in the fridge.

"What's for lunch today, Col?"

That's another one of his passions; he can't resist food that's been marked down in supermarkets because the sell-by date has nearly gone. Consequently, his lunches consist of daring taste sensations dictated by the contents of the Tesco's reduced section.

"Today we have a fantastic piece of roasted lamb that's only just slipped by its expiry date but smelled fine this morning, and a small salad of roast peppers, rocket, and new potatoes—although the rocket's not as lively as I'd like it to be. But then you can't have everything."

Colin's a good cook but you have to have a cast-iron stomach to dine at his house.

"So," he looks me up and down, "what's the story? You look amazing. Coffee or tea?"

"Coffee, please, easy on the bleach. There's nothing to tell, really. I cleaned out my closet, and this is what I had left. You like?"

"Very much so, Ouise." (He always calls me Ouise [pronounced Weezy], the name Louise being too long and complicated to say in its entirety.) "And it's about time. I was beginning to fear for your sex life. What does Himself think?"

"He hasn't seen me today, he was asleep. And you know I have no sex life. I'm married."

"Well, I'd buy yourself some extra condoms, darling, and be prepared to walk bowlegged for a few days. He's going to think it's Christmas!"

"Colin Riley! Don't be wicked!" I laugh. "Remember, the Baby Jesus can hear you!" But inside I feel strange, almost sick. I don't know if I want to go there again.

But that's another dangerous thing about being Catholic; we believe in miracles.

When I get home that evening, I decide to give it a go. After all, it's been a long time. The flat is empty, but I spot my husband poking about in the back garden, wearing a pair of rubber gloves. Sneaking into the bathroom, I fix my hair and adjust my makeup. It's so rare that I do this. It's so rare that I even try to be interesting to him anymore. I'm not quite sure of what to do with myself or how to begin, so I go into the living room and perch on the edge of the sofa.

It's like waiting in a doctor's surgery.

My husband and I puzzle over this room; obsess about it. We spend endless hours trying to rearrange it so that it feels warm, comfortable and inviting. We make drawings, sketch plans, cut out little paper models to scale and move them around on pieces of paper with all the intensity of two world-class chess masters. But the result is the same. Wind howls around the sofa. An ocean of parquet stretches between the green armchair and the coffee table. (I've seen guests land on their stomachs reaching for a cup of tea.) And the dining room table lurks in the corner like an instrument of torture rescued from the Spanish Inquisition. (Dinner parties confirm this to be true.)

I pick up a magazine and am flicking through the pages when he comes in.

"Hello!" he calls.

"Hey, I'm in here!" My throat is tight so it comes out a bit higher than normal.

He pokes his head round the corner. Still wearing the rubber gloves, he's now got the bedroom waste bin in his hands.

"Louise," he begins.

"Yes?" I rise slowly so he can see the full glory of my form-fitting dress, smiling in a playful, naughty way. It's a risk. Either I look like a complete sex goddess or Jack Nicholson in *The Shining*.

My husband stands immobilized. He looks cute and confused in his faded, baggy sweatpants. I giggle and take a step forward. "Yes," I say again, only softer this time, like I'm answering a question, not asking one.

We're standing quite close now; there's only the waste bin between us. I can smell the damp warmth of his hair and the clean, fresh perfume of the clothing softener we use on his sweatshirt. I gaze into his eyes and for a moment everything shifts and melts. I'm smiling for real now, with my whole being and I know I don't look like Jack Nicholson. Raising my hand, my pretty, delicate hand, I move forward to caress the gentle slope of his cheek, when suddenly I see something that stops me.

As my hand draws closer, his body tenses. He's standing just there in front of me, but somehow, without ever moving, he begins to recede. A look sweeps across his face, hardening his features into a facade of detachment. It's the look of every child who has been forced to endure an unpleasant but un-avoidable physical punishment, a spontaneous expression of utter resignation.

I step back in amazement, my hand poised in the air like a Barbie doll. My husband looks up in surprise and our eyes meet. The air around us condenses into a vacuum, thick with shame and humiliation, impossible to endure.

My husband is the first to recover, his face a mask of indig-nation.

He holds up the waste bin. "Louise, what is *this*?"

I look at the contents of the bin. I'm staring at it but I seem to have a hard time seeing it. "Garbage." That's the best I can come up with.

He reaches in, pulls out a printer paper box and wields it aloft. "And this?"

He's really got me now. "More garbage?"

He rolls his eyes and sighs the sigh of all sighs. The "shall I repeat this for the mentally impaired?" sigh. "All right, look." He places the crumpled box back into the bin. "Now what do you see?"

My eyes are welling up with tears. I blink them back. "I see a box in a bin."

"No, Louise, what you see is a box taking up the *whole* of the bin. Every single bit of room."

"So what? It's a bin. Empty it!" I despise him. There's no way I'm going to cry. Ever.

"And who's going to do that? Me, that's who."

"Not necessarily."

"Please." He rolls his eyes again. I'm married to a Jewish mother.

"You don't have to. You don't have to be the self-appointed garbage monitor. Somehow we'd survive."

"You just don't get it, do you? All I'm asking is that when you have an extra large piece of rubbish, could you please use the kitchen bin. All right? Is that understood?"

"An extra large piece of rubbish."

"Yes. And don't be that way, you know exactly what I'm talking about."

"Of course." I feel cold. I want to climb under the covers and go to sleep.

"So, we're in agreement?"

"Yes, large garbage in big bin. Understood."

"It's not much to ask."

"No, it certainly isn't."

He turns to go but pauses when he reaches the door. "That dress . . . ," he begins.

"Yes?" Heat rushes to my face and I wish I weren't so pale, so transparent.

"It's . . . what I mean to say is, you look very nice."

I stare at him across the sea of parquet. "Thank you."

"But if you want to change into something more suitable, maybe we can start clearing that path in the garden. After all, it's really a job we should do together."

He lingers by the doorway, waiting for some sort of response.

There's nothing to say.

"Well, whenever you're ready, then."

He turns and walks back into the garden.

And I am alone.

∞

That night, I stay up and read, searching for clues through the pages of *Elegance*. There must be a way out of this. Someone as wise and experienced as Madame Dariaux must be able to advise me. I'm certain, quite certain, it wasn't always this way. If I can just find the key, the moment I should've turned left instead of right or said yes instead of no, then I'll be able to understand what I did wrong.

And then the rest is easy.

I simply reverse it.

D

❦

Daughters

Little daughters are understandably the pride and joy of their mothers, but they are very often also, alas, the reflection of their mother's inelegance. When you see a poor child all ringletted, beribboned, and loaded down with a handbag, an umbrella, and earrings, or wearing crepe-soled shoes with a velvet dress, you can be certain that her mother hasn't the slightest bit of taste.

It is a serious handicap to be brought up this way, because a child must be endowed with a very strong personality of her own in order to rid herself of the bad habits that have been inculcated during her early years. The more simply a little girl is dressed——sweaters and skirts in the winter, Empire-style cotton dresses in the summer——the more chic she is. It is never too early to learn that discretion and simplicity are the foundations of elegance.

When I was about nine, I was taken out of my Catholic day school and sent to an all girls' preparatory school. There I met Lisa Finegold, who became my best friend for a year and a half and my fashion idol for a lifetime. Her mother, Nancy, was from New York, which made her sophisticated. Pencil thin, with long brown hair and elegant features, she moved as if she were made of fine bone china.

My own mother was experimenting with unisex dressing that year, to my intense mortification. She'd read a book on Communist China and been so impressed by the austerity of their lifestyle that she emulated it by wearing the same red tartan pantsuit every day for a month. (This was in the seventies.) While Nancy Finegold never ventured from the house in anything but stilettos, my mother regularly rounded us all up for long, rigorous hikes in the woods, dressed in thick moccasins she'd made herself and one of her favorite Greenpeace T-shirts. I longed for her to grow her hair long and even dug out an old wig she'd bought in the sixties but she stubbornly refused to alter her trademark crop. "It's not that important," she'd say. But I couldn't help secretly wishing she was from New York and made of bone china too.

Lisa had her own bedroom, complete with a huge, extra frilly canopy bed, just like in *Gone With the Wind*. It had pillows covered in lace that you didn't sleep on; they were just for show. Rows of beautiful china dolls were carefully seated along her mantelpiece and in the corner stood a mahogany and glass display case filled with her collection of porcelain miniatures.

Then there were Lisa's clothes, which her mother bought in massive shopping sprees in New York. Most of them were dry clean only and hung on silk-covered hangers in neat rows. Everything was pressed, clean, and more amazingly, the right size. She didn't own a single hand-me-down.

Until I met Lisa, all my friends were exactly like me. We shared rooms begrudgingly with our siblings, drawing invisible lines down the center of the floor, not unlike the battlelines of the Civil War, in a vain effort to gain some autonomy and an identity of our own. We slept in bunk beds on pillows you put your head on and could drool over and that were machine washable for when you got sick. Even the furniture was made out of hard-wearing, wipeable surfaces, the kind of furnishings you could jump off of or on to without a second thought. And our collections were living: spiders, slugs, bugs, and worms. They were displayed in jars and cardboard boxes stored in the cool mud underneath the porch steps in the backyard. There are many backyard badges of courage, of which touching and capturing a gigantic slug after a thunderstorm is only one.

During recess, Lisa and I would link arms and walk round the edge of the playground in endless circles (Lisa never ran or played tag or did anything involving sweat) and I would ply her for more and more details about her day. I dreamt regularly of my own parents dying in a horrible car accident and, at the height of my inconsolable grief, being adopted by the Finegolds and becoming Lisa's sister.

The first time Lisa asked me home to play, I felt like I'd fallen into a dream world. The housekeeper answered the door and was wearing an apron, just like Alice on *The Brady Bunch*. She made us lunch and not only was it hot, but it consisted of spaghetti and homemade sauce she'd actually cooked herself— not out of a jar. If that wasn't enough, we even had tapioca pudding for dessert, which was sweet and bumply and, Lisa claimed, made with frog's eggs, which is why she wouldn't touch it and why I got two helpings.

Finally we went up to Lisa's room and sat on the bed. It was quite a concoction when fully made; you couldn't really touch it without ruining the effect, so we sat along the edge, not in the middle. Lisa smoothed down the folds of her skirt and looked bored. (This was her most attractive quality, her incredible capacity for boredom.)

"Why don't we play dolls?" I suggested, eagerly eyeing her marvelous collection. I'd already chosen which ones would be ballerinas and which ones would be possessed by the devil. *The Exorcist* had come out that year and although we were too young to see it, my brother and sister and I were fascinated by the idea of being possessed, vomiting green stuff, and speaking in scary voices. Also, it contrasted nicely with the ballet theme.

"Why don't we make the ones with dark hair be possessed and all the blond ones ballerinas?"

There was a moment's silence and Lisa looked at me like I was speaking a foreign language.

"Or the other way around?" I was flexible.

"You don't *play* with them," she said. "You just *look* at them."

I wanted to ask why but my desire to impress her prevented me from calling attention to the fact that I wasn't completely *au fait* with the etiquette of owning china dolls.

"Oh yeah. Right. OK, well, why don't we make a miniature world underneath the bed? We can take all the miniatures out of the cabinet and if we get some green tissues, we can make a pond and then we can use the bedside table and it's like they go into the World of the Giants . . ."

I could tell by the pained expression on her face that I was losing her.

"Louise," she began, and then stopped.

Lisa couldn't explain her world to me any better than I could understand it. And she had never had to before. Finally, like a child reciting a catechism, she said, "Some things are to look at, not to touch."

"Oh." I didn't get it at all.

She smiled at me. So I smiled back. We sat there smiling at each other, both thinking the other insane.

"I know," she said at last. "Let's go up to the attic and dress the dog in baby clothes."

Luckily, there are some human experiences that transcend cultural divides.

Then one day the Finegolds invited me out to dinner. In honor of the occasion, I wore my best dress, which was made to my exact specifications by Grandma Irene. We chose the pattern and the material together, a crisp, white cotton covered in bright blue and red flowers, and she made little cap sleeves trimmed with lace and smocked the front of it by hand.

I brought the dress to school with me on a hanger and hung it in my locker. Occasionally I'd show it to one of the other girls but I wanted it to be a surprise for Lisa, certain that once she saw me in it, she'd come up with the idea of us being sisters all on her own.

After school we went to her house and played, which, that day, consisted of taking all the miniature figures out of the glass cabinet, looking at them, and then putting them back in exactly the same way. After a while, we heard someone come in and Lisa said, "It's time to get ready." We put on our dresses, brushed each other's hair, and went downstairs. Lisa didn't say anything about my dress and I didn't say anything about hers, which was in black velvet with a creamy, satin sash. It was understood that we both looked fabulous.

In the kitchen we found Dr. Finegold eating tapioca pudding from a serving bowl in the refrigerator. Tall and slim, with black, wavy hair, a romantic mustache and soft, dark eyes, he was easily the most beautiful man I'd ever seen. He owned an enormous collection of tortoises that he kept in various tanks and plastic pools in the basement, which I thought were cool but Lisa thought were gross. And best of all, he loved to play the piano.

"Daddy, don't do that," Lisa admonished halfheartedly. (Even her parents were just minor irritations.)

"Our little secret," he said, tossing the spoon into the sink. "I know; why don't I play you girls a little tune?"

We went into the living room and he began to play. I danced around the piano and we laughed, egging each other on. I'd turn a pirouette and he'd shout, "Go on, do another one!" He'd do a massive run and I'd clap and make him do it again. Lisa wasn't very good at dancing; it was part of her whole horror of physical activity, so she stood by the side of the piano, sulking and being bored. Dr. Finegold sang "Mona Lisa," which I thought was hysterical and Lisa ignored him. All in all, we had a great time.

We didn't even hear Nancy come in but suddenly she was there and Dr. Finegold stopped playing. I stood beaming and panting to catch my breath. This was it, I'd just turned four pirouettes and was wearing the most beautiful dress in the world. If ever they were going to want to adopt me, it was now.

Nancy Finegold stood in silence in the doorway. "I think you girls ought to get ready," she said at last.

"We are ready, Mama." Lisa's voice was unusually quiet.

She turned to me. "Is that what you're wearing?"

I nodded. Was this a trick question?

She turned her back to me and spoke to Lisa. "Don't you have something she could borrow?"

I felt myself go cold; the way you do when someone talks about you as if you were a chair.

"Nan!" Dr. Finegold interrupted.

She registered him with distaste. "Don't be so dramatic, Mel." Bending down to examine my dress more closely, she smiled sweetly. "That dress is fine, Louise, but Lisa has one that will be better."

"Mom!" The horror on Lisa's face was unmistakable; she'd obviously never been asked to share anything before.

Nancy Finegold was a genius trapped in a world of idiots. She sighed in exasperation, rolling her eyes in the grown up version of Lisa's favorite expression. "All right, fine! What about a cardigan then?"

Dr. Finegold walked away and Lisa stared dejectedly at the floor.

In her full-length mink coat and slender high heels, Mrs. Finegold seemed too thin to stand upright for long. Her huge brown eyes scanned the room for any sign of affirmation or weakness and, finding nothing, she opened her mouth to speak but nothing came out. She closed it again in such a way that she reminded me of a ventriloquist's dummy and for one terrible moment I thought I would laugh. Her exquisite hands clenched in frustration and then fell limply by her side, the gold bangles rattling against one another, as if someone had suddenly let go of the strings.

I couldn't bear it. "I'll wear a cardigan," I offered.

She stared at me for a moment and then smiled, triumphant. She gave Lisa a shove. "Go on. Run upstairs and grab one of your blue cardigans."

Lisa extracted herself with all the speed of one of my giant slugs.

Now there was just the two of us. I stared at her, but she didn't look at me. Instead, she knelt down and pulled up my knee socks, folding the tops over in two perfectly even strips. I could smell her perfume, her hair spray, and the musky, almost aluminum scent of the fur coat she wore as she smoothed down my hair with her hand. I had wanted to be touched by her for months, to run up and wrap my arms around her, to bury my head against her shoulder and tell her how much I loved her. And now, at last, I was the whole focus of her attention. And I couldn't move.

Some things are to look at, not to touch. Nancy Finegold was one of them.

We went out to dinner and I wore the cardigan.

My father came to pick me up in the old brown family station wagon and when I jumped in the front seat, I felt free and very, very old.

"How'd it go, Pea?" he asked. "Did they like your dress?"

"I don't think they understood it, Da."

He laughed. "What's there to understand?"

"Everything," I said.

Absolutely everything.

E

❦

Expecting

The period during which a woman is expecting a baby is not always, it must be admitted, the most propitious one for elegance. A bad complexion, an expanding waistline, a silhouette becoming a bit awkward towards the end, all add up to an image that is not always a joy to contemplate in the mirror. But since almost every woman is obliged to go through it at one time or another, it is better to accept the situation with good humour and to make the most of it.

A good plan is to buy only a few things for your maternity wardrobe and to wear the same dresses over and over again until you are quite fed up with them. This way you can give them away afterwards without the slightest regret. Above all, don't try to have them taken in at the seams after you have recovered your normal figure. The clothes you have worn throughout these long months will disgust you for the rest of your days.

My husband and I are entertaining friends, a couple we haven't seen in a long time. We haven't seen them because they have children, twin girls. My husband and I don't do children very well. No matter how much we try to hide it, we're clearly horrified. I keep staring at them like I'm going to pass out and he's permanently on guard, brandishing a washcloth like he's ready to mop up toxic waste. Very quickly the couple feel as if they've defiled the sanitized sanctuary of our pristine living room and decide that the twins need to go home for a nap after only forty-five minutes in our company. Everyone's relieved, even the babies, who are only nine months old. Their faces noticeably relax as they're loaded into the car.

Our friends are all having children now; we're the odd ones out. They've stopped asking us about it; stopped smiling and saying, "But surely *someday* you'll want a family." By now it's obvious that only an act of God could make us parents. We wave to them as they drive away and then walk back into our barren household—the one with the dust-free living room and the bed the size of Kansas.

"Thank God that's over," my husband says, bending down to pick up something from the floor. It's a single, pale blue baby sock, still warm and smelling of baby. He hands it to me. I don't know what to do with it or where to put it, so I throw it away.

"Yes," I agree. "Thank God."

The first time I was pregnant, I was sixteen and it was before the creation of home pregnancy tests. I had to see a doctor to tell me what I already knew. You don't have to have been pregnant before to know that there's something strange going on. I was throwing up in the mornings and, in fact, all through the day and I started noticing strange discharges I'd never encountered before. Things smelled different, tasted wrong, and I'd gone off pizza. For the first time in my life, I was forced into paying attention to my body. I was possessed, like in the *Invasion of the Body Snatchers,* and it wasn't going to go away.

I couldn't go to the family physician—not to the same man

who'd vaccinated me against smallpox and measured my growth against a chart on the wall covered with smiling, cartoon animals. I was sick but I had to hide it. But by now I was used to hiding all the most important facts of my day.

I was used to hiding the fact that I threw up my food after each meal by going upstairs to the guest bathroom and sticking my fingers down my throat. I was used to hiding the little black speed pills I took every morning, the ones I bought from Sarah Blatz, a fat, redheaded girl who played on the girls' field-hockey team and who was prescribed them by her doctor to lose weight. And I was used to hiding where I went in the evenings from my parents, what I did, and especially who with.

My friend Mary took me to see her doctor—a female physician in another part of town. She had a growth chart on her wall too, but she'd never measured me before, so that was OK.

Mary was frightened; she wasn't used to concealing things or maybe she was just used to covering up all the normal things, like that she'd gone all the way with her boyfriend, the one she'd been going steady with for a year and a half, or that she'd got drunk at a friend's party last Saturday and had to spend the night.

I didn't have a boyfriend; I got pregnant from a guy who never called again and I was drunk every Saturday night.

After school, Mary drove me to the doctor's in her mother's custom built silver Cadillac, the one with the horn that played the theme from *The Godfather* when you pressed it. (Her father was in the meat trade.) Every once in a while she'd press it and we'd laugh, more out of politeness than anything else. She was obviously trying her best to cheer me up and I was grateful for her kindness.

The doctor took a blood test and examined me as I sat in my little paper gown on the crinkly paper strip that covered the examining table. The office was on the seventh floor of a modern block, overlooking the traffic that led into the mall below. I concentrated on the pale blue of the sky as she felt my breasts and shook her head sadly.

"They're pregnanty," she announced. "We'll get the test back tomorrow, but I can tell you right now, you're pregnant."

I know, I thought. I know.

Mary wanted me to tell her mom because that's what she would do. But I knew I'd have to do the rest on my own. I made an appointment but had to wait another month before I could have the abortion.

In the meantime, I told my parents I had an ulcer, which they believed without questioning. Every morning at around 4:30 A.M., I was sick. And every morning, my father woke up at 4:15 and made me a small bowl of porridge to settle my stomach, which he placed by the side of my bed. Then he'd pad off upstairs in his red robe, feeling his way in the darkness to catch another hour and a half's sleep. He never asked if he should do that; he just did it. Like so many things in our house, even acts of kindness occurred in silence. I wondered if he would do the same thing if he knew the truth. I think he would.

My skin got bad and my mouth tasted metallic. In my locker at school, I kept an enormous box of saltines, which I ate in the hundreds. My diet diminished to saltines, mashed potatoes, and porridge. Anything else was just too exciting. No matter how much I ate, I still got sick. And no matter how often I threw up, I was still hungry. I was more afraid of gaining weight than of being pregnant.

The operation cost $230. My parents gave me $200 in cash after I managed to convince them that I needed a new winter coat, and the rest of it I paid for out of my allowance.

Finally the day came, a Saturday morning in early March. It was raining, softly misting when I left the house.

I told my parents I was going to go shopping with my friend Anne and then I drove myself to the clinic and checked in. It was early, around 9 A.M. The waiting room was full of flowered cushions, pleasant prints, and bright, soft colors. There were little clusters of people—a young couple holding hands and whispering to one another, a girl with her family. They'd obviously tried to make the waiting room as sympathetic and normal looking as possible, but despite that, no one wanted to look at one another.

You had to meet with a counselor before you did it. They took us in one at a time, in such a way that you never passed any of the other women in the hall. I was led into a little office where a young woman with short brown hair was waiting for me.

I cannot remember her name or how she introduced herself but I can remember her deliberate, almost institutionalized kindness. And I recall her asking if I was alone, and saying yes.

My mouth was dry and sticky. The office was like a closet, with no windows. There was a table and two chairs and a chart on the wall with a diagram of the female anatomy. Even here they'd done their best to make it seem normal and wholesome by painting the walls pink. It was like a beauty parlor for abortions. There were no sounds at all in the room, no traffic noise, no distant conversations. Just the woman and me.

"I'm here to tell you about the operation and what to expect," she began.

I nodded.

She took out a red plastic model of a uterus cut in half.

"This is a model of a uterus," she said.

I nodded again. I wondered where she'd got it, what kind of

company made these sorts of things, and what other models they had in their catalog.

She started to talk and point at the model. I could hear her voice, and see her hands moving, but my mind had gone numb. I just stared at the plastic uterus, thinking how red it was and how a real one couldn't possibly be that red.

"Excuse me," I interrupted after a while. "I'm going to be sick."

"Of course," she said.

I went and threw up in a little cubicle next door. There seemed to be cubicles everywhere—clean, little rooms filled with women throwing up. When I came back, she continued where she left off. She was obviously used to people throwing up in the middle of her presentation.

"During the operation, what we will do is remove the lining of the uterus, creating a kind of non-biological miscarriage. You will have all the symptoms of a miscarriage—heavy bleeding, cramps, and hormonal imbalance. This will make you feel a little more fragile than normal. It's important for you to rest afterwards and take it easy for a few days. Is some-one coming to pick you up?"

I stared at her.

"Did you drive yourself?" she repeated.

The room was perfectly still. She had no makeup on. I tried to imagine her in a bar, talking to a stranger, way past closing time. I couldn't.

She waited. She was used to waiting.

I started to open my mouth; it tasted like yellow sick. I closed it again and tried to swallow.

"Would you like some water?"

I shook my head; it would only make me throw up again.

"You don't have to do this," she said at last.

She was looking at me with her clean, fresh face, the face of a mother on a children's aspirin commercial.

I started to cry and she was used to that too.

I hated myself because I knew we would all be doing it. She passed me a Kleenex. Twenty minutes from now, she'd be passing a Kleenex to someone else, the girl with the boyfriend perhaps.

"Maybe you'd like to think about it some more," she offered. Freedom of choice.

"No." I was done crying. "I've made up my mind."

It was exactly as she said it would be. An hour later I was lying in a hospital version of a La-Z-Boy chair, drinking sugary tea and eating cookies.

Four hours later I was shopping for a new winter coat with my friend Anne, using a credit card I'd stolen from my parents.

"Your ulcer seems to be better," my father remarked a week later.

"Yes, Da. I believe it's gone."

And it is gone. Until the next time.

There's a coat that hangs in the front hall cloak room of my parents' house. It's a single-breasted, navy blue winter coat; a classic cut in immaculate condition. It's been there for years but no one's noticed. It has never been worn.

F

❧

Fur

If women are honest with themselves, they would admit that the fascination they feel for furs is not only due to the warmth they provide. After all, a fur is never just a fur—it is also, more than any other garment I can think of, a symbol and a mink coat is the most easily identifiable symbol of them all. It stands for achievement, both for the man who bought it and the woman who wears it, as well as status and undeniable luxury. It has been said with a great deal of truth that a mink is the feminine Legion of Honour.

Furs are important milestones in a woman's life, and in general they are purchased only after a great deal of thought and many comparisons. So make your selection with care. After all, men come and go but a good fur is a destiny.

There's a story about a famous opera diva rehearsing for a production of *Tosca* at the Met. At the end of the rehearsal, she sends her dresser to collect her things and the poor woman comes back clutching a black wool coat.

The star is appalled. She tosses her head and fixes the woman with an icy stare. "Honey, you know I don't wear no *cloth* coats!"

Divas and minks have a lot in common. You have to kill something to make a mink. Its beauty is horrible to behold. Divas are like that too. And while you don't have to be a diva to wear a mink, it helps.

I got my first mink when I was nineteen years old. It was given to me by a friend of my mother's, whose own mother had recently died of Alzheimer's. She'd been a tiny woman and no one else in the family could wear the coat. Or wanted to.

It was a full-length mink; glossy, heavy, stinking of musk when it rained. It was the most un-PC garment it was possible to own. And yet it had both authority and a powerful, threatening glamour. People reacted violently to it; they were infuriated, offended, jealous, or lustful. It was a coat of almost Biblical symbolism. It hid nothing, accommodated no one. If you hated it, it was there to be hated. If you loved it, it couldn't care less. The very thing that made it repulsive was the same thing that gave it its splendor. And it fit me like a glove.

The trouble with a coat like that, is it can take over your life; dominate your whole personality. If you don't know who you are, you can easily become a mink coat.

I had a boyfriend at the time. He'd been a car thief in high school and was now two years ahead of me in drama school. He wore a denim jacket that had been in police chases, that still had bloodstains on it from when he'd been arrested. Badly worn, it hung together in places by threads.

We looked liked brother and sister, he and I, with the same pale hair and green eyes. Neither of us knew who we were or who we wanted to be, so we became actors. We spent our nights eating at an all-night diner called Chief's, he in his threadbare denim and me in my mink, smoking cigarettes, drinking beer with our eggs, and arguing about iambic pentameter and if Pinter was really a genius or just a fraud. We were going to be great actors, famous and rich. We made up stories about ourselves, wore costumes, acted in scenes. And we were our own favorite characters.

Only, I was always the mink and he was always the denim jacket. We met wearing them, parted wearing them and despite all the drinking, fucking, and fighting, we just couldn't manage to take them off.

He performed Romeo in his end-of-term project with a black eye. He got it smashing in the face of a man who propositioned me in an all-night drinking club over the Christmas break. It was three o'clock in the morning. We'd been drinking since six. The man had said something I hadn't quite heard and then all of a sudden we were outside in the bitter cold.

They rolled around in the frozen black snow in the middle of the road, punching and kicking, blood forming pale pink pools between the patches of dark grit. A crowd gathered and cheered them on, shouting and jeering—full of exactly the kind of people you'd expect to be strolling around at three in the morning.

I hated to be upstaged. Pulling the mink around me tightly, I walked away, staggering in my high heels over the snowdrifts to the car.

We were doing a close-up, just the mink and me, when I saw him running towards me, limping. His nose was bleeding and his knuckles smashed. The guy had been wearing a ring, and the side of his face was cut.

"You cunt!" he shouted across the parking lot. "You filthy, fucking cunt!"

So, we're starting with Mamet.

DENIM JACKET: I fucking defend your fucking honor
    and you fucking walk away!
MINK: Get in the car.

DENIM JACKET: Fuck you!

MINK: Get in the fucking car!

DENIM JACKET: I said, fuck you! Or maybe you didn't fucking hear me. Maybe you were too busy walking the fuck away!

MINK: I didn't ask you to fight him, did I?

DENIM JACKET: No man takes that.

MINK: It was about me!

DENIM JACKET: No man fucking takes that, understand? You're my girlfriend. A man says something to you, he says it to me. Understand?

MINK: Fuck you!

DENIM JACKET: Fuck you too.

(Pinter pause)

DENIM JACKET: You walked away.

MINK: I couldn't watch you do it, baby. *(Tears welling up in eyes; gin tears; three o'clock in the morning tears.)* I just couldn't watch you get hurt.

(Grabs me by the shoulders; moving rapidly into Tennessee Williams territory now.)

DENIM JACKET: You gotta have faith in me, Louie. Please. *(Bloody head on mink)* I need you to have faith in me. *(sotto voce)* I need you, baby. I need you.

(Curtain)

Only the curtain never fell.

We broke up just before I came to England, exhausted. I

discovered I wasn't a diva, that I didn't have the endurance for grand opera. And there are only so many ways you can say "Fuck you" to someone before you start to really mean it.

I had imagined that passion, drama, and love were all one and the same—proof that the others existed. But the opposite was true: drama and passion are just very clever disguises for a love that has never taken root.

I gave the mink away to a friend in New York. It was a heavy coat to wear and I was relieved to get rid of it. But very soon after it was gone, I began to feel that something was missing.

I thought I could change my character as easily as I could change my coat.

But I've been searching for the right one ever since.

G

❦

Girl Friends

It is a good idea never to go shopping for clothes with a girl friend. Since she is often an unwitting rival as well, she will unconsciously demolish everything that suits you best. Even if she is the most loyal friend in the world, if she simply adores you, and if her only desire is for you to be the most beautiful, I remain just as firm in my opinion: shop alone, and turn only to specialists for guidance. Although they may not be unmercenary, at least they are not emotionally involved.

I particularly dread these kinds of girl friends:

1. The one who wants to be just like you, who is struck by the same love-at-first-sight for the same dress, who excuses herself in advance by saying, "I hope you don't mind, darling, and anyway, we don't go out together very much, and we can always telephone beforehand to make sure we don't wear it at the same time, etc. etc. . . ." You are furious but don't dare show it and you return the dress the next day.

2. The friend with a more modest budget than yours, who couldn't dream of buying the same kind of clothes as you

(the truth is that she dreams of nothing else). Perhaps you think it is a real treat for her to go shopping with you. Personally, I call it mental cruelty, and I am always painfully embarrassed by the role of second fiddle that certain women reserve for their best friend. Besides, her presence is of absolutely no use to you at all, because this kind of friend always approves of everything you select, and will agree with even greater enthusiasm if it happens to be something that isn't very becoming.

3. Finally, the friend who lives for clothes and whose advice you seek. This spoilt and self-confident woman will monopolize the attention of the shop assistants, who are quick to scent a good customer. You find yourself forgotten by everybody, trying to decide what looks best not on you, but on your friend.

Moral: Always shop alone. Women who shop with their friends may be popular, but elegant they are *NOT.*

I'm on my way to Notting Hill to see a friend I write with, Nicki Sands. We began working on a screenplay together about a year ago. Neither of us are really writers, which is probably why we aren't making a lot of progress on the project. We meet religiously twice a week, loitering around in a kind of career cul de sac. However, writing does provide us with a useful alibi, instantly deflecting any embarrassing questions such as, "So, what do you do?"

Nicki used to be a model in the late seventies and early eighties and now she lives with a record producer in an enormous double-fronted house in Notting Hill. They openly despise one another. Neither one of them is obliged to work, so they while away the hours wandering from room to room, looking for new ways to torture each other.

I arrive around ten-thirty to find Nicki and Dan milling about in their Santa Fe–style kitchen. They own a cappuccino machine that neither of them can work and are standing in front of the faux adobe wood-burning hearth and indoor barbecue unit holding their empty cups.

Every once in a while, one of them will have a go and the other will provide a running commentary.

"That's right, put the coffee in and turn the knob . . . No! No, no, no, no, no!"

"Shut up!"

"Jesus, you're doing it wrong *again*!"

"No, I'm not!"

"Steam, there's meant to be steam!"

"Shut up! What is it with you?"

"What is it with me? What *is* it? I've been up since six and I still haven't had a fucking cup of coffee!"

Reading the instructions is considered cheating.

After a while, Dan gives up and makes a Nescafé. The three-hundred-pound triumph of Italian engineering has won again. Nicki and I decide to go out for coffee and discuss plot development. But what we really do is sit in Tom's, a café and organic food shop around the corner, and hash over Nicki's failing relationship in detail.

"He thinks he looks young!" she hisses at me, leaning dramatically across the table, as if discretion were a consideration. "I mean, he said to me the other day, 'I don't think I look a day past thirty-five.' I nearly choked on my cappuccino!" (They must have been out.)

She's speaking to me but her eyes never leave the door, just in case someone thinner, prettier, or more chic walks in. This almost never happens. I'm just beginning to confide to her that I think maybe my husband and I might have a serious problem too, when suddenly she screams, grabs my arm violently, and yanks me across the table. "My God! Louise!" she gasps. "That's the handbag I was telling you about! There!"

I smile and nod.

I'm used to Nicki by now. And I'm used to her ignoring me.

Nicki is one of these women who only has one girlfriend at a time. She wears friends out with her constant demands for attention but is too competitive to tolerate more than one extra female in her life. I've known this for a while. However, cultivating friends has never been my forte. Although I'm perfectly sociable—happy to spend an hour or so in idle chitchat with any number of people, the thing I'm not terribly good at is the kind of honest self-revelation and shared intimacies that are the backbone of a lasting female friendship. I long to be open and informal, if only my life weren't such a mess. But now is not the time. After all, if I started confiding my innermost problems to someone, I'd have to do something about them. And I'm not ready for that yet. Someday, when I've pulled myself together, maybe I'll have a real chum of the heart.

In the meantime, I'm not expected to share any deep personal confidences with Nicki; I'm only required to show up and tag along. And tagging along will do me just fine. It's easy, undemanding—we talk about nothing more taxing than new lipstick formulations and, even though I could never afford it, the benefits of Pilates versus Hatha yoga techniques. And there's a certain amount of glamour involved in these weekly escapes. I enjoy basking in the chaotic splendor and excess of Nicki World, complete with multimillion-pound homes, £100 face crèmes, and £4 organic lattes while clinging perversely to the reassuring knowledge that, for all their money, Nicki and Dan are still incredibly unhappy. When your own life remains a baffling, unresolved puzzle, there are few things more comforting than to be surrounded by fellow struggling souls.

When we've downed enough caffeine to bring us to tears, we walk back to Nicki's and dump our bags in the Moroccan-style living room. Almost everything that Nicki and Dan lose is eventually discovered lying camouflaged against the overwhelming profusion of kilim cushions that populate this room. They've even managed to create curtains out of old Oriental carpets, so that sitting in it is like being swallowed by a giant carpetbag.

Then we climb up to Nicki's Victorian study and she sits in front of her computer, which folds out from a unit made to look like an antique dressing table and I sit on the daybed. The daybed is an original; painfully uncomfortable and obviously designed to keep Victorian ladies very much awake.

"OK. Right." Nicki turns on the computer, clicks into our file, and pages down to where we left off.

"Here we are, page fifteen," she announces triumphantly.

No matter how much work we do or how often we meet, we're always on page fifteen.

"OK, so how did we leave it then?" I try to gather my enthusiasm.

"Jan was just about to reveal to Aaron why she'd left home."

"Oh, yeah. Good. And what did we decide about that?"

Nicki checks through the notes we made at coffee.

"You know, I don't think we came to any firm conclusions about that one."

"Did we have any ideas?"

She flicks through again. "I'm not really seeing anything that can be called a *solid* idea."

"Oh. OK. Never mind." I haul myself out of the sagging center of the daybed. "Right. Let's get brainstorming!"

The room goes dead. A dog barks somewhere in the distance. Nicki gnaws at a hangnail.

Suddenly, like the voice of God, the sound of Dionne Warwick singing "Walk On By" floats down the stairs. Nicki's on her feet in a flash.

"My God, I can't *believe* he's doing that now! The bastard!"

"Doing what?" I ask.

"He's playing Dionne Warwick!" she shrieks. Flinging the door open, she screams up the stairs, "I know what you're doing, you bastard! I *know* what you're doing!"

"My God, Nicki, what's he doing?" I'm missing the point badly.

"He's *exercising!*" she screams, rolling her eyes. "Don't you understand? The bastard will be bouncing all over the treadmill next!" She cradles her head in her beautifully manicured hands. "I'm getting a tension headache. I can feel it right *here*." She points very specifically to the top of her left temple. "I can't work this way. I just can't. Do you mind? I *have* to get out of here."

So we go shopping.

Shopping with Nicki takes stamina. It takes patience. And it takes great fortitude.

I'm fine as long as we stick to coffee shops and her house but as soon as we go shopping, real, proper clothes shopping, the enormous gulf between her life and mine is ruthlessly revealed. Suddenly all the cuddly *Hello* glamour and intimacy we've shared evaporates and I'm keenly aware of a sharp, insurmountable shift in status.

Firstly, she's tall, incredibly slender, with long legs and a handsome bust. So it's like, well, like shopping with a model.

Secondly, she shops at Prada and Loewe, Harvey Nichols, and Jo Malone—stores well beyond my meager budget. I'm used to doing my Columbo impression, shambling around the changing rooms of Harvey Nichols in my secondhand trench coat while she parades through the department in her knickers, grabbing piles of garments in all conceivable colors and styles. The shop assistants love her. They look upon me as a badly groomed pet.

Occasionally, Nicki encourages me to try something on. There are awful moments, embedded in my memory, of standing in front of a changing room mirror in a badly fitting dress, my legs unshaven, wearing a pair of worn-out Keds, only to have Nicki emerge from the neighboring cubicle in exactly the same dress (but a size smaller), looking, yes, like a model.

It's the shop assistants I feel for most. They avert their eyes and smile and lie. The minutes stretch like years while they desperately try to make a sale to one of us, to both of us, and then neither of us.

Nicki frowns, pouts, and checks for nonexistent panty lines while I crawl backwards into the cubicle, desperate to hide again under my trench coat and brown beret. Later, I help her carry her bags from the shop. She smiles and pats me on the head and I listen to how hard it is to find clothes that fit when you're really a size six and nearly five foot nine on the way back home in the car.

If she shot me, it would be quicker and less painful.

That's our normal routine, only it's about to change.

Thanks to Madame Dariaux, the next time I meet her, I'm not wearing a brown beret or my secondhand trench. And I've already been shopping. By myself.

I've been thinking about it for a while, building up to it. Normally, I don't even allow myself to window shop; I tell myself I don't have the money and therefore it's torture even to look. Or I tell myself I'm too fat; I'll shop when I'm taller (when I'm five foot nine and a size six). But ever since I wore the navy pinafore dress into work, Colin's been hounding me, calling me the Vixen. And then on Saturday, the most extraordinary thing happened.

Someone noticed me.

A man.

I was on my lunch break and famished. Not just hungry but ravenous. I'd run to Pret A Manger and bought a tuna salad and a chocolate brownie. Then, back in the theater, I hid inside the empty auditorium, tucked away in one of the ancient red velvet boxes to eat. Eating is, in fact, putting it politely. What I was actually doing was savaging my food, complete with little grunting noises; leaning in close to the plastic container for maximum intake in the minimum amount of time. It was the kind of eating a girl only does on her own, usually in front of the television, dressed in a pair of pajamas she hasn't been out of all day. Except, I wasn't alone; there was someone watching me.

I didn't recognize him. Wearing jeans and a faded blue sweatshirt, he had dark, almost black hair and brown, heavy eyes.

He just stood there, hands crammed into his pockets, staring at me. And when I caught sight of him, I nearly choked on a caper.

"That's a funny place to eat," he smiled.

Oh God, a techy, I thought disparagingly. One of those guys who paint scenery while exposing their bum cracks. Piss off and leave me alone.

"If I go upstairs, they'll nick my brownie and I'm really hungry," I explained curtly. I turned my attention once again to the total annihilation of my feast but he continued to stand there, digging his hands ever deeper into his pockets and rocking back and forth on his heels.

"Are you new here? I don't recognize you," he continued amiably.

"No. I work in the box office." I finished each sentence like I was finishing the conversation but he lingered on, enduring my silence and indifference. I picked lamely at my food. He was putting me off my stride—I felt self-conscious and all too aware of the fact I was eating my tuna salad with a spoon.

He asked me some more questions, about the box office hours and what I thought of the company, but mostly he stared at me. I couldn't figure out what he was doing but it made me nervous and uncomfortable. Eventually, I threw my salad away and made my excuses. Back in the box office, I ranted to Colin about my ruined lunch.

"Well, my little Vixen, what do you expect?" He laughed, pouring me a cup of sugary tea. "He likes you."

"Me?! Get *real*, Col."

"Face facts, Ouise. The man fancies you. And by the way, he isn't just a techy; he's our new hotshot director and his name's Oliver Wendt. Bit of a dish, if you ask me."

I felt odd—slightly ill, tingly and adolescent.

"Fancies me?" I echoed.

Colin gave me a hug from behind. "Yes, Louise. Fancies you. Better get used to it."

When I left the theater at the end of the day, Oliver Wendt was having a cigarette on the front steps of the building.

For someone I'd never noticed before, he suddenly seemed to be everywhere.

"Good night, Louise," he called after me.

I stopped and turned. "You know my name."

"That's right," he said, stubbing the cigarette end out under his heel. "And my name's Oliver, so now you know mine." He was looking straight into my eyes. I felt my heart pounding in my chest, echoing around the seemingly hollow recess of my head. I turned away and smiled to myself.

"Good night, Oliver," I called and as my voice drifted off behind me, I felt sure he was smiling too.

I walked home as slowly as I could, reluctant to lose the buzz of adrenaline that coursed through my limbs. And that night, as I lay beside my husband in bed, for once I didn't fall into a coma of sleep.

Sunday I got up early, long before my husband was conscious and made my way to Oxford Street. I went to Topshop and wandered around the cavernous store for hours, mesmerized by the video screens, pulsating music, and vast selection of clothing.

At last, after trying on what was easily half the stock, I settled on a pair of steely gray wide-legged trousers and a pale pink fitted cardigan top. Then, invigorated by my purchases, I walked across the street to Jones and bought a pair of black ankle boots with a kitten heel. And suddenly, in a single afternoon, the thing I had never allowed myself to do was done. The brown beret and secondhand trench coat were gone and I emerged, butterfly-like in all my Topshop glory.

Monday, I'm due to meet Nicki in Tom's at noon. I get to Tom's a little late, and Nicki's already there, guzzling a latte with all the desperation of a junkie. She looks up and I wave. But instead of waving back, she just frowns at me. Something's wrong with this picture.

"Sorry I'm late," I say, piling my coat on the chair between us. "Been here long?"

She's examining me, her eyes registering every detail of my being. "You look different," she concludes.

"Yes," I smile, pleased she's noticed.

"Those trousers are *new!*" This is not an observation but an indignant accusation.

"Yes." I pull out a chair and swivel my hips proudly.

"When did you go shopping?" she demands.

"On Sunday."

I sit down and a young man with spiky hair and an apron comes over to take my order.

"And what can I get for you?" He's smiling and his eyes are gleaming. Normally I have to wave my hands in the air like an air traffic controller before anyone takes any notice of me, so this makes a nice change. I smile back.

"What's good today?" I ask.

"Well . . . there's the soup, which today is roasted red pepper and avocado, it's a cold soup but then"—he winks at me—"you seem like a cold soup kind a person."

"Do I indeed!" I giggle.

Nicki can't stand it. "We don't have time for that! We've got work to do."

"I could bring it right away," he offers. So accommodating.

"That would be great, and an orange juice please. Thanks."

"No trouble. Freshly squeezed?"

"Of course."

"I should've known," he smiles.

"Excuse me!" Nicki throws her cup down onto the saucer.

"I ordered something almost twenty minutes ago, if you don't mind!"

"Certainly." He winks at me again as he leaves. Nicki's outraged.

"The service here is appalling. And the food's gone right downhill. God, I've had enough of this. Come on." She slaps a fiver down on the table. "Let's go to Angelo's instead." She pulls on her black Prada duffle coat and storms down the steps.

"I'm sorry," I say to the spiky haired young man as I run to catch her up at the door.

Nicki's cooling her heels in the street. "Listen, let's just go home," she says. "I can make us something to eat."

"Fine," I agree and we walk to her house in silence.

When we arrive, Dan's sending a fax in the kitchen.

"Hey, Louise. You look great! Have you lost weight?"

"No, thanks Dan. Just got some new trousers."

"They're really cute. Turn around."

I do a little pirouette and Nicki rolls her eyes. She throws her coat on top of the dog and pushes past us.

"For God's sake, Dan. They're just a pair of trousers," she hisses, chucking things out of the fridge onto the counter.

"Where'd you get them?" he persists.

"Dan!" She pelts some organic, vine grown tomatoes into a wooden bowl. "Who cares?"

"Topshop," I tell him.

"Topshop!" He stands amazed. "My girls shop at Topshop!"

"No, they do not." Nicki slams the fridge door. "No one you know shops at Topshop."

"They do now. How much were they?"

"Nothing, thirty-five pounds."

"No way!" The whole concept of buying a garment for as little as thirty-five pounds is new to him.

"Dan, leave us alone. We've got work to do," Nicki commands, pointing to the door.

But he lingers on, unfazed. "Why don't you shop at Topshop, Nicks?"

"Don't call me Nicks." She's chopping something with a knife and pieces are flying everywhere.

"Come on," he persists, "why don't you go buy a cute pair of trousers like Louise?"

She turns, knife raised, eyes narrowed into two tiny little slits. "Because, my darling, I don't need to shop at Topshop. I can afford to buy decent clothes from a proper designer. We all do the best we can with what we have and Louise has done very well. It's not easy for girls on a budget and then of course, certain figures are, shall we say, more challenging than others." She turns back and the knife hits the cutting board with a crack.

For a moment, there's absolute silence. Dan stares at Nicki in disbelief.

"My God, but you're a rude bitch," he says at last.

Nicki turns around again and looks at me. Her eyes are dead, like a shark. "I didn't mean it that way. I just meant . . ."

Dan turns to go. "I'm sorry, Louise. I really am."

"Don't you dare apologize for me!" she shouts after him.

He's gone and the kitchen is quiet. "So." She turns to face me, smiling. When she speaks, her voice is like honey. "Would you like tuna in your salad?"

"No. No, thank you," is all I can say.

She swivels around and continues chopping. "Suit yourself."

Nicki and I never get beyond page fifteen. We decide we have artistic differences and have gone in different directions. We never noticed it before, but now it's all we can see.

Considering that I used to see her twice a week, I should miss her more than I do.

H

❦

Husbands

There are three types of husbands:

1. The Blind Man, who says, "Isn't that a new suit, darling?" when he at last notices the ensemble you have been wearing for the past two years. There really isn't any point in discussing him, so let's leave him in peace. At least he has one advantage: he lets you dress as you please.

2. The Ideal Husband, who notices everything, is genuinely interested in your clothes, makes suggestions, understands fashion, appreciates it, enjoys discussing it, knows just what suits you best and what you need, and admires you more than all the other women in the world. If you possess this dream man, hang on to him. He is extremely rare.

3. The Dictator, who knows far better than you what is becoming to you and decides if the current styles are good or not and which shop or dressmaker you ought to go to. This type of man's ideas on fashion are sometimes up to date, but most often he has been so

impressed with the way his mother used to dress that his taste is, to say the least, about twenty years behind the times.

Whatever type of husband you have, my advice is to make the best of it and to try to tame your expectations of him. Even the most devoted man is bound to be distracted at times and forgetful, despite all the efforts you have made to charm him. If you are wise, then you will allow it to pass unnoticed. It is better to develop a strong sense of your own style than to rely too heavily on the opinion of another . . . even that of your husband.

I'm handing my husband, the Blind Man, a fresh cup of tea. I walk across the living room and place his cup on the small round table beside him.

He looks up.

"You've lost weight," he observes.

I stand like a rabbit frozen in the headlights of a car. "Yes," I concede.

And for a moment I think he's going to notice. For a very long second it looks like he's going to register the fact that slowly but surely everything about me has changed. I'm wearing my hair differently. I've bought several new items of clothing. I've started to seriously go to the gym. For weeks now I've been making dozens of tiny, little adjustments and silently waiting for some sort of response.

And now here it is; he's noticed.

And then, just as quickly, I don't want to know. After years of being invisible, the sudden spotlight of my husband's attention is too much to bear. It infuriates me.

As it happens, I'm in luck.

"Don't get too thin," he says, disappearing again behind the Sunday papers. I breathe a sigh of relief. I'm safe.

I pick up the Style section of the *Sunday Times* and perch on the edge of the sofa with it. Wait a minute, I think. Why is that a relief? What are my motives for changing the way I look if I don't even want my husband to notice?

I'm doing a pretty good imitation of a woman reading the paper, but what I'm really doing is gathering my thoughts about me.

I'm changing. Fast. It started off gradually enough, but now it's snowballing. I can't explain it; things that were perfectly acceptable a minute ago are suddenly intolerable. At first it was only the clothes but now it's seeping into everything—the way I eat, sleep, think. I steal a glance at the figure hidden behind a wall of newsprint on the other side of the room. Here's the rub: can I hide it from him? And do I want to?

I can hear him chuckling. "That television show Clive's in has got *terrible* reviews."

Clive Foster is my husband's arch-rival and we hate him. I say "we" because this is part of the glue that keeps the relationship afloat. There's a kind of camaraderie in tearing successful people down, like a shared hobby. And Clive is one of our favorites. Not only is he a similar physical type to my husband, which means they're always up for the same roles, but he's also considerably more successful. If that weren't reason enough, they're at present sharing a stage night after night in *The Importance of Being Earnest*. My husband spends most of the evening trying to upstage him and Clive retaliates by cutting off his laugh lines. It's an ugly business. But mostly we hate Clive because he's out there, enthusiastic and determined and that's deeply threatening to people like us.

He laughs again. "My God! They've even singled him out!

'Clive Foster is horrifically miscast in the role of Ellerby'! Splendid!"

"Poor Clive," I murmur.

Poor Clive?

Unexpectedly, I feel for Clive. Yes, Clive, who used to be the household embodiment of all that is evil and loathsome. Suddenly, getting what you want, thrusting yourself center stage, and taking risks doesn't seem so offensive. What is distasteful is the way we hide behind our own sterile mediocrity and take pleasure in the failings of someone who at least has the courage to try.

That's when I start to lose the plot.

"Poor Clive," I say again, only louder this time.

The paper comes down and my husband looks at me like I'm crazy. "Poor Clive? What, are you mad? The man's a beast!"

Here's where I should chime in. But I don't.

"And why is that?"

"Louie, what's wrong with you? You know why." The paper goes up again.

I feel a totally unreasonable fury building inside me. I should let this go. I should allow it to pass unnoticed. But I don't. "Pardon me . . . I seem to have forgotten exactly why Clive is so offensive."

No response.

Come on, let it go. I pick up the Style section for a second time, then, for reasons beyond my control, put it down again.

"Is it perhaps because he's not the way you would like him to be? Because he has the balls to be openly ambitious?"

The paper stays in place; his voice resonates behind it. "You're being ridiculous. I'm not having this conversation with you."

"Not having this conversation? Not *having* . . . you don't get to choose which conversations we have or don't have!"

The paper remains. "I don't need to talk to you when you're being unreasonable."

I can feel myself flushing; my heart is pounding so loudly, I almost scream the next words. "I'm not unreasonable!"

He snorts from behind the paper. "Listen to yourself."

I lose it. Before I know it, I'm on the other side of the room, tearing at the paper that divides us. My husband stares at me with a mixture of horror and disbelief. When I speak, my voice is hoarse and I have a hard time catching my breath. "Don't you *ever* ignore me again! Conversations are over when we are done talking. *We!*"

My hand is crumpling the paper, shredding it. He grabs my wrist. "Fuck off," he says, matter-of-factly. "Fuck off, Louise."

I reel backwards. He's smoothing back the paper with his hand and I reach forward, grab the whole section, and throw it across the room. He's going to notice me now.

"If you don't want to talk to me, why did you marry me in the first place?"

He stares at me in disgust.

"You call this talking? Is this what you call the art of conversation?" He turns hyper-English. "I'm perfectly happy to talk to you in a calm, reasonable manner."

"No, you're not! I just tried and all you said is, 'I'm not having this conversation with you.' We are *never* having this conversation. We've *not* had more conversations than anyone I know! And why are you the arbiter of all that's calm and reasonable? Why can't we have an unreasonable conversation? Why can't we say anything we want?"

He's cold and calm, blinking at me with his pale blue eyes. "Like what?"

I start to feel foolish, awkward. And then it comes out—out of nowhere. "We never fuck."

The world melts; goes all Salvador Dalí. I've reached new heights of absurdity. He laughs at me in amazement. "What's that got to do with Clive or his TV show?"

I'm crazy—I sound crazy. But what I'm saying is true. I say it again.

"We never fuck."

He stops laughing quite suddenly, like Anthony Hopkins playing a psychopath. "So what. Plenty of people don't have sex all the time."

My breath is slowing and I'm calming down. I say another true thing. "You're not attracted to me."

He considers this. "You're a very attractive woman, Louise, when you're not behaving like a banshee." He shrugs his shoulders and employs his customer service voice, the one he uses to extract refunds from unwilling sales assistants. "I'm sorry that I disappoint you sexually. I obviously don't have the same sex drive you have." The word "sex" hisses with disdain.

I feel ashamed for being so base. Only, I'm tired of feeling ashamed.

I say one last true thing. "I don't think my sex drive's unusual."

He stands, walks to the door and smiles graciously. "Then it's me." He does a little half bow. "I am The Defective One."

He rises above me and my brute animal sex drive. I am, after all, common—from Pittsburgh, where people fuck and fight and fart. The Three F's.

"Where are you going?" I sound plaintive and hollow.

"I'm going into the garden. Unless there's anything else you'd like to say to me." He's playing the end of a Noel Coward scene. "I so enjoy these Sunday morning conversations."

Fuck Noel Coward.

"I think we should see a marriage counselor," I blurt out.

He looks me up and down. "Feel free."

"But we need to go together."

"Louise, you are the one with the problem. My marriage is fine."

Once again, I find I'm alone in the barren wasteland of the living room. The torn paper is the only evidence of life.

The words "If you are wise, then you will allow it to pass unnoticed" swim around and around in my brain. I'm not wise. But I don't know why.

I go into the bedroom and look out the window; he's pulling weeds in the back garden. How can he do that? How can he carry on with basic domestic tasks when everything between us is deteriorating? But he does.

I watch him rearranging the garbage bins at the back of the building in order of size and fullness. He does it carefully, earnestly. He needs to. He needs to believe it matters. That he's protecting us from all sorts of chaos—the chaos of dusty surfaces, the violence of unevenly stacked books, the irreparable damage of a fruit bowl found to contain an onion next to an apple. He's an errant knight, on a quest to save a lady who doesn't want to be saved. Who doesn't even want to be a lady and who'd rather sleep with the dragon than sleep with him.

And that's when it hits me. I go back to the moment when he comments on my weight loss. I freeze-frame it in my mind's eye. And there, there it is, clear as day. The truth is I don't want him to notice me, to cuddle me, or touch me, or say how pretty I am. I just want him to leave me alone.

After all that, I don't want to fuck him either.

We have both been blind.

I'm sitting on the edge of the biggest bed you can buy in the United Kingdom.

The zip has come undone, the beds are drifting and soon the walls of the bedroom will not be able to contain the sleeping figures that are floating apart.

In the weeks that follow, I become obsessed by Oliver Wendt, otherwise known as The Man Who Can See Me.

I spend inordinate amounts of time wandering around the theater on the off chance that I'll encounter him and then running away when I do. I find myself lurking, like a stalker, outside of his favorite pub, standing across the street in the darkness, glued to the spot by desperate, confused lust. The weird thing is (and I don't really get this at the time), is that the lust I feel is for myself—the self I see in his eyes. I don't really want to talk to him, or know him; I just want to be seen by him.

"Do those reports need to go downstairs? I'll take them."

"But, Louise, you've only just come back from there. We can take them down later."

"Oh, it's no trouble, no trouble at all."

And I'm off, roaming around the building like a creature from a fairy tale, doomed by some evil curse to wander the earth forever in search of her own reflection.

This continues for a while. We see each other, we stare at each other, and I run away. And then one day, when I absolutely can't stand it anymore, I invite myself out for a drink with him.

He's smoking in the foyer. It's the opening night of a new play and the revolve on the stage isn't working properly. He's got all the techys putting in overtime while he works his way through a pack of Marlboro Lights.

I'm meant to be gone. Or rather, I'm not even meant to be in today. But that's how it is for me during this time. I find myself "popping into work" for no reason—hanging about in the foyer, walking around the halls, possessed and saucer-eyed, one millimeter away from hysteria at all times.

I spot him and then race immediately to the Upper Circle Ladies and check my makeup. Then I check it again.

I take deep breaths, pray, and then saunter over to my Nemesis.

"Hey, how are you?"

What this costs me, you'll never know. My voice is about three octaves higher than normal and my hands are shaking. This doesn't prevent me, however, from imagining that I'm the sexiest, most alluring creature on the planet and that I'm in fact part of a living movie, complete with thrilling soundtrack, mood lighting, and a cracking script.

He eyes me in that way smokers do when they exhale, not quite winking, not quite frowning, just avoiding the stinging smoke of their own fags. "Great, Louise. What about you?"

Ah! He speaks! My heart convulses, palpitates, chokes on secondary smoke.

"I'm, well, . . . I'm thirsty," I rejoin, tossing my hair back. "That's how I am."

He stares at me like I'm demented. "Thirsty?"

I smile. How different it is when he looks at me like I'm demented than when my husband does!

"Yes," I persist. "Ever so thirsty. One might even say parched."

And then the penny drops, almost audibly. He laughs and swings the door open. We walk out in the cool evening air and cross the road to his favorite pub. He buys me a drink and we sit on dangerously high bar stools, attempting to make conversation.

Alas, every relationship has its Waterloo. Conversation proved to be ours.

It's difficult to have a conversation if your basic premise is not to reveal anything about yourself. He asks me a question, for example: where do I come from or what am I doing in London and I try, in the most charming and amusing way possible, not to tell him point blank that I'm married. I twist my hand around like a claw on the bar, trying to hide my wedding band. I don't know why I don't take it off. I guess I can't. It's as simple as that. So I sit there, with my hand in a casual fist, giggling maniacally and volleying each question with another one.

"So, how long have you been in London?"

"I don't know—ages. What's your favorite color?"

"My favorite color?"

(It's charming to be infantile . . . isn't it?)

He lights another cigarette. "Ah . . . well, that'll be green, I guess. What about you?"

"Hot pink and the color of gold sequins."

"That'll be gold, won't it?"

"Well, not really. Not flat gold. I only like sequined gold." Oh God, I'm trying *way* too hard. I shove the claw that passes for my hand into my hair and examine the bottles behind the bar like an alcoholic out of change. Please, please don't let there be a moment of silence! What can we talk about, what can we . . . "What about your father?"

He raises an eyebrow and gives me what I take to be the Look of Total Riveted Fascination. "What was he like?"

"Old. What about yours?"

That was quick.

"Honest," I say forlornly, caught off guard. "My father's a very honest man."

And because I've said something true, he looks at me with real interest.

"That's a good quality."

"Yes . . . I suppose it is." And I stare at my drink like it's a crystal ball, going to tell me my future.

We last about twenty minutes before Oliver excuses himself on the grounds that the opening night won't occur if he doesn't sort a few things out. Like the set.

We walk back as slowly as possible without actually stopping in the middle of the road.

"So, when can I buy you a real drink?" he ventures, squinting sideways at me through a stream of smoke.

"I'm . . . I'm not sure . . . ," I stammer.

Strange as it seems, I'm caught off guard. It's one thing for me to fantasize and project like a mad woman; it's quite another for the object of my delusions to respond. And besides, what am I doing? I can't make a date, I'm married! But there's another voice in my head, a soft, compelling voice whispering, "Hey! What's the problem? Chill out. It's not like you're sleeping with him . . . you're . . . you're just . . . having a drink, that's all. Right?"

And then I'm back in the movie again, trying my best to play the femme fatale.

"I think I'd like to go somewhere I've never been," I parry, smoldering at him from behind a sheaf of Veronica Lake hair.

The "Are you demented?" look is back.

"Well," he sounds irritated, "how am I meant to know where you've been?"

Good point.

I shrug my shoulders nonchalantly and walk straight into a restaurant placard. "Oh, Jesus! I'm so sorry! Fuck! What am I doing? I'm apologizing to a wooden sign!" He watches as I struggle to detach myself from the specials of the day. Once free, he takes my arm with the kind of solicitous authority usually reserved for the elderly and steers me back safely to the theater entrance.

"About that drink . . ." He waits, but I can't think. It has to be somewhere perfect, somewhere private, somewhere away from restaurant advertisments and people who know me . . .

He's starting to get restless.

"Why don't I give it some thought?" I suggest.

"Please do."

He smiles and with that disappears into the rapidly filling foyer. I stand transfixed on the front steps, my heart pounding, palms sweating. The crowd engulfs me, swirling around me like fast moving water around a stone in a brook.

I've done it. I've taken hold of my life and for better or worse, nothing will ever be the same again.

A week later, I drop a small note into Oliver Wendt's mailbox. In the bottom right-hand corner of an emerald green card I've written,

I've never been to the Ritz.

The days pass and I hear nothing.

Nothing at all.

I

❧

Ideal Wardrobe

For an Elegant Woman

9 A.M.   Tweed skirts in the brown autumn shades and harmonizing sweaters, worn under a fur coat of one of the casual varieties. Brown shoes with medium heels and a
capacious brown alligator bag. (A really elegant
woman never wears black in the morning.)

1 P.M.   A fur-trimmed suit in a plain colour (neither brown nor
black) and a matching fur hat. Underneath the jacket,
a harmonizing sweater, jersey blouse, or sleeveless dress.

3 P.M.   A wool dress in a becoming shade that matches or con-
trasts with: A pretty town coat in a vivid colour.

6 P.M.   A black wool dress, not very décolleté. It will take you
everywhere, from the bistro to the theatre, stopping en
route for all the informal dinner parties on your social
calendar.

7 P.M.   A black crepe dress, this one quite décolleté, for more
formal dinners and more elegant restaurants. A white
mink hat.

8 P.M.   *A matching coat and dress that is called a "cocktail ensemble" in Paris, but in reality is often far too dressy for the occasion, although perfect for theatre first nights and elegant black-tie dinner parties.*

10 P.M.   *A long formal evening dress that can be worn all the year round (which means you should avoid velvet and prints).*

9 A.M. I'm at the top of Whitehall, wearing a navy gabardine suit, with a brown V-neck knitted top from Kookai and a pair of black T-bar shoes. The Kookai top is beautifully formfitting but has a tendency to unravel under the arms. Must remember to keep my jacket on. Am popping into Sushi Express for my breakfast—a fruit smoothie and an order of green tea to take away. Part of my new regime. I will not eat sugar today. I will not. I buy an extra banana, just in case. The sun is blinding as I race across the street to catch the light. I'm good at running in high-heeled shoes now—I have to be. I've been promoted to manager in the box office and spend all day running up and down the stairs between the window in the lobby and the office upstairs. A bit of a wild-card candidate for the job, no one was more surprised than I was when I got it. It's been a huge boost to my self-confidence. And the constant activity is a godsend. My husband and I have, as far as I can tell, stopped talking. The new job makes it easier for us to pretend that we are too busy or just too tired to communicate. Neither of us is ready to hear what the other has to say.

1 P.M. I'm in the changing room of the gym, along with about thirty other women, all of whom have only an hour to squeeze themselves into their lycra ensembles, work themselves up into a sweat, shower, dry their hair, and tear back to

the office. Since I renewed my membership several months ago, I've managed, miraculously, to show up four times a week. Not since my dancing days have I pursued any form of fitness with this much success. And it's starting to show.

The gym locker room is also where you learn about the reality of other women's bodies and wardrobes. We all spend as much time surreptitiously examining each other as we do on the treadmill. Everyone freezes simultaneously as the tall, tanned blonde emerges from the shower. We pretend to be adjusting our hair but really . . . yes! She does have cellulite!

Life is full of surprises. Who would've guessed that the anchorwoman with the Armani suit and the mobile phone attached to her ear ("I'm at the gym! T-H-E G-Y-M!"), would wear dingy white M&S knickers with a black see-through bra? But the surprise transformation of the week goes to the mousy haired, be-fringed girl in the 1984 Laura Ashley floral ensemble who undresses to reveal a bright pink silk bra and knicker set with matching garter belt, stockings and a pair of legs that would make Ute Lemper weep. Even the tall blonde stands agape in the center of the shower room. I pull on a bright blue crop top, a matching pair of stretch trousers and some hideously expensive Nike trainers. I'm sure I burn more calories just trying to squeeze myself into this outfit than the whole workout put together.

3 P.M. I'm back in the office, showered, hair not quite dry (competition for the three blow dryers is fierce), and back in my navy suit. The only difference is, I've given up on my black T-bar shoes. There's only so long a woman can be expected to bounce around on the balls of her feet before someone has to die. The temperature has shot up and my jacket is hanging over the back of my chair, leaving the unraveling Kookai top in full view. I will repair it. I will. Tomorrow. In the meantime,

I'll just get rid of this stray thread that's hanging down . . . I watch with a strange sense of detachment as half the remaining sleeve comes undone in my hand.

I'm meant to be completing a weekly sales report but have hit my midafternoon slump. This is a biological glitch that renders me incredibly depressed between the hours of three and four o'clock each afternoon without fail. My theory is that I'm genetically programmed to have a nap at this time but unfortunately don't live in a climate that favors siestas. The consequences are dramatic. The will to live seeps away and instead of focusing on figures and performance breakdowns, I'm visualizing various methods of suicide. Dangling from a rope, passed out on a bed, floating in a stream. Or a drastic haircut.

The phone rings on the desk opposite, and as I scramble to get it, my foot catches on an invisible snag in the gray carpet tiles. My stockings run and I still manage to miss the call. Luckily, Colin puts the kettle on (he's intuitive in this area) and magics up a box of shortbread cookies. ("Two for the price of one, darling. Only *slightly* crushed.") I desperately grapple for my spare emergency banana and find it at the bottom of my handbag, beaten into a kind of brown pulp. Fuck it. Spirits rise with the sugar intake and Colin assures me that Sinéad O'Connor was a fluke; that most women would be unable to successfully carry off a shaved head with any real sense of style. Unless they had ambitions of a professional wrestling career.

6 P.M. never fails to bring with it an inevitable second wind. The malaise that immersed the office at 4:45—that hopeless hour when going home seems like just a cruel, unsubstantiated rumor—evaporates and at 5:55 is replaced by a carnival atmosphere. There's dancing, singing, the telling of jokes. Colleagues pat each other on the back and hold the door open

for one another as they run, laughing and singing, out of the office. The night shift takes over, looking like they've just been sentenced to life imprisonment. I've got just over an hour to go home and get changed before I'm due at the theater for the opening night of my husband's new play. He's having dinner after the show with his agent and the director and they expect me to be there, proud and supportive in my role as "the wife." I feel a headache coming on just thinking about it. I decide to take off my stockings, as the run is just too bad for public display, and force my swollen feet back inside the T-bar shoes. On goes the jacket and I'm tearing out the door, flapping my way down Whitehall towards home.

7 P.M. I've had a quick shower and am reapplying my makeup. In an effort to look striking and sophisticated (I was reading *Vogue* on the loo), I've penciled in my brows with kohl pencil and now look like Bert from *Sesame Street*. I try to compensate for my unibrow by applying a thick coat of red lipstick and before I know it, am a dead ringer for Bette Davis in *Whatever Happened to Baby Jane?* As I'm frantically wiping it all off with wads of toilet paper, it occurs to me that ten minutes before you're due somewhere is obviously a bad time to experiment with your look. I manage to tone my makeup down to a Joan Crawford level and am searching through my underwear drawer for a pair of matching hold ups. Will I ever get out of the habit of saving runned tights "just in case"? Finally locate matching pair and step into my new Little Black Dress, a strappy, short Karen Millen design in thick, black stretch satin, which was the very first purchase I made after my promotion. I'm Audrey in this dress and love it more than anything in the world. However, do NOT feel the same way about black T-bar shoes, as I slip them back on my aching feet. Grabbing a little black satin evening bag I found in the sales, I

try unsuccessfully to cram the entire contents of my purse inside and then relent, telling myself that it's OK, I probably won't need my address book, a needle and thread, and seven tampons for a single evening out. (My period isn't due for a week.) Force myself to make do with a lipstick, a compact, and my change purse, but not before doing a brief visualization exercise I learned from reading *Feel the Fear But Do It Anyway*. I'm only fifteen minutes late as I hail a cab to the theater.

8 P.M. I'm standing alone, like a total lemon at the theater bar when magically spot two old friends, Stephan and Carlos. Stephan's a set designer and Carlos works in the wig department of the RSC. They're buying and suddenly things start to look up. After all, I'm going to need a few drinks to make it through the entire evening as half of the happiest, nonspeaking couple on earth. The bell goes. Go on then, just one more.

God, that bartender is cute.

10 P.M. Supper with husband's agent and the director at the Ivy. A little bit tipsy. My husband is still not talking to me (this is Advanced Silence) but did rescue me from drowning in the tub. Don't normally bathe this much but seems I kept missing my mouth at dinner.

May go back to acting. Flirted all night with the director, who couldn't keep his eyes off me. Think I made quite an impression.

3 A.M. Wonder what Oliver Wendt is doing and who with.

J

❦

Jewellery

The contents of a woman's jewellery box are a chronicle of her past——more telling than her underwear drawer, bathroom cabinet or even the contents of her handbag. The story the jewellery box tells is a romance and hopefully for you, it is a grand and passionate one.

Jewellery is the only element of an ensemble whose sole purpose is elegance, and elegance in jewellery is a highly individual matter. It is therefore impossible to say that only a particular kind of jewellery should be worn. One thing however is certain: an elegant woman, even if she adores jewellery as much as I do, should never indulge her fancy to the point of resembling a Christmas tree dripping with ornaments.

Finally, a word to would be husbands: an engagement ring is often the only genuine jewel a woman owns, so please, invest in one of a respectable size. The shock of paying for a good quality ring will evaporate the instant you see your thrilled fiancée proudly displaying it to all of her friends and relations. And secondly, do not underestimate the advantages of buying only from the very best. A ring box from Cartier, Asprey, or Tiffany's will be prized almost as much as the ring itself. And this is one occasion where you do not want to be accused of economising!

*   *   *

I close the book and lean it softly against my chest. Imagine receiving a box from Cartier or Asprey! As for Tiffany's, I've never been in—not even to browse. I wonder what it looks like inside. Or what it's like to walk in on the arm of a man who loves you, knowing that when you come out, you'll be wearing a diamond ring or maybe a sapphire surrounded by brilliants. I gaze at my hand resting on the duvet and try to envisage a sparkling, bright diamond solitaire on my fourth finger. Closing one eye, I concentrate as hard as I can but still, all I see is the pink, slightly wrinkly flesh where my finger and knuckle meet.

I look over at my husband, who's reading in bed next to me and watch as he furiously gnaws away at a nonexistent hangnail on his thumb. He's reading the evening paper as if it's written in code, scowling as he diligently scours its pages for clues.

He never gave me an engagement ring.

It slipped his mind.

He had planned to ask me to marry him, but evidently in much the same way that you plan to keep a dental appointment. Later, he claimed not to know that when you propose, it's customary to present the woman with a ring.

I told myself at the time that we were beyond romantic gestures; unorthodox; unique. And we congratulated ourselves for not indulging in any of the common, more banal expressions of love. I even looked the word "romance" up in the dictionary once, I was so obsessed with justifying its absence from our relationship.

"A picturesque falsehood," I read out, closing the book triumphantly. "See, it's not real. Romance is a lie."

And he nodded sagely. How reassuring, to know the emptiness surrounding us is real.

But as I sit here, pretending I can see a diamond on my

bare finger, it occurs to me that intellect can be a terrible, deceptive thing.

I remember the day he asked me to marry him. We were in Paris in the middle of a heat wave. He'd just finished the run of a play where he was a dog, scrabbling around on all fours and had badly hurt his knee. He was limping around with a stick and I had a cold. The French love suppositories. All the cold medicines seemed to involve inserting something into your bottom, so I preferred to sniffle and sneeze as we stumbled around the great city, determined to absorb its beauty.

The relationship had come to a standstill several months ago. I knew he was going to propose because there was nowhere else for it to go and I was deeply irritated that he hadn't asked me yet. I was tired and ill and wanted to go back to the room, take off my dress and lie down. But I knew he was measuring each place we went as a potential setting for the proposal. So I stumbled on, pretending to find everything charming, lest my bad attitude spoil the moment and delay it further.

And I wore a dress because that's what you wore when someone proposed to you.

We drifted through the landscape of Paris, hoping to find on a bench or in a narrow alleyway the reason for our continued association. Eventually we came to sit under the shade of some trees in the Jardins du Luxembourg.

"You're not happy," he said at last.

"I'm afraid," I conceded.

He waited patiently in the stifling heat.

"Remember when we first met," I began, feeling a wave of nausea building, "and you had a . . . a friendship . . ."

He pressed his eyes closed against the burning sun. "That's over," he said. "You know that's over."

"Yes, but it's what's behind it that scares me."

He kept them closed. "There's nothing behind it, Louise. We've been all through this."

But it wouldn't go away; it was like a third person on the bench between us.

"I'm only saying, I mean, as a reflection of your true self . . . ," I persisted.

He opened his eyes. "There is no 'true self.' I am who I make myself. It was a normal friendship."

"But you had to break up with him. When we met, you broke up with him. Friends are pleased when you meet someone. They stick around, get to know them. You don't meet them in the park one wet Wednesday afternoon and quietly inform them that 'things have changed.' They don't disappear— not when they've been calling you every day for years . . ."

He grabbed my wrist. "What do you want from me? What is it that you actually want? Do you want me to pretend it never happened? Is that it?"

"No, but don't you understand? How do I know it won't happen again?" I tried to pull away, but he held on tightly.

"Because I won't let it. I just won't let it." His voice was defiant but his eyes looked exhausted, lost. "I promise you, Louise, I promise I won't let you down."

He let go and my arm dropped limply by my side. I stared at the sandy walkway. Everything inside me was telling me to leave, to walk away.

We're in Paris. It's romantic. A French family walks by, complete with small children and grandparents, as if they'd been cued in by an unseen director.

I say it quietly, but I say it. "What if that's your true nature. You cannot, no matter how hard you try, deny your true nature."

He rises slowly and holds out his hand. "I'm not going to have this conversation again. Either you accept me the way I am or not. It's up to you."

I get up. I tell myself I'm crazy, stupid. He loves me, doesn't he? He says the words, doesn't he? I have a cold; I'm being dramatic.

And I don't want to be alone.

We walk. We stumble on, into the heat. It never becomes more comfortable.

The next night he proposes to me in the middle of La Pont des Arts and I accept.

I close the book and look again at my husband. He's completing the crossword, methodically crossing out each clue as he goes, writing the answers in pen.

He has kept his promise; he has not let me down.

1. We've always lived comfortably, in the best neighbor-hoods, often within walking distance of the West End.
2. He's never been rude to me in public or, to the best of my knowledge, unfaithful.
3. He's looked after me, managing the household finances, taking care of me when I've been ill, constantly seeking to improve our home and the comfort of our living conditions.
4. He does the laundry. I regularly come home to find my clothes neatly folded and stacked on the bed.
5. When he's working in the West End, he picks up the Sunday papers outside Charing Cross on his way home on Saturday night so that we can stay up late and read them together.
6. We often go for long walks together late at night, all over London, when the city is transformed by stillness.

7. He's a good companion.
8. And he has brought me the perfect cup of tea every morning in bed for the past five years.

Who am I to say this isn't love?

❧

The first time I saw him, it was at the opening night party of *The Fourth of July*. It was my first big professional role and I was ecstatic with the feeling that I'd made it; I'd arrived. The audience had given us a standing ovation and everyone was certain the play would transfer into the West End. I was wearing my favorite red dress, a long swirling concoction of silk crepe that flowed and clung to the body. The lilting, pulsating rhythms of Latin music filled the house in Ladbroke Grove where we were celebrating, and some of the guys were mixing pitchers of margaritas in the kitchen. The rest of us were dancing on the patio, swaying and turning with our arms outstretched, laughing too loudly in the cool, early autumn air.

When he appeared, a gate crasher from another theater, tall and slender, with light hair and pale blue eyes, I barely noticed him. He wasn't my type. He was in a new play at the Albery and doing well for himself. But I had other plans. My live-in boyfriend had cheated on me a few months earlier. I ignored it at the time, but tonight, wearing my red dress and drinking too many margaritas, I was determined to pull.

I don't know how or why I came to be kissing him. But the next morning, nursing a violent hangover and lying very, very still on the cold, flat futon in the studio flat I shared with my cheating boyfriend, I realized I'd made a mistake.

I called to let him know I'd fucked up, that it was just something stupid and to laugh it off but he must've heard the confusion and fear in my voice. "Let's meet for a coffee" he said. "Tell me what's really bothering you. Maybe I can help."

And so we met in a little Polish tearoom off the Finchley Road, where they served lemon tea in glasses and the air was thick with the fug of goulash soup. It rained and we sat at a tiny corner table and he listened while I told him the whole, sordid tale of my unfaithful boyfriend. I apologized for "behaving badly," and he nodded and said it was all understandable under the circumstances. And then we walked, very slowly and for a long time through the quiet streets of West Hampstead. He told me he'd ring me again, to see how I was doing.

The next day we met in the outdoor café in Regent's Park. It was too cold to sit outside, but we did anyway. Moving indoors required more commitment than we were prepared to make, so we perched gingerly on the edge of the wooden benches, shivering. And again, I told him things I hadn't intended telling anyone and he listened. All the feelings that had been bottled up for the past six months came crashing forward and I didn't think I'd be able to bear it.

The day after that we met on the other side of Regent's Park and walked until we came to a street in Fitzrovia. He stopped and said, "This is where my flat is." I followed him up the winding stairs and we sat on a sofa in the front room. It was a tiny flat but everything was immaculate, spotless. It was so different from the studio I shared with my boyfriend, crammed full of books, papers, and clothes. There was space to breathe here, everything was visible. We talked and I cried and told him I didn't know what to do. He held me, and I stayed curled up in his arms for a very long time.

Then we went into his bedroom.

The bed was made so tightly, so perfectly, that there were

no creases anywhere. The books on the shelf were in alphabetical order. Everything was white—the bedclothes, the carpet, the bookshelf, the desk. He took out a volume of poems. We sat on the bed and he read to me "The Love Song of J. Alfred Prufrock." And when he finished, there were tears on his cheeks.

And there, in the clean, white, untouched room, we tore at each other's clothes, grabbing and pulling, twisting the perfect sheets, shattering the silence.

When it was over, we dressed again, quickly, without looking at one another, and walked back into the safe neutrality of the park.

And, there, under the sheltering boughs of a chestnut tree, an hour after we made love, he told me that he had been thinking . . . that when he had broken up with his previous girlfriend, it was because he suspected . . . that he was afraid he might be . . . well, that there might be something wrong with him.

We didn't speak for weeks after that. The play transferred into the West End. I left my boyfriend and slept on the sofa in a girlfriend's flat. But every day I thought of him, of how he'd listened to me and held me and how peaceful and serene the cool white world was where he lived.

And then he rang.

We met in the same outdoor café, only this time we moved inside where it was warm. After an embarrassed silence, I started to say, fumbling for words, how I thought we could probably still be friends, when he reached across the table and took hold of my hands.

His eyes were feverish and the words came spilling out on top of one another, in a disjointed torrent I struggled to keep up with. Never before had he been so animated, so passionate, or alive. He had just been afraid, he said, he could see that now. For so long—too long—he'd been on his own in the apartment, day after day, just waiting for something to happen, for some sign. He'd been overwhelmed by depression, suicidal even and hadn't known what to do. Which way to go. The men . . . he'd tried, but it had repulsed him. He'd been disgusted. Ashamed. But it had all been just a red herring, nothing more than a phantom. The truth, the real truth, was that he had just been afraid to love anyone.

But that was over.

Now he loved me.

He held my hands tighter. He'd tried to forget me, but he couldn't. I haunted him, whispered to him, thoughts of me swam around in his head day and night.

He pulled me closer and looked into my eyes. I'd never know how desperate, how lonely, how hopeless it had all been. Or how I'd changed him. Changed him to the very core.

Laughing, suddenly euphoric, he showered my face with kisses and told me how he knew, as soon as he saw me in my bright red dress, that I was the one for him. And how all he wanted to do was to help me, take care of me, look after me.

"Please, Louise! Rumple the bed sheets! Pile the sink high with dirty dishes! Hang your red dress from the center of the ceiling in my empty, cold bedroom! But most of all stay."

I smiled, leant forward and kissed him.

He seemed the kindest, most gentle person I had ever known.

"You look tired," Mrs. P. says, breaking the silence between us.

I stare up at the ceiling. "I'm not sleeping very well," I say at last.

She expects me to go on but I don't. I'm too tired to talk, too tired to do anything but curl up on the dreaded daybed and fall asleep. There's a tiny spider attempting to scale the elaborate molding in the corner; I watch as it slips back over the same few inches, again and again.

"Why do you think you're sleeping so badly?" Her voice is frustrated, tense. I feel for her, having to play such an active role in our session. She must've imagined herself as a kind of female Freud, curing patients of deep-seated traumas and neurosis. But instead she gets to watch me take a nap.

"My husband . . . we're . . ." I yawn and force my eyes to stay open. "We're falling apart. The whole thing is falling apart. And I can't sleep anymore when he's there."

"What does that mean? 'Falling apart'?"

I shift onto my side and pull my knees up towards my chest. I can't get comfortable. "It means the glue that used to stick us together isn't there anymore."

"And what glue is that?"

The answer flashes in my brain almost instantly, but I think a moment longer because it's not the one I'm expecting.

"Fear," I say.

"Fear of what?"

The spider tries again. And fails.

"Fear of being alone."

She crosses her legs. "And what's wrong with being alone?"

The spider has given up. I watch as it descends slowly from the ceiling on an invisible silk thread.

"I don't know. I used to think everything was wrong with being alone. That I would die, kind of literally implode with loneliness. But lately, lately I'm not so sure."

"Louise, do you love your husband?" Her voice is challenging, hard.

I'm quiet for a long time. A gust of wind blows through the

open window and the spider wavers, dangling precariously. It couldn't be more fragile.

"Love isn't the point. As a matter of fact, it only makes it more confusing. It's not a matter of loving or not loving. I've changed. And it isn't enough just to be safe anymore."

"And is that what you were before? Safe?"

"That's what I thought. But now I see that I was afraid." I close my eyes again; I'm getting a headache. "It's like that thing, that thing that when you know something, you can't ever go back and pretend you don't know it. You can never go back to the way you were before."

"But you can move forward," she reminds me.

Yes, I think. But at what cost?

Weeks later, I come home from work to find my husband sitting, still in his overcoat, on the living room sofa. He looks dreadful, as he has done for weeks. By some strange, sick law of nature, as I become more attractive, he declines. It's as if only one of us is allowed to be appealing at a time. His eyes are ringed with dark circles, his hair wild and unkempt and he seems to have forgotten that razors exist. He should be gone, at the theater getting ready to go on, but he's not. He's here instead.

"Oh!" I say when I see him sitting there, staring into the middle distance. "You'd better go hadn't you?"

But he just looks at me, like some feral animal that's been trapped in the house by accident.

I should feel concern, or worry but the truth is I'm more irritated than anything else. We have an unspoken agreement, an arrangement that each of us has been honoring for months now: I go to work in the day and he's gone in the evening when I get home. He's now on my time and I don't want him here.

But I sit down anyway, in the green chair, and wait.

"We need to talk," he says at last.

Here it is, the conversation we've been avoiding for months. I feel sick and yet strangely exhilarated, calm even. "Fine," I agree. "You start."

He stares at me for another long moment and when he speaks, his voice is accusatory. "You're different. You've changed. And I feel like I've done something wrong but I don't know what it is. What have I done wrong, Louise? What is it that I've done?"

I take a deep breath. "You're right; I have changed but it's all been good. Surely you can see that?"

"All I see is that you're more concerned with the way you look."

"But that's good. I look better than ever before—you should be proud of me."

"I liked you better before. You were easier to be around."

"You mean less demanding."

"I mean less vain," he contradicts. "Less self-obsessed."

It's starting to get ugly. I can feel myself balking against every word he speaks. It's hard to believe that this is the same man that only six months ago, I would've given my right arm to please.

"You know what? People are supposed to change," I remind him. "It's a good thing. You're just used to me not giving a shit what I look like. The truth is, you like me better when I'm depressed. Well, I don't want to be depressed anymore. I don't want to spend my whole life hiding and feeling ashamed and apologizing for myself. I have a right to look good and to be happy. And I have a right to change!" I'm shaking, my whole body quivering with the force of my declaration. "Anyway, the problem isn't about me changing. I think the real problem is that we don't really want the same things anymore."

"Like what?" He sounds crushed.

"Like . . . I don't know . . . everything. I mean, we're not going to have children, right? So what are we going to do? Just sit around in this flat of ours, hunting for the perfect lamp shade and growing old?"

"Is that really so bad?"

He just doesn't get it. "Yes! Yes, it is that bad! Can't you see that it's bad for us to be sitting around here like two pensioners with no surprises, no passion, no hope, just waiting to die? I mean, doesn't that strike you as bad?"

For a moment it looks as if he's going to cry and when he speaks, his voice is hoarse. "Is that really the way you see our life together? Is that really what you think? That we're like two old pensioners?"

I know I'm hurting him. But if we don't speak honestly now, we never will. "Yes, that's exactly what I think."

He sits, motionless, cradling his head in his hands. Silence stretches out before us, vast and insurmountable. Then suddenly, quite suddenly, he pulls himself onto his feet and I watch in horror as he crosses the floor and kneels in front of me.

"I should have done this earlier, Louise. I'm so sorry. I've been very selfish." He's looking up at me, his eyes two enormous pools. I feel sick.

He reaches in his pocket and pulls out a tiny, clear plastic bag.

"Perhaps we haven't been very passionate . . . I'm not very good at showing you how important you are to me. I'm sorry. I'd like to make it up to you." And he puts the little plastic bag into my lap.

There, floating amidst the emptiness, are three tiny colored stones. It's a surreal moment; I can't quite figure out how we went from discussing our life together to this bizarre, makeshift proposal.

"I got them from Hatton Garden. We can have them made into a ring."

I should say something—act surprised or pleased, but instead I just stare at the packet, unable to form any cohesive thought other than shock and dismay.

"Louise, I'm here . . . on my knees before you. I know we've been having difficulties. And . . ."

I have the uneasy feeling he's rehearsed this; he's looking down now, taking a pregnant pause.

"And I want you to have this, to know that I love you, that I'm sorry."

He looks up at me again.

It's my cue. My head is pounding; say something nice, something conciliatory, it screams at me. But when I speak, my voice is cold and flat.

"Exactly *what* do you want me to have? Some colored stones in a bag?"

He blinks at me.

"This isn't a ring, is it?"

"Yes, but . . . but it could be."

"But it isn't. What kind of stones are these?"

He shakes his head. "I don't know the names."

And then I find myself doing something very unexpected; I hand the bag back to him. "Why don't you get up," I say.

He stares at me in amazement. "Louise, please!"

"Please what?" I'm suddenly overwhelmingly angry. I want him off the floor. I don't want to be a part of this charade anymore. It's offensive. All of it; the stones, the speech. "Why are you doing this?" I demand. "Why are you even doing this now, after all this time?"

"I . . . I'm doing it because I don't want you to leave."

"Why?" I persist. "What difference does it make whether I stay or go?"

He just kneels there, staring at me.

"Be honest, you don't really want me, do you? I mean, it's not like you want to *touch* me, do you?"

"I do want to touch you," he says, his eyes not meeting mine.

"Then why don't you?"

But he just shakes his head, over and over.

And I snap.

"Why are you doing this?" I shout, my voice so loud and shrill it doesn't even sound like it's coming from me. "Just tell me! Say it! Why?"

"Because," he whispers, his hands trembling as they cover his face, "I cannot trust myself when you're gone."

My husband and I are having a "trial separation."

Colin is looking for someone to rent his spare room. I tell him that person is me and he blinks in surprise and asks, wide-eyed, if there's anything he can do. No, I say, there's nothing to be done. And of that I'm sure.

It's been months now—months of conversations, arguments, silences, tears. We have "given it one more week" again and again and again. It's like trying to amputate a limb with a spoon.

We make it to the end of the month, to the end of another excruciating month, and then I move out.

It's a Tuesday. My husband offers to help me pack my bags.

"I'm not going on holiday," I tell him, repulsed and amazed that he can imagine us standing side by side, taking things off of hangers and folding them into piles. He stares at me numbly.

"I'm leaving you," I explain, saying the words slowly and loudly, the way you speak to a deaf person. "This is me packing my bags and leaving you." But he just blinks.

"I'll pay for the cab," he says. He reaches for his wallet and examines the notes. I watch as he calculates in his head how much he can spare. He puts back the twenty for later. And I

want to hit him, to cry, to tear through the fabric of our life together like it's a badly painted backdrop and get to the point at
last. He fumbles. Pulls out a tenner. And we've been here before; we've been right here, in this same, exact spot for a very
long time.

I let him put the money on the table. I turn and walk into
the bedroom and take down my suitcase, the one I brought to
England when I thought I was going to be a famous actress,
and start filling it with clothes.

My husband goes out for a walk and when he comes back I'm
gone.

❧

Colin lives with his roommate Ria, a glassblower and
gallery manager, in South London, beyond the urban chic of
Brixton. Gone are the exclusive cafés and lunchtime concerts
of Westminster, replaced by the gaudy splendor of the
Streatham Mega Bowl and the late night Mecca Bingo parlor.

The cab driver helps me to unload my bags and haul them
up the front steps. I ring the bell and the door opens to reveal
Colin in his bathrobe, hair wet from the shower and Madonna
blaring in the background.

"I'm sorry, Col." I stare at the misshapen collection of bags,
suddenly too overwhelming and unwieldy to move. "What
am I doing? What have I done?"

He wraps an arm gently around my shoulders. "Come inside. Sit down. And I'll make us a nice, hot cup of tea."

K

❦

Knitwear

Few women can resist the temptation of a soft new pullover in a luscious shade, and how right they are! If you feel the cold, as I do, then it is really the only garment that will keep you comfortable and content from morning till night, in all kinds of seasons, in both the country and in town. The sweater is the grand-mère of the fashion world: warm, loving, and totally forgiving. (Unless, of course, you are afflicted with a very large bust. Then it is in your interest to stick to less clinging fabrics.)

Made from silk for the warmer days and of cashmere when it becomes bitter, a good sweater has no rival. And with a little care and attention, it will last years and years without the slightest sign of age. In these whirlwind times of changing fashions, it is reassuring to know that a camel or navy twin set will continue to be elegant for seasons to come. It is a perfect example of the modern trend towards ease and comfort.

During the first days at Colin's, I fall into a kind of stupor, going to work in a daze and returning to spend the evening rolled into a little ball on my bed, crying and staring at the ceiling. The garment of choice during this bleak period is, morbidly enough, a worn navy cashmere sweater of my husband's. For years I've had a clandestine relationship with this sweater, curling into its warm, forgiving softness like a child clings to a favorite blanket. I used to sneak it from his closet when he was out at the theater, racing to return it when I heard his key turn in the lock.

I hadn't intended to steal it and I'm not even sure why I did. It was draped over a chair in the corner of the bedroom and I just slipped it into my case along with the rest of my clothes. It's his favorite; it will be missed. And maybe that has something to do with it. Perhaps I'm waiting to see which one of us he wants back first.

Then the blue envelopes started to come, letters from my husband.

I'm sorry . . . I've failed you . . . so sorry.

They go on and on, saturated with regret and remorse but not one of them asking me to come home.

I had expected something more. A grand gesture: he'd appear in a cab in the middle of the night and insist upon taking me home. Or he might ambush me as I left the theater, his arms filled with roses. Part of me dreads the idea of spotting him, thin and haggard, lingering on a street corner, waiting for me. But I dread even more the empty corners that appear, with haunting regularity as the days go by, and the consciousness of the resigned ease with which he's let me go. The letters are not declarations of love or pleas for resolution or even promises for the future but persistent, miserable apologies to which there is really no reply. He's letting me know, in his own quiet way, that all the street corners will be empty from now on.

I sit in my room crying, choking and spluttering, rocking

back and forth, blowing my nose on roll after roll of toilet tissue. I cannot go back but I cannot bear to be where I am. Colin tries to coax me out with various culinary delights— nearly new bourbon biscuits, slightly crushed chocolate éclairs and chicken korma made fresh from a jar (special offer, two for the price of one). But I've lost my appetite. Instead, I stagger down to the Indian shop on the corner to buy single cans of spaghetti, eating them, more often than not, straight from the tin.

Even Ria, who's never met me before and who has more than enough reason to be wary of the obscene lack of mental health in her new roommate, makes a few tentative overtures. She offers to help me unpack my bags and make my bed up with some pretty linen and even lends me a delicate, 1930s lamp from her collection of prized objects. But it's no use. I don't want to unpack my bags. My bed is far too small to bother with pretty sheets and as for decorating the room, who cares. It's over. I'm finished. Over the years I've transformed from a budding, young actress into a bitter, disillusioned box office manager, selling tickets to plays I could have been in. I'm thirty-two years old, living in a broom cupboard with a theater queen and a spinster.

I take a few days off of work. And then a few more. When I do show up, eyes red and swollen from crying, I have the concentration of a three-year-old. The same things must be repeated three and four times before I can take them on board. I make mistakes. My colleagues cover for me, finally delegating simple, manual tasks for me to blunder instead. All decisions seem completely overwhelming, even simple ones, like what kind of sandwich to have for lunch. I sidestep this quandary by not eating at all. My weight plummets and I can't find the energy to wash my hair or organize clean shirts.

I wear the same dress day after day, like a uniform. But I don't care. All I want to do is go home, close my bedroom door, and fall asleep in the sweater that still smells of him, feels like him, reminds me of him.

And then, well into my third week of unbridled wretchedness, the sweater goes missing.

One morning it's where I left it in a loving, crumpled heap on the corner of my bed and by that afternoon, it's gone. I search frantically throughout the whole of my tiny room, flinging the contents out of my half-unpacked bags and tearing the sheets off my bed. Then I expand my hunt to the living room and its environs, overturning sofa cushions and rifling through the laundry basket. It isn't until I've exhausted every possibility and am bordering on hysteria that it occurs to me: I'm not dealing with a simple case of a misplaced sweater, I'm dealing with a kidnapping.

Suspiciously, both of my new roommates have retired early for the night. I knock on Colin's door first.

"It wasn't me!" he shouts over his new Robbie Williams CD.

"But you know about it, you traitor!" I rage, stamping down the hall to pound on Ria's door.

"Ria, I believe you have something that belongs to me and I want it back!"

A tiny, sullen voice answers firmly, "No."

I'm flabbergasted. "What do you mean 'No'! That's *my* sweater! You have to return it!"

"No. It's bad for house morale."

Now I'm stunned. "You cheeky little fart! How can it be bad for house morale? It's got nothing to do with house morale!" I rattle the doorknob threateningly.

She opens the door a crack. Five feet tall in her stocking feet,

Ria peers at me like a mischievous elf. "It has everything to do with house morale when one person has completely given up even trying to pull themselves together."

Colin's head pops out from behind his door too. "She has a point, Louie."

It's more than I can bear. My eyes sting and my throat's so tight I can hardly breathe. "I don't want to discuss it. Just give it back to me. I'm not in the mood for jokes."

Ria takes my hand. "But darling, believe me, this . . . this . . . overindulgence is not the way to mend a broken heart. You're doing yourself more harm than good."

I pull my hand away. "What does it matter what I do, as long as I'm quiet and pay my rent? What difference could it possibly make to you! Why should you care, anyway?"

"Louise . . ." She's taken aback but I can't help myself.

"Don't! Don't even pretend you care about what happens to me! Do you realize . . . have you even *noticed* that my own husband hasn't rung once since I arrived? Do you know what that means? Do you have any *idea*?"

"Honey, I'm sorry—"

"He doesn't want me back!" I point out to her, tears rolling down my face. "He doesn't even want the fucking sweater back!"

I run into my room and slam the door. I'm acting like a child, throwing a temper tantrum. Shocked as I am at the violence of my reaction, any shred of self control has disappeared. I curl up on the bed, sobbing pathetically into my pillow, beating my fists into the mattress. I'm as powerless and impotent as a child.

Suddenly, I'm seized by an overwhelming sense of déjà vu. And memory from long ago.

This isn't the first time I've stolen a sweater.

The first one was my father's—an ancient moss green pullover of his which hung in the laundry room by the garage. He wore it when doing chores, but in its heyday, it had been to countless fraternity parties and dates during his college years. It was his constant companion during the long nights of studying for law school and the more it deteriorated, the more he loved it. When my mother finally exiled it from his daily wardrobe, it lingered on, waiting patiently for him, like a once fine show dog grown old in all its shabby, soft splendor.

The most enduring image I have of my father is of distraction. His mind was always elsewhere. A whirlwind of activity, he could lose weight just getting dressed in the morning. "I have a list of things to do today" was his constant refrain. "A list of things to do." And he'd be off. He'd set himself heroic, impossible tasks to accomplish. "I'll rewire the house by dinner time" (my father was not an electrician). Or "I'm sure there's a way of building an indoor pool by yourself." And then he'd disappear. There was always one more job that had to be done, some final thing that needed urgent attention, one more essential bit of home improvement that absolutely must be completed by dusk. With only his faithful green sweater to keep him warm, he'd vanish into the sunset, never to be seen again, lost in a blur of perpetual motion.

It wasn't easy to get my father's attention, but you could steal his sweater if you were desperate.

Trouble is, we were all desperate and the competition for that sweater was fierce.

Traditionally, my mother had first dibs. But she had other, more effective ammunition in her armory. She had perfected a fail proof technique to grab my father's attention that the rest of us could only marvel at. Since my father loved to fix things, she'd deduced that the best way to secure his attention was to be broken. Accordingly, she suffered from strange, debilitating headaches that could strike without a moment's warning and last anywhere from twenty minutes to two weeks, as required. It was genius. If he was going to be distracted, he could be distracted with her. As a consequence, she pretty much had a copyright on any form of illness in our family. Occasionally my brother or sister would do a weak imitation, a kind of tribute to the master, but it's hard to compete with someone who isn't afraid to pass out.

Effective as it was, it had its downside. By the year I turned seventeen, my mother got fed up with the invalid routine. It must have dawned on her that she was worth more and that made her angry. So angry that she stopped talking to my father altogether. It was known as the Year of Silence.

It was a dismal time aggravated by their refusal to admit it was happening.

"Mom, why are you and Dad not talking?"

"We are talking. We just don't have anything to say."

His voice was on a frequency she no longer registered. Anger hung over the household like a thunderstorm that refused to break, the pressure building day by day. My father still fixed things, probably even more so now that he didn't have all the diversions of conversation, but my mother greeted each accomplishment with sphinxlike indifference. We were all horrified to see how easy it was to vanish from her affections. The invisible man had finally disappeared altogether.

During this time, my Dad and I became friends. We drove into school together in the mornings and there, in the sanctuary of the car, he listened to my endless Bowie compilation tapes and quizzed me about my studies. When I read Dickens, he bought a volume and read it too. And that's when I started to wear the moss green sweater by the door.

One day I came home from school with it on and my mother saw me.

"Don't wear that again," she warned. She had a way of saying things.

I tossed my hair out of my heavily lined eyes. "Why not?" I challenged.

My mother said nothing. Her silence could spill out in all directions.

"What difference does it make to you, Mom," I persisted. "It's not like you wear it anymore."

She gave me a look. "Just don't."

The next day I wore it again.

This went on for some weeks. My mother warned me. I ignored her. My father was nowhere to be seen.

And then, on my seventeenth birthday, I came home from school with my father and my best friend. My mother was standing in the kitchen with a birthday cake she'd picked up on her way home from work and as I walked in, her face fell. There I was, holding my father's hand, laughing and wearing the sweater. She brushed past my father, grabbed my arm, her fingernails digging into my flesh, and dragged me into the hall.

"That doesn't belong to you!" she hissed, barely able to control the venom in her voice. "Do you understand me? *That doesn't belong to you!*" She stared at me, a strange, fierce stare. At last she let go of my arm.

I didn't wear the sweater after that. It went back on its hook in the laundry room and hung there uneventfully for several months.

Then one spring afternoon, I noticed my mother wearing it while she and my dad washed the car. My father was vacuuming the interior, all his attention on the task in hand, and my mother was emptying out a pail of dirty, black water. To any-one else they looked like a normal couple engaging in a tradi-tional Sunday afternoon chore. But I saw a different picture.

My mother had given up. The Year of Silence had failed. My father probably didn't even notice she'd nicked the sweater, he was so intent on completing his list of things to do. But she was back to stealing what she could from him—moments of com-panionship and the intimacy of the sweater.

She was right; it didn't belong to me. Things you have to steal never do.

Now the sun is setting outside. I sit up on my bed and blow my nose. When I open my bedroom door folded there neatly on the floor, is the navy blue sweater.

Stepping over it, I walk into the living room, where Colin and Ria are watching a late night chat show about royal impersonators. Colin mutes the sound and they both look up at me.

"I'm sorry," I begin. "You were right about the . . . the sweater thing . . . it isn't helping." I'm staring at my shoes. I've never had to apologize as an adult for having a temper tantrum before. It's much harder and more humbling than I thought. "The truth is, I'm not very good at being on my own . . ." Even as I say it, this seems like the understatement of the year, "I don't really know how to . . . you know, do it."

For a moment, I think they're going to laugh. And then Colin reaches out and takes my hand.

"None of us do. But you're not alone, Ouise. We're here and we've been where you are now. Two years ago when Alan left me, all I wanted to do was open a vein."

"And believe it or not, I was actually engaged at one time," Ria adds quietly.

I look at her in surprise. Tiny, capable, emotionally concise,

Ria seems above the messy realm of failed relationships. "And what did you do when it was over?" I ask. It's almost impossible to imagine her wading through the same histrionic wreckage I'm having such difficulty navigating.

She smiles at Col. "I cried, like you. And then I came here, like you. I knew Colin through a friend of a friend and when Alan left, he needed a roommate. The rest is history."

Colin gives my hand a little squeeze. "Welcome to Mother Riley's Home for Wayward Women. It gets better, kid. Believe me. The trick is to stay in the game long enough to be around when the good stuff starts happening again. You'll see. Suit up and show up. Even if you feel like the whole world can see that you're made of little pieces, badly glued together."

Ria nods. "And, when in doubt, bathe."

And so, in the absence of any direction of my own, I take their advice.

Ria runs me a tub with lavender oil in it while Colin grills us up some sausages and mashes potatoes. He and Ria argue over which CD to listen to (*The Goldberg Variations* vs. *Massive Club Hits Volume 2*) and the Bach wins, but only on account of me being suicidal. Colin sets the table with the mismatched silverware and china his favorite grandmother left him when she died. And while I bathe, Ria makes my bed with the pretty linen sheets she offered earlier and even begins to hang up some of my clothes. When I emerge, freshly scrubbed in my bathrobe, they both applaud.

That night the bed seems softer and more comfortable than before, the street outside more tranquil. Moonlight shines through the narrow slats of the venetian blind, forming little rectangles of pale light on the carpet and the gentle rustling of the wind through the leaves is the only sound to be heard. I fell into a heavy sleep, no doubt induced by the potent combination of a hot bath and sausages, and when I wake up, I feel oddly refreshed, despite the constant, aching heaviness in my heart. After ironing a shirt, I put on a clean trouser suit and catch the bus into work with Colin on time. I may still feel like a hollow shell but at least I don't look like one.

A week later, I post the sweater back to my husband with a brief note.

I took this by mistake. Sorry for the inconvenience.

As comforting as it's been, I don't want it anymore.
After all, it never really belonged to me.

I sit, very deliberately, on the edge of the daybed in my therapist's office. She's upped my sessions since I left my husband and the last few times I've simply refused to engage in the conversation about lying down. I've decided there's nothing wrong with wanting to sit up and am tired of wasting sessions talking about it. I find my decision liberating but there are consequences, ripples in the dynamic of the relationship that all have to do with status.

Mrs. P. closes the door and sits down. She waits for me to lie down and I don't. I smile at her but she doesn't smile back. Instead, she looks at my shoes.

"Those shoes are very high," she says. I'm wearing the pair of black suede T-bar shoes from Bertie. They are high, but also very sexy.

"Yes, that's true."

She can't take her eyes off these shoes. I cross my legs and one foot dangles elegantly, making my ankle seem fragile and tiny. I love it, but Mrs. P. seems disturbed.

"They must be very hard to walk in," she adds.

"They're fine once you get used to them, not nearly as treacherous as they seem. But no, they're not really walking shoes," I laugh. Her smile is tense. Why are we talking about shoes?

Of course, I can't help but look at her shoes now. They're from Marks & Spencer, the kind you try on while you're nipping in to buy preshelled peas. They're flat and beige with a crepe sole. She catches my eye and shifts her legs defensively.

"Your fashion sense has changed dramatically," she concludes.

"I think that's a good thing."

She peers at me over her glasses.

"I'm dressing more like a confident woman," I explain.

"And how does a confident woman dress?" Her voice is challenging.

"Like she knows she's a woman and she likes it. Like she expects people to notice her." I smooth a crease out of my suit skirt. "Also, I have a more demanding job now," I remind her, "and I'm required to look a bit more professional."

"Yes." She nods her head but gives the impression of being somehow unconvinced. What am I trying to convince her of?

"So why didn't you dress 'like a confident woman' before?"

"Because I wasn't confident, I suppose. And there was no one there to notice anyway." We've been down this road before and I don't like it. Automatically my eyes scan around for the tissues. There they are on the faux mahogany coffee table; all I need to do is reach across. How handy. Do they teach that at psychiatry school—where to place the tissues? If they're too close, is that considered enabling?

"What about your husband?" She's staring at me but I can't decipher the look. It's neither kind nor indifferent. I feel a mass of pressure building in my chest, tearing at my throat. I swallow, breathe, and then I say it out loud to another person for the first time.

"My husband is gay."

It comes out sounding like a very mundane fact, like I've

said "I'll have some chips." This strikes me as odd and I find myself flashing her this funny, little smile, a kind of awkward, half smirk. I know it's inappropriate, but knowing that only seems to fuel it. I try to will the corner of my mouth down with some success but it pops up again, this time accompanied by a little fart of a laugh. My hand shoots up instantly to cover my mouth but it's too late. The smirk explodes into a fit of giggles, hysterical and oddly hyena-like.

Mrs. P. stares at me impassively. She reminds me of every nun who ever taught me at school. "Louise," her voice is stone cold sober, "why are you laughing?"

I'm six again, in church.

"I'm not," I say, stupidly, pressing my hand into my mouth.

"Yes, you are."

"No, not anymore." I straighten up. Think sad thoughts, car crashes, dead parents. Dead parents, dead parents, dead parents.

"Louise . . ."

Oh fuck! My face explodes again and I throw myself into a ball on the daybed. "Excuse me," I stammer.

"Louise . . ."

I'm making noises I've never even heard before.

"Louise!"

"Yes?"

"Why are you laughing?"

I manage to lift my head up. "Wouldn't you?" I whisper hoarsely.

"Wouldn't I what, Louise?"

The temperature seems to have plummeted ten degrees in the last second. I feel small and cold; my voice sounds like a child's. "Laugh if you married a gay man."

The silence that follows is crushing; it's the silence of my childhood, my mother's silence, which isn't silence at all, but the howling vacuum of the absence of response.

She's looking at me again with that look I can't quite get and then she says, "No. I don't think I would."

The light has drained from the sky. My face is wet and my eyes stinging. "Try it," I mumble, dabbing my eyes with one of the recycled tissues. "It's hysterical."

"What makes you think your husband is gay?" she asks.

I'm tired. I want to go home. "He told me. He said he thought he was gay, or at best bisexual when we met."

I'm leaving here and going straight to the off-license.

"But that does not mean he's gay."

I've got mascara in my eyes and it's burning. Am I deaf? "Pardon?"

"I said," she repeats, "that it doesn't mean he's gay."

Oh.

"What does it mean then?"

"Well"—she's the one crossing her legs now—"it means that he's questioning his sexuality, what it means to be a man. It does not mean he's gay."

Wait a minute.

"I'm just telling you what he told me. Don't you think he knows if he's gay or not? Also, we don't fuck. Don't you think that's significant?"

"There are many reasons why sexual relations cease in married couples." She adjusts her glasses and cocks her head to one side. "Why do you think they've stopped?"

"Well"—I cock my head too—"I think they've stopped because my husband is gay and because he's not interested. Let's face it, if you want to do something, you usually find a way of doing it. We don't fuck because we don't want to, it's as simple as that."

She arches an eyebrow. "So you don't want to fuck either."

"Being rejected twenty-four hours a day is not an aphrodisiac. It's humiliating." And then I add, somewhat defensively, "There's nothing wrong with me."

She cocks her head the other way, like a parrot. "And yet you claim to have married a gay man."

"Yeah, well, apart from that." What is it with her? This isn't at all what I expected. I feel like I've fallen into an episode of *Perry Mason.* "And I'm not *claiming*, I'm telling you what I know to be true."

She's looking at me over her glasses again.

"Look," I continue, "he doesn't want to be gay, it's damned inconvenient for him—he's a very conservative guy, from a very conservative family. And I come along and we fuck and he tells me this thing and I'm so crazy with fear of being alone and I say, 'No, you're not. Look, I've fixed you.' And he loves that because that's his problem solved and we get married and someone's got to be crazy because you can't marry a straight woman to a gay man without someone going mad, so it gets to be me. Get it?"

She says nothing.

I hate her.

"Well, I do. And that's something."

"You seem angry," she observes.

I'm clutching handfuls of chenille throw in both fists. "Angry? Yeah, just slightly. Just slightly pissed off."

She removes a piece of lint from her skirt. "And why do you think that is?"

I can't believe her. I want to throw things, to rip those lousy pictures off the wall and smash them into her face. "Why? Haven't you heard a thing I've said? *I'm married to a gay man!*"

She considers this. "That's your perception of the situation."

I can't stand it. "What does that mean, 'my perception'? You know what, it's a lot more than my perception, it's my *experience*—my hard-earned experience of the situation, whether you believe it or not. I'M NOT CRAZY! My experiences are real. I don't need you or anyone else to verify them for me. If ever I was crazy, it was when I believed that someone like you, with your . . . your incredible mediocrity, could help me!"

I'm on my feet.

"Anger can be very healthy," she says.

"Fuck you," I say, putting on my coat.

Her kids' university fees are walking out the door. She stands too. "I think we're making real progress, Louise. But you may be feeling a little unsupported at the moment and we should think about increasing your sessions."

I turn and take her hand in mine. We've never touched before; I feel her recoil but don't care. "Thank you for all your help. Extra sessions won't be necessary. You've taught me that my biggest mistake is giving my power away to people who haven't got a fucking clue."

I let go of her hand and it drops limply by her side.

She's speechless. Only she manages to talk anyway. "Louise, what are you doing? You can't finish your therapy just like that! We should discuss this over a series of sessions . . . we need to resolve the relationship . . ."

I feel sorry for her; she's pathetic.

"No, no we don't. We don't need to talk, we don't need to

discuss, or resolve. Send me a bill. Buy yourself a decent pair of shoes. Do something for a change. Talk is cheap."

I open the door.

And walk through it.

Why is it easier to walk away in high heels?

L

❧

Lingerie

The number of articles worn by a fashionable woman has considerably diminished since the beginning of the century. However, even though a woman's lingerie may be reduced to two pieces, they should at least be matching. It is the height of negligence to wear a white brassiere with a black girdle, or the reverse. Bright-coloured undergarments are charming, but of course can only be worn under dresses which are opaque or dark. In the summer, it is preferable to stick to white. If you are extremely refined and rich, your underclothes might match the colour of your outer ensemble.

Women are making a mistake in neglecting this potential added attraction to their charms. In short: when you dress, think always that later on you will be undressing and in front of whom. After all, nothing betrays a woman more than her lingerie; it is infinitely more revealing than a thousand hours spent on a psychiatrist's couch.

One final word: this is not an area in which you throw discretion to the wind. Do not confuse beautiful lingerie, the kind that supports well and remains fresh, with the cheap, vulgar stuff of men's magazines. Fascinating? I'm certain. But elegant it is NOT. A man likes to think that his wife is attractive and dis-

*cerning even when he is not looking, and surely, that is the image
you want him to have at all times and the one that will excite his
deepest admiration.*

One day, after I'd hung out my washing on the clothes-drying
rack in the kitchen, Ria takes me aside.

"Louise, what are these?" She points to a pair of ancient
Sloggi briefs that are clinging in gray exhausted resignation to
the line. (No matter how many I toss out, The Curse of The
Dingy Knicker haunts me, mysteriously refilling my drawers
with shabby underwear.)

Not since my early childhood, when I was young enough to
wet my pants, has anyone called such dramatic attention to my
knickers. I look them over closely.

"Knickers?" I offer, hesitantly. (Even I have to question
their identity.)

"No," she says firmly, taking me by the hand. "Those are
not knickers. Come with me, I want to show you something."

And she leads me into her room—a sanctuary not to be violated for anything less than fire, burglary, or extreme acts of
God. Within its walls she's created the most wonderful of girly
havens. Her bed is antique mahogany, covered in a collection
of tapestry cushions and swathes of fabric she's gleaned from
markets all over London. The walls are covered with photographs and original paintings, and everywhere there are objects chosen to entice and delight—milky bone china cups,
slender handblown champagne flutes, printed silk scarves,
satin Emma Hope slippers, piles of multicolored hat boxes,
and stacks of art books upon which she's placed scented candles and fresh flowers. The window box is planted with a vast
collection of herbs and flowers that perfume the air through

the enormous sash window. And, although it's a small room, Ria has managed by a thousand clever touches to pay tribute to each of the senses which have been deprived during the other ten hours of the day.

I watch as she kneels by the bed and pulls out a flat pink box tied with a black silk ribbon from Agent Provocateur.

"These," she says opening the box carefully, "are knickers."

And there, wrapped in gauzy tissue paper, lie a black lace bra and panty set, hand embroidered throughout with the tiniest, most delicate scarlet poppies. The poppies, flowers of intoxication, of vibrant sensuality, are so minuscule, so exquisitely, mind-achingly small, that they're nothing but a whispered double entendre, a knowing little wink of a sexual joke. They glow in luminous silk thread against the inky, flat blackness of the hand finished lace, weaving their way sinuously around the curve of each breast and fanning outward, almost sprouting from the crotch of the panties. Here is lingerie which is cunningly, knowingly erotic, with or without the company of a man.

We worship in silence for a moment.

"Do you actually *wear* those?" I whisper. (I don't know why I'm whispering; maybe because I've never had another woman show me her underwear before.)

"No." She places the lid back on the box and carefully reties the ribbon. "I mean, I hope to someday."

I'm fascinated. "Did you buy them for yourself?"

She blushes. "No, someone bought them for me." She says it with such finality that I know it's pointless to ask who. "But in a way," she continues quickly, "that's not the point. Of course, not every pair of knickers is going to be gorgeous—you wouldn't even want that. But . . ."—and here she looks me sternly in the eye—"everything you own should do its job with some semblance of grace and dignity. Underwear isn't just underwear, Louise; it's the true garment of your secret sexual self. And nasty knickers completely sabotage your sexual self esteem."

I nod solemnly and try to figure out why my mother didn't initiate me into these feminine mysteries years ago. Then I recall the state of her underwear drawer.

"You have seen greatness," Ria smiles. "Now please, go and buy some proper pants."

We walk back into the kitchen to make dinner and I watch in wonder as she unpacks her groceries: tuna steaks she'd selected from the fishmonger, new potatoes authentically covered in black Jersey dirt, fresh mint, fragrant and soft, and perfect raspberries for the dressing on her salad. Ria never does bulk shops; she only buys food on the day, depending on her mood. Preparing each course languidly, in a kind of meditative state, she arranges her plate with careful aesthetic consideration.

Everything is specific and sacred in Ria's world. That's the mark of a true artist.

The most remarkable thing is she's only cooking for herself. I can imagine going to such trouble for a dinner party or a special occasion but just for me . . . ?

I reach for another tin of Safeway's own brand of ravioli and look up at the ancient Victorian drying rack on the ceiling and the worn collection of undergarments that normally fill my lingerie drawer. I can only describe them as "Catholic knickers," that is, garments specially designed to repel the lustful advances of the opposite sex. Ria's right—I can't possibly continue to wear them.

I think of Madame Dariaux, and her enigmatic advice fills my mind: "When you dress, think always that later on you will be undressing and in front of whom."

Undressing. With my husband, that always meant changing into my nightgown in the bathroom and scuttling to bed with the lights out. I close my eyes for a moment and try to imagine slowly undressing in front of Oliver Wendt, his dark eyes watching me steadily through a cloud of silver smoke. But before I know it, the fantasy short-circuits and I'm back in the bathroom again in my Snoopy nightshirt.

Right. Actions speak louder than words. I reel the drying rack down from the ceiling, pull the offending articles off the line, and stuff them into the waste bin. There's no way I'm undressing in front of Oliver Wendt in a pair of gray Sloggi panties.

The next day, I head off for Agent Provocateur, in search of a new, improved sexual identity and a decent bra. It proves much more difficult than I imagined.

The shop is all hot pink and black lace—a tongue in cheek version of a naughty lingerie store. The girls behind the counter are voluptuous, sexy and indifferent, their blouses unbuttoned to expose the curves of their ample bosoms, and the gasping vocals of "Je t'aime" play in the background. Gingerly, I sift through scraps of sheer lace and satin floating on pink silk hangers—tiny slips in pastel candy colors with white maribou trim and matching G-strings, saucy lace bras and suspender belts, boned bustiers that finish just below the breasts, French knickers and sheer peekaboo bras. Under the pink glow of the lights, everything has a slightly sinister, Barbie-esque feel to it. I don't know when Ria received the embroidered set she showed me, but they're gone now. I contemplate a fairly conservative silk camisole and knicker set but cannot bring myself to try them on. The truth is, just looking at it makes me feel shy and awkward, let alone wearing it. After half an hour of loitering about like a dirty old man in a video shop, I leave with nothing.

Walking across Soho, I try to recall the last time I had sex and draw a blank. Standing stock still in the center of Soho Square, I really, *really* concentrate and still nothing. If this isn't bad enough, I expand the field to include "even with myself" and my memory remains a flat, empty screen. Apart from my childish fantasies about Oliver Wendt, which always end in a kind of slow fade, Vaseline kiss, I'm nothing more than a kind of secondhand virgin. A prude. Frigid.

Depressing as this is (and it is deeply depressing), I'm faced with an even more pressing problem: I've chucked away all my knickers.

There's nothing for it. Having failed to identify my sexual self at Agent Provocateur, I have no alternative. Let's face it, when your secret sexual self resides at Marks & Spencer, things are looking pretty grim.

I'm dragging myself across town to Marks when the sky begins to darken ominously. I quicken my pace. When the raindrops harden into a torrent of hailstones, I dodge into a doorway for cover. After standing there for several minutes, wincing and pressing myself against the window for protection, I notice that the shop is none other than La Perla.

Despite being convinced that my destiny now lies firmly within the walls of a convent, I go in.

Now this is lingerie of a completely different class. There's nothing seedy or vulgar here. The shop itself has the bright, golden sheen of a very expensive pearl, with creamy white walls and pale marble floors. La Perla carries no peekaboo bras or crotchless panties and not a hint of black lace or marabou in sight. This is the genuine article. Luxurious lingerie that's attractive and comfortable enough to wear every day—if only you could afford it.

A man and a woman are shopping together. They're a

handsome couple, youngish and probably Italian, both beautifully dressed in the kind of flawless, casual tailoring the Italians excel at. He's selecting various panties for her to try on: silk G-strings, hipsters, and the tiniest of thongs, while she's tossing her long, dark hair and looking rather bored, as if they do this every day and she'd much rather be at home, watching TV. I feel slightly voyeuristic watching them shop but still make a mental note of each item he selects. Is this what men like?

But you can't expect to walk into a shop like La Perla and just browse. Moments after I step across the threshold, a saleswoman descends upon me. Disturbingly, she's the very image of Madame Dariaux on the back of my book, with the same aristocratic nose, imperious gaze, and sculptural Margaret Thatcher hairstyle. She clears her throat and looks down at me while I stand, gaping up at her.

"You look as though you may need some help." She speaks slowly and carefully, as if she's weighing even these simple words.

I cannot get over the resemblance. "I . . . yes . . . I need some new knickers, ah, I mean lingerie," I stumble, "and I can't decide which ones. . . ."

Before I know it, she's got her arms round my chest and is measuring me.

"You are a thirty-two B and"—she looks me up and down—"I'd say a size ten should be adequate below. What would you like them for? Are they to go with a specific outfit? A strapless dress, perhaps?"

"No, no, just for real life."

"Well then, white is best, I think." And she points me away from the exotic silks the Italians are admiring and in the direction of a distinctly modest range.

I'm back where I started, but at five times the price. I follow her anyway and she hands me a white bra and a pair of briefs. "Would you like to try them on?" she asks.

Oh, hell, why not? "Yes. Fine."

She shows me into a changing cubicle the size of my bedroom, complete with a little white velvet settee and soft, amber lighting.

"See how you get on," she says, closing the curtain brusquely.

Just being in the changing room is soothing and relaxing. I sit down on the settee and peel off my coat, shaking the rain from my hair. Then I slip off my shoes and begin to undress. The La Perla pieces fit well, smooth and seamless, and have an attractive clean shape, with tasteful, lace detailing. They're sleek and figure enhancing. But are they sexy?

I turn and look at the back view. No problems there. I do a little twirl. Very nice really. I shorten one of the bra straps. Stroking the smooth silk of the cups, I adjust my breasts so that they sit a little bit higher and smile approvingly at my reflection. And that's when I notice that the curtain hasn't quite closed and the handsome Italian is watching me, quite unashamedly, while he waits for his wife to emerge.

I see him and he sees me. However, he doesn't move or look away. Instead, he smiles very slowly and gives me the slightest nod. His wife is calling him, and he answers quite calmly, without averting his gaze.

My heart is pounding, I feel flushed and at the same time unusually languid. My conscious mind protests "How dare he!" but there's another, much more mischievous side that's secretly excited and thrilled. There's a rattle of the curtain and the saleswoman clears her throat outside. "What do you think?"

"Fine," I say, my voice much softer and deeper than normal. She pokes her head round the corner.

"Um," she nods approvingly. "Perfect. How many would you like?"

"Well . . ." I look back in the mirror.

The Italian has gone.

I buy three sets in white, two in nude, and two in black. I'm overdrawn for a month, but it's worth it.

I have, at long last, found my secret sexual self and she's a little naughtier and a great deal more expensive than I anticipated.

Now when I'm dressing, I'm only too happy to think that later on, I'll be undressing. The only question that remains is, in front of whom?

M

❧

Makeup

Ah! Wouldn't it be marvellous if none of us needed it? But, alas, while some beauties are born, most of us are made. Makeup is a kind of clothing for the face, and in the city a woman would no more think of showing herself without makeup than she would care to walk down the street completely undressed. Nothing is more effective for brightening a woman's visage and putting that final bit of polish to her look than a dash of lipstick, a sweep of black mascara, or a rosy hint of rouge.

However, while fashions in makeup may come and go, there are some things that remain forever déclassé. To be perfectly frank, too much is always too much. It is worth noting that people are meant to be complimenting you on the beauty of your eyes, not your eye makeup. And if you find you cannot embrace a man without leaving a trail of powder on his suit lapel (an event too hideous for words!), then it's time to reconsider your motives, as well as your methods. Makeup is capable of many ingenious enhancements but it will not make you impervious to age or disappointment or a thousand other insecurities that plague the female mind. By all means, be quick to make the most of what makeup

*can, reasonably, do for your appearance but also be clever enough
to know when to stop.*

Suddenly I wake up one morning to discover that, in addition
to dealing with a failed marriage, a new job, a, shall we say,
challenging financial independence, and the certainty that I
will end up alone for the rest of my life, I now, just as a pièce
de résistance, have the skin of an adolescent girl—pink, oily,
and erupting in spots.

Not only is my life veering dangerously out of control but
now my face is as well. A girl can happily avoid any connection
with reality as long as she looks OK. But when that fails, drastic action must be taken.

And that means makeup. Lots of it.

Rising at daybreak on my day off, I catch a bus into town
and arrive at Selfridges's cosmetic emporium just as the store
opens. Hidden behind sunglasses, head bowed, I weave
through the maze of displays and bored perfume promotions
girls until I arrive at the only cosmetic solution I know for
Problem Skin.

There's the same clinical freshness about the display, the
same assistants dressed in white lab coats, the same pale green
and frosted glass bottles. After so many years and halfway
around the world, I'm back where I started.

My mother, also a traumatized survivor of teenage acne,
first steered me towards an identical counter when I was
twelve. She was not about to let me suffer the way she had all
those years ago, in the age before oil-free makeup formulations
and mildly medicated soap bars. Her hand firmly gripping my
shoulder, she guided me through the makeup department of
Horne's Department Store until we arrived in front of the
same glowing white stand. "Pardon me, my daughter has

acne," she announced, to my intense mortification. "And we'd like to know what you can do about it."

Of course the worst thing you can do is march up to a sales counter and announce that you need help.

The first hour we were there, the makeup assistant, who was at least forty-five and appeared to be wearing all the products in the range at once, insisted on diagnosing my skin type using the then high-tech Skin Analysis Station, which was on a separate little island in the center of the cosmetics room. It consisted of two high white stools and a plastic, illuminated box with some sliding panels on it, under the headings of Oily, Combination, and Dry skin. We sat on the stools and she put on a white lab coat and took out a pad and pen and began asking me a series of very serious questions like, "Is your skin dry and flaky?" To which my mother persisted with the refrain, "She's oily! Oily! She's got really oily skin!"

The assistant nodded knowingly and slid the panel in the illuminated box over to the pale green, astringent-colored section marked OILY. Then she moved on to the next question. "Would you say your pores are small, normal, or large?"

"Well, just have a look." My mother gave my head a push and the next thing I knew, the assistant and I were staring at each other's pores.

"Yes, large," she confirmed, just as I was thinking hers were the size of a house. And again she pushed the panel over to the oily section.

By now a small crowd was gathering, so novel was the sight of the Skin Analysis Station in action, especially in one so young and so in need of emergency attention. The assistant, deftly playing to the crowd, raised her voice, shouting the next question across the entire ground floor. "So, how many times a day do you need to moisturize?"

"Moisturize?" My mother shouted right back. "You don't understand; she's oily! OILY! The last thing she needs is moisture!" And the women in the crowd, indeed, even a few of the men in the gentleman's shoe department across the aisle, shook their heads in sympathy.

When every panel had finally, scientifically revealed that, yes, I did indeed have oily skin, the assistant tore the sheet off her pad, removed her lab coat, and led us back in a cloud of perfume to the purchase counter. "Fortunately, we have a number of extremely effective products to combat the oily skin condition," she began. The next forty-five minutes are a blur.

And that's how I came to look like a twelve-year-old version of Joan Collins.

Now, hovering just beyond the jurisdiction of the white-lab-coated assistants, I'm on the verge of doing it again. I remove my glasses and take a deep breath. Desperate times require desperate measures.

An hour later, I'm armed with a new collection of lotions, astringents, smudge-proof foundations, cover-up sticks, oil-removing blotting pads, blushers, a quad of eye shadows (three of which I don't like), and a free lipstick in a shade I'll never use. From now on, the words "fresh faced" are just a distant memory. So is the balance in my bank book.

However, there are some things that even one's best Joan Collins impersonation can't remedy.

The next day at work I check my mailbox and discover nothing. Yet again. No note or sign from Oliver Wendt, who I haven't seen in weeks. What have I done wrong? Upstairs at my desk, I stare blankly at my e-mail screen, replaying the whole sequence of events in my head. Over and over.

It's been ages since I left the note, the note I now seriously regret. I feel like a complete twat. Worse, I still think of him all the time, still wander the halls of the theater, hoping to see him, still fail to find any other man attractive, still cling to this old obsession.

If Oliver Wendt can see me, I must exist. This is the philosophical premise upon which I've built my new life. And now that I exist, I'm allowed to participate in the whole dynamic of living without apology—to take up space and time, to want things, to reach, to try, to fail. However, it seems impossible to me that I should come this far, make so many changes, and yet miss out on possessing Oliver himself. He's the prize, the reward I get for so much effort, the reason that I've gone to all this trouble.

I must love him. I think about him all the time.

Or am I really thinking of him thinking of me? Is Oliver merely a reflective surface in which I've caught sight of my own image for the first time?

Suddenly, my phone rings. Could this be it, at long last? I take a deep breath, my heart pounding as I reach for the receiver.

"Phoenix Theatre box office," I purr, in the smoothest, calmest tones I can manage. "How can I help?"

There's a pause.

"It's me," my husband says. "We need to talk."

I meet him for lunch at the Spaghetti House restaurant next to the theater. We're both unable to conceal our shock at seeing each other. He looks drained, thin and exhausted, and I resemble a pantomime dame. We stand together by the doorway, awkward, uncertain of how to greet each other and afraid to look each other in the eye.

Now we're seated in a corner booth. The food we order arrives and sits there, untouched. After what seems like hours of painful chitchat and loaded silences, he finally asks, "So, what are we going to do?"

This isn't a subject I'm ready to discuss, although I suspect we both know the answer. I toy with my cutlery, trying to balance my knife on its flat edge. "I'm not sure," I stall. "What would you like to do?" The knife falls and I catch sight of my reflection on the blade. The distorted face of a fun house mirror stares back at me.

"I take it you're not coming back." He's trying to force my hand. It's all too abrupt, too sudden, and too real.

The waiter brings us our coffee. I wrap my hands around the warm china cup for comfort.

"Nothing's changed," I say at last. I sound vague even to myself.

He sighs in frustration. An awkward silence ensues.

I pick up my teaspoon and am about to stir in some milk when, again, my image, pale and warped, is reflected back to me in the curved bowl of the spoon. I bury it immediately in the sugar bowl.

"I've been to see a lawyer." He's undeterred by my evasiveness. "Just as a precautionary measure."

I open my mouth to say something. Nothing comes out.

"Tell me honestly, have you met someone else?"

I look up, startled. And there, in the darkened glass behind him, I see myself again, my face red and flushed, almost unrecognizable behind the mask of makeup.

"You're blushing."

"No! No, I'm just shocked that, that you would even think such a thing!" I fumble, certain he can read my guilty thoughts.

"Well, then maybe we can repair the damage, don't you think?" He reaches across the table and touches my hand.

"I'm sorry." I struggle to push my chair away from the table. "I really . . . really can't do this right now." My head pounds and my hands shake as I reach for my bag.

"Louise, we need to talk about this!"

"Yes, yes, I know." I stand up. "But please, not now!" The words trail over my shoulder as I head for the door.

I run all the way back to the theater and into the safety of the Upper Circle Ladies. Splashing my face with water, I fill the palm of my hand with cheap, pink hand soap, and scrub my face clean. My makeup dissolves, mascara running and lipstick smearing to form grotesque shapes. And suddenly I'm sobbing into the warm water.

It's all gone wrong. And all the makeup in the world can't hide it.

That night at home, I lock the door and sit, with my pen and Post-its, making notes of Madame Dariaux's words of wisdom. If I just concentrate, if I can just get it right, everything will become clear. And I'll know what to do.

The next day at work, I get a call from the foyer to say there's someone waiting to see me. "Is it a man?" I ask cautiously.

"Nope." The security guard suppresses a burp. "It's some old tart."

Mona stands imperiously in the center of the lobby, smoking a cigarette and peering disdainfully at the poster for the season of new lesbian writing we're hosting next month. She has a gray fox-trimmed cashmere wrap thrown around her shoulders and a tiny green Harrods bag dangling from her wrist.

Every inch of me wants to turn and run back up the stairs before she can see me.

No such luck.

She turns, looks up, and her face expands into a slow, Cheshire cat grin.

"Louise!" she cries, as if we're not so much mother and daughter-in-law as two long-lost lovers, and a moment later, I'm enveloped into a full Mona embrace, a kind of suffocation by cashmere and Fracas.

When I disengage myself, she holds me at arm's length and gestures dramatically. "But darling, you're not well, are you? All this nonsense is clearly making you ill. Look! You're nothing but skin and bone! Doesn't that Calvin you're staying with have any food?"

"It's good to see you Mona," I lie. "And it's Colin; my roommate's name is Colin."

"Well, that's settled! I'm definitely taking you out to lunch! We'll go anywhere you like—the Ivy, Le Caprice . . . you name it and we'll go get some *proper* food into you!"

She pulls me across the foyer but I manage to twist free. "I'm sorry, Mona but I can't. I just got on duty and I don't have another break for ages."

"Well then, a coffee. Just for five minutes." Her hand is on the small of my back, pushing me firmly towards the door. I feel like a leaf, small, brown, and weightless, being forced downstream in the direction of some treacherous waterfall. In the five years that I've known Mona, I've never managed to defy her and it doesn't look as if I'll be able to start now.

We sit in Café Nero across the street from the theater. Mona orders a double espresso and I drink still water, turning the glass bottle around and around, peeling the label off in long strips while she talks.

"Louise . . . ," she begins and I know, just from the tone of her voice, that this is not a conversation I'm going to enjoy. Sensing this, she stops and starts again. "First of all, this is for you!" She places the Harrods bag grandly on the table between us and my whole insides collapse with mortification.

"Really, you shouldn't have." My voice is as flat as a pancake.

The last thing I want to do is have to go through the whole dumb show of pleasure and gratitude in front of Mona. Not today. Not ever.

"Well, it's not actually *from* Harrods . . . I got it in a little shop in Hampstead, but I had the bag at home and I thought it might be *fun*."

I'm not sure why it's fun to make something look like it comes from a different, more expensive store but it does somehow make the whole charade easier to bear; the knowledge that the gift is not, in fact, an extravagant gesture, but only a trinket parading as such. Inside the bag there's a tiny tissue paper parcel. I unwrap it to discover a silver brooch in the shape of a fish.

"Oh. How thoughtful. Really, really lovely."

"I thought you might like it, you being a Pisces and all. I don't know if you believe in that sort of thing but . . . it's *fun*."

Everything's fun today. We're having a wonderful time.

"How lovely," I say again, re-wrapping the fish and putting it back in the Harrods bag. I haven't got the energy to tell her my birthday's in June.

I peel another bit of the label and watch as she takes a small, enamel vial from her purse and carefully shakes two tiny saccharine tablets into her coffee. Her spoon clips the edge of the cup with a brisk, clicking sound.

"Well, I won't ask how you are, Louise; this whole thing has clearly affected you very badly. And of course, I'm here to offer you my help and guidance. There comes a time in every woman's life when she needs the advice and assistance of, shall we say, a more *experienced* confidante."

I continue peeling.

She clears her throat. "Let me be frank with you. All marriages go through bad patches—that's just part of the deal, isn't it? For better or for worse. Am I right?"

She pauses but without effect.

"Louise, I know my son can be difficult. He's sensitive, an artist. His father, God rest his soul, was the same way. But you and I are women, we're the adults here. Am I right? Certainly, we'd all like life to be about romance and flowers and all the rest of it but sometimes it just isn't that way. There's a lot more to making a relationship work than just sex!" She laughs awkwardly. "Sometimes marriage is more about kindness, shared interests; a kind of sympathy for one another . . ."

It's not working. She stares into the small, black darkness of her coffee for a moment and when she speaks again, her voice is tired and drained.

"I know my son. I know he's . . . difficult. But he does love you, Louise. In his way."

I stare at the table.

She sighs heavily and looks me in the eye. Her voice turns bitter. "You're not making this very easy are you?"

"It isn't easy," I say.

She smiles, lips stretched across teeth. "No, no of course not. But have you thought about where you're going to go? What you're going to do? This situation may not be ideal, but after all, you're old enough to realize that there's more than one kind of love in the world. You're going to have to learn to take the rough with the smooth."

I push the chair away from the table and stand up. "I'm sorry, Mona, I really have to go. Thank you very much for the pin."

She doesn't move. "You're very welcome, Louise. It's a

pleasure." Then she reaches out and grabs my hand. "Just think about what I said. Sometimes the best thing to do, the *smartest* thing, is just kiss and make up."

She lets go and I turn and walk out of the coffee shop.

That night, Colin and I are riding home on the bus, when he looks at me and says, "Stay still, there's something on your cheek." And he reaches out a finger and begins brushing away at something.

I recoil violently. "Don't touch it!" I snap. "Just leave it alone."

But he won't. "No, Ouise, there's just this little dark mark," and he licks his finger, the way your mother used to do when you were a kid, and begins to rub even harder. "Hold still, I've almost got it."

But I know what he's after and it isn't a mark, it's a suppu-rating boil that's taken a good ten minutes and two different products to hide and now he's only making it worse.

I push him off. "Just leave it I said! Can't you understand English? Get off me!"

The bus lurches up to our stop and I race down the aisle ahead of him, while he struggles, laden with shopping, behind me. "What's gotten into you, anyway?" he says as we clamber off. "Why are you so touchy?"

"I'm not touchy. I just don't want to be touched," I retort, walking, or rather running as quickly as I can down the street away from him.

"Fine! If you want to walk around with a big, black mark on your face, then great. I was only trying to help. God, Louise, you are really getting to be really hard work, do you know that?"

"Who cares," I hiss, suddenly irritable beyond all reason. I turn the key in the front door and stomp upstairs.

As the door swings closed he catches it with his foot. "I care!" But by then I'm in the flat and halfway to my room. I make it, just as he reaches the landing, and slam the door behind me. But he follows me, bursting in with all his shopping before I can stop him. "I care!" he shouts again.

And then stops.

And looks around.

Everywhere, on the mirror, on the wall, are little yellow Post-its.

Reminding me of what is elegant.

And what is not.

"Jesus, Louise, what's all this about?"

"Nothing," I say, suddenly quiet. "It has to do with a book I'm reading."

"What book?" He puts his shopping down. "Honey, this ain't normal."

"Yeah, well, I'm not normal, not normal at all. There's something wrong with me." I lift up my hair and show him my cheek. "See that? That isn't a mark, it's a spot. Loads of them. If Oliver Wendt should see me like this . . ."

"Oliver Wendt? What's he got to do with anything?"

"Nothing."

I've gone too far.

Oh, fuck it.

"Only I met him for a drink and he said he'd take me out, so I left him this note, and I haven't heard anything. Nothing. He's obviously avoiding me. He probably saw me and thought, What am I doing with this loser?"

Colin sits carefully on the edge of the bed. "He's in Australia, Ouise. He was sent to direct *Gale Force* in Australia."

"Oh," I say, stupidly. It never occurred to me that he might be away.

"What's all this?" he gestures to the yellow Post-its. And before I can stop him, he reaches out and plucks one off the wall. " 'Beauty is no guarantee of happiness,' " he reads aloud, " 'strive instead for elegance, style, and grace.' What is that supposed to mean? Louise?"

He's talking to me but his voice seems far away. I've been here, exactly here, before.

"Ouise?"

But the only thing I can say is, "It isn't working. No matter what I do, it isn't working. I'll never be elegant. Never get it right. It's all gone terribly, terribly wrong."

"Honey, sit down." Colin yanks my hand and my knees bend forward, landing me abruptly on the bed. "Tell me, what's this all about?"

I hand him the book, my bible, from where I keep it, in pride of place, on my bedside table. And then, almost immediately, I regret it.

"*Elegance*," he reads out loud, flicking the pages open. "What is this? Some sort of ancient self-help book?" He riffles through it, as if it were nothing more than an amusing oddity.

"Never mind." I try to take the book back but he holds it aloft, just beyond my reach.

"Not so fast! Are you honestly telling me you think this woman, this, what's her knickers, Madame Dariaux, knows what it means to be elegant? That she's got something you lack? By the way, she has Margaret Thatcher hair."

"Does not!" I punch his shoulder, a little harder than I'd intended.

He swats me back. "Does too! Listen, Ouise, that book is just one woman's opinion. And by the looks of it, one woman's opinion from a completely different age! What does she know anyway? Has she ever had to go through what you're going through? Has she ever left her husband and had to build her life from scratch? Why are you torturing yourself? Because that's what all this is: torture. Don't you have any confidence to trust your own instincts? So what if you make mistakes or have a few spots! Jesus, if I'd just left my husband I'd have a whole lot more than just a few spots!"

"You don't understand! None of you! It isn't about a few spots! Or about taking the rough with the smooth! Or any of that crap! Now give it back to me!" Again, I grab for the book and again, he holds it just out of my reach.

"No. First tell me, why is being elegant so important anyway?"

"Because . . . because . . ." My mind goes blank, folding in on itself, collapsing with frustration. "Jesus! Why don't you just fuck off, Colin!" I explode. "Stop being so fucking self-righteous and leave me alone!"

He stares at me a moment. Then he thrusts the book back at me and stands up, gathering his shopping together. "Fine." His voice is cold. "Have it your way."

He strides out of the room and the door slams behind him. And I'm alone, with my book, my Post-its, my spots, and my faux Harrods fish pin.

I've never been so rude to anyone in my life. Clutching the book, my hands shaking, I try to grasp what just happened. Why am I overreacting this way? Why can't I answer his question like a reasonable person? And why, after all that, is it so important to me to be elegant?

And then it comes, emerging slowly out of the darkness of my mind. Perhaps if only I'd been more of a woman, maybe he would've been more of a man.

When I finally dare to step out of my room, I find Colin making a shepherd's pie and listening to football on the radio in the kitchen. I stand in the doorway a while, watching him mash potatoes and he ignores me. So I move into the center of the kitchen, where I become a real obstacle and refuse to budge.

"Forgive me. I was wrong. And rude. And a bitch."

He stops what he's doing for a moment and stares at the floor.

"I was wrong and rude and a bitch," I repeat.

He looks up. "It's not just that. I'm worried about you. You're acting crazy."

"I know. I *am* crazy. Please, Col. Don't hate me. I'll get rid of the Post-its, put the book away. Only, please, forgive me! Say we're still friends."

"Come here." He steps forward and wraps his arms around me. "Listen, Ouise, no matter what happens between you and me, no matter what we say or do, there's one thing I can promise you. We will *always* make up."

He held me for a very long time.

A week later, my husband and I decide to file for divorce.

And shortly afterwards, my face begins to clear.

N

∾

Negligees

One of the most baffling points of inconsistency in many otherwise elegant women is the way they completely neglect their appearance during the hours of intimacy in their own homes—which is the very time and place where they ought to be at their most attractive.

For every woman who, at the end of the day, removes her makeup and replaces it with a lighter one, ties a ribbon in her well-brushed hair, and slips into a pretty, long dressing-gown or housecoat with matching slippers, how many dress for an evening at home in a shabby dressing-gown, their heads bristling with curlers, cream spread over their faces (when it isn't a green or black masque), and with huge shapeless mules on their feet? It makes you wonder whom the result of all this beauty care is meant to impress—undoubtedly the trades-people they will see when doing their shopping the next morning. In the meantime, the poor husband learns to avoid looking at his scarecrow-wife and fixes his gaze instead on the sports page of the newspaper or in contemplation of the television screen.

After all, isn't this really what beauty parlours were created for—so your poor, dear husband might be spared the horror of having to see everything?

*   *   *

I'm thirty-two and for the first time in my adult life I'm living with people I'm not sleeping with, commonly referred to as flatmates. We share the kitchen, bathroom, and living room.

Communal living doesn't come easily for me. At first I make a few faux pas. I don't understand how to shop for myself, or how to sit in the living room with the others and watch TV. I am, however, very good at doing the washing up and taking out the garbage. Every day is a learning experience. I learn from Colin how to organize three people's shopping in a single fridge. ("Stack from large to small, sweetie. Think upwards, upwards!") And Ria teaches me how to take a bath, with candles, special soap, bath salts, and loofah scrubs. "You're communing with yourself," she instructs. "The water is your emotional life. If you're in and out, your relationships will never succeed."

Oh. OK.

The one thing they both do is chip in and buy me a new robe, under the guise of an extremely belated Christmas gift.

"We have something for you," Colin says one evening when we're all making dinner together. And he presents me with a bulky, wrapped package. Ria's smiling and looking at her shoes.

"Oh, my God! Guys! You shouldn't have!" I'm thrilled to bits, giggling and tearing the paper like a kid. When I open it up, it appears to be a giant towel.

"Wow," I say, wondering why they've bought me a towel. "This is great. You shouldn't have."

"I'm glad you like it," Colin says, looking at Ria, who's trying so hard not to laugh she has to turn away. "By the way, Louise, it's a robe."

"Ahh! Yeah, I can see that now! It's great," I say, noticing how enormous it seems. And blue. And shapeless. "Yeah, fantastic but you guys, I already have a robe. My little white one. You've seen it, haven't you?" I look at both of them, but they're not looking at me. All of a sudden the floor is deeply intriguing.

This is weird.

"You have seen my robe, Col? Haven't you?"

Colin clears his throat. "Yes, darling, we've all seen it. As a matter of fact, when Mick was over the other night and you were coming out of the bathroom, he saw it too. And he's straight. The thing about that robe is that it's fine if you're trying to seduce someone . . ."

"But," Ria finishes his sentence, "not really appropriate for communal living."

I can feel my face burning, my hands tingling. "What are you saying? What's wrong with it? Is it see-through? What?"

"What we're saying," continues Ria, "and maybe we're not doing it terribly tactfully is . . ."

"We can see your tits," Colin concludes.

"Absolutely," Ria says.

"Oh my God!" I curl up into a little ball of shame on the floor, clutching the enormous, thick, terry cloth robe. "Oh God! I'm so sorry! How . . . how embarrassing!"

"Calm down, sweetie." Colin strokes my hair and laughs. "They're lovely, really. Just a bit distracting when you're having your tea in the morning."

I look up sheepishly. "I'm so sorry, really, I had no idea. All these years I've been wearing it, no one's said anything . . . nothing's ever . . . I mean . . ." I drift off, not sure how to continue.

Apparently, I'd been strolling around in a see-through garment for months, but like a modern-day, sexual version of the *Emperor's New Clothes,* I'd been oblivious to my nakedness.

After years of living with a man who's completely immune to me physically, I've apparently concluded that everyone is. In the absence of any response, I've pretended to be clothed, but in fact, I've been just begging for some kind of reaction.

And here it is.

Thing is, it isn't the first time. When I go out dancing with Colin and his friends, he shimmies around me, pulling up the straps on my Morgan halter neck. And Ria has met me by the door a few times, brandishing a cardigan and refusing to let me leave until I cover up. Until now, I've managed to ignore these unrelated incidents, but suddenly the focus has been pulled in, sharply, and I can see clearly. It's like my radar's broken. After so many years of hiding, the pendulum's swung completely the other way and I'm an overnight exhibitionist, shouting, "Look at me! Notice me! I'm alive! Here are my tits to prove it!" How pathetic and degrading. And yet I've done it again and again.

And now I'm the subject of some bizarre flatmate intervention.

I bury my head underneath the mountain of terry cloth Colin's calling a robe. I want to hide here forever—to pass out from embarrassment and never come to.

There's just one thing I want to know before I do. "Are they really lovely?"

"I'm sorry?" Colin asks.

I clear my throat. I shouldn't need to know this, but I do. "I said, are they really lovely?"

"Are what?" Ria and Col look at one another, confused.

I'm staring intently at the blue swirl that separates the red rectangle on the Oriental rug. The pattern repeats itself again and again, all along the edge of the design.

"My breasts." My voice is suddenly choked, just barely above a whisper. "You said . . . you said they were lovely."

There's a long, astonished silence. And I find that I'm crying—the blue swirl is melting into the red rectangle. I blink and they separate again.

It's Ria who says, "They are lovely and you're lovely. Lovely enough to put your clothes back on, Louise."

O

⋙

Occasions

There are numerous occasions in life when even the most unassuming, least clothes-conscious woman realizes that it can be of real importance socially for her to be well dressed. Suddenly seized with panic at the idea that she will be the centre of attention, she wonders in anguish, "Whatever shall I wear?" and rushes out to buy any kind of new dress she can find.

Whatever the ceremony at which you or your husband may be required to play a leading role—such as godparent at a christening, committee member of a charity ball, or merely as a guest at the Christmas office party—you should always adopt simplicity as the best policy and not try to radically transform your appearance for this special event. It would only astonish everyone, and on this particular occasion you do not want to cause a sensation, but simply to present a pleasing and attractive appearance.

One Saturday morning, I awake to the sound of muffled voices. Shuffling into the hallway, wearing my new, guaranteed opaque robe, I pause to listen by the living room door.

"And you think they're getting a divorce?" This is a woman's voice, but one I don't know.

"Yes," Colin says, "it's pretty much certain now."

The woman sighs. "Sex or money, darling. Mark my words. It always comes down to sex or money."

I knock gently. "Hello? Sorry to disturb you."

Colin rises and the woman, slim and tiny with flaming red hair, smiles at me. She's wearing a tweed skirt with an emerald green twin set and she sits with her ankles crossed, her feet arched delicately.

"Morning Ouise! Did we wake you? I don't believe you've met. This is my mother."

I grin apologetically, aware of how bedraggled I look and badly in need of coffee. "It's a pleasure to meet you, Mrs. Riley." I cross and shake her tiny hand.

"Please, call me Ada." Her voice, smooth and cultured, betrays just the slightest hint of an Irish accent.

"I'm about to make some coffee, can I get you some?" I offer.

"No." She rises. "I really should be getting on before your father misses me. It was lovely to meet you, Louise."

Colin holds her coat out and she steps into it. "I'll see you out, Mum." And I hear them whispering as they make their way down the steps.

When Colin returns, he joins me in the kitchen.

"Your mum's an early riser. What was all that about?" I ask, pouring a bowl of cereal.

He leans his head on the door frame and closes his eyes. "It's my father. He's playing up again."

Colin's father, Patrick Riley, was once a famous Irish tenor and his mother, Ada, a dancer in the Royal Ballet. They met at Covent Garden in the fifties and were married shortly afterwards. Very quickly, five children followed, of which Colin is the youngest. However, Patrick's career came to a sudden and tragic halt when he lost his voice during a performance of *Cavalleria Rusticana* in the late sixties. Unable to conceive of a career in anything else but music, he struggled to support his family as a voice coach and music teacher, but never fully recovered from the loss of prestige from his Covent Garden days. Always highly sensitive, he began to succumb to dark periods of depression and locked himself away in his study for days on end. As he grew older and his children left the family home, his mood swings became increasingly violent; sudden, uncontrollable outbursts were followed by tears and pathetic promises that he would "pull himself together." But he was unable to effect any real or lasting changes on his own. The family rarely spoke of "Da's condition," but lately things had been worse and Ada was beside herself. And he was always particularly bad around the anniversary of his final, devastating performance, which was in a month's time.

"Mum thinks that maybe we should organize some kind of tribute to him. You know, gather all his friends and family and have a party to celebrate his career, but I don't know. It could go either way; either he could really enjoy it or it might just send him into another bad bout of morbid reflection—though, chances are, he's going to no matter what we do." He shook his head. "I just don't know, Ouise. I really don't know what to do."

"It's a tough one." I poured him out a cup of coffee. "I wish I could help."

"Well, there is one thing . . ." He hesitated.

"Just name it."

"If she does decide to go ahead with this whole thing, will you come with me?"

"Sure, Col. No problem. Although she might just want family only, don't you think?"

He studied the kitchen floor a moment. "And their part-ners," he added quietly.

"Partners?"

He looked up. "You see, I've never really told them I'm gay."

For a moment I thought I would laugh. "And you don't think they know?"

He sighed heavily. "It isn't a matter of them knowing, Louise. But they're not of a generation that find it necessary to discuss these things. Do you understand? What they know or don't know is not really my concern. My *telling* them doesn't help. We all get along better when it just isn't an issue."

"And how do you accomplish that?"

"I just don't put it in their faces and they don't ask."

"That's fine now, while you're single, but what about when you have a boyfriend?"

"Louise," he seemed tired and irritable, "trust me on this one. They don't want to know. They want me to be happy but they don't want to know. Some things are just better left un-said."

Three days later, Colin confirmed that his mother had de-cided to go ahead with her plan; the party was to be held in their large family home and would be a surprise. And in the weeks that followed, Colin spent every spare moment coordi-nating arrangements between his mother and fellow siblings. They planned a buffet supper, a jazz trio for dancing, and Ada had arranged for some of Patrick's star pupils to sing. Family and friends were scheduled to arrive from as far away as Dublin, and Colins's brother Ewan had managed to find some old film footage of his father singing in *La Bohème*, which he'd had restored, to be screened at the end of the evening. The phone rang constantly and there was a buzz of real excitement in the air. The energy and enthusiasm with which the Riley clan launched themselves into Patrick's party was unparalleled.

A week before the big night, Colin cornered me as I was doing the washing up. "I think we ought to talk about what we're going to wear."

I handed him a tea towel. "Good plan. Let's start with you."

"Well," he polished off a few glasses, stacking them on the kitchen shelf, "I'm thinking maybe my navy pinstripe, a pale blue shirt, and a red tie. You know, something very conservative, formal but not too formal. . . . what do you think?"

I looked at him in surprise. "You own a navy pinstripe suit? I can't imagine you wearing anything so somber!"

He smiled. "Well, I'll have to have it cleaned, but yes, it does exist. Alan bought it for me when he was trying to persuade me to go into banking. I tried to convince Mum to make it a black tie evening—everyone looks better in black tie—but she says that not everyone will have a tux, and I'm sure she has a point."

"*Banking!* I can't imagine you trying to control anyone's spending, Col!"

He laughed. "Now it's your turn. What did you have in mind?"

"Well," I hesitated, "I'm not really sure. I've got my little black Karen Millen dress."

"Hummm." I could tell by the way he was concentrating on the drying that it wasn't quite what he had in mind.

"But then again, it may be a little . . . how do you say it?"

"Tight?" he volunteered.

I turned to face him. "Tight?!"

"Well, then, formfitting. A little close, shall we say."

I glared at him. "Colin, there's absolutely nothing wrong with that dress. Or the way it fits me!"

"Yes, yes, yes, yes! Of course! I love it, Ouise! Really, I do. But I'm thinking something a little more subdued, a little more restrained . . . what's the word I'm looking for? A little more Catholic."

"Like what? A habit?"

He sighed and put the tea towel down. "You have to understand, Louise, this is my family we're talking about. When it comes right down to it, they're a little old-fashioned. Traditional even. Despite the show biz roots. You and I are going as kind of a team, right? I'm wearing the blue pinstripe and you can wear something that goes with that look . . . don't you think?"

I frowned at him. This was not the Colin I knew. Suddenly it was as if he'd been abducted and replaced by an evil twin— one that wanted us to perform some sort of bizarre charade for his parents.

And then it hit me.

"Colin, did you by any chance tell them that I was your girlfriend?"

He picked up the tea towel again and started drying as if his life depended on it. "No! No, of course not!"

"Really? 'Cause you're acting really weird."

He avoided my gaze and began stacking plates together. "Absolutely not, Louise! Really!"

"But you didn't *not* tell them I was your girlfriend either. That's it, isn't it? You were going to just say nothing and let them draw their own conclusions."

He put the plates down. "Is that really so bad?"

I shook my head. "Why are you doing this, Col? You do know, don't you, that you have nothing to be ashamed of?"

He closed his eyes and passed a hand wearily over them. "This is not the occasion, Louise, when I come out to my family. Can you understand that? This party, this night, is not about me. All I'm asking is that we blend in, that we remain anonymous. Just for this one night. Look, I'm not going to try to pass you off as my girlfriend, OK? As far as anyone's concerned you're my friend and my roommate, all right? But all I want is for this one night to go smoothly. Can you understand that?"

I can.

I wrap my arms around him. "Listen, I'll wear anything you like, OK? And we'll have a good time and the whole evening will be a terrific success. Just wait and see."

He gives me a squeeze. "I did take the liberty of borrowing something from the wardrobe department." He dives into the living room and comes back clutching a shopping bag. He hands it to me. "Go on, see if you like it."

I reach in and pull out an original Diane von Furstenberg wraparound dress in a bold crimson print. "Wow," I say, holding it up against me. "It's kind of incredible."

He beams at me. "*Now* you look like a banker's wife!"

However, Colin and I never get to wear our carefully chosen outfits.

Two days before the party, while Colin is delivering spare plates and cutlery to his mother, they hear a strange noise from Patrick's study. They discover him, slumped in a heap on the carpet, having swallowed a fatal dose of tranquilizers. There is no note.

Colin spends a week at his mother's, helping with arrangements, and then, after the funeral, Ada departs for Ireland, to stay with family.

The day Colin comes back to the flat, Ria and I both take the day off. He comes in and goes straight to bed for four hours, while Ria and I busy ourselves baking scones. (She bakes. I watch.) When he finally wakes up, eyes swollen and red, we make a fresh pot of tea and try our best to force-feed him the scones and when that doesn't work, we just sit there, in the living room, watching the sun melt behind the London skyline and listening to an old recording of Patrick singing famous Italian arias. The record ends and we sit in silence in the dark. And then Ria turns a light on and goes into the kitchen to make us all cheese on toast. Colin lies down and rests his head in my lap.

"He was so much trouble," he says. "So unpredictable to be around. And yet I don't know what we'll do without him."

I gently stroke his hair.

I want to tell him I understand, but I don't. I'm one of the lucky ones.

When I was thirteen, I came home from school one day to find my mother sitting in one of the living room chairs in her nightgown. She should've been dressed. And at work. But she wasn't. She was here instead—pale, drawn, her eyes glassy and swollen. The nightgown she was wearing was faded and damp. It clung to her thin frame and there was some sort of stain on the front. My mother was never home when I got back from school.

I asked her if she was all right and she ignored me, staring straight ahead, her head wobbling on her neck as if it might fall off at any moment. I stood directly in front of her and asked again, but she looked at me as if she didn't recognize me and blinked slowly. Far too slowly. Then her mouth just fell open and in a single, horrible instant, I realized she was dying. The world seemed to move in slow motion; I felt my backpack slide off my arms and onto the floor and although I was running, my feet were made of lead. I pulled at the phone on the wall and dialed a number. A voice came on the line and I could hear myself screaming our address, telling them to hurry and as I turned, I saw her slump forward, head on chest, a thin strand of drool sliding its way slowly down her chin. I let go of the phone and it crashed against the wall as she crumpled to a heap on the floor.

Minutes later, the ambulance team arrived. I was rocking her back and forth in my arms, trying to get her to wake up. They pulled her away from me, strapped her onto a stretcher, and put an oxygen mask over her mouth. Then they searched the bathroom until they found some bottles. In a matter of minutes, they were gone. A neighbor came over, Mrs. Klavin- ski, and rang my father. She was Polish, and although she was just trying to be helpful, her English wasn't very good. When my sister and brother came home, she greeted them with the news that my mother had a "sickness of the head and was tak- ing to hospital."

It was months before she came home.

And when she did, she was different. Better.

And as I held Col, I thought of all the secret preparations that had been made over the past month and of how he and his mother found Patrick too late. And I thought again, for the thousand millionth time, of what would've happened if I'd been late home from school that day. If I'd loitered by the bus stop, staring at the boys from St. Andrew's or landed myself in detention and not come home at all.

Later that night, I rang home. Sitting in the darkness by the window, I listened to the phone ring thousands of miles away. Then I heard a click and my mother's voice came on the line.

"Hello?"

"Hello, Mom."

"Louise! What's the time? It's kinda late there, isn't it?"

"A little."

"Are you all right?"

"Yeah, Mom, I'm fine. I just called to see how you are."

"Great, Kiddo. Couldn't be better. Your father's a bit of a pain *dans le derrière* but I'm being very firm with him, so we'll soon have that under control. It's all about this new shed he wants to build in the backyard. Did you know your sister's trying for another baby? No luck yet, but I'll keep you posted. How's the job? I spent the whole day planting bulbs, which I have a feeling the deer are just going to eat again. But I try every year, so I can't start giving up now, can I?"

"Absolutely not."

"So, Kiddo." I hear her lighting a cigarette. "What's the occasion?"

I look out the window. The world outside is still and black.

"No occasion, Mom. I just called to hear your voice."

P

Pounds

Every springtime the fashion magazines and women's pages invent new diets which, if they are followed to the letter, guarantee a slender figure and, consequently, elegance. Although it isn't necessarily indispensable to be as skinny as a mannequin in order to be elegant, it is probably true that the list of the Ten Best Dressed Women is also a list of the Ten Hungriest Women.

Slimming is practically a new religion. It used to be practiced very discreetly, almost clandestinely, and the early followers contented themselves with a moderate slenderness which still allowed for a few soft curves. But the sect has gained new converts every day until it now confidently decrees that salvation is impossible for the few remaining infidels who do not believe in the string bean silhouette and the skinny look.

Should you or should you not convert to this new religion? Perhaps, but at what cost? Dieters can become drearily obsessive about their new found vocation. I recommend that you weigh not just yourself but your priorities as well. After all, God made you the way you are and there is no point fighting nature to the extent that you alienate all your friends and fam-

ily with endless rules and regulations concerning what you can and cannot eat.

Being slender is undoubtedly elegant but neurotic self-obsession is NOT.

I'm standing in the queue at Starbucks, trying to figure out the fat grams, calorie content, and carbohydrate index of a fat-reduced blueberry muffin. All I really want, though, is a slice of double fudge chocolate cake. I'm irritable and confused, looking at the cake like a hypnotized lemming. Ria's asking me what I want so that we can order and the queue behind me's getting restless and the girl behind the counter is rolling her eyes. What I want to do is to punch through the glass case and grab the whole cake and run howling into the street with it like a creature from a Hammer horror film.

But I don't.

No, I do the right thing. Because the world is divided into right and wrong, good and bad, fat and thin. So I order a double espresso instead with no sugar.

And when Ria asks, "Are you sure?" because she saw me eyeing the cake, I snap at her, "Yes, yes that's it!" like I hate her, because I do. I hate her and anyone else who can order anything they want without going through a thousand mental gymnastics—who can walk up to the spotty Spanish girl behind the counter and say, "I'll have an iced latte and a slice of double fudge chocolate cake" without taking a roller-coaster ride to hell and back from waves of guilt and panic.

So I order the double espresso instead, get completely psychotic on caffeine, and walk around in a sweaty, twitching cloud of resentment all day long because yet again, I've denied myself. And there are three meals in a day, a day's twenty-four hours long and they follow each other, day after day after day, until you die. And that's an awfully long time not to have what you want.

I went on my first diet when I was nine. Being a dancer, we were encouraged to starve ourselves. I remember our teacher sitting us down, talking to us about how it was time to start watching our weight. She taught us how to carry little jars of honey and teaspoons in our ballet bags so that when we'd been dancing all day with nothing to eat and felt like fainting, we could pop a teaspoon of honey into our mouths to keep us going. So we all carried leaky little jars of honey that came undone and coated our leotards in thick, sugary goo.

We used to sit in the changing room, listening avidly to the diet tips of the older girls. You must eat only low-fat yogurt, diet soda, coffee, and baked potatoes with nothing on them. Or only protein and vegetables, as much as you want but less is better. However, all too often we ended up eating hamburgers at McDonald's after class, and if you were going to have a hamburger, you might as well have fries and a shake. But that was OK, because we'd all learnt from Melissa Formby the wonderful invention of throwing up everything after you ate. She'd only just discovered this magical solution herself and was now giving master classes on how to best achieve the results you wanted with the least amount of effort.

"Always drink a glass of water very quickly beforehand," she instructed us. "And then use your longest finger. A little nail doesn't hurt. And think of something gross. If you can think of something *really* gross, then you don't have to waste too much time and that keeps your mother from getting suspicious."

We nodded. How wise she was.

"Oh, and use a private toilet. Especially until you learn how to do it quietly."

Good one. We were, after all, as dancers always learning how to do things quietly—how to jump across a room and land without a sound, how to bourée on bloody point shoes without so much as a whisper, how to stretch your leg up around your ear without screaming. Piece of cake.

By the time I was thirteen, I'd developed my own little variation on this theme. I'd have one meal a day, usually something completely disgusting and devoid of any nutritional value, like chocolate cake, covered in M&M's, with ice cream and chocolate sauce for breakfast and I'd take speed, coffee, and diet soda the rest of the day. If I had any food after my one meal, I'd chuck it up in the guest room toilet.

This went on for quite a while until one night, high on speed and having just watched a particularly depressing Bergman film about necrophilia, I scoffed down a whole box of nasty, white sugar biscuits and then threw them up again. I sat, shaking on the bathroom floor, certain that I didn't want to live anymore. Or, at least, that I didn't want to live like this. I could no longer bear the twenty-four-hour obsession about what I was going to eat, when I was going to eat it, and worst of all, what I wasn't allowed to eat. (I'd already tried laxatives, with disastrous results.) So I resolved that whatever I ate would stay down, for better or worse. And a new chapter in my dieting history began.

When I got married, I kept my eating habits a secret. But with my husband away every evening onstage, it was easy to get into a routine of bingeing in his absence.

We're in Stratford; he's with the RSC. We have a new place to live, he has a new job, and I'm on a new diet. It's like the Hay Diet, only it's with organic food. Every day I eat about twenty-six pounds of grimy, misshapen, hairy fruits and vegetables. I have wind constantly and smell like a cabbage.

The rules are easy. (Diets have rules, like games. There's no difference really, this one's Twister with food.) You can have carbohydrates with vegetables and dairy but not with protein. And you can have protein only with vegetables. And fruit, well, fruit's so dangerous that you can only have it on its own, several hours before or after eating anything. So, that's steak and salad, chicken and salad, fish and salad. But not cheese. Cheese is evil. The devil's work. I'm allowed some strange form of organic goat's cheese curd but there's only one shop in Notting Hill that sells it and it tastes like glue. And for lunch, salad. Salad with rice, salad with nuts, salad with bread. When I say bread, what I really mean is a gluten-free yeast-free loaf of millet and linseed. It looks like a brick but if you toast it, it's really quite crunchy. (In the absence of any taste, texture will have to do.) And no sugar of any kind, no caffeine, and no fat.

The book makes it seem quite simple. Actually, more than just simple; like you'd be an idiot to eat any other way. There's a couple in their seventies laughing hysterically on the front cover and running a marathon. Completely caffeine free. I feel inadequate just looking at it. There's a strong emphasis on beans. Bean and cabbage soup, flavored with garlic. They could've warned me that I was going to explode. I have to lock myself in my room with the window open. My husband sleeps on the couch.

You're meant to eat as many things raw as you can. I'm munching on a fortune's worth of crudités all day long and all I manage is to feel bloated and hungry at the same time. I'm dreaming of hamburgers, chips, shepherd's pie. I wake up gnawing at my pillow. Watching other people eat becomes an erotic experience for me. Staring in the window of McDonald's like a Peeping Tom, I'm glued to the spot, ready to kill for a Happy Meal.

It's meant to get better. I'm meant to be full of life and energy. My skin's meant to glow. But all that happens is I get a vicious case of irritable bowel syndrome. I'm doubled over with pain and my husband takes me to the doctor.

"What are you eating?" the doctor asks after he's examined me.

"Well, today I had gluten-free muesli and rice milk, broccoli and chicken stir-fry with ginger, some raw carrots, a little rye toast with soya spread and sugarless raspberry jam . . ."

He raises a hand to stop me; he's already late for his golf.

"Good God!" He looks at me in disgust. "Eat a potato, woman! Have a sausage roll! No wonder you can't stand up straight."

"But . . . but . . ." I can't believe it. Doesn't he want to be running a marathon when he's seventy?

Apparently not.

By the time I came to live with Colin and Ria, I was so confused from a lifetime of dieting that I felt beyond repair or redemption. The only difference was that now there was no place to hide it. We shared a kitchen, often ate together, and while Colin was happy to tease me about my strange meals and occasionally force-feed me chicken curry and steamed jam pudding, Ria observed my eating habits in silence, quietly noting all the things I would rather she'd forgotten.

Then one night, she finds me in the kitchen.

It's half past two and I'm sitting in my pajamas, stuffing cookies into my mouth. They're her cookies; she'd been given them at Christmas, several months ago, and not having much of a sweet tooth, she'd let them sit there, going stale on a shelf above the sink. Normally I wouldn't touch her food without asking her, but I'd woken up, suddenly scared and starving and didn't have any of my own food left. I was afraid to buy it

in case I ended up eating it all in one go. I hate myself for stealing stale biscuits. They're the kind I would normally have
gone out of my way to avoid. But here I am, crouched in the
dark, cramming them into my mouth when she comes in and
turns on the light.

I blink stupidly, like a wild animal caught stealing from a
garbage pail. I can't bear to be seen eating, even at the best of
times, but it's absolutely essential that these midnight raids remain secret.

"What are you doing?"

I scramble up from the floor and try to smile. "I'm sorry.
Really."

"But what are you doing?" she asks. Again.

I want to die, to disappear, to be sucked away into the ether.
I'm still holding the bag, so I put it on the counter, my hand
moving in slow motion, as if not holding it will make it all go
away.

"Those are old," she says. "Why are you eating them? And
why are you eating them in the dark?"

"I was hungry. I'm sorry. I'll replace them. Buy some
more."

"Louise, I don't like those biscuits; that's why I never ate
them. The biscuits don't matter. But what you're doing is
strange."

"I know. I'm sorry. I won't do it again."

She looks at me carefully. "Yes. Yes you will."

It's half past two and there's nothing, no noise of passing
traffic, no distant drilling to whisk the words away. They hang
there, solid between us, and for some reason I can't explain, I
don't lie or wheedle, laugh or protest.

"You're right," I hear myself say.

How odd that you're saying that, I think in my head. No

one's meant to know and now here you are, saying it out loud. But it doesn't stop there.

"I can't eat," the voice goes on, speaking through me, like a ventriloquist's dummy. "I don't, don't really know how."

We stand there. A breeze blows in through the open kitchen window, out of the solid blackness that pressed against the house. Cold and fluid, like mercury, it races between us, running its fingers through Ria's hair and making it dance around her face. Her white cotton nightgown billows up around her like a sail and for a moment she isn't earthbound at all but weightless and floating, like an apparition pasted against the poorly fitted kitchen cabinets. Then it darts away, brushing past us impatiently on its way to more exotic locations and we're alone again. Ria's nightgown drifts silently back around her ankles and her hair lands gently in place on her head.

"Are you still hungry?" she asks.

"No."

"Well, why don't we go to bed then." She holds out her hand and I take it. "You think too much, Louise. You're not really meant to think so much." And she leads me back through the darkness to my room.

The world is full of advice about how to eat, but here's a novel idea.

Have three normal meals a day. Eat what you really want. Stop when you're full.

I'll admit, sometimes that's easy and sometimes it's very, very hard.

But, in Madame Dariaux's immortal words: "God made you the way you are."

And in Ria's: "Get over it."

2

❦

Quality / Quantity

One of the most striking differences between a well-dressed Englishwoman and a well-dressed Parisian is in the size of their respective wardrobes. The Englishwoman would probably be astonished by the very limited number of garments hanging in the Frenchwoman's wardrobe, but she would also be bound to observe that each one is of excellent quality, expensive perhaps by British standards, and perfectly adapted to the life a Frenchwoman leads. She wears them over and over again, discarding them only when they are worn or outmoded, and she considers it a compliment (as it is meant to be) when her best friend says, "I'm so glad you decided to wear your red dress—I've always loved it!"

Foreign visitors are often shocked by the high prices in the Paris shops, and they wonder how a young career girl, for example, who earns no more than her British counterpart, can afford to carry an alligator handbag and to wear a suit from the Balmain boutique. The answer is that she buys very few garments: her goal is to possess a single perfect ensemble for each of the different occasions in her life, rather than a wide choice of clothes to suit every passing mood.

I wonder if the Englishwoman wouldn't profit by replacing once in a while her penchant for quantity with a quest for quality. She might find that not only is her elegance increased, but also the enjoyment and even the confidence that she gets from her clothes.

Colin and I have adopted a new catchphrase and a new philosophy, which is essentially this: life's too short. Not staggeringly original, but nevertheless, it fits the bill.

I'm not sure quite when we reached this conclusion, but the pivotal moment might well have taken place on the top deck of the number 159 bus. We were riding into work together one rainy morning, jammed in with all the other rush hour commuters. Everything was wet; the windows were fogged up, the seats soaking, sopping umbrellas littered the aisles. Colin was squashed into the seat next to me. On his lap he balanced a large plastic bag filled with Patrick's old suits to drop off at a charity shop, while simultaneously trying to keep his backpack and umbrella from rolling into the aisle with each jolt of the bus. I was sitting next to him, my feet damp and freezing inside a pair of newly ruined suede loafers.

I opened my post to discover yet another batch of divorce papers as the bus lurched forward and then screeched to a sudden halt, pitching me into the back of a well-dressed black man in the seat in front. "So sorry!" I apologized, gingerly retrieving my letters from where they had landed on the floor.

"That's quite all right," he smiled amiably. "Not your fault."

I smiled back.

"If I may disturb you just a moment longer," he continued, "I'd like to tell you about the joy of living in the light of the salvation of Christ."

And that is the exact moment I think it happened. I looked at Col and he looked at me.

"Life's too short," Colin said, perhaps the first full sentence he'd uttered that day, and I was inclined to agree.

"What are we doing anyway?" he continued, suddenly unstoppable in his indignation. "What are we waiting for? I'm tired of death. I'm tired of taking the bus into work. I'm tired of sitting at home in the evening, waiting for the right guy to come up and knock at my door."

"I'm tired of divorce!" I chipped in. "And I'm tired of wet shoes!"

"To hell with wet shoes!" He stood up and pushed the bell. "I'm tired of playing it safe! Goddammit, Ouise, we're young, we're sexy, we're talented! You know what, life's just too fucking short and I think it's about high time we had some fun!"

"OK."

We got off the bus and caught a cab instead.

And that's how it began. Suddenly being a grown-up was just too difficult, so we gave up. At the same time, I decided to give the sane, sober, fashion advice of Madame Dariaux a break as well. The thought of saving all of one's pennies for the perfect cashmere cardigan seemed too old, too responsible, and to take far, far too long. I wanted to be one of the girls with as many outfits as she had men for a change—gay, dazzling, voracious, and in the thick of life. Like Colin, I was tired of waiting for time to heal my heart and make me feel normal. And, like Col, I was ready for drastic action.

That's when I decided that trying to be elegant wasn't working anymore. I wanted to be fashionable instead.

It's a Thursday night and Col and I are out with twenty of our new best friends at a bar called Cube. Cube is just like Mink Bikini, only Mink Bikini was hot last month and Cube is hot now. The place is packed, heaving with spiky haired media types, dressed in gray, unisex clothing, sulking, lanky would-be models in torn Chloe-style T-shirts and spike heels, and ad men in black Armani suits with bold, neon ties—all shouting, jostling, spilling drinks on one another and tripping over the Swedish-style lime green ottomans that constitute the lounge area.

The soundtrack is surreal, spacey French remixes of KC and the Sunshine Band, dubbed over by Vanessa Paradis. And there are loads of saucy little features to keep the customers amused, including a discreetly hidden video camera tucked away in the men's toilet and a not so discreetly displayed video screen transmitting all the evidence in the ladies' (forewarned is forearmed). There's also a large electronic billboard above the entrance that projects different messages every time someone walks in the door. "Jesus loves you but he won't leave his wife," it bleeps, like an automated fortune cookie. "Is it love or is it lust?" it bleeps again as a young woman ducks in out of the black rain, shaking her hair and pulling down her micromini. Someone calls out "Lust!" across the room and we all laugh while she stands, frozen like a rabbit caught in headlights, unaware of the cartoon captions lurking just above her head.

There's a definite buzz. We've all made it. We survived the doorman and the two Gucci clad female bouncers, who stand poised, dripping with boredom and fatigue, ready to reject anyone too ugly, too fat, too old, or too "yesterday" (retro looks not withstanding). We celebrate this fact by waving twenty-pound notes furiously at the blue-haired, tattooed barmen, giggling at the drunken media men peeing (unbeknownst to them) on video and flirting with the obnoxious ad men, who in turn, flirt with the sulking models, who in turn flirt with no one.

I'm wearing a black pencil skirt from Kookai that's almost exactly like this season's Prada, a tiny, sheer, layered vest top like the one they're showing at Versace (only mine's from a stall in Brixton Market), and a pair of painfully high single-strap hot pink mules from Office, which are the spitting image of the Manolos Kate's wearing in this month's *Vogue*. My hair's blown dry into a single sheet of heavy, blond straightness, with a "natural" looking center part that took me only fifty minutes and three different hair products to achieve. My lipstick is Mac, my toenail polish Chanel, and I smell like a mixture of wild figs and French wisteria, which is meant to be both sexy and unisex at the same time. I've come a long, long way from the navy pinafore dress. And I'm as hot as they come.

Unfortunately, not everyone I invite is. A few of my friends almost don't make it past the doormen. They simply just don't understand that you need to look the part.

Darren's a music student; he's carrying an old smelly black gym bag and wearing a yellow Rupert Bear scarf. If this weren't bad enough, he's got on a bright red Gap puffa jacket that's easily ten years old and is holding his travel card like it's a press pass at a catwalk show.

The Gucci brigade salivates as he ambles unsuspectingly up to the door. I lurch into action, descending upon him like a tornado, whisking off his jacket and scarf, quickly tucking his bus pass into his breast pocket (he whimpers when I suggest we put it in his bag), and smoothing down his white-boy Afro rather unsuccessfully with the palm of my hand. Then I hand the whole bundle, bag and all, to the repulsed Norwegian coat check boy, who touches the Rupert Bear scarf as if it were medical waste and insists on giving us a separate ticket for each item, as if to punish us both for Darren's appalling lack of taste as well as his complete inability to travel light. The Gucci Girls narrow their eyes and one is about to speak, but she relents, waving us on and pursing her lips in a terse little smile as if to say: "You owe me one."

I'm left with Darren, bemused and bewildered, and not a little overwhelmed, who turns to me, clutching his bouquet of coat check tags and says, "I didn't know, Louie . . . you know, that it was *that* kind of place."

I laugh like Cruella DeVil and shove him towards the bar. "Don't be silly, darling!" I scream above the lethargic intoning of Ms. Paradis. "Let's get you a drink and look! You can watch people come in and laugh at the things above their heads!"

"Really?" He looks up at the billboard with all the savoir faire of a six-year old on their first trip to Disneyland. "Soooo cool! Louie, walk in so I can see what it says!"

"No, Darren," I say firmly, pushing him harder in the direction of the bar and away from the Gucci danger zone. "You only walk in once. You have to wait for someone new to come in. Those are the rules."

"Wow," he says, reverently. "We're in a place with *rules*."

Fashion is all about rules, as are fashionable places. We didn't want to have drinks at the local pub across the street from work. We wanted it to be different. Rules make it different—give us something to do, something to focus on instead of one another. And it's a success. Everyone's thrilled to be here, shouting to one another at point-blank range, spending too much money on expensive rounds of drinks, trying to dance between the tables and falling into strangers' laps. We get drunker and drunker, run out of cash and the credit cards come out. I'm flitting between groups of people, having half conversations— catching a verb here, an adjective there and throwing out my fair share in return.

"Fantastic!" I shout, blowing air kisses across the room to a man I saw peeing on video.

"Absolutely *screaming* at each other!" I interject, stealing the punch line from Colin's story, along with a sip of his martini.

"Really, *really* repulsive!" I stage-whisper behind my hand to a girlfriend as we watch one of the models ooze her way across the room to the ladies'.

Everything I utter comes with an exclamation point attached to it. I talk to no one for very long but we hug each other a lot and say things like, "We really must get together sometime!" And later on in the evening, when standing upright is becoming a bit of a challenge, we grab each other, bury our faces in each other's necks and sob, "I love you! I really, really do!" And then attempt to look each other meaningfully in the eye, which isn't easy when you're seeing double.

The next morning I'm trying to recover from my hangover, drinking coffee and munching on piles of toast with Ria. She couldn't make it last night. I went round to the gallery where she works to meet her, but she cried off at the last minute; said she wasn't in the mood for all those people, all that noise.

"You're never going to meet anyone if all you do is hang around the house," I lecture, waggling a finger at her across the kitchen.

She turns another page of the magazine she's reading. "And who did you meet?"

I have a hazy recollection of a loud agent pulling at my arm, a married photographer who wanted to do some "art shots" of me and another girl, a bisexual ex-army man . . .

"That's not the point," I snap, finding it difficult to butter my toast without shaking too much. "I'm out there; I'm in the game. You've gotta be in the game, Ria. Take it from me, I know."

"Aha," she murmurs, turning another page and smiling like the Mona Lisa.

She's looking at *Vogue* and as I sit down, I note, with considerable irritation, that they've dumped the whole seventies retro look and are now pushing a bouffant-debutante-meets-punk-rock-chick story that renders all my carefully researched knockoffs completely useless. The models are photographed skulking around in £700 Pucci shifts with torn fishnets and fat, absolutely enormous hair. It's not just a new look but a whole new ethos. I feel unnerved. How can they do this? I've only just learnt how to blow-dry my hair flat.

"I don't know why anyone would even bother to spend that much money on designer pieces!" I fume, wondering if I still have any fishnets lurking in my lingerie drawer. "In another few months, that look will be dead anyway. What's the point of spending seven hundred quid on something you can get from Topshop for thirty-five pounds in two weeks' time? Pass the sugar, please."

Ria pushes it across the table without looking up.

"I'm serious. What's the point?" I continue, furiously filling my coffee with spoonfuls of sugar. "Who would bother to spend that sort of money just to stay in fashion?"

"Well," she says quietly, sipping her tea, "first off, fashion is not the same as style. Secondly, a person might easily spend seven hundred pounds on something that was the real thing."

"The real thing?"

Is she being condescending?

"And what exactly is the real thing?" I ask. I can feel myself just picking a fight; someone has to pay for all the time I've wasted in Miss Selfridge.

"The real thing is what remains when fashion is gone," she continues, pouring herself a second cup of tea. "It has staying

power, character. It's a pair of well-tailored trousers, a perfectly fitted suit, a black cashmere polo neck . . ."

"Oh, right! You mean *boring clothes!*" I correct her, frustrated beyond belief that my new red snakeskin ankle boots are
already passé and she's talking to me about black polo necks as
if they were the Zen of fashion.

"Classics," she parries.

I glare at her. Has she been reading my book? Either that or
she's actually channeling for Madame Dariaux. "Classics are
for when you've given up," I point out. "Given up going out,
given up dancing, given up being fashionable. If you want to
be sexy and young, you have to be fashionable."

"Or perhaps," she says, eyeing me slyly, "they're the kinds
of things that appeal to you only when you've grown up."

A weighty silence descends between us. I hate her. And I
despise black polo-neck sweaters.

"So, how was it last night?" she asks, quickly changing the
subject.

I let her score her point; after all, I reason, she's obviously
one of those people who's already given up and it would be
rude to continue.

"It was great last night. Really, really good. Everyone was
there—Colin, Sanam, Nelson, Darren." I have a flash of inspiration. "You should come next time. I think you and Darren would really get along."

She wrinkles her nose at me. "We'll see."

I shrug my shoulders. "Sure. Maybe next time."

And I think about how staid she is with her home cooked
dinners and her piles of art catalogs, bless her. Doesn't she
know the clock is ticking? I pat her affectionately on the head
before I disappear down to Brixton Market in search of something vaguely Pucci that I can wear next Friday night.

Then, one Sunday, I find myself alone in the house with Ria. I'm suffering from a particularly irritating and persistent cold and have reluctantly canceled all my weekend plans in favor of sleeping face down on top of my duvet all afternoon. I linger in a coma-like state most of the day until the afternoon wanes and the sun sets. When I finally pad into the kitchen to make some dinner, I run into Ria, who's emerging for the same purpose after an afternoon of reading. We move effortlessly around the narrow galley together, ducking out of each other's way, sharing utensils, talking when we want to and comfortable in our silence when we don't. I'm struck by the easy calmness that I'm enjoying in her company.

We turn the television on and as luck would have it, a huge costume drama is airing its first episode that night. We nestle into the enormous, sagging sofa together and settle down to an evening of heaving bosoms and bursting bustiers.

A heated debate ensues over whether or not the oppressed virgin should really have a fringe or not and we disagree violently about the sexiness of the leading man. (Is it possible to love a man whose hair is bigger than yours? I think not but Ria believes it's all a matter of proportion.) And we agree unequivocally that there are, in fact, only three extras in the whole series that the production team just dress in different clothes and force into the back of each shot.

When the evening's over, I discover, much to my surprise, that I feel better and more refreshed than I have in a long time and yet we've done nothing, gone nowhere, said very little. I find myself eagerly looking forward to next Sunday and then the Sunday after that.

And very quickly Sundays become the most cherished day of the week.

It's a year later and Ria's birthday.

Colin and his new boyfriend, Andy, and I are taking her out to dinner. I'm wearing my red silk Joseph dress, and a matching cashmere cardigan. I've worn it a thousand times already this summer; it's my "summer outfit." But it's so perfect, so beautifully cut, that I don't mind if everyone's seen it before.

Ria's already waiting outside our favorite restaurant, Villandry, when I arrive. She, Andy, and Colin are sipping champagne and chatting in the warm glow of the late afternoon sun. She's holding a bouquet of flowers they gave her at work and she looks crisp and fresh in her white linen shirt and trousers. It's not a big party, just the four of us, but her face is beaming as I get out of the cab and she's so excited that when we sit down, she can hardly eat. I've asked them to make a cake for her, which they bring out with coffee. It's a solid, almost impenetrable block of pure chocolate with "Happy Birthday Ria" written on it in pink icing and a single, slender candle. When we sing "Happy Birthday," she turns bright red and starts to cry.

I've seen Ria a thousand times since I first met her. We know each other so well now that we can finish each other's sentences. I hand her my gift. It's a book about Barbara Hepworth she's been wanting for a long, long time.

And I know this. I know that she's wanted this book. I know that she'll order fish to start with and fish for her main course. I know she'll only have one glass of champagne because she doesn't really drink and that she's been lusting after that crisp, white linen blouse she's wearing for ages. I know what shoe size she wears, why she doesn't like the Underground, and how anything, beautifully done, can make her cry.

She's the real thing. A classic. A real black cashmere polo neck of a friend.

And after all, life's too short for anything else.

R

Restaurants

The question, "Where are we going tonight?" is never an idle one. It provides valuable information that will allow you to tailor your appearance to best suit the surroundings in which you find yourself over the course of the evening and it is just as unthinkable for an elegant woman to arrive at a restaurant for dinner in the wrong attire as it would be for her to turn up an hour late.

For example: if you are being treated to a glamorous evening in a fashionable bistro, prepare yourself for food that is really quite average but clientele that are sure to be wearing the very latest styles. You will feel most comfortable if you follow suit and choose something along the lines of a chic, little black dress, augmented with very fashionable, up to date accessories. If, however, your escort has selected a celebrated, well-established venue, then I would suggest you dress in whatever you own that's conservative, luxurious, and perhaps even a little banal. By all means, fling a mink stole over your shoulders and deck yourself in diamonds——this is exactly what he would expect. And besides, your more avant-garde, stylish ensemble will most likely be wasted on the older, affluent clientele, who are really only there to eat.

Never forget that when you are dressing for dinner, you are

*dressing not just for yourself, but also for the pleasure and comfort
of the gentleman taking you. And when a man is spending a
small fortune on an evening, he usually likes to be surrounded by
lavish decor, delectable cuisine, and a companion who looks as if
she blends in perfectly with both.*

And then it happens. Long after I'd left the fateful note,
Oliver Wendt makes a rare and brief appearance in the lobby.
I'm on my hands and knees counting programs in one of the
storage cupboards when I suddenly become aware of the smell
of cigarette smoke behind me. I turn to find him staring down
at me, lounging against the door frame and blowing a trail of
hazy smoke rings into the dusty sunlight that filters in from
the stained glass window above the main door. He looks
tanned and relaxed in his pale blue shirt and jeans.

"I guess you'd have to wear a tie at the Ritz," he ponders,
gazing reflectively at the slowly dissolving rings and flicking
his ash into one of the battered brass urns with a practiced
flick of the wrist.

I swallow hard. Easy does it, girl. Cool and aloof. Cool and
aloof.

"I suppose so," I answer, arching an eyebrow. "That is, of
course, if a person were actually going to the Ritz."

I smile coyly.

He smiles coyly.

And then suddenly my hands begin to shake. I turn bright
red and try to mask it by gripping the stack of programs as
tightly as possible. But somehow it only makes it worse. I'm
possessed; my hands have a life all their own and I can only
grin stupidly as the pile suddenly erupts and shoots across the
foyer as if under some supernatural attack.

"Shit!" I say as coolly and aloofly as possible, scrambling to pick them up. Oliver grins, places his cigarette carefully in the corner of his mouth, and stoops down to help me.

"You really have a knack with inanimate objects," he observes.

"I'm not normally this bad," I defend myself, furiously piling the programs together. I wish I were dead. "There are times, believe it or not, when I'm downright graceful."

"Let's hope Friday is one of those times," he replies, piling the programs swiftly into a spare box.

I freeze.

"Friday?" I try to sound casual and nonplussed. Unfortunately, my voice takes on a strange vibrato and it comes out more like Edith Evans delivering the famous handbag line in *The Importance of Being Earnest*. He appears not to notice.

After we finish stacking the programs, he lifts up the box. "Where would you like them?" he asks, ignoring my question.

"Ahh . . ." I'm having difficulty concentrating. "Ahh . . . here. Just here is fine."

He looks at me. "Here," he repeats.

"Yes, please, that would be great," I smile.

"But you just took them from here."

"Oh! OK . . . Well, what about there then." I point wildly to a spot across the foyer. "Let's take them over there!"

He hauls them over to the designated spot and puts them down.

"Thank you so much! That's terrific!" I gush. I'll have to wait until he leaves before I could move them back again.

"You're welcome." He draws hard on his cigarette.

We contemplate the box in silence for a moment.

"So, Friday," he begins; now it's his voice that sounds oddly Edith Evans. He shifts from one foot to the other. "I mean, that is, unless you have other plans."

"No," I stand numbly, trying my best not to throw up or fall down or destroy anything. "No," I pretend to be going over my social diary in my head, "I guess I could do Friday."

"Right then. Shall I collect you?" He makes it sound like a parcel.

"No, no!" I'm horrified at the thought of him seeing my home, especially my broom cupboard bedroom and Colin's dubious collection of objets d'art. "Why don't I meet you there."

"Seven o'clock?"

My mouth is dry. "Seven is fine," I croak.

"Then I'll see you there," he says, heading into the auditorium.

Suddenly I feel like the victim of a hit-and-run. "Yes, but where?" I call after him.

He turns and grins. "Somewhere I've never been before, Louise. The Ritz."

And then it's all over. He's gone. And there's only an impossibly tidy box of programs and a bit of fag ash left to confirm that he'd been there at all.

∞

"I guess you have to wear something pretty swell when you go to the Ritz," I chirrup to Colin when I arrive home that evening, eyes sparkling.

He's dusting the flat, and in particular, his prized collection of china figurines. There they all are, carefully lined up on the dining table: the naughty shepherd and shepherdess, the leaping tiger, the emaciated Don Quixote tilting at a windmill. He looks up.

"The Ritz! Well, I suppose, darling. Boys like me don't get much past Walthamstow KFC on a good night out. And who," he adds, grinning slyly, "would be taking my little Americano to the Ritz?"

I skip gleefully into my room. "Oh, no one. Only his name starts with an *O* and ends in *liver Wendt*!"

"My lord, he *is* straight! Hallelujah! Oh, Ouise! My own little Ouise!" He clutches the dust rag he's holding dramatically to his chest. "My little girl's all growed up! Next thing I know you'll be leaving me!"

"Col, stop rehearsing for *Coronation Street* and come help me."

"I don't know why I should," he sulks. "You never let me finish a scene."

A moment later he pokes his head round the door to find me tossing everything I own out of my wardrobe onto the bed.

"So, what are you going to wear?" I can feel him examining my room. The Post-its are gone now, but that's not the only thing troubling him. "Lord, don't you *ever* dust?" he despairs, his eye falling on my overcrowded bedside table. Shaking his head, he perches on the edge of the bed and starts wiping my perfume bottles with an air of quiet resignation. It's Colin's curse that he's unable to pass by any surface without inspecting it for dust.

"I just don't know . . . ," I fret. "I have nothing . . . absolutely nothing!" I chuck another pile onto the bed.

"I have an idea. When you're done throwing everything, we can put it all back, arranged in color-coded sections. Look," he smiles, holding his handiwork up to the light. "Now, just look at that and tell me it doesn't look better! You can even read the name on it now, *Amerige*."

"Colin! You're not paying attention to a word I'm saying! I don't have a thing to wear!"

"Don't be such a silly moo, of course you do!" He flicks his cloth over the lamp shade in a single, absentminded gesture. "But I can tell right now we're going to need a cup of good strong tea before we can make any real progress. Oh Ouise!" He shakes his head in disbelief as I throw another blouse onto the bed. "I don't know how a girl like you can still be using wire hangers! One would think you were raised by a pack of gypsies." And with that, he disappears into the kitchen to put the kettle on.

A few minutes later he's back with two "doubles," as he calls them, which are like espressos, only with tea; a specialty of his achieved by cramming a whole handful of PG Tips into a very small teapot and allowing them to brew until the color of tar. He claims it's how the British won the war, which brings troops of twitching, sweaty caffeine junkies to mind.

"Now." He settles onto the only available corner of the bed left. "Let's proceed logically. Option number one, please."

"Well, there's this." I hold up a tweed suit. "With this little top," I add, pointing to a black lace button-down shirt.

"Hummmmmm." He purses his lips and taps them with his forefinger. "Very mixed messages. Very 'I'm a prude, oops! No I'm not,' if you get my drift. Kinda 'Do I, don't I.' A little bit, 'Why Miss Jones, you're beautiful!' And just a touch 'Ooooo, matron!' Which, personally, I like. Only thing is, they don't seem to match."

"All right. What about this one?" I hold up a black evening dress.

"Louise, it's got a bow on it. How can a woman in her thirties own anything with a bow on it?"

"I thought it made me look young," I protest, weakly.

"Young is one thing; infantile is another." He waves it away.

"OK, fine. There's always my Pucci-look skirt and halter neck." I hold them up. He dismisses them as well.

"Ouise, that look is soooooo dead."

"What can I do?" I sink into a dejected mass on the floor.

"Whatever happened to that little black dress of yours? You know the one."

I shake my head. "The Karen Millen. I ripped a seam dancing at Mink Bikini and never had it repaired."

"Well, what would Madame What's Her Knickers say in a case like this?"

I look at him. "Col! You're the last person I would expect to send me back to Madame Dariaux!"

"Well, angel, you don't *have* to be completely psychotic about it—you could just read it and take the advice with a pinch of salt like a normal person."

I stick my tongue out at him. "I don't think so."

He shrugs his shoulders. "Then there's really nothing for it. You're going to have to borrow something from Ria."

"Ria! You must be joking!" I try to laugh, but a hollow choking sound comes out instead. Colin blinks at me, unmoved.

"Face facts, Ouise. It's a class joint and you, I'm sorry to say, ain't got no class clothes. No offense, sweetie, you're cute and sexy, but when we're talking about a two hundred–pound evening, we need Audrey Hepburn not Barbara Windsor. And," he goes on, raising a hand to silence me, "no matter what you think of our tiny dictator, you must admit, she's always beautifully dressed."

"She wears *old people clothes!*" I shout, trying very hard to resist the urge to pitch my tea at his head.

"Ahhaa! But that's just where you're wrong, my little bargain basement friend! Ria wears classics and the Ritz is a classic kind of place. Your aim is to blend into your surroundings, angel. Blend and become, blend and become . . . repeat after me. Ousie," his look is stern, "trust me on this. I'm an old queen, I know what I'm talking about."

"You're thirty-five, Colin."

"Yes, but in gay boy years that's sixty-five and shopping with a trolley."

"You're missing the point entirely! I don't want to blend in; I want to stand out! I've been waiting months for him to ask me out. I want him to notice me!"

"No." He shakes his head and waggles a finger at me as if I were an erring dog. "Not at the Ritz. Believe me, darling, you really *do* want to blend in, you just don't know it. And he has noticed you or else you wouldn't be going there in the first place."

"But if he saw how sexy I was . . ." I begin. But Colin continues to shake his head no.

"I'll think about it," I sulk.

"Do. Now," he stands up eagerly, "shall we color code these clothes?"

"No, not now. I want to be alone." I push him towards the door.

"Now, Ouise, you're not angry are you? Babe?"

I shove him out and slam the door shut.

"Ouise?" He presses his eye to the keyhole but I put my hand over it. "Don't be mad, it's for your own good. Even Audrey was nothing until she met Givenchy."

"With all due respect," I respond haughtily, "I am thirty-two years old, Colin, and I think I can dress myself. Now, if you don't mind, I'd like a little privacy."

Ask Ria for clothes! Honestly!

As I pick up my faux Pucci mini and rummage around for my sheer layered vest top, my eyes fall on the copy of *Elegance*, where it sits on top of a stack of books balanced against the windowsill. Perhaps Colin's right. Maybe it wouldn't do any harm to consult the oracle one more time.

I pick it up and hold it a moment, staring at the well-worn gray cover and feeling the familiar weight of it in my hands. I think of all the hours I've poured over its pages, searching for answers and advice. I was desperate then. But I'm not desperate now. After all, he's asked me out, hasn't he? I must be doing something right.

Still, I hesitate. Flipping the book open, I riffle through until I come to *R*.

"Dress in whatever you own that's conservative, luxurious, and perhaps even a little banal."

I look again at the tweed suit on my bed. OK. Why not give it a try? Moments later, I'm examining my reflection in the wardrobe mirror. Adorned top to bottom in brown tweed, I look not just conservative but positively *embalmed*. Attack of the Sexless Librarian. I take off the suit and throw it back on my bed in frustration.

There's nothing for it; rummaging around in the back of my wardrobe, I locate the damaged Karen Millen dress. I'm just going to have to repair it myself. And while I'm here, I toss my copy of *Elegance* behind a stack of old T-shirts and close the door.

I've waited far too long to let this opportunity go to waste.

And I don't need help from anyone.

∞

It's Friday night. I emerge from Green Park tube station waxed, shaved, depilated, exfoliated, refined, defined, moisturized, and volumized. I am, in supermarket terms, washed and ready to eat.

Getting dressed was nothing short of a nightmare. I figured

I had one shot at this and one shot only, therefore, I'd better not leave anything to chance. If I was going to successfully seduce Oliver Wendt, I'd better bring out the big guns. So, I've highlighted a few of my assets.

Although I'm not the world's greatest seamstress (or even in the top five thousand), I have managed to stitch together the torn seam of the black Karen Millen dress. Exhilarated after completing my task with such a relative amount of ease, I then decide to go that one step further. After all, if the dress looks sexy just above the knee, imagine how much more effective it will be if I take it up a few more inches. So much more Versace. And tonight I'm determined to give even Liz Hurley a run for her money in the glamour stakes. To finish the look off, I've got on strappy high heels to make me look taller, fishnets to make my legs look thinner, and a new, inflatable push-up bra aptly named Vavoom. Then I backcombed my hair to make it look fuller, sprinkled my eyes with gold glitter dust to bring out their color, and dusted my cleavage with a little blush. I'm not dressed so much as armed. He cannot fail to appreciate my natural charms.

However, impressive though I am in an MTV kind of way, I'm attracting a little more attention than I'd like traveling on the tube from Brixton. I'm practically chased down the platform by a Rasta who wants to sell me his travel card, calling out after me, "Oooo, I think you look *fancy*, girl!" This isn't quite the reaction I'm after.

I stand outside Green Park tube station with my black overcoat buttoned to the chin feeling more than a little peculiar. Compared with the hysteria of blow-drying, plucking, ironing, etc., showing up seems something of an anti-climax.

It's seven o'clock. I turn and make my way towards the Ritz.

I walk in from the cold, damp darkness of the park, past an army of uniformed doormen in coats ornamented with gleaming brass buttons and stiff epaulettes, bellhops in pillbox hats, and foyer attendants in morning suits.

The first thing I notice is how golden everything is. The light is, in fact, blinding, bedazzling. It sparkles across mirrors, bounces off crystal chandeliers, glitters over gilt surfaces. I stop for a moment, clinging to a corner of the front desk like a drunk while I catch my breath and allow my eyes to gradually adjust.

The second thing I take in is the sheer grandiosity of the place—the bold, unassailable authority of so many rococo flourishes gathered unblushingly into a single location. Pudgy, rosy-cheeked cherubs romp across pale blue skies on cream-colored clouds not unlike junior members of the Conservative party set loose at a party conference. Chandeliers blaze above velvet covered Louis Quatorze furniture. The atmosphere vibrates with self-assurance. There's the sound of a piano playing unobtrusively in the next room. "Isn't It Romantic?" it inquires softly. And it is.

And then I become aware of something else; it's as if gravity pulls harder at the Ritz. Everyone seems to be moving just a little bit slower than normal people do. I notice a blond woman sitting at a small table in the corner. She's dressed in an off the shoulder black cocktail dress, ornamented by a single strand of pearls. She could be twenty-five, thirty-five, an immaculate forty. She's engaged in conversation with an elegant man in his fifties, who could equally be her father, her husband, or her lover. He's handing her a small turquoise Tiffany bag which seems to float between his hand and hers. She smiles. He smiles. She opens the box and laughs a little before closing it again, and they exchange a knowing look. There is nothing hurried or impulsive about the transaction—they move in a kind of emotional slow motion, brought about by a drug more potent than Prozac or Valium. It's affluence itself that evens out their lives into a single, pale sheet of fine water-marked paper.

Gradually I become aware that all around me life defining moments are being played out against the plush emerald velvet seats—proposals, anniversaries, infidelities. It's no wonder that everyone is moving so slowly.

And here I am, about to join this exclusive club and engage in a life defining moment of my own.

I see him before he sees me. He's sitting, forlornly, at one of the small round tables in the lounge, drinking a beer from a glass and pulling awkwardly at his tie. It's an old school tie—I can tell by the bizarre combination of colors. And at that moment I realize, with a dreadful, sinking feeling in the pit of my stomach, that I've made a terrible mistake.

S

&

Sex

Unconsciously or not, men and women indulge in all sorts of artifices in order to attract each other, and the sad truth is that women almost always employ far less discretion than men. In fact, it is often in attempting to exploit their natural advantages that they destroy all hopes of elegance. So called sexy styles are never truly elegant, but only suitable for the vamps of gangster films or comic strips.

A kind of mythology seems to have been built up concerning men's preferences in fashion, with the result that many a young woman who deliberately dresses to attract masculine admiration often inspires only astonishment. To separate once and for all the fact from the fiction, this is:

What Is Really Attractive to Men:

- full skirts, tiny waists, and a long-legged look
- clothes that are in fashion, but not avant-garde; men follow the fashion trends more than you may realize
- furs, and a general air of luxury
- almost any shade of blue; white; very pale and very dark grey; certain men hate to see their wives in black; others adore it

- perfume——but modern men appreciate lighter perfumes than their fathers did, subtle sophisticated blends rather than simpler scents

What Men Think They Like (But Only in the Cinema):

- revealingly tight skirts and aggressively pointed bosoms
- false eyelashes
- "femme fatale" lingerie
- musky, oriental scents
- spike heels
- yards of black fringe and miles of red chiffon flounces

In short, men enjoy being envied, but they hate feeling conspicuous. *And they particularly dislike vulgarity in the woman they love.*

I ring Ria from the telephone in the ladies' loo.

"Louise? What is it? Where are you?"

"Ria, Ria, I've made a mistake, a terrible mistake!" I'm choked with tears.

"Calm down, baby. Where are you?"

"I'm at the Ritz."

"The bastard hasn't stood you up, has he?"

"No, no, he's here but . . ." I can almost taste the shame, "it's me. I . . . I'm *all wrong!*"

"Wrong? What do you mean?"

"I look like something out of Studio 54! I'm wearing my black Karen Millen dress."

"Yes? What's wrong with that?"

"I've . . . I've shortened it, Ria."

"By how much? An inch? Two inches?"

"Try five," I whisper.

There's a long silence.

"Oh Louise!" I can actually hear her shaking her head.

"Ria, you've got to help me!" I plead. "He's my destiny. I know it. But I can't go to dinner at the Ritz like this!"

She sighs. "All right," she says at last. "Stay where you are. I mean, no, go out, speak to him; it's rude to keep him waiting. But whatever you do, don't take your coat off! I'm on my way." And then she hangs up.

When I walk back to the lounge, he's still there. He stands up to greet me, holding his tie to his chest, as if he fears it might fall off into the cocktail peanuts. I smile a frozen head of death smile, pull my coat more tightly around me, and laugh like a hyena on helium.

"I'm so sorry I'm late . . . I just had to . . . to . . ."

"Quite right," he smiles, pulling out a green velvet chair for me. "Please." He motions to the chair again and then moves behind me. "Shall I take your coat?"

I recoil as from a hot flame. "No! No!" I hiss, coming over all Glenn Close. Then, seeing the look of shock on his face, force my mouth back into the death grin and say with as much softness as I can muster, "It's just that I'm so awfully cold." I thud into the chair like a sack of potatoes.

He motions to the waiter. Act like a normal person, act like a normal person, I berate myself in my head. Pull yourself together.

Right, I think. I'll fake it. He doesn't know what I'm wearing underneath this coat—I could be draped in Dior and dripping in diamonds. From this moment on, I am the blond woman with the Tiffany box.

"And what would Mademoiselle like?" purrs the waiter.

I straighten my shoulders, sit up, and cross my legs. "I'd very much like a glass of Chablis please."

Oliver smiles. "A glass of Chablis for the lady and another Heineken for me," he orders.

"Very good, sir." He dissolves into the golden ether.

Oliver looks at me admiringly and straightens the top of his tie. "I think we're going to have a good time tonight. I mean, I had my doubts about coming to a place like this. I'm not really a suit and tie kinda guy. To be honest with you, I like the atmosphere, the way people look. I guess I'm really a secret snob," he laughs.

I laugh gaily, fighting the desperate desire to sob outright. "Who isn't?" I parry lightly. I am the Tiffany woman, I am the Tiffany woman. "I love the Ritz. It's so quiet and discreet."

He looks at me carefully. "I thought you'd never been here before."

I am still the Tiffany woman, still the Tiffany woman. "Ah, yes, well now that I'm here, I find I love it. And it is discreet," I flounder. "Discretion is so undervalued, don't you think?" I sound like the straight man in an Oscar Wilde play.

"True enough." He passes me the peanuts.

I decline with a gentle wave of the hand. Women with Tiffany boxes do not require peanuts; they've undoubtedly had smoked salmon sandwiches at lunch.

The threat of a silence stretches out in front of us. When in doubt, ask a question. "Tell me about your day," I invite him, eager to abandon any more metaphysical discussion of the merits of discretion.

"Well," he begins, "everyone at work teased me today because I was wearing a suit." He smiles. "They wanted to know who I was trying to seduce."

My heart skips a beat. "And what did you tell them?"

"I told them I was meeting someone at the Ritz and that since they couldn't understand the concept of a suit and tie, they'd better just leave it. Of course, it didn't keep them from following me around all day trying to prize your name out of me."

Sudden panic. "And did you tell them?" I try to sound light and easy.

He sips his Heineken. "Well, I don't know about you, but I think discretion is so undervalued nowadays. Besides which, I decided that a girl with such refined tastes wasn't to be revealed lightly."

I want to say, Not all my tastes are refined, but I sip my Chablis instead. And then I spot Ria's diminutive figure scurrying past us, glaring at me significantly. The calvary has arrived!

I jump up. "Will you excuse me a moment?"

"Ah, sure . . . are you all right?"

"Oh, yes! Absolutely! It is a little warm in here after all. So I will check my coat." I smile and speed off to the ladies' where Ria's leaning against the sink, trying to catch her breath.

"Sorry, I ran all the way from the gallery," she gasps, fanning her face with her hand. "He's a bit of all right, isn't he? How's it going?"

"Uh, OK. Fine. I think. Truth is, I don't know."

"Hum, maybe you just need to relax. OK, let's see the damage," she sighs.

I open my coat, feeling very much like a flasher on a Sunday afternoon jaunt. She shudders and seems to deflate inwardly for a second, then rallies and looks me sternly in the eye. "I just want you to know I have never done this before and I will never, I repeat, *never* do this again. Right," she continues grimly, "there's only one thing for it; we'll have to swap. Get your kit off."

And she begins to undress. The ancient cloakroom attendant is completely unfazed by this bizarre transaction. Ria's come straight from work. My heart sinks at the austerity of the black Sonia Nuttal skirt and fitted gabardine top she's wearing. But then again, she's none too thrilled by the homemade micromini I hand her and flatly refuses to wear it under any circumstances. "If I die in a car accident, I'd rather people found me wearing nothing but my underwear," she says, slipping it into her handbag.

Three minutes later, I'm magically transformed from Sweet Charity into a real life Tiffany woman. The skirt which seemed so stark in its simplicity drapes across the moving figure with stunning fluidity. And the fitted top's bateau neckline frames my creamy pale shoulders in a subtly sexy way.

Ria regards me uncertainly. "Here." She hands me a tissue. "Rub off your lipstick. Hurry!" Then she carefully removes the gold, glitter eye shadow from my lids.

"My face looks chalky and washed out," I protest.

"Hush!" She pulls out a soft crimson lipstick and paints on a sweet red mouth. To my surprise, I actually look younger. Then she wets her hands and begins to smooth down my hair. I watch in horror as she undoes in thirty seconds what's taken forty-five minutes of blow-drying to achieve. But as she flattens my hair into a sleek little bob, it occurs to me I looked more confident without my rigidly coiffed mane.

"Now, what else?" She eyes me carefully. "This has to go." And she strips me of my sparkling necklace and earrings, slipping her own Georg Jensen silver cuff on my wrist instead.

"There!" Standing back to admire her handiwork, she pulls her overcoat around her. "You're a woman. Not a Barbie doll.

Let that be a lesson to you. Now get out there or he'll think you're a drug addict."

I hug her and force a twenty into her hand for the cab ride home. "Ria, I can't thank you enough, you're so kind, so amazing. You've worked miracles!"

She pushes me towards the door. "No one else but you, Louise. And remember, we must never, *ever* speak of this again."

At last, almost an hour after I arrived, I'm finally able to check my coat. As the decaying attendant hands me the tag, she leans forward and whispers, "Now *that's* a real friend."

I sashay forth in my chic reincarnation and sit down once again next to the would-be man of my dreams. Only, something strange happens, something unexpected. Clothes make the woman and Ria's clothes certainly transformed me. I feel more vulnerable. More exposed. No big hairdo, no sexual trimmings, no cartoon makeup mask to hide behind.

Oliver seems different too. He's ordered another Heineken in my absence and he's smoking a cigarette, playing with his lighter.

"You look stunning. I'm glad you decided to take off your coat." He smiles and it occurs to me that he's proud to be seen with me. However, his next question catches me off guard. "May I ask you something?"

"Of course."

"Are you married?"

There you have it; proof that gravity does pull harder at the Ritz.

"Yes." I feel awkward and detached—like the gig is up; I've been found out posing as a young, single woman. "We're getting a divorce. Right now we're separated."

He looks at me intently. "What happened?"

"Nothing happened." I don't really want to go down this avenue. "We didn't get on."

Any hope of sexual frisson drifts away. An uncomfortable cloud of seriousness descends. "And what do you want from me?" he demands.

And to this day, I will always shudder when I think of my response.

I look at him, sitting in the Ritz, sucking on a cigarette and I think of all the times I've wandered around the empty theater, hoping I'd run into him, imagining he felt the same way.

"To play," I say. It sounds plaintive, so I smile and try to make it seem cute, sexy, and enticing. "You know, like when you were a kid—just to play, have fun."

He's looking at me very seriously, not at all like a kid having fun.

"I see," he says at last and leans back in his chair again.

I'm an actress. I've auditioned for the role of mistress but the director remains unconvinced.

"I was with someone for seven years," he begins.

I feel as if I'm falling, very quickly, from a great height. This is not the conversation I imagined during all those months of obsession. Apparently we're not about to embark on a romantic, sparkling, magical evening. We're going to talk about the exes instead.

"We almost got married." He taps a packet of Marlboro Reds against the table. "Mind if I smoke?"

I shake my head no. After all, he's already started.

"She was pregnant. And lost the baby." He motions to the waiter. "Want another drink?"

I stare at my untouched glass of Chablis. "No. Thank you."

"Another Heineken," he orders. "And a whiskey chaser." The waiter nods and vanishes once more.

"Her name was Angela. She was amazing."

And suddenly it's all over.

Before it's even begun.

He smokes and drinks and tells me about how accomplished Angela was, of her courage and poise. He shows me the lighter she bought him one year for Christmas and makes me feel how heavy it is to hold. He talks about how difficult it is to pay two mortgages—she still lives in the house they once shared, while he moved out to a tiny studio flat not far away. And how she criticized his drinking; told him he was an alcoholic, but he's sure it's just a phase.

I smile and nod my head and play with the Georg Jensen cuff on my wrist. And in the golden light of the music filled lobby in the world's greatest hotel, impeccably dressed, beautifully coiffed, and ten pounds lighter than I've ever been, I finally realize I'm not going to get what I want. I'm not going to be saved by a thrilling, all-consuming relationship with Oliver Wendt. And even looking like the Tiffany woman can't protect me from all the gross realities that loom before me. I've left my husband and it's too late to scuttle back. I'll go home tonight and wake up tomorrow and there will be nothing there to distract me.

I'm alone. I've lived in absolute terror of just this moment and here it is—as cool and detached as a note scribbled in an appointment diary.

Friday, March 18th, 8:21 P.M.— you discover you are alone. Really.

Thing is, what happens at 8:22?

And for the first time, perhaps, since I've laid eyes on him, I have a real look at Oliver Wendt. He has a paunch. There are heavy, dark circles under his eyes. He's chain smoking and ordering another drink. But most of all, he's sitting with a beautiful woman, talking about someone who left him four years ago.

I have to smile.

Friday, March 18th, 8:22 P.M.—you discover you're better off. Really.

I think this is what's known as a moment of clarity. My grandmother used to comfort my widowed aunt by saying, "Better to go alone than to be badly accompanied." That always used to frighten me. But tonight, it starts to make perfect sense.

After a while I stand up, put my hand out and thank Oliver for agreeing so kindly to meet me.

"But I thought . . . ," he stammers, rising, "I thought that we might actually have dinner together—get to know one another."

"You're still in love with Angela," I remind him.

He seems genuinely shocked to hear it. "No, I'm not! I'm sure I'm not. I mean, I'll always love her, of course—"

"Besides which," I interrupt him, "I think that on this occasion, I'd rather dine alone."

And as he stands, swaying slightly in front of me, I realize he's drunk.

"I made a mistake," he says, blinking. "I . . . I've fucked up, haven't I?"

I don't know what to do or say. He seems pathetic, baffled and out of his depth.

"Would you like a cab?" I ask him quietly.

"Yes, yes, I guess that's the thing to do," he mumbles,

searching in vain for a coat he didn't bring, unable to look me in the eye.

We walk outside into the bracing cold and the doorman waves down a black cab and opens the door for him. He stands in front of me for a moment, wavering, and then suddenly demands hoarsely, "Kiss me."

There they are, the words I'd dreamt of. I feel myself go numb inside. And automatically, without thinking, I tilt my cheek towards him. He blinks, obviously shocked by my reading of this request, but he kisses it anyway, brushing his dry lips against my skin. Then he falls into the cab and the doorman slams the door shut. I watch as it lurches away into the darkness.

I walk slowly back inside. This isn't at all what I'd planned. What do I do now? I stand alone in the center of the lobby. Should I just get my coat and leave?

What would a woman of substance do in a case like this?

The maître d' smiles as I approach. "Good evening, Madam."

"Good evening."

"Table for one?" he asks, as if it were the most natural thing in the world.

"Yes, please," I say. "Table for one."

T

❧

Tan

Although I sincerely hope that I don't need to warn you about
the dangers of over sunning yourself and ruining your complexion,
I hardly imagine my own advice will dissuade you, especially if
you are intent upon spending your summer holidays looking like
a burnt piece of toast. There used to be a time when a deep tan
was absolutely essential upon returning from holiday to excite the
envy of all of one's poor friends who were condemned to spend
their summer months in the city. But modern travel means that
nowadays everyone has access to sunny climes and a tanned complexion is in no way unique or exclusive. So really, what is the
point?

While a lightly sun-tanned complexion creates an agreeable
impression of health, an overcooked epidermis is very ageing and
even inelegant upon one's return to the city at the end of the summer. In order to be attractive, a deep tan requires the open air,
very décolleté necklines, and bright, clear colours (particularly
blue, yellow, and white). The rather neutral shades of town ap-
parel often make a sun-tanned bathing beauty look more like an
off-duty field hand and there's nothing even remotely elegant
about that!

*   *   *

There comes a time in every woman's life when she's finally ready to move on.

The debacle with Oliver Wendt helped. But now, two weeks later, my decree nisi has arrived in the post, as stark and impersonal as a gas bill. The message is more than clear. I'm single—not just waiting for someone to return my phone call, but completely unattached to anyone in any way, either by old, lingering ties or by any shred of hope for the future. And now that the focus is firmly on me and my life, it's become clear that my time at the Phoenix Theatre Company is drawing to a close too.

Once this job was a haven. I started out as an usher, working weekends for extra pocket money when I first got married. Now I was one of two rotating box office managers (or rather, a Deputy Head of Sales, as they liked to call it). I can't deny that if things had worked out a little differently with Mr. Wendt, I might still be happily compiling sales reports with a ridiculous grin on my face, but now that the thought of bumping into him in the hallway fails to fill me with delight, I'm forced to concentrate on the job in hand. And the job in hand is dull.

"I'm thinking of making a career move," I say to Colin one lunchtime.

"Oh?" He picks at his lunch. "Fireman or policeman?"

"Well, there's a position going in the development department of the Royal Opera House." I hesitate. "Actually, I applied for it a while ago. And I've got an interview next week."

I wait anxiously for his response; after all, we've been working together for years. But he just sighs wearily. "Sounds perfect, Ouise. Let me know how you get on."

He pushes the same forkful of leftover fish pie from one side of his plate to another. Something is definitely wrong. I expected him to be disappointed or excited but nothing prepared me for his complete and utter disinterest. "Col, I can't help noticing that you seem a bit distracted today. Are you all right?" I ask.

He shakes his head sadly. "Nothing for it, I'm afraid."

"Nothing for what?" I persist.

He looks up at me with the most wayward, hopeless expression I've ever seen. "Oldest story in the book, Ouise. I'm in love."

I laugh with relief. "But that's wonderful! You should be over the moon! Right?"

He pushes his plate away and looks more despondent than ever. "Yeah, right. Thing is, he doesn't even know I exist. To him, I'm just some filthy old queen."

I have visions of a seventeen-year-old still shambling about in his school uniform. "How old is he?"

"Twenty-three," he confirms, with all the enthusiasm of a prisoner repeating his sentence.

"But that's fine, darling. What's wrong with that? You frightened me. I thought for a moment you'd been loitering by the school gates."

He shakes his head again. "You don't understand, Louise. This boy's an Adonis; an absolute god. The only way a boy like that's ever going to look at me twice is if I'm a rich sugar daddy. And let's face it, three Armani T-shirts, a flat in Streatham, and a monthly bus pass do not a sugar daddy make."

I can't believe what I'm hearing. "Shame on you, Col! How dare you speak like that! Not only are you demeaning yourself, but you're also being incredibly harsh on him. Do you really think so little of both of you? If that's the way you honestly think he is, I wonder that you're bothering to pursue him at all!"

"I'm not pursuing; I'm pining," he corrects me. "Which is exactly why I'm allowed to form bitter and twisted judgments about the object of my desire. Besides, I don't expect you to understand," he adds grandly. "I'm suffering from a condition that you can only guess at, Louise—a love that dare not speak its name."

I ignore this last bit of drama. "And where did you meet this Adonis?" I imagine some gyrating figure at Heaven or one of the pulsating pelvises from GAY.

But Colin blushes and begins fumbling with the strap on his backpack like a fourteen-year-old. "He's . . . I met him the day you sent me over to Copy Cat with the autumn-season proofs."

"The printer man?" I can't believe it. "Col, are you in love with Andy the printer man?"

He looks at me in surprise. "You know his name?"

"Of course! He's a total sweetie! He looks after our account; I've known him for ages."

"Andy." He repeats his name softly, as if invoking some magical being.

"Col, this isn't a love that dare not speak its name; it's Andy the printer man! He's a darling. Just ask him out!"

We're back to more fourteen-year-old mumbling. "Well, I'll . . . I'll certainly think about it . . ."

"Don't think, act!" I urge him.

He mumbles a bit more and the words "but," "can't," and "Adonis" are tossed around a few more times.

"Anyway, what's all this about an interview?" he says suddenly, obviously desperate to change the subject.

"I'm sorry I didn't tell you earlier, but I thought there'd be no point in mentioning it if I didn't get one."

"And in the development department." He's really listening now. "Very posh!"

I smile, and he reaches out and takes my hand.

"So you're leaving us, are you?"

I nod. "Time to move on, darling. Time to move on."

In the days that follow, I proceed to do what I always do when big changes are afoot: I panic. I panic about my background, my age, my lack of experience, my qualifications, my hair, my outfit for the interview, what will happen if I do get the job, what will happen if I don't, what they might ask me, and, most of all, how I'll respond to all these fictional questions. I sit alone at a table in the staff canteen, answering them at some length until one of my colleagues confesses I'm starting to frighten them and asks me to stop.

Colin, in the meantime, seems to have taken on a new lease of life. Not only has his depression lifted, but he positively glows with renewed health and vigor. When at last I lift my head long enough from my own obsessions to notice, I'm amazed to find him a man transformed.

"You seem well." I eye him as he bounces from his desk to the stationery cupboard in a single bound.

He just smiles at me.

"Have you lost weight?" There's something about him I can't quite place; a subtle difference I can't put my finger on. It's infuriating. I'm actually starting to feel jealous of him. And in my already heightened state, it's more than I can bear.

"C'mon," I snap. "What is it? What have you done?"

"Jesus, Ouise! Take a chill pill, why don't you!" He giggles, and then, seeing the look of psychopathic dementia cross my face, adds gently, "I was going to tell you about it anyway. It's a new self-tanning solution and it's amazing; makes you look ten years younger and ten pounds lighter overnight! I'll tell you, darling, it's just the boost you and the rest of rain-soaked London needs." He leans forward. "I'm even going to stop by the print shop on my way home and see if I can't lure Andy out for a drink! Really, you ought to try it. It's done wonders for my self-esteem."

I look at him skeptically. "You can't be talking about that orange stuff in a bottle?"

He taps the side of his nose. "When I get home tonight, IF I get home tonight, I'll show you everything. I promise." And he skips away from me before I can respond.

That night, sitting alone on the bus home, I wonder if, on the eve of my interview, I might not avail myself of a little bottled self-esteem too. Having rehearsed every conceivable outcome and scenario I can think of, including those involving fire, acts of terrorism, and the sudden, debilitating loss of feeling in one's limbs, I'm still no closer to feeling comfortable or confident about my big day. Besides, it's transformed Colin so completely and subtly that what could be the harm? I decide to take him up on his offer.

By twelve-thirty that night, Colin still hasn't come home. If ever I needed proof that the self tan works, this is it. However, having waited patiently for him for three and a half hours, I'm now reaching a fever pitch of anxiety about sleep deprivation and the importance of getting an early night. So, in a fit of hysteria and more determined than ever to appear for my interview as a sun-kissed goddess, I decide to raid Colin's bathroom shelf myself. After all, I hardly need an instruction manual and personal assistant to help me slap on a little fake tan.

Colin's shelf in the bathroom is stacked with more beauty products than Ria's and mine combined. It's not easy being a gay man. In the cutthroat world of Soho bars and one-night stands, only the youngest and fittest survive. There are toners, moisturizers, blemish sticks, foundation, cover-up crayons, and pot after pot of anti-aging creams, along with all the normal male grooming products of shaving creams, deodorants, and a stunning, completely comprehensive range of after-shaves and colognes which he arranges in alphabetical order, from Armani to YSL along the bathroom window ledge. It takes me a while to find what I'm looking for but eventually I discover the magical bottle of self-tanning lotion, tucked away behind an extra-large bottle of Regain shampoo.

I sit down on the side of the tub to read the instructions.

First prepare skin with Exfoliating Scrub and Moisture Surge Skin Balm.

I search again through Colin's massive collection of lotions and potions; they're nowhere to be found. Typical. You buy one product and they always make it sound as if you need to buy ten more. Well, if Colin has achieved such stunning results without them, so can I. I move on to the next section.

Then apply tanning lotion in smooth, even strokes, one limb at a time, to prevent streaking. The use of plastic gloves is highly recommended.

Plastic gloves? I look around the bathroom. Apart from a pair of old yellow rubber gloves crumpled in a heap by the bathroom cleanser, there are no other gloves to be seen. It's probably not that big a deal. They're most likely just being overly cautious in case someone suffers from some strange allergy. Besides, I can always wash it off.

Avoid contact with all fabrics and surfaces until completely dry. Formulation should be completely dry within ten minutes.

Sounds easy enough. Let's get cracking!

I strip off my clothes and begin slathering the stuff on. It looks a lot darker than I anticipated, as a matter of fact, it's like covering myself in oily mud. I consult the bottle again.

Color will appear initially darker but will rinse off in the morning to reveal silky, smooth skin and a golden, natural-looking tan.

Great. Right on target. I smooth some onto my face and neck and then stand, naked, in the middle of the bathroom waiting for it to dry. A half an hour later, it's still tacky to the touch but after forty-five minutes I decide that the definition of "dry" can probably be stretched to include "not absolutely sopping wet." Finally, somewhere around one-thirty or two in the morning, I fall into bed and drift into a deep, exhausted sleep.

The next morning, I stumble into the kitchen for a cup of coffee and am greeted by a horrified scream. "My God, Louise! What have you done to yourself?"

I'd almost forgotten. "Don't panic, Ria," I reassure her, "it's this fantastic new tanning lotion. As soon as I have a shower, you'll see. It washes off and all I'm left with is a glorious, golden glow."

"You look like an extra from *Quest for Fire*." She shakes her head skeptically. "And your hands, Louise, they're orange!"

I look down; my palms are at least two shades deeper orange than the rest of my hands, obviously from slathering the lotion on without the recommended plastic gloves. The effect is disturbingly simian. My confidence is starting to wane. I put my coffee down and jam them into my pockets. "I'm telling you

Ria, it all washes off! Look, I'll prove it to you." And I stride into the bathroom and turn on the shower.

Ten minutes later, I emerge, wet and triumphant. "See," I gloat, "what did I tell you? Do I look ten pounds lighter and ten years younger or what?"

She continues to stare at me in horror. "You're orange," she says at last. "A kind of *stripy* orange."

She's starting to really annoy me. "Ha ha ha. Very funny, Ria."

But she just shakes her head. "No, Louise. Not ha ha ha at all."

I run into my room and stare at myself in the mirror. She's right. My body's covered in bizarre orange tidemarks that don't make me look either ten pounds lighter or younger but definitely do give the impression I might easily glow in the dark. "Shit! What am I going to do?" I panic. "Ria, what can I possibly do?"

An evil little smile creeps across her face. "Apply for a job in Willy Wonka's Chocolate Factory?"

I glare at her and then, much to my shame, start to cry. "I have an interview at eleven o'clock!" I wail, two huge tears rolling down my cheeks. "At the Royal Opera House, and they probably don't hire orange people!"

"OK, OK, calm down. No more jokes, I promise. Come on." She takes my hand and leads me back into the bathroom. After ferreting around in a wicker basket for a few minutes, she comes up clutching a giant loofah. "Get back in the tub," she orders. "If we're lucky, we might be able to scrub it off."

I've never been treated for radiation contamination, but I imagine that standing, naked and shivering in a tub while somebody you never, *ever* intended to see you naked scrapes off the top three layers of your skin with a dry, rough object is all just part of the fun. Memorable as this attempt is in the humiliation stakes, it hardly puts a dent in the ginger tinge that's masquerading as my "natural-looking golden tan."

Finally we both give up. "Look Louise, as much as I've enjoyed this rare chance to indulge in some serious female bonding, I've got to go to work and you've got an interview. Face it: you're just going to have to tough it out."

I wrap my raw limbs carefully in a bath towel. "I could always reschedule. Say I got food poisoning or something."

She shrugs her shoulders. "It's up to you. Though, if they're interviewing today, they might easily find someone before they meet you. And it always looks a bit dodgy when someone can't turn up for an interview."

She's right. I have to go.

To minimize the damage I wear a navy trouser suit, hiding my monkey hands in the deep pockets. The pretty red dress I'd had dry cleaned and the new pair of Kurt Geiger shoes I'd splashed out on beckon but involve far too much skin exposure. Besides, as Ria points out, red and orange don't really mix. After buttoning my blouse right up under my chin, I'm left with only my curiously carroty face to deal with. Foundation only makes it look chalky, but luckily a thin dusting of translucent powder does wonders to tone down the neon quality of the tidemarks. By ten to ten, I'm out of the door, heading for the bus stop, just praying I won't be interviewed in a room with fluorescent lighting.

An hour later, I've been installed on a bench outside of one of the private bars, waiting to be called in. Eventually, a woman in her mid-forties emerges, shaking the hand of another candidate.

"Lovely to meet you, Portia," she smiles. "We'll be in touch. And please, do send my love to your father!"

The girl, at least ten years younger than me and sporting a perfectly normal skin shade, lopes off down the corridor, her long blond hair swinging behind her. My heart sinks. I wish I'd called in sick with food poisoning after all.

Then the woman turns to me. "Louise Cassova?"

"Canova," I correct her, standing and holding out my hand. "It's Italian."

"How lovely." She eyes my monkey paw warily and I jam it back in my pocket. "Would you like to come through?" I follow her into the empty bar. She gestures to a table and chairs by the window. "Please have a seat. My name is Charlotte Thorne, the Head of Human Resources. The Head of Development, Robert Brooks, will be joining us in a moment but I thought I might ask you a few questions myself."

I nod eagerly and feel my face stretching into a petrified grin of sheer terror.

She sits down and opens the file of résumés in front of her. "I see you were one of the lucky ones who got away over the Easter break." She makes small talk while she rummages through her pile of papers. "Where did you go?"

"I'm sorry?"

"I couldn't help noticing your tan. Did you go somewhere nice?" She's located what she was looking for and now gives me her full attention, folding her hands neatly in front of her on the table.

I freeze. Where do people who went away over Easter go? The Cayman Islands? Skiing? She sits there blinking at me. I can practically hear time slipping away while I stare blankly at her. "Well, no. No, I didn't get away this time . . . it's just . . . just . . . well, you know how we Italians are! A few sunny days and we're as brown as can be!"

I laugh inanely and she smiles, launching swiftly into her

standard line of attack. "Lucky you. So tell me, Louise, what makes you think you'd like to be part of our team here at the Royal?"

Fortunately, this *is* one of the questions I've prepared for. I take a deep breath. "Well, Charlotte, I guess the bottom line is, I'm just so passionate about the arts . . ." and I go on to bludgeon her with my enthusiasm until Mr. Brooks appears.

All in all, it goes better than I could've imagined, though, after Ms. Thorne introduces me as "multicultural," there are a few sticky moments when he insists on speaking to me in Italian (of which I'm entirely ignorant) and regales me with stories of his student adventures in Florence (where I've never been). But somehow my total ignorance escapes him; he's on a mission. And, despite the fact that I giggle nervously each time he addresses me, he seems to have taken a shine to me.

"Although we're a great British institution, we're also one of the world's leading international houses, Ms. Canova." (He rolls my surname out with such zealous attention to what he imagines the authentic pronunciation is, that I barely recognize it.) "And I feel that it's about time we reflected that in our personnel." He pumps my hand vigorously. "I'm certain we'll be seeing you again."

I exit the building as quickly as I can, before he has time to recall another secluded art collection or remote café in Florence I really must be familiar with.

Having made my escape, I stand panting with relief on the front steps, when a handsome young man stops me.

"Excuse me, do you have a light?"

I'm so shell-shocked that I just stare at him. "A light?" I repeat, as if he's speaking in code.

"Yes, you know, for a cigarette?" he prompts.

"Oh!" My mind kicks into gear. "Yes, of course! Let me have a look." And I rummage around in the bottom of my bag until I find a battered box of matches, bizarrely enough, some I'd pinched from the Ritz. I fumble to strike one and notice, to my embarrassment, that my hands are shaking violently.

I strike one and my hand wobbles dangerously towards his face. "Pardon me," he intervenes, gently steadying my wrist before leaning in. "I hope you don't mind."

"No, no. I'm sorry. I've just come out of an interview and I'm still a little shaky," I confess.

He smiles. "Please, allow me to return the favor." He offers me one of his cigarettes. "You look like maybe you could use one."

I hesitate. "I'm not really a smoker."

"Quite right," he nods. "Filthy habit. Absolutely disgusting." I watch as he takes a long, luxurious drag.

"Well, maybe just one wouldn't hurt."

He lights it for me and we stand a moment, smoking. It's only twelve-thirty, but it's already been quite a long day.

"So, how'd it go?" he asks, leaning casually against a poster for *Swan Lake*. And suddenly, smiling in the warm sunlight, it strikes me that he's easily the most beautiful man I've ever seen. Slim and not terribly tall, he's graced with a mass of wild, dark hair and even darker, enormous black eyes. When he smiles, his full lips relax into a sanguine grin that's both mischievous and completely benign.

I realize I've been staring at him. "I'm sorry," I apologize, coming to. "You were asking?"

"The job . . . do you think you got it?"

I shake my head. "I have no idea. Impossible to say. Do you work here?"

"Only for the summer. I'm a classical pianist. My sister

works here, and she managed to wrangle me a job playing for the Royal Ballet rehearsals. I'm studying in Paris this autumn and the money's really quite good."

"Gosh, the Royal Ballet, Paris. You must be wonderful!"

He grins, suddenly shy. "I'm lucky," he confesses. "Have you been to Paris?" He quickly changes the subject. "It's my favorite city in the world! You haven't lived unless you've idled away an entire afternoon sipping champagne and smoking cigarettes in a café on the Boulevard St. Germain!"

I laugh. "I've been to Paris but somehow I never got around to that."

"Then you must go again," he says softly.

I look up and catch his eye. He smiles again and I feel myself blushing.

"Do you like the ballet?" he asks.

"I love it. Or at least, I used to love it, many years ago. I haven't been in a very long time."

"Here." He reaches into his back pocket and pulls out a ticket. "I don't know what you're doing for the rest of the afternoon, but there's a dress rehearsal for *Swan Lake* going on at the moment. They give me these tickets and I always forget about them until it's too late. Speaking of which," he checks his watch, "I was due in rehearsal five minutes ago."

"That's so kind of you . . ." I falter, caught off guard by his generosity.

He stubs his cigarette out under his heel and turns to go. "Enjoy! And you never know, maybe you will get the job and I'll get to see more of you!"

A moment later, he's gone.

I take another drag. This is certainly turning out to be an unusual day, especially for one that had started off so disastrously.

I had planned to go straight home and hide for the rest of the afternoon. I look again at the ticket in my hand.

It's been a long time since I've been to the ballet. Eighteen years, in fact. That was the summer I stopped dancing. The same summer my mother tried to commit suicide.

I'd been asked to audition for the local ballet company that year. But when the day came, I never showed up. I blamed my mother; told myself I had too much to think about, that I needed to look after her.

Perhaps I couldn't bear to try and fail. Or perhaps I just wanted to be a normal teenager for once, without the pressure of establishing a whole career before the age of sixteen. It was her dream that I become a dancer. But after that summer, there seemed no point.

I'd failed.

Taking a deep breath, I exhale slowly and close my eyes. Long rows of girls stretch their legs in impossible positions on the barre. Rosin crunches beneath my feet. The air is thick with sweat and concentration. And there's music. Always music.

I flick my eyes open again.

Eighteen years is a long time to feel like a failure.

I take one last drag on my cigarette before throwing it away. Then I turn and walk inside.

"I'm afraid you're too late to take your seat," the young girl ushering informs me, "however, you are allowed to stand at the back of the dress circle until the end of the first act."

As I follow her up the grand central staircase, I notice how her jacket is just that bit too big, the way mine was when I used to usher at the Phoenix.

"Are you a student?" I ask as we reach the top.

She nods. "A singer at the Royal Academy. Only one year left."

I think about all the plays I've watched, standing at the back of the stalls in my ill-fitting jacket.

"Good luck!" I whisper as she opens the door and I slip inside.

And there, tucked into the warm, black curve of the circle, surrounded by the overwhelming music of Tchaikovsky, another equally unexpected thing happens.

As I stand there in the darkness, watching some of the finest dancers in the world, it gradually occurs to me that it's OK that I'm not one of them.

I couldn't have changed my mother anyway. No matter how hard I danced.

Darcy Bussell leaps across the stage, defying gravity—defying all the laws of nature—and a soaring, light-headed joy overwhelms me.

I haven't failed anyone. Least of all myself.

∞

Two days later, I'm called in for a second interview. And that afternoon, I become the first orange person to be hired by the Royal Opera House.

U

❦

Uniformity

*Thanks to the high standard of living in the Occident and the per-
fection of mass-produced Western fashions, an untrained observer
must have the impression that every woman is dressed exactly alike.
I do not know the origin of this modern form of modesty, which
has swept through the feminine population from San Francisco to
Paris, and which seems to cause all women to want to resemble
each other——even though at the same time they are spending
more and more on clothes, cosmetics, and hair dressers! But if you
really enjoy being dressed exactly like everybody else, then your future is rosy. Uniformity is the natural by-product of an automized
society, and——who knows?——perhaps one day individuality
will be considered a crime. In the meantime, you can always join
the Army.*

We don't dress for who we are, so much as who we would like
to be.

In London, different streets and different parts of town
have different uniforms. Soho has a dress code just as much
as the City or the King's Road. And then there are places
where these worlds collide. The theater is one of them.

A really hot production will have an audience as mixed as they come—conservative businessmen, aging Sloane rangers, hippie chic students, Notting Hill bohos, Prada and Armani clad minimalists, gay, straight, young, old, all mashed in together and yet as clearly defined as if they're wearing big labeled T-shirts.

It's a Friday night in early June. I'm sipping lukewarm white wine, being jostled to and fro in the bar of the Royal Court in residence at the Ambassadors Theatre and chatting to my friend Sandy, who, in a Cassandra-like fit of foresight, managed to book these tickets ages ago. It's a full house and the bar is heaving when the bells start to go and Sandy decides, the way certain women must, that two minutes before curtain up is the ideal time for a trip to the loo. The throng oozes its way slowly towards the auditorium and suddenly I catch a glimpse of a profile that seems familiar. It belongs to a smartly dressed man. He's leaning forward, listening with great intensity to what another, younger man is saying to him.

My mind is strangely blank. Yes, I *do* know him but from *where*?

And then that thing happens that sometimes occurs in great and dreadful moments where everything falls away—the crowd, the noise, the bells, and there is only the horrific, curious detail of the moment.

I do know that man.

It's my ex-husband.

I stare, mesmerized, as he turns around and laughs, slapping his friend on the shoulder.

I wouldn't have recognized him.

Couldn't have recognized him.

Everything about him is utterly, completely different. His hair is cropped short. Not cut, mind you, as in, I popped down to the barber's but *cropped*, as in I just nipped into Nicky Clarke's. And dyed. Pale, honey-colored highlights. He's wearing a pair of fitted dark brown velvet jeans and a Hugo Boss pale blue turtlenecked sweater with the neck worn slouchy and high, as if he's just this moment pulled it on over his head. Slung casually over his arm, is a softly tailored black leather jacket and his feet are adorned with a pair of Camper bowling shoes.

He isn't just dressed; he's groomed, styled.

Here is the man whose wardrobe consisted of shirts his mother had bought him from Marks & Spencer for Christmas, worn without being pressed, cuffs frayed and tattered until they literally fell off his body. Who found it physically painful to buy a new pair of shoes. And now he's transformed, floating butterfly-like over to the crowded bar to leave his glass, and wearing this season's hot item—the bowling shoes—without so much as a glimmer of discomfort or a trace of irony.

He's a changed man but one I recognize.

It's the uniform. I know it. I've seen it before.

My head is a vacuum, imploding. If I don't move, he won't see me. So I freeze, standing so rigidly that even the tables and chairs look animated in my presence. And I watch, holding my breath, as they press their way into the auditorium, chatting easily, completely unaware of my existence. He moves with unexpected fluidity, almost gliding up the stairs. I'm sick and fascinated at the same time.

Suddenly Sandy is by my side again, searching for the tickets in her wallet, panicking that she doesn't have change for the program seller, wondering out loud if she should fold her coat and put it under her seat or if she should pop it into the coat check. And before I know it, we're sitting, crammed next to a couple of German tourists clutching their knapsacks on their knees. The lights are dimming when I realize I'm still holding my glass of warm wine.

I can't remember anything about the first act. Intent on locating the silhouette of my ex-husband's head, I spent the whole of it looking through the audience, trying to discern his distinctive new haircut from the haircuts around him. I think I see him and then I don't. And I want to see him. To stare at him. I cannot—or rather won't—believe my eyes. So I stare into the blackness of the auditorium rather than at the brightly lit stage. The audience leans forward in fascination, laughs in all the right places, gasps during the climax, but still I can't find him.

Finally the first act ends and the lights come up.

"That was amazing!" Sandy gushes, completely enthralled. "Don't you think that was absolutely amazing?"

I spot them. There they are, walking up the center aisle. Laughing.

"Incredible," I mummer.

Sandy's standing up, brushing off her skirt. "Shall we?"

It's his friend I'm looking at now; same cropped haircut, same Camper bowling shoes, but young, younger than I'd realized. His face has that hyper-neatness. Does he pluck his eyebrows? And he's wearing a pair of Diesel jeans and a tight black T-shirt. They're walking past now. I hold my breath. Sandy's pushing me towards the end of our row and we slot in behind them. The cologne the young one's wearing wafts around me, clean and light, and then I watch as he reaches up and places his hand briefly against the back of my ex-husband's neck.

It's a small gesture: quick, casual. But it stops me dead in my tracks. A kind of slow motion close-up shot of the thing I never wanted to see. I'm staring, not at the hand, but at my ex-husband's reaction.

There is none. It's apparently normal for him to be touched in this way.

I cannot make my feet move forward anymore. The crowd is clogging up on the steps behind me.

"Are you all right?" Sandy asks, giving me a gentle shove. But I'm glued to the spot.

"I forgot my program," I croak, turning back against the tide, away from the bar. "I just want to grab my program."

And I stumble down the steps, past my row, to the front of the stage, where I lean, heart pounding, against the front of the orchestra pit.

I know. I know now.

I always knew, but now I really know.

You can't tell a book by its cover, but you can learn a lot about a person from their shoes.

V

Veils

Somewhat out of fashion at the moment (and I cannot imagine why), veils are one of the most flattering feminine adornments. If you wish to appear at once seductive, mysterious, and incredibly sophisticated, a veil will serve your purposes admirably. The unique charm of this accessory is that it allows even the most plain, uninspiring creature to look as if she's Anna Karenina, or at the very least, Garbo. And the very fact that part of the face is hidden from view creates a certain frisson that is both exciting and intriguing. Whether you choose a large, coarse veil, or a fine, delicate wisp of tulle, makes no difference. Women who wear veils are creatures with a past, a secret. And what could be more elegant than that?

"But I don't wear hats," I protest. "No one wears hats any more!"

"They do at Ascot," Colin says firmly. "You won't even get in unless you have a hat on your head, so you might as well get over it. Now, be a darling and pass me that piece of sandpaper, will you?"

I bend down and riffle through the collection of tools, dirty rags, and toxic potions Colin's using to strip the paint off the living room door. I come across something rough and brown and hand it to him. "This is such a total bore!" I sulk. "I don't even know why I have to go to this stupid event anyway. Corporate entertaining is turning out to be incredibly dull!"

"Well," Colin douses a toothbrush in turpentine and works it vigorously into the molding, "you didn't need to take the job at the Royal, did you? You could've always turned down the chance to make more money, work in a thrilling environment in one of the leading artistic institutions in the country, and own even more fantastic pairs of shoes. No one's twisting your arm. Utter mediocrity and a return to a life of ass-aching boredom is only a short phone call away . . ."

"Fine, I get your point." I flounce into an armchair.

Colin looks up at me sternly. "Don't you flounce at me, Missy. What's gotten into you anyway? You should be pleased, excited! Most girls would be thrilled to be going to Ascot and getting paid for it!"

"Most English girls," I correct him bitterly.

He frowns. "What has that got to do with anything?"

"Everything! Oh God, you just don't understand, do you!" I bury my face in my hands dramatically.

Colin puts down the toothbrush and eyes me warily. "Louie, is someone maybe just the tiniest bit premenstrual?"

"No!" I snap. "And don't be so condescending!"

"I think I'm doing pretty well," he counters. "Especially considering that I'm rooming with Dr. Jekyll and Mrs. Hyde. One minute you're thrilled to bits to get the job of your dreams and the next you're spitting flames because someone's taking you to one of the most sought after social events of the year and all you have to do is shove a hat on your head! Quite frankly, you've been in a foul mood all week and if your period isn't coming, you'd better have a pretty damned good excuse."

We sit in silence, glowering at one another.

"I'm sorry," I say. Finally. "It's just much . . . much harder than I thought." How can I explain it to him? "The trouble is, Col, I'm not English."

"I've got news for you Louise. You never were."

"Ha ha. No, I'm serious. These girls, they're like, how can I put it? Professionally English. Like the whole point of them is how English they are. For starters, they've all got names like Flora, Poppy, Hyacinth, and Ginista. It's like working in an herbaceous border. And this is just something they do to pass the time before they marry their City boyfriends. A job they got through Daddy, who either knows the artistic director or *is* the artistic director."

"Meeeeeeooooooooooow, Louie! Put the claws away!"

"It's not that they're not nice," I acquiesce, trying to control myself (and not succeeding). "They're fine in a sort of inbred, mutant kind of way. It's just that all we seem to do is entertain the fathers and mothers of their old school chums. For example: the head of Investment Banking at Goldman Sachs is Flora's best friend's dad. They spend all evening talking about his son at Eton and her brother at Harrow. The next day he books a season box and donates a check that's so large they're obliged to engrave his name all over the building—I'm talking on *every* conceivable surface!"

"And what, exactly, has this got to do with you?"

"I can't compete, Col! I just can't compete! Plus," I add bitterly, "they've all got legs *and* tits, which is just too, too unfair!"

He smiles at me. "You're jealous."

"Of course I'm jealous!" I rage. "But I'm also out of my depth! I can't do all this public school stuff. I've never been shooting, or to the races, or to Annabel's or Tramps or had my picture in *Harpers & Queen*. No one's ever invited me to their place in the country and I wouldn't know what to do once I got there! I'm from Pittsburgh, for Christ's sake! And now we're going to Ascot to entertain clients from BP and Reuters. I just know it's going to be like a kind of living hell, with hats and rules and strange insider knowledge I know absolutely nothing about."

He squeezes my knee. "Louise, that's why these girls are so useful in that profession; their upbringing and education guarantees that they have a certain number of connections. But they hired you for a reason. I suggest that you keep your eyes on your own paper. You're too old for this kind of bullshit. Plus, my dear, I hate to be the one to tell you, but it's really rather unattractive." He looks at me significantly. "Now, why don't you do me a favor and clean up that awful mess you made in the kitchen. Andy's coming round later and I don't want him thinking I live in a tip."

And with that, he goes back to his toothbrush and turpentine.

Two days later, I'm languishing at my desk, picking soggy tomatoes out of my calorie controlled BLT sandwich and attempting halfheartedly to jazz up my standard corporate begging letter without sounding too pathetic, when Poppy lurches over, all five foot ten inches of her, and invites me to join her for a session of hat shopping. A tangled assortment of arms and legs, she resembles an embarrassed giraffe as she tosses her long fringe out of her eyes and smiles at me shyly.

"I have absolutely *nothing* I can wear!" She slouches against my desk, pulling at the cuffs of her blouse in a vain attempt to make them cover her wrists. "I mean I have this really poxy hat from my sister's wedding last year but she insisted it had to be lilac."

Suddenly there's a scream from behind the felt partition that separates the desks. "*Noooooooo!*" Flora's blond bobbed head appears. "You *so* didn't tell me that Lavender was married!"

"Tell you!" Poppy rolls her eyes. "Flora, you were *there!*"

"Oh!" She's shocked to hear it. "Did I give them silver place card holders in the shape of pigs?"

"Pineapples," Poppy corrects her.

"I gave them pineapples? That's not like me." She frowns, chewing vigorously on the end of her pen. "Who did I go with?"

"Flora! You are such a cadet! Went to boarding school at like, three," she whispers to me behind her hand. "You gave them silver *pineapple* place card holders from Smythson's and you went with Jeremy Bourne-Houthwaite. Remember, you were practically engaged to him once."

The light goes on in Flora's pale blue eyes. "Oh! Lippy Houthwaite! Of course!" And they both start giggling uncontrollably.

"Lippy Houthwaite?" I'm not certain I really wanted to know.

"I'm telling you, Louise, he had the most *enormous* lips," Flora explains. "I mean, kissing him was like being attacked by a Labrador. I've never been so damp in all my life!"

And they giggle even harder until Poppy begins to choke. I pat her on the back.

"So, if you gals are going shopping, I *soooo* need to come with you," Flora pleads.

"Fine, where shall we go?" I ask.

"Lock's," they chirp in unison and then shout "Snap!" at one another, falling into hysterics again and pounding their feet into the floor.

Any minute now, I think, I'm definitely going to have an out of body experience.

"Lock's on St. James's Street," Poppy explains, when she's gained what, for her, passes as composure. "It's *the* place to go for a good, proper hat." She eyes me sternly, which, I must say, is odd coming from Poppy; she and any form of gravitas are not natural partners. "You don't want a *fancy* hat, do you?" (She says "fancy" the way that football thugs say the word "poof.")

"Well, no . . . ," I hesitate, secretly thinking that a fancy hat is exactly what I want; the fanciest, most stunning hat money can buy.

"No, you want a *proper* hat!" Flora nods her pale head with surprising vigor. "A proper English hat!" she adds significantly, like a Mason dropping a code word into casual conversation. There it is—the *E* word. I give way immediately.

"Oh yes! Absolutely!" I agree, overwhelmed by the strange feeling that any moment they might launch into an impromptu version of "Rule Britannia" and I don't know the words. I smile and they smile back at me. (This is my latest defense mechanism for dealing with anything that goes completely over my head. It also means I spend most of my day grinning like an idiot.)

I'm not quite sure what they meant by "proper" or "English," but it's clearly the antidote to "fancy," which, for reasons I'm too foreign to understand, is definitely beyond the pale. If I can just survive this latest shopping excursion, I'm bound to be initiated into some of the most elusive elements of the English upper-class social code.

"No fancy hats for me!" I cry gaily.

And perhaps, just a little prematurely.

It's not until later on that afternoon when I came face to face with Flora and Poppy's idea of a proper English hat that I begin to regret my earlier enthusiasm. They're all the size of small planets.

"Here, try this one," Flora says, jamming a colossal pink candy floss confection on my head. It slides down below my eyebrows and when it comes to a stop, the enormous brim sags listlessly over my shoulders.

They stand back in admiration.

"That is stunning!" Poppy gasps. "Simply stunning!"

I try to position myself in front of the mirror so that I can see the whole thing but only manage to knock over a pile of foldable Panamas some two feet away with my incredible brim.

"It seems a little large," I point out.

"Large!" Flora frowns. "But that's the whole point!"

"A big brim makes your hips look smaller," Poppy explains. *"And,"* she whispers conspiratorially, "you don't have to fix your hair."

"And if it's mammoth," Flora adds brightly, "you don't even need makeup!"

"I see." Hat as one stop dressing.

And then they try on a couple of equally daunting head meringues and I notice that even when we're standing brim to brim, there's a good three feet between our bodies. Then I get it. Like hedgerows and newspapers on the tube, these hats are primarily there to protect one's privacy—just another manifestation of that impenetrable English reserve.

I'm far more attracted to a small collection in the corner: trim, chic little creations to be worn at a jaunty angle by a confident woman. Brilliant jewel colors—emerald green, sapphire blue, ruby red, are decorated with feathers, curling in bold shapes around the head.

"What about these?" I venture.

Poppy wrinkles her nose at me. "A bit fancy, don't you think?"

Flora reaches over and picks one up. "That's going to do absolutely nothing for your hips."

"I like them." (What is it with English women and their hips?) In a fit of defiance, I try one on.

To be honest, it looks a bit silly. Even I can see that. The emerald feather that had seemed so striking on the white, hairless mannequin sprouts like some bizarre growth from the back of my head. It dangles eerily over one eye with a razor sharp point that threatens to stab anyone who comes too close. No matter where I put it, it retains the same sculptural rigidity, making me look more like an amateur performance artist than a sophisticated femme fatale.

Poppy curls her lip. Flora narrows her eyes.

"Quite frankly, it just tries too hard," Poppy says.

"She's right," Flora agrees.

And then she delivers the coup de grâce. "It looks a bit *common*."

There can be no insult more scathing than the accusation of being common. Even I, puppy dog exile from the home of the free, land of the brave, shudder inwardly at the finality of this sentence. And of course there are few things considered more common among the English upper classes than something that tries too hard. After all, effort itself is working class. Shamefaced, I whisk the hat off and the subject's dropped.

Poppy and Flora make their selections in a matter of minutes, deciding only between huge hats and obscenely huge hats, while I linger listlessly.

"Coming back to the office?" Poppy asks while Flora flags down a cab (they're unable to walk and carry their hatboxes at the same time).

"I, ah . . . I think I'll just have a peek at Fortnum's," I stall. As I watch them lumber merrily into their cab and head towards Piccadilly, I'm more disappointed than ever.

I wander up to Fortnum's. On the first floor they have a hat department rather like the one at Lock's, and once again, I try to make a selection from one of the wide-brimmed varieties. I'm peering sheepishly out from underneath a particularly vile pastel creation when I hear a voice behind me exclaim, "My dear, with all due respect, that really isn't you."

I turn around to face a very elegantly dressed, diminutive older woman. She has on a cream cashmere coat, draped over a classic, ivory Chanel suit and is carrying an alligator Kelly bag. She smiles at me and her remarkable blue eyes sparkle mischievously.

"It is none of my business, of course," she says, in a very refined Austrian accent. "However, I hate to see such folly in one so young. I must say," she continues, "it is rare to see someone of your age even looking at hats. I was of the impression that they were considered *très passé*."

"I'm going to Ascot," I explain, removing the offensive article from my head. "I need a hat and the girls I'm going with are all wearing these. I'm not quite sure of what's expected, of what's . . . best."

"I see," she nods. "You are American?"

"Yes, that's right," I confess, as if it were my guilty secret.

She pulls herself up to her full height (which put her at about five foot). "Those sorts of hats are good on English women; they are tall and don't like to attend to their hair properly. I would suggest that you wear something a little chicer, smaller. Something perhaps with a veil." She turns and hands me a small navy cloche with a dramatic loosely woven veil attached to the brim. "Something like this."

I put it on. Instantly, I'm perfectly aloof. The veil intervenes between myself and the outside world, creating a superior modesty that is at once seductive and impenetrable. And incredibly chic.

She smiles triumphantly. "Now, you see! That's much better."

I can't take my eyes off myself, I look so film star-ish. But still I hesitate. "It's just, well, the other girls won't be wearing this sort of thing," I falter. "It might be a little out of place, a little too . . ."

She raises her hand to stop me. "As I said, it is none of my business. But in my experience, it is best not to try too hard to be like the English. Being English is, after all, a club not even the English can get into. And they will not respect you for it."

And with that she turns and disappears among the women's lingerie, vanishing completely somewhere between the cashmere bathrobes and the Egyptian cotton nightdresses.

Suddenly, I panic—the only voice of sanity I've encountered all day is disappearing. "Wait!" I call out and run after her.

Almost instantly I find myself face to face with what appears to be a transvestite member of the senior sales staff. I say transvestite because she's built like a linebacker for the New Zealand All Blacks squeezed into an outsize polyester suit.

Folding her enormous hands across her chest, she glares at me. "And would Madame like to *buy* the hat?" she demands significantly, raising a single, omnipotent hairy eyebrow.

I reach for my head, and as my hand lands on the navy cloche, my heart sinks.

"Oh! I'm sorry! I didn't realize . . ." I stammer, feeling my face flush. I smile in what I imagine must be a winning fashion. "I was just . . . just looking for someone and I forgot I had this on my head and . . . and I . . ."

It isn't working. She's looking at me like I'm a criminal. I'm beginning to feel like a criminal.

I giggle stupidly. "Oh, really! You can't honestly imagine that I meant to . . ." (How can I put this?) "to . . . *abduct* the hat!"

She stares at me unblinkingly and exhales in a kind of snorting fashion reminiscent of a bull just before it charges.

I try a different tack.

I whip the hat off of my head and thrust it at her defiantly. (When in doubt, act like a spoilt child.) "Here!" I roll my eyes and do my best to seem indignant and superior. "Here is your hat! Now, I am sorry but I really must go!"

And just as I'm about to flounce past her and hurl myself headlong down the steps in a frantic, suicidal bid for freedom, my little Austrian friend reemerges.

"So. Are you taking it?" she asks, oblivious to the embarrassment of my current situation. "It is really quite the best one."

I'm about to respond when I notice that something is happening to the saleswoman. She blushes and flounders. "Lady Castle!" Her monstrous eyebrow shoots up to her hairline. "I do apologize . . . a simple misunderstanding, I'm sure . . . I mean . . . what a pleasure it is to see you!"

Lady Castle nods in her direction, otherwise ignoring her. "It is the best one, don't you agree?"

"Oh, yes . . ." She's desperate to appear accommodating. "It's undeniably a very sophisticated . . . a very . . . uh, unique design. . . ." I watch as my former foe melts to a jelly on the floor.

"Lady Castle, I want to thank you so much for helping me to make a selection." I pluck the hat back triumphantly. "Your advice has been invaluable."

"It is no trouble at all," she assures me. "I have a great deal of experience in these things. I have found a hat with a veil very useful in the past. It's flattering and a little mysterious. That sets one apart."

"Well, that's just it," I confide. "I already feel set apart— a little too set apart in fact. What I was trying to do was to fit in."

She shakes her head vigorously. "Fitting in is for school-girls. Being different is not a crime, my dear, but an asset."

I shrug my shoulders and smile wryly. "I'm not so sure."

Lady Castle looks appalled. "But of course it is! You are an individual! A woman with a past, a history. No one can take that away from you!"

I'm intrigued. She speaks so passionately, with such assurance that once again, I'm flooded with the feeling that I don't want to let her go.

"Would you allow me to buy you a cup of tea?" I offer, sounding, even to myself, like an archaic figure from a P. G. Wodehouse novel.

She accepts my invitation without a moment's hesitation, as if it's only natural that she should be invited to tea by a total stranger that she's just met in the hat department of one of the better department stores. This remarkable self-assurance is exactly the quality I feel I lack. And so, after I'd bought my hat we go downstairs to the splendor of Fortnum's tearoom, where Lady Castle promptly and unapologetically orders a full after-noon tea, complete with toasted tea cakes and scones.

I watch and listen in complete fascination as she recounts her history in England while effortlessly negotiating the business of serving tea with all the ease of one for whom it is a daily habit.

"The English are wonderful people. I adore them," she

says, adding a slice of lemon to her tea. "If it weren't for the English, I wouldn't be alive. It's as simple as that. During the war, I was sent from Austria when I was just a child. My mother put me on a train and I left. The only one to make it out alive. The only one," she repeats softly. "I do not know why I should be so lucky, only that I am. The English are my family now." She carefully presses the lemon against the side of her china cup with her teaspoon. "But like most families, it is not always easy."

"But you are a Lady now," I point out emphatically. "Surely that makes all the difference."

Again she looks surprised. "But, my dear, I always *was* a lady! Even when I was a scrawny, immigrant child who couldn't speak a word of English! I did not need to wait for a Lord to ask me to marry him before I became a Lady!"

"But what I mean"—I struggle to put it into words—"what I mean is, now that you are a Lady, you're one of them . . . you're not an outsider anymore."

"Outside, inside . . . you make too much of this thing." She takes a sip of Darjeeling, her sharp eyes never leaving my face. "What people respond to, what is such a mistake, is not that you are different, but that you are *ashamed* that you are different."

She smiles and pops another fruit tart on her plate. "These pastries! Really, they are too good! I shall have to fast this evening to make up for it. Do things with style, Louise. Your own style. And believe me, no one will care where you come from."

Back at the office, the hat is more of a miss than a hit with the girls.

"It's ever so serious," Flora turns it over in her hands like it's a bomb.

"Yes, it's certainly very adult," Poppy agrees. "You're a braver man than I," she adds, handing it back to me quickly.

I put it back into its box, undaunted.

"Cup of tea, anyone?" I offer.

"Oh yes please!" they chorus, ecstatic in the way only the English can be about tea.

That night, as I maneuver the hatbox in place on top of my wardrobe, I'm struck by the persistent feeling that I've met Lady Castle somewhere before. I sit down on the edge of my bed and concentrate. Who does she remind me of?

Then suddenly, it came to me. I open my wardrobe and unearth my volume of *Elegance*. Flicking it open, I browse through the gems of timeless advice. Lady Castle reminds me of Madame Dariaux and I realize with a twinge how much I've been missing her. She'd become real to me and even when I resented the unfailing accuracy of her wisdom, she's never let me down. I've been foolish to exile her and now carefully dust the book down and return it to its place of pride on my bedside table.

When the big day arrives, I discover that Lady Castle is right. I pair the hat with a very simply cut navy raw silk dress and matching jacket; the hat is, of course, the star of the show. Sure enough, amidst a sea of three-foot brims, I'm distinguished and aloof. And I have the additional bonus of being able to slip easily through the crowd, which is undoubtedly more elegant. The veil itself has the most surprising effect. It bestows upon me an instant status that's beyond anything I could've predicted. Men are incredibly solicitous, fascinated by it, and women intrigued. And as I walk towards Flora and Poppy across the Royal Enclosure, I see Flora's jaw drop, even from beneath the formidable brim of her candy floss creation.

"Oh Louise!" she cries, clutching at my arm forlornly. "You look exactly the way I would've liked to if only I could!"

And for the first time, I see them in a completely different light. They seem strangely vulnerable amid the daunting crush of morning suits and designer dresses; small and young with only their huge hats to protect them. And I think of Lady Castle's words: inside, outside, it makes no difference.

It's a long, thrilling, and exhausting day. The weather, so often gray and dismal in early June, turns out to be stunning and the clients genuinely appear to be having a good time. It's almost four o'clock before I can slip away for a few moments peace on my own. I'm strolling slowly through the crowd, wondering if I dare to place a bet, when I catch sight of a familiar face.

"Hello!" I say. It's the young man who'd given me the ticket on the opera house steps, only this time he's dressed in full morning suit.

"Hello!" He beams back. "What happened, did you get the job?"

"Yes, yes I did, and I just wanted to thank you so much for giving me that ticket. I can't tell you how amazing it was!" The crowd presses around us, pulling us in opposite directions as the bells sound.

"Look, I've got to quickly place this bet for my grandfather before the next race," he shouts over the noise of the throng. "Fancy a drink?"

"I can't," I shout back, just as the bells sound again. "I've got to get back in a minute. Run or you'll miss your chance!"

He pulls away, fighting his way to the shortest queue, but before I lose sight of him completely he turns and yells across the betting hall, "By the way, you look absolutely incredible!" Which results in a good-natured flurry of "Hear! Hear!" from some of the gentlemen around him.

He stands grinning at me and a moment later melts into the crowd.

My whole body's tingling, and as I make my way back to the Royal Enclosure, there's a definite spring in my step.

Ascot is a feast of fashion statements, some disastrous, others delightful. However, despite the vast variety, I'm surprised to see very few women wearing hats with veils. As a matter of fact, Lady Castle is wearing the only other one I spot all day. It's a small silver gray pillbox with a stunning swathe of black net falling across the face. Just below, her perfectly drawn matte red lips smile playfully and she gives me the slightest hint of a wink.

"I am really quite impressed!" She takes my arm as I approach. "*You* look like a lady—these others may *be* ladies, but you look like one. A real Wallis Simpson! Horrible woman, of course, but so beautifully dressed, you cannot imagine! Now," she steers me towards her box, "you must allow me to introduce you to some people. I have a feeling you might find them interesting." She swings me around to face a small, squat, red-faced man who's holding his glass of champagne as if it's a beer mug. "This is Fredrick von Hassel, Louise. Mr. Von Hassel has a passion for early music."

He thrusts a swollen pink paw at me, which I shake.

"Fredrick collects Caravaggios," Lady Castle continues. "I understand that the Royal Opera is mounting a new production of *Orfeo*. Is that correct?"

Before I have a chance to speak, Mr. Von Hassel is away.

"Nobody stages Monteverdi correctly!" he barks. "They are always trying to make a statement. To update the story. It is a great tale of love and death!" he shouts, his face growing redder by the second. "I cannot stand to see these productions! I object to them! I really object!"

Here is a moment when a veil really comes in handy. I blink. I smile. I take the liberty of brushing some of Mr. Von Hassel's spittle off my lapel and then quietly say, "That's such a shame. Especially as Caravaggio is the inspiration behind the design of our new production and I would love to have your opinion of it."

I think it's the exaggerated glamour of the veil that gives me the courage to turn away. Bold gestures as well as lingering silences come more easily behind a wall of mesh.

He's by my side in an instant.

"Caravaggio?" he stammers. "Please, I am most eager to hear more!"

The Von Hassel productions of early music are really one of the highlights of the winter season each year. They're thoughtful, intimate, and beautifully produced. More often than not, they're completely sold out months in advance. So book early.

And you might want to ask for seats in the Castle Box.

$\mathscr{W}$

❈

Weekends

After five days of gradual asphyxiation in town, an ever increasing number of city dwellers escape to the country for the weekend to fill their lungs with forty-eight hours' worth of fresh air.

As a result, an entire industry has been built around this desire for pastoral leisure, and never before have so many sports clothes been sold.

However it's important to note that 48 hours in a country house require almost the same number of clothes as a holiday abroad and if one is to be a pleasant and social guest, not one of the items in your overnight case will be optional.

These will include an attractive suit of the sporty variety, either of tweed or linen in the summer for travelling down, sensible, flat heeled shoes, a sturdy pair of boots for walking, a pretty silk dressing gown——never sheer or revealing in any way——for breakfast, a pair of trousers with a matching fitted shirt, a warm sweater or cardigan, a long evening dress for formal suppers or a shorter, more casual one for evenings en famille, a lightweight cotton dress and matching sandals for exploring the country side, a pair of mannish silk pyjamas, and above all, a hot water bottle in a soft cover, some of your favourite soap and a secret sup-

ply of biscuits. (It is impossible to know when and if you will ever be fed!)

This list will be longer and more complicated if your hostess expects you to engage in any kind of sport. Naturally riding will require that you come prepared with riding boots and jodhpurs, tennis means you should be dressed in a clean, white skirt, shirt, and shoes and, whatever you do, don't forget to bring along your racquet, golf clubs, or any other equipment that's necessary for a good game. You will not endear yourself to anyone if you're forced to borrow bits and pieces of the appropriate attire from either the hostess or other house guests.

So be warned and be prepared. Weekends away are the Waterloo of many a friendship. And you may ask yourself if it's worth all the trouble. I'm not an outdoor woman myself but I'm always incredibly refreshed and pleased after a weekend away, if only because I realize how wonderful and easy living in town really is!

After Ascot, I acquire a reputation in the office as a sophisticate. I nickname Flora and Poppy the Flower People, and they in turn call me Shanghai Lil in honor of my veiled success.

"It took more than one man to change my name to Shanghai Lil," Poppy intones at me every morning as I stroll in, clutching my double caffè latte. I wink at her, force my voice down two octaves, and sing the opening lines of "Falling in Love Again" until it becomes too murderously low for me to continue. And bit by bit, we grew accustomed to each other, then to appreciate one another, and finally to be friends. Despite our different backgrounds, I soon discover that my little Flower People have just as many secret vices as I do: Poppy's sole ambition in life is to meet a man she can wear high heels next to, hopefully while seducing him at her weekly salsa class, while Flora harbors a dangerous obsession with old reruns of *Dallas*. When we get bored (which is often), she regales us with stunning impersonations of Sue Ellen emerging from blackout, which Poppy claims are just a bit too realistic for comfort.

So it's not a complete surprise when, one steaming Thursday afternoon in August, Poppy casually asks if I'd like to spend the weekend with her and Flora at her family's country home in Berkshire.

"Nothing fancy," she says. "But it will give us a chance to get some fresh air and it's very relaxed down there. We can just laze about . . ."

The thought of escaping from London into the cool, green oasis of the English countryside is too intoxicating for words. I have visions of tea tables set up under a leafy canopy of chestnut trees, of hammocks swinging gently in the breeze, of dinner al fresco under the stars, accompanied only by a chorus of crickets, of girls in white dresses with blue satin sashes . . . essentially, I lose the plot.

"That sounds amazing!" I sigh.

"Great!" Poppy says. "We'll go tomorrow night after work. Flora's driving, so I'd suggest no solid food until we arrive . . . *if* we arrive! Really, Louise!" she beams, "I'm so pleased you're coming! It's only a small house party."

"House party?" I come to with a jolt. A weekend away is one thing; a house party is another animal altogether.

She sees the terror on my face. "But only small, teensy even," she assures me quickly. "Just my brother and his wife, Mum and Dad, my sister, Lavender, and her husband, who's a terrible bore and a bit of a letch, so stay clear, my other brother Tarquin, who's just been expelled from Eton so you're not to mention anything to do with school, school friends, academic hopes for the future, gap years, books, uniforms, Prince William, rugby, or alcohol in front of my parents. As a matter of fact, best to shun him altogether. It's what we'll all be doing. It's easier that way. Then there's you, me, and Flora, Flora's brother Eddie, who plays the piano, my grandparents, my mother's sister Hazel, my cousin Daisy, her friend Sacha, and possibly the Drews, who are friends of my aunt's and are thinking about getting a divorce." She smiles brightly. "So no one, really. It will be *so* cool!"

"Cool," I echo. "Really, really cool." But my heart sags like an empty, old Wellington boot.

I've never been good at staying at other people's houses. Even when I was a kid, I was terrible at sleepovers. And what is a house party if not one great big adult sleepover? I panic if I can't eat what I want when I want, and I'm extremely bad-tempered about sharing bathroom facilities. Creeping around corridors in the middle of the night, listening at bathroom doors for any sign of life, trying to pee as quietly as you can in case the walls are paper thin, all send shivers down my spine. In addition, I'm terrified that I'll be expected to participate in one of those country sports that require years of training. And special clothes. Like riding, shooting, or golf. I can see everyone else in impeccable hunt gear flying over fences while I plod along on an aging mule half a mile behind them.

"It will be brilliant," Poppy enthuses. "*And* we can play charades!"

Life can be so cruel.

"What can I do?" I duck down behind the felt partition and whisper into the phone to Colin. "I already said yes!"

"Sweetie, you go, of course. Honestly, don't be so silly. The whole trick of it is just to be prepared."

"Col, you don't understand!" I hiss. "I'm not good at communal living. It took me months just to get used to you and Ria!"

He sighs. "Fine. Tonight when you get home, we'll go over it all and I'll help you pack, all right? But no backing out! Truth is, with Ria at her sister's this weekend, Andy and I can finally have the house to ourselves—he's already gone to Marks & Spencer and I get to choose which videos we're watching."

"OK, OK. It's a deal," I agree. Nice to know that at least one of us has a love life.

When I arrive home that night, Colin greets me at the door with an ice cold glass of Chablis.

"Oh, you angel!" I collapse gratefully onto the couch. "How did you know?"

"I always know," he grins, settling down next to me. "Now look, I hope you don't mind but I borrowed your fashion book, Madame Thingy, just to have a look through. And I've come up with a few ideas. Here's what I think you're going to need, as a kind of bare minimum." And he hands me several pages of A4 notepaper.

I look at him. "You've got to be kidding."

He smiles. "Have another sip and try to keep an open mind, will you?"

The list is thoughtfully divided into "style sections":

For Traveling Down:
1 pair jeans—not too tatty
1 simple cashmere pullover
1 plain white T-shirt (+ 2 spare)
1 pair loafer-style driving shoes

"I won't actually be driving, Col."

"It's just a suggestion. Want some crisps?"

"Yes, please."

He disappears into the kitchen.

For Country Walks:
1 pair Wellington boots
1 Barbour or Barbour-style coat
Previous jeans, new T-shirt, cashmere pullover

"This is impossible! I don't have a pair of Wellingtons, let alone a cashmere pullover. And Barbour jackets stink to high heaven!"

"When in Rome, Ouise. Plain or cheese and onion?"

"Cheese and onion, please." I return to the list, which I'm beginning to hate.

For Town and Evening:
1 casual linen dress (for going into town)
1 simple jersey evening sheath for formal meals

"A simple jersey evening sheath? Have you ever *seen* a simple jersey evening sheath? I haven't." This is getting grim. "Col, you don't actually think they're going to dress for dinner . . . do you?"

He emerges with a bowl of crisps and hands them to me. "Well, you never know."

For Bed:
1 pair midweight pyjamas and matching robe
Slippers
Clean and matching knickers—just in case someone walks in on you by accident

"Col!"

"It could happen to anyone, Louise." He stretches out his long legs and pops a crisp in his mouth.

For Sport:
Tennis whites, tennis shoes, and racket
Riding boots (can borrow)
Bathing suit

I put the list down, my head reeling.

"This is just too much! I can't just go out and buy a tennis outfit or riding boots or even Wellingtons. I mean, surely they'll let me off the hook if I don't have all this gear . . ."

He stares at me. An unyielding silence settles between us.

I try a different tack. "There must be other people in the party who aren't going riding, or shooting, or whatever they do in the country. A special outfit to walk in? I just don't get that. I mean, not everyone's robe is going to match their pajamas, not everyone is going to spend tonight bleaching their knickers just in case the lock on the bathroom door doesn't work. I can't be the only one!"

He shrugs his shoulders. "Look, you asked for my help. Here it is. I can't help it if that's what people wear in the country, can I? You're welcome to go down there with nothing but a fresh pair of knickers but what if they do dress for dinner, huh? What are you going to do then?"

I'm just about to tell him when Ria lets herself in the front door.

"What's all this about?" She throws herself down on the sofa next to me and helps herself to some crisps.

I sigh heavily. "I've been invited by Poppy for a weekend at her country house and it turns out it's a whole house party full of strangers and I'm not sure what to take or what I need and Colin's trying to help me . . ."

She takes a sip of my wine. "Well, I just hope you've got a pair of Wellingtons."

Shit.

Later that evening, I unearth my sky blue nylon overnight bag and plop it on the bed. I'd bought it in the LA airport sometime in the eighties when I'd stocked up on too many plastic flip-flops to fit into my suitcase. It sags open in all its garish glory, like a soiled, battered mouth, covered in airline stickers and boarding tags. I strip off the excess tags but it still looks cheap and ridiculously bright. I'm distinctly uninspired.

Next I open my wardrobe and consider what I own that might actually be suitable. A pair of flared Diesel jeans, a cropped Morgan cardigan, a leather shift dress that makes more noise when I move than a military demonstration in Red Square.

Then I remember that Colin had consulted my old friend Madame Dariaux when making his list. Sitting on the bed, I open to *W* and read her advice.

Be warned and be prepared.

My heart sinks. Colin is right after all. And as I sit there, holding my book, I begin to wonder if I will ever graduate from Madame Dariaux's tutelage. Just when I think I've got it sussed, some new, unexpected dilemma comes careering along. Part of me longs to chuck a few pairs of clean pants into my blue nylon bag and be done with it. And yet I can't. I've come too far. If I've learnt one thing, it's that being elegant is just a matter of being willing to make an extra effort and enter into the spirit of things—of life—with enthusiasm and grace. And after all, if this is how people dress for a weekend away, then it's not going to kill me to give it a try.

I knock on Ria's door.

"Yep?"

I poke my head round the corner. "Do you know anyone who has a pair of Wellingtons I could borrow?"

She smiles. "I think my sister has a pair. I'll see what I can do."

Come Friday afternoon, after a day of frantic bargaining and begging, I've finally managed to pack a reasonable sized bag (that's using the word reasonable liberally) for my weekend away. I'm pretty well prepared for just about every occasion, except for tennis, which I've resolved to solve by posing as a fascinated bystander. Otherwise, although I'll never be accused of demonstrating the height of casual country chic, I can console myself that at least my pajama tops match my pajama bottoms and I've managed to pack a dress that shouldn't crease too badly and both an outdoor and an indoor pair of shoes. As a matter of fact, I'm inwardly congratulating myself on how well I've done, taking everything in my stride, when Flora pulls up outside the office in her aging, sunshine yellow Beetle convertible and toots the horn.

"She's here!" Poppy's whole face shines with joy as she leans out of the office window and waves. And then I suddenly remember the thing I've forgotten.

"Shit! Shit, shit, shit! I can't believe it!"

"What is it?" Poppy says, rushing to turn off her computer and set the answering machine.

"Listen, I've forgotten to get a gift for your mum and dad." I grab my wallet from my massive cherry-red straw handbag and race towards the door. "Be an angel and pop my bag in the trunk for me. I won't be a minute, I swear! Tell Flora to wait!" And I run frantically down the steps towards the staff exit.

One of the brilliant things about working at the Royal Opera House is that you're right in the center of Covent Garden. It takes me just fifteen minutes to pop into Penhaligon's, buy a gift-wrapped box set of scented candles, and tear back to the car where Flora and Poppy are waiting.

"Ready?" Flora's revving her engine and slipping on her pink plastic shades.

"Ready!" I shout, throwing myself into the backseat.

The car lurches forward, barely missing a Big Issue seller, and we're off, speeding out of London, racing towards a greener, pleasanter land in the dappled light of the warm evening sun.

Somewhere between Oxford and Reading we turn off the main road and fall, like Alice in Wonderland, into the surreal, impenetrable rabbit warren of secondary roads that weave across the countryside, hugging the hedgerows as they twist from one bizarrely named enclave to another. Three Mile Cross, Rotherfield Peppard, Nettlebed, Russell's Water, Gallowstree Common—the names are not so much destinations as roads not taken in a mystical, magical journey worthy of J. R. R. Tolkien or C. S. Lewis. We pass Tutts Clump, narrowly escape Rotten Row and are headed towards a fate known as Sheffield's Bottom when Flora takes a sharp right. We skid off the road and onto a paved driveway that extends for a quarter of a mile through parkland, bordered on either side by an avenue of ancient chestnut trees. As we near the house, the parkland gives way to a rolling green carpet of immaculately manicured lawn and there, sprawled before us is Poppy's family home—a huge Queen Anne house of red brick and leaded glass windows, complete with two narrow turrets and a set of snarling gargoyles posed above the solid oak door.

I'm not certain if it's the unbelievable size of the place or Flora's driving, but suddenly I'm finding it very difficult to catch my breath.

"We're here!" Poppy jumps out of the front seat with surprising agility for a girl of her size.

"My God, Poppy!" I gasp. "You live here?"

"It *is* nice," she concedes. "But it's full of damp and costs a fortune to heat . . . not a patch on my little cubbyhole in Notting Hill."

She pushes the car seat forward and I try to step out. However, my knees are shaking so much that I collapse onto the drive instead.

"Oopsy-daisy!" Flora picks me up off the gravel, completely unfazed (people evidently always fall out of the cars she drives). "Deep breaths, Louise, it will pass. Isn't this air terrific?"

And the next thing I know, I'm surrounded by dogs. Not just two or three but easily twelve of various breeds and sizes, jumping, barking, licking, and sniffing in that overly intimate way you dearly wish they wouldn't and all smelling quite distinctly, quite strongly of dog. In the midst of this canine cloud, a woman with absolutely no sign of ever owning a chin emerges, towering above even Poppy in a pair of old Wellingtons and brandishing a pair of lethal looking pruning shears.

"Down!" She booms in a voice that could rule an empire (or destroy one). "Down, boys! Jasper! No! NO! Just push him off," she instructs me. "He hasn't been done yet and he's a *terrible* nuisance."

"Mummy!" Poppy leans forward across the sea of waggling tails in an attempt to kiss her mother on the cheek. However, this noble effort is thwarted not just by the dogs but by Mrs. Simpson-Stock herself, who performs a swift side step, thus neatly avoiding any form of physical intimacy. The move throws Poppy off balance and she lands heavily on her mother's shoulder.

"Honestly, Poppy!" she snorts, pushing her away. "Still as clumsy as ever!"

"Yes, Mummy," Poppy giggles. "You know me!"

"Hello Flora." Mummy's hand shoots forward as if it were spring-loaded. She shakes Flora's hand so violently that her blond bob bounces up and down and her sunglasses fly off her head, lost in a sea of dog. Next she turns her fearsome hospitality to me. "And you must be The American!" she bellows, giving me the same brain-addling handshake.

"Louise, Mummy. Her name's Louise," Poppy corrects her.

"Yes, well, Louise, welcome to Lower Slaughter. Just make yourself at home. We have only a few rules here. First off, supper is seven-thirty for eight P.M. Sharp. And secondly, no feeding the dogs! They're fat enough, aren't you boys, aren't you my lovely little babies! Yessssssssss! And thirdly, no strangers in the gun room. If someone's going to get their head blown off, I'd prefer it was a member of my own family. Understood?"

"Absolutely," I joke. "We have similar rules about guns in my family too."

She stares at me stonily.

No one makes a sound. Even the dogs sense I've made a faux pas and freeze mid-wag. Somewhere in the distance a peacock cries eerily. Wind whistles through the chestnut trees. Time, who waits for no man, is apparently quite accustomed to standing still for Mrs. Simpson-Stock.

"Yes. Well. Be that as it may," she says finally, and the film starts rolling again. "Poppy will show you to your rooms. I expect that you will actually *sleep* in yours this time, Flora," she adds, raising an eyebrow significantly, to which Flora responds by turning several shades of crimson and giggling nervously.

In a desperate bid to repair the damage I've already done, I thrust the Penhaligon's gift box towards her. "These are for you," I smile; the very essence of obsequiousness. "Just a little something to say thank you."

"Very much obliged," she replies brusquely, taking the box and tucking it neatly under her arm without so much as a glance. "Bound to be scented candles or soap. All anyone ever brings me is scented candles and soap. I'm certain I'm the cleanest, freshest smelling woman in Christendom. But you're very kind. A well brought up young woman. Don't expect such civilized manners from an American. Now, I must finish pruning these rosebushes before supper. Remember, eight P.M. sharp. And Poppy, for Christ's sake! Don't slouch! Come on, boys!"

And she tramps off, engulfed in the cloud of dogs.

We stand in silence a moment, more shell-shocked than anything until Poppy heaves a long sigh. "Isn't she a darling? I think she adores you already."

"Bit of a favorite," Flora confirms. "It was two years before she even spoke to me."

Poppy unhands the bags from the trunk. She slams it shut and gathers her things. "Shall we go in and I'll show you around?"

I stare at the pile of luggage. Something's missing. "Where's my case?"

She and Flora look at each other.

"What case?" Flora says.

The whole bottom of my stomach falls away. "The blue nylon case I brought to the office. The one I asked you to put in the trunk for me."

There's that damned peacock again.

Poppy opens her mouth, then shuts it again. She looks confused. "But when you said put your bag in, I thought you meant that," she explains, pointing to the cherry-red straw bag. "I thought that was your weekend bag."

My throat is dry. "*That* is my handbag," I croak.

Silence.

"It *is* an awfully big handbag." Flora's trying to be helpful. She's not.

"Oops!" Poppy laughs awkwardly, slapping me on the back a little too roughly. "Never mind! You can borrow some clothes from Flora and me. I'm sure we'll find you something!"

I'm drifting into a coma of despair. All my easy adaptability, instantly vanishes.

"Come on, Louise! Don't look so glum!" Flora says. "It's not the end of the world! I'm sure I've got a pair of knickers you can borrow and those trousers you're wearing," she eyes my "not too tatty" jeans, "well, I'm sure they're just fine . . . dinner isn't, well, *too* formal and as long as you don't go riding in them . . ." Her voice trails off as she begins to comprehend the reality of spending a whole weekend at Lower Slaughter with nothing but a pair of jeans and a cardigan.

We stand in silence for a moment, staring at the blank space on the driveway where my bag should be.

"I *am* sorry," Poppy apologizes softly, putting her arm around my shoulders and easing me gently towards the front door. "We'll sort something out, I promise."

But as well meaning as they are, all I can think of is how

they're at least six inches taller than I am. How will I ever manage without my borrowed Wellingtons and my carefully folded crease-proof dress?

Poppy shows me to a room on the east side of the house that's decorated in pre-war Liberty prints and has the kind of sloping ceiling and uneven floorboards that conspire to attack even the most docile visitor. The bed groans in protest when I sit on it.

"There's a lav just down the hall and Flora and I are right next to you." Her voice is gentle and kind, as if trying to console an elderly relative. "Why don't you have a rest and I'll knock on your door when it's time for dinner?"

"Wonderful!" I force a smile. "I'll just have a lie down."

They leave and I sink onto the bed. A gentle breeze wafts in through the open window and suddenly I deflate like a balloon, utterly worn out. Much to my shame, stinging tears well up in my eyes. The tears of a disappointed eight-year-old who wants to go home. Resistance is useless. I curl up into a little ball and surrender. All my expectations of another dazzling Ascot-type triumph dissolve. For all my fastidious planning, I couldn't have reckoned on this. I'm going to end up being uncomfortable and badly dressed all weekend, shambling about like a homeless person in the same outfit for three days. I punch the pillow in frustration and a blizzard of feathers spurts out, covering the duvet and part of the floor.

That's all I need. Sobbing bitterly now, I crouch down and try in vain to gather up the dusty feathers whirring around me.

So here I am, scrambling around on my hands and knees, drowning in a sea of self-pity and non-waterproof mascara, when slowly I become aware of the sound of piano music drifting in through the open window. It begins softly, delicately, building in a series of intricate themes. Slowly it gathers strength and force, finally exploding in a pile of octaves, furiously stacked one upon another, and then subsiding, softening, melting, and beginning the cycle all over again.

I kneel on the floor, transfixed. Perhaps it's a recording or maybe someone's listening to the radio. But after a while the piece ends and then a particularly tricky bit is repeated; it's played over and over until the pianist gains confidence and clarity. And I realize with a shock that the music is live.

I stop crying. Or rather, I simply forget to continue. Getting up from the floor, I push the bedroom door open and creep downstairs, following the music like a hypnotized child trailing after the Pied Piper, moving as quietly as possible so as not to break the spell.

Most of the guests are out on the lawn, playing croquet or collapsed into loungers. The house itself is abandoned. A warm zephyr blows in through the open windows, gathering and releasing the sheer curtains with silent, invisible hands, almost in time with the music.

At the bottom of the stairs, I turn a corner and follow the corridor along until I come to a long narrow room, bordered on one side by a wall of windows and on the other by floor-to-ceiling bookshelves. At the far end of the room, there's an elegant early twentieth-century Steinway grand piano. And there, unmistakable, even with his back towards me, sits the young man from the Opera House steps.

Playing with a kind of tremendous fury, oblivious to everything around him, his long fingers glide over the keyboard with unbelievable speed; one moment attacking, the next caressing in a dazzling display of technical and interpretive brilliance. The total assurance of his playing is nothing less than heroic. Nothing is measured or hesitant. Even the softer passages display a level of involvement and commitment uncommon in everyday life. I hover a moment in the doorway. Nothing, not even an act of God is likely to distract him, so I steal in.

And as I stand, listening in the corner, a remarkable transformation takes place. My shoulders release and sink forward. The tight thread knotted in my head begins to unravel. And gradually I'm aware of the even, steady sound of my own breathing. The last rays of the shocking pink sunset glow over the lawn, outlining his shoulders and highlighting his dark hair. They radiate around his fine features like a halo of golden light, too beautiful to be real.

Only he is real.

And then, incredibly, even the all-pervading smell of dog vanishes and is replaced instead by the delicate perfume of the late summer roses that wind around the open glass doors.

I don't know how long I've been there, maybe a few minutes, maybe half an hour, but after a while he stops playing and turns around.

"Oh, hello," he smiles. "Fancy seeing you here! Have you been there long?"

"Yes, well, no . . ." I hesitate, "not long enough. That is, you play so beautifully."

"Thank you," he tilts his head shyly. "Fourth Ballade. Chopin. My favorite. Or, actually no," he corrects himself, apparently unable to let such a shocking inaccuracy slide. "Beethoven's my real favorite, and then Chopin, Brahms, and you can't beat Rachmaninoff. Do you like him?" he plays a few bars of Rachmaninoff's Third Piano Concerto. "Isn't that amazing? And this bit . . ." he launches into another passage. "This is the absolute best bit of all!" he shouts above the crashing chords. "You've gotta love it!"

"Yes, it's amazing," I agree, laughing. His eagerness and delight is infectious.

"See and wait! Wait! Listen to these octaves!" He pounds away, fingers flying. "I saw someone break a finger once playing those—isn't that incredible! Ruined his whole career!" And he smiles again as if it were the most wonderful news in the world. "Do you know any Prokofiev?"

"Only *Romeo and Juliet* and *Love of Three Oranges*," I admit.

"I love *Romeo and Juliet*!" For a moment I think he's going to explode with excitement. "Mercutio's death scene—so tragic!" Again he begins to play, filling the room with the dramatic, halting march that characterizes the end of act two, replacing a whole orchestra with an intricate transcription for single piano.

Curling up in a nearby armchair, I make myself comfortable and bask in the light of his enthusiasm and astonishing talent.

I can't recall the last time I saw someone enjoying something so much, so openly. Perhaps it's my age or just the people I hang out with, but almost everyone I know seems to be an aspiring cynic. We stand at the edges of our experiences, smoking cigarettes and trying to convince each other that we've seen this, done that and it isn't so hot anyway. It's considered uncool to be passionate, if not downright gauche. And on the occasions when one of us does become excited, it's under duress, both embarrassing and brief. It's considered unrealistic; a kind of madness that descends and has to be apologized for the next day. "Real life" is, after all, a serious and rather dull business. And the more serious and dull, the more "real" it is.

I don't know how we all collectively came to the conclusion

that this is the way adults behave but as I watch him play, I feel an aching in my chest: an intense longing to let go of my eternal pessimism and trade it instead for the easy joy before me. The rapture I hear right now.

He finishes Mercutio's death scene and is launching into the flowing, ominous passages of the balcony scene when I hear someone crossing the wooden floor.

"There you are!" I look up to find Flora standing over me, wearing a floral dress. "I've been looking for you everywhere. It's almost time for supper." She offers me a hand, pulling me out of the armchair with a good, solid all girls hockey team yank. "I see you've met my brother Eddie. Eddie!" she shouts. "Eddie shut up, for Christ sake!" He stops playing and swivels round indignantly.

"Oh, it's only you, Old Bag," he says, giving her a wink.

"Nice to see you too, Waste of Space," she counters, grinning. "I hope he hasn't been boring you senseless. He can pound that piano until you just want to bludgeon him to death, can't you?"

He nods happily.

She looks at me and frowns. "Geez, Louise, what's happened to you? You look an absolute fright! You're covered in feathers and there's mascara all down your face! What've you been doing to her, you brute!" She turns to Eddie, hands on hips.

"Nothing, I swear!" he protests. "It's the music! My music has been known to bring tears to the eyes of many a lovely lady! And to cause the occasional molt," he adds.

I'd completely forgotten about the exploding pillow tantrum. I catch sight of myself in one of the huge gilt mirrors hanging between the pairs of French doors. I look like I've been tarred and feathered by a group of minimalists. "Shit!"

"Well put!" Eddie laughs.

I'm blushing.

"Well, there's only a few minutes before supper," Flora says, glancing at her watch. "So I'd clean up if I were you. I put a spare skirt on your bed."

"Thanks," I murmur, racing towards the door. I can't get out of there fast enough.

My mind is reeling as I bound up the stairs. Eddie, the man from the opera house steps, is Flora's brother! And he's here! Why does this have to be the weekend I have no decent clothes?

I dive into the bathroom, splash my face with water, rinse away the trails of mascara, and pull the feathers out of my hair. Three minutes to eight. Shit, shit, shit! I tear off my jeans, pull on the skirt Flora left for me, and look in the mirror. Barefaced, without a hint of makeup, and dressed in a T-shirt, elasticized floral skirt and loafers, I look like an escapee from a special needs home. I sob in despair. One more minute to go. Damn it! I pull the T-shirt out to cover the rouched waistband, grab the red lipstick out of my handbag and paint on a lovely red clown mouth, which I dab down desperately with a tissue. The grandfather clock in the front hallway chimes ominously. Eight o'clock. Fuck! I grab my cardigan, throw it around my shoulders and tear out of my bedroom.

I skid down the main staircase, coming to a halt at the bottom, unsure of which way to go. There's laughter somewhere to my left. As I speed down the hallway, the noise becames louder and louder. The doorway to an open lounge is only ten feet away. The clock is just striking eight. I might just make it! Rounding the doorway, I prepare myself to smile winningly at the assembled guests when suddenly I'm hit by a wall of jumping dogs. Before I know it, I'm down on the Aubusson, covered in canines.

"No running in the house!" Mrs. Simpson-Stock roars. "How many times do I have to say it! Down, boys, down! Heel! Sit! STOP! Here," she offers me a hand and pulls me up. "You're late. Everyone, this is Poppy's friend Eleanor."

"Louise, Mummy."

"Yes, well, whatever. She's American," she concludes by way of explanation and they all nod their heads knowingly.

Poppy comes to my rescue. "Why don't I get you a Pimm's and introduce you to everyone later?" she suggests, taking me under her arm and guiding me to the drinks table.

"Thank you, that would be lovely," I rasp, shamefaced. As we cross the room in total silence, I scan its boarders as discreetly as I can for any sign of Eddie. Is it possible that I've escaped humiliating myself in front of him for a second time? My heart lifts at the thought. I search the room once more just to be sure. He's definitely missing. I'm so relieved I even manage a smile when Poppy hands me a glass filled to the brim with fruit salad and cucumbers floating in a sugary amber liquid.

"Cheers everyone!" she toasts, raising her glass.

"Cheers!" they shout back, maneuvering their faces so that they're able to drink the liquid without disturbing the complicated mass of foliage. It's like taking a sip out of a vase full of flowers. With my track record, I decide it's best for everyone if I give it a miss.

I stand there holding my glass, trying to blend in with the other guests when a youngish man with very blond hair and no discernible eyelashes swaggers over. He has on a purple and white pinstriped shirt and a pair of canary yellow corduroy trousers that, like the sun, can't be looked at directly without severe damage to the eyes.

"Yah, hello. My name's Piers, Lavender's better half," he introduces himself, gesturing to a drained, angry looking young woman in the corner who's clutching her drink so violently, she might easily shatter the glass. "So," he smirks at me. "You're American. Tell us why your presidents are all such dumb pricks?" He tries punctuating this sparkling opening gambit by taking a swift swig of his drink but miscalculates and lands a bit of cucumber in his eye instead.

I hesitate. "Well, politics isn't really an interest of mine . . ."

"Well, what I want to know," he continues, undeterred, "is how they can be allowed to continue in office when it's clear that they're all total liars? I mean they're all a walking mass of contradictions . . ."

"I really don't follow the presidential follies," I interrupt, wishing he wouldn't stand so close. "It's not a topic upon which I have an opinion."

"Well, regardless of that," he waggles a thick pink finger in my face, "the thing that gets me is how the most powerful man in the world, I mean, we're talking about a man who's got more nuclear capability—right?—than all the other world powers combined, can be allowed to say whatever he wants, even lie directly to the Supreme Court of America, on, like, national television! It's like everything in America is one great big bloody Oprah Winfrey show! And that's another thing I hate!" he rants, his voice filling the room. "This whole country is getting to be just like America! We've completely lost our national identity! We're just like some faded, secondhand rip-off of Your Country!" He points at me accusingly. "Like we're just some unofficial, bastard fifty-third state! I mean, how do you explain that?"

He turns to the rest of the room for affirmation. "Special re-

lationship with Britain! 'Special relationship' my arse! As far
as I can see, the whole 'special relationship' is built around us
doing what you tell us to do! And what's more—"

"Oh, shut up, Piers!" Lavender hisses across the room.
"You're boring the poor girl senseless. And everyone else."

He rolls his eyes. "No, I'm not, darling. Elsie and I are having a very nice, very civil conversation about her president.
And, for your information, politics is not boring, yah? It's just
boring for you because you have a brain the size of a pea and
don't understand, like, long words all strung together in a
row."

For a moment I thought Lavender was going to chuck her
glass at his head. "Piers! How can you be so rude!" she
screams. "If you ask me, the President of the United States
isn't the only one who's a prick!"

"Language, Lavender!" Mrs. Simpson-Stock glares at her.
"A lady never swears!"

"But Mummy!"

"*Never!*" her mother growls and Lavender sits down
abruptly, like one of her mother's dogs.

A mortified silence ensues. The rest of the guests, too
daunted to speak, sit holding their drinks like third-class tro-
phies, staring with pretend fascination as the dogs savage what
appears to be a small woodland animal in the center of the
floor. Piers pokes his tongue out at Lavender. She responds by
sticking two fingers up at him when her mother isn't looking.

Mrs. Simpson-Stock twists her wristwatch around, frowning at it intensely, the way people do when they haven't got
their glasses. "Flora, honestly! Where is that brother of yours?
We can't sit around here all day making polite conversation!"

"Certainly not," Flora giggles nervously and Mrs.
Simpson-Stock shoots her a look Medusa would be proud of.

"I'll go get him!" I offer, desperate to get away from Piers's searing political insights. "I think he might be in the piano room."

"Yes, well, whatever," she waves me on. "But no running in the halls! Understood?"

I nod obediently, hand my glass to Poppy and make my escape.

I wander through the long corridors until I reach the music room, only this time it's empty. I walk out of the French doors onto the lawn and there, sleeping in a lounger, is Eddie.

He's the only person I've ever seen who sleeps with a smile on his face.

His eyes flick open and he smiles even wider. "I'm late, aren't I?"

I nod. Even this piece of information seems to please him enormously. He stretches his arms out langorously above his head. "Shall I kidnap you? We can escape down to the local pub instead and finally have our drink. I'll even buy you a packet of crisps," he offers.

I'm sorely tempted. "I don't dare. I'm already in trouble. I've been caught running in the house."

"No!!!" He gasps in mock horror. "Not actually *in* the house! Were you pulled over?"

"Worse. The dogs got me."

He winces violently. "Oooo! *Nasty*! Smelly little vermin."

"Too right," I confirm. "They just went for me."

He leans in and lowers his voice. "Rumor has it that she gets a new one every time *He* has an affair. They're really just walking, wagging, weeing versions of her own pent up fury and betrayal."

"Noooooooooooo waaaaayyy! I didn't even know there was a *He*!"

"Only a rumor, mind you," he taps the side of his nose.

"About the dogs, you mean?"

"No, about the husband," he winks. "See! See what a font of knowledge I am! How dashing and debonair! And full of malicious gossip! How can you turn me down? How can you miss this enchanting opportunity to be alone with me over a Scotch egg and a game of darts?"

"But I'm dressed like a librarian," I point out, completely baffled and thrilled by his persistence. "And besides, I . . . I just can't . . . they're all waiting in there with glasses of . . . I don't know . . . fruit salad and sugar water. We can't just *leave*." I sound pathetic even to me.

He surveys me sadly. "Now, is this the spirit that won the West? Walked on the moon? Bombed the shit out of Vietnam?"

"No," I admit.

"I didn't think so," he comments gravely. "What *is* the world coming to! Come on," he sighs. "Well, then. Here's to the Voice of Reason. If only she'd mind her own bloody business!" He stands up and offers me his arm with exaggerated formality. "Shall we?"

I take it and we walk back, through the empty hallways to the lounge. Just before we enter, he gives my hand a little squeeze. "Just between you and me," he whispers, "I think we missed a wonderful chance to really fuck these people off."

"Just between you and me," I whisper back, "I think you're absolutely right."

And with that we sweep into the lounge and on to one of the most painful meals of my life.

It's not just that there's more cutlery surrounding my plate than I know what to do with, or that the "Summer Gazpacho" soup turns out to be cold tinned Campbell's cream of tomato with additional chunks of raw onion, or even that a cloud of floating dog hair descends upon every course. No, the most painful aspect is the halting, stilted attempts at conversation, made more torturous by the rigid social observance of turning first to your right and then to your left to ply your neighbors with half-hearted queries about summer holiday plans and observations on the state of the weather.

The dining room, which possesses all the dark grandeur of an Italian morgue, is surprisingly cold, despite the time of year. I perch, shivering next to Poppy's deaf grandfather on one side and an increasingly drunk Lavender on the other.

In a show of resolute social decorum, she swings round to face me. "Going on holiday?" she snaps, her gaze glued to the white wine bottle as it makes its way around the table. (Despite the number of guests, only two bottles of wine appear, one red, one white, and the mounting tension as they're passed from hand to hand is almost unbearable.)

"I don't think so. What about you?"

"Never go anywhere," she spits bitterly. "Piers thinks we ought to save money. He's under the impression that we're going to have children, although I can't imagine how."

Not really sure what to say, I watch as her hands clutch and unclutch the linen napkin in her lap.

"At least the weather's been nice," I hear myself bleat.

"Fucking fantastic." She grasps the bottle eagerly with both hands when it finally arrives, draining the remains into her glass. "Thank God!" she gasps, her whole body collapsing in relief.

The Summer Gazpacho is followed by a fish course that looks more like a medical sample on a petri dish than anything else. Minuscule shreds of smoked salmon are dotted on piles of shredded iceberg lettuce, then completely overwhelmed by generous dollops of mayonnaise and chopped gherkin. In the corner of each plate is a little triangle of dried brown bread with curly corners where the crusts have been cut off. After that, shavings of lamb are accompanied by tinned peas and roasted potatoes, which manage the culinary distinction of being simultaneously burnt and undercooked. We're rationed to three per plate; they stand sentinel-like around the gray, cooling slivers of meat. There's an even more violent scramble for the gravy than the wine, with the result that half the table have plates swimming in the stuff while the rest of us are left to negotiate the horror unaided. We poke, push, and pull at the lamb until it snaps into rubbery little parcels, which can be chewed for fifteen minutes or more without dissolving.

Poppy's grandfather turns to me and smiles. "Going on holiday this year?" he shouts.

Having survived a stint at a local community theater, where the over-sixties used to yell at the actors if they couldn't hear, I fancy myself as a bit of an old hand when it comes to dealing with the hard of hearing. I smile. "No!" I bellow back. "I'm not going this year!"

He recoils and straightens his tie defensively. "You don't have to shout!" he booms. "I'm not deaf, you know!"

The whole dining room freezes, focusing its collective horror upon me.

"Oh! I'm so sorry!" I flounder. "I didn't mean to offend you . . ."

"What?" He fiddles with his hearing aid. "Stop mumbling, girl! Filthy American accent! You people always slur your words! What is it Churchill said, 'A people divided by a common language!' Ha, ha, ha! Too right!"

Suddenly a green grape bounces off his head.

"Hey!" he dithers indignantly.

I look in the direction of the grape's flight path, at Eddie who's staring at his plate and pushing his peas around with incredible intensity. He doesn't dare glance up at me. But he looks as though any minute his face might explode.

"What's going on here?" Poppy's grandfather demands. "Is that a grape? Why don't I have a bloody grape! I fought in the war! I *deserve* to have a grape! Who's hoarding the grapes!"

"Father," Mrs. Simpson-Stock rolls her eyes heavenward, "no one's hoarding the grapes. They're in the center of the table. Center of the table!" she shouts automatically. "And don't scream, you're upsetting the dogs."

"Bugger the dogs!" He lurches forward and appropriates a bunch, clutching them protectively to his chest. "Next bastard to chuck a grape is going to get more than he bargained for!" he threatens, eyeing the assembled party suspiciously. "Never saw a grape during the war. Or even a tomato. Here." He passes me half a handful. "If it weren't for your scruffy dough-boys, none of us would even be here, let alone eating grapes!"

"Thank you." I've obviously risen in his estimation, though why remains a mystery. (Perhaps the "special relation-ship" between Britain and America only really flourishes under attack.)

Pudding is a large, gooey sherry trifle, followed by thimbles full of lukewarm Nescafé. At 9:47, we're finally released. Mrs. Simpson-Stock rises and sweeps back into the lounge, escorted by her furry entourage. The rest of us bolt after her, leaving only her father behind, popping grapes into his mouth, savor-ing the possession rather more than the flavor.

Once in the hallway, Poppy turns to me. "Fancy a fag on the terrace?" she whispers. Flora opens her cardigan and flashes a hip flask she's tucked into the waistband of her skirt.

"C'mon!" she giggles and the three of us bypass the rest of the party, slipping out in the moonlight.

"Head for the oak!" Poppy hisses and we kick off our shoes and run across the cool, damp lawn to the enormous, ancient oak in the center. Under its canopy of branches, we throw ourselves down, panting and laughing.

"God! What I wouldn't give for a packet of Smarties!" Flora sighs, passing the flask.

"Ahhh! Or a giant box of Cadbury's chocolate biscuits!" Poppy says.

"So," I laugh, "I'm not the only one who's starving!"

"As a matter of fact," Poppy says, "that's one of the main reasons we come down here. When I've put on a few pounds, I just head home for the weekend. Cheaper than a spa and much, much more effective."

"Actually, Pops, your mother's true calling may be saving chronic overeaters," says Flora. "A few family dinners at Lower Slaughter and you'll never look at food the same way again. And she could put the dogs on patrol at night to keep clients from escaping to the nearest all-night mini-mart."

"There's an all-night mini-mart?" I say, sitting up.

"Miles away," they chorus.

"Oh." I collapse once more. "Poor Poppy! Please don't tell me you were actually raised on this food!"

Poppy takes a long swig and passes the flask. "What can I say? I was the only kid at boarding school who thought that school dinners were heaven. I used to weep with joy over boiled cabbage, stringy beef, and semolina pudding. Never wanted to go home for the holidays."

We lean back and gaze up at the stars through the branches of the oak, leaves fluttering in a soft, cool breeze. A chorus of crickets sing gently. And all is quiet except for the sound of our grumbling stomachs.

The next morning, I awake to the thunderous chords of Beethoven's *Hammerklavier*. Eddie's obviously an early riser. However, it goes rapidly downhill from there. I do my pre-coffee stagger into the bathroom, only to discover that there's no hot water. Evidently, Mrs. Simpson-Stock is a passionate morning person. She rises at dawn, refreshes herself with a quick splash, and can't understand why anyone would require more, taking an unnaturally hostile view of people whose morning routines include such extravagances as hot baths and showers. Like many British raised during or just after the war, she regards a bath as the ultimate luxury and hot water as downright frivolous. If you really want to inflame her, all you need to do is mention the disturbing trend among the young to wash their hair every day and she's catapulted into a hysteria second only to her feelings on animal quarantine laws and the decline of the Women's Institute.

So I crouched naked in the tub, shivering as I sprayed myself with icy water from the handheld shower attachment. It's one way to wake up fast.

I prefer coffee.

Now dressed in the jeans and T-shirt, I make my way downstairs in search of food. If there's one meal the English excel at, it's breakfast. I'm dreaming of silver urns filled with steaming piles of scrambled eggs, sizzling sausages, bacon, grilled tomatoes, creamy mushrooms, and piles of warm toast. The dining room, however, is completely empty. Not a sausage in sight. I wander tentatively into the kitchen, where I find an enormous woman wading through piles of dirty dishes.

"Hello?" I venture. Where did all these plates come from?

"Hello, to you." She doesn't bother to turn around.

"Ah, so, what do people do around here for breakfast?" I wonder aloud.

"They turn up on time," she says brusquely. "Need to be down here by eight A.M. at the latest."

"Oh." I spot the remains of crispy bacon and fluffy eggs being scraped into the bin.

"There's cereal on the table and some milk in the fridge," she dismisses me.

And that is that.

I eat and make my way into the music room.

"Hey!" I shout to Eddie, who's pounding away.

"Morning!" he shouts back, not slowing his pace.

"Where is everyone?" I yell.

"Out killing things! Louise! Just listen! This theme is the best!"

"Killing things?" I echo.

"It's what they do in the country to have fun," he beams. "You know, chase 'em, shoot 'em, fish 'em, trap 'em . . . otherwise known as the joys of country life." He pauses a moment, seeing I'm at a bit of a loss. "Not everyone's out butchering the wildlife. I think Flora and Poppy are sunning themselves in the garden. At least, that's what they're calling it. More likely they've passed out trying to recover from a couple of very mysterious hangovers."

"I'd better join them, if only to offer them my sympathy." I don't want to disturb him further. "Thanks, Eddie."

"Or"—he stops and looks up at me—"we could always take a walk."

"Are you sure?" Do I sound too delighted?

"Absolutely," he says. "There's only so much of me that Beethoven can take in a day and I think he's had it up to here."

"Then I'd love to," I agree, "only, I'm warning you, I'm not much of an outdoors person."

"You'll be fine," he assures me. "Only, I don't suppose you have a pair of Wellingtons, do you? It's just you never know what you're going to walk into out there."

"Well, no . . ." I think of the pair I'd borrowed, comfortably installed in my office, next to my dinner dress, fresh T-shirts, and clean knickers.

"What a relief!" He grins. "There's a certain type of girl who owns her own Wellingtons and I'm glad you're not it!"

"And what type of girl is that?"

"The same type of girl who always has a clean hankie, the right bus fare, and matching socks. A girl who owns her own Wellingtons is afraid of looking ridiculous, afraid of getting mud on her feet and that's a terrible thing."

"But you said we needed them!"

"Absolutely—it's perfectly foul out there, Louise!" He stands at the French doors, hand shading his eyes, a dauntless explorer looking towards the woodland beyond the lawn. "But just because we need them doesn't mean we *want* them. We shall use them under protest, under duress, and with the complete understanding that we welcome mud, wouldn't be caught dead using a clean hankie when we have a perfectly good shirtsleeve, and would catch a cab over the bus every time. In short, with our integrity intact."

"Our integrity?"

"Yup, our integrity demands that we have boots but recoils at them being ours." He's leading me down a corridor I haven't seen before.

"That's a bit tenuous." I trip along, laughing beside him. "Amusing, but you're not making sense."

"There you go again! Sense, sense, sense! What is this obsession with sense! Nothing of great beauty in this world makes sense! Now, 'Let us go then, you and I . . .' "

He begins quoting Eliot and I join in " '. . . when the evening is spread out against the sky like a patient etherized upon a table.' "

We arrive at the boot room. It's a kind of giant closet filled from top to bottom with moldy pairs of mismatched Wellingtons in all conceivable colors and sizes. Along the walls, wooden pegs hold row after row of waxed Barbour coats; my eyes water from the chemical stench of the waxed coating.

"My God, Eddie! How can people wear those things!" I gasp, pinching my nose. "I can't even get anywhere near them!"

"Why the Barbour waxed jacket is the very emblem of English country life!" he proclaims as he chucks various rejects across the room. "They repel not only water, but also any form of human contact. Perfect!"

We find one black and one green welly for him and two left-footed red wellies for me. It's not easy to walk with two left feet; there's a distinct tendency to move in a circle. Only by turning my right foot outward at a ninety-degree angle do I manage to make any progress at all.

I start to sulk.

"*Courage, mon amour!*" he cries. "Remember our integrity!"

"I've got two left feet," I remind him. "You haven't got two left feet!"

He gives me one of his fetching, quirky looks. (Already I'm building a file of his expressions to go over when I'm not with him.) "You are old, you are old, you shall wear the bottoms of your trousers rolled."

I stick my tongue out at him.

We tramp (or rather he tramps, I limp) across the lawn until we come to a grassy lane leading to the riverbank.

"Smell that air!" Eddie sighs.

Someone has been riding that morning and the air smells of horse manure.

"Look at that view!" he cries.

We stop for a moment, look up, and then continue to shuffle along.

"Feel the sun on your face!" he beams exuberantly.

We both turn our faces upwards and walk straight into a cloud of midges. We dodge the manure. We duck the midges. We run off the trail to avoid the midges but the horses have been there too. Both midges and manure are remarkably adhesive.

Piers, Lavender's self-proclaimed better half, is fishing by the river's edge. Somehow he's managed to bag the only matching pair of Wellingtons and has exchanged his brilliant canary yellow corduroys for moleskin trousers and is even sporting a tweed fishing cap. It was all very Constable-ish. He clearly shops at a store with a "What to Wear in the Country" section. He waves a be-Barboured arm, signaling for us to be quiet. This is what it's all about: a man, a stream, a smelly coat. A moment of almost overwhelming pastoral beauty. Moments later, he reels in a fish and begins clubbing it to death with a small leather bat he keeps in his pocket.

I had no idea that fish screamed but they do.

"Well, that was lovely. Just lovely," Eddie says. "Shall we go back?"

"Yes, why don't we," I agree.

Fifteen minutes of rural bliss is enough for anyone.

Back at the house we peel off our boots and flop down on the grass. Lunch seems miles away. On the lawn, a heated game of croquet is going on between Mrs. Simpson-Stock, her father, and Lavender. The game is considerably hampered by the participation of the dogs chasing after each ball and whom the elderly man regards as a free target, whacking his mallet around indiscriminately and with some effect. They in turn feel free to savage his leg. Under the old oak, the dozing figures of Poppy and Flora are pretty much where I left them the night before.

"Now what should we do?" I ask, pulling lazily at a blade of grass.

"Let's take a nap," he suggests.

And that's what we do. He takes off his sweater, bunches it up in a ball, and slips it under our heads. Side by side, our eyes closed, we bask in the warm heat of the sun. After a while, I'm aware of the sound of Eddie gently snoring next to me. And it's a wonderful sound; a soft, whistly little sigh of a snore. I open one eye to see if he's still smiling, and he is.

I smile too and close my eyes again.

How strange! I think, just as I'm dozing off. Why is it that I can sleep next to Eddie and yet I needed a bed the size of a football pitch to sleep with my husband? And as I snuggle closer to him, he turns and throws an arm over me. It must be the country air, I conclude, dreamily. It obviously has an intoxicating effect.

And that's how I learnt that the great secret of surviving a country weekend isn't the right clothes or the right equipment or even an enormous secret stash of food. It does, however, have everything to do with the company you keep.

The next evening, Poppy, Flora, and I drive back to London. Sitting in the backseat, I stare out of the window at the patches of green countryside as they flash by. I feel strangely melancholic and agitated. I should be overjoyed to be returning to civilization, but I'm not.

"So." Flora looks at me significantly in the rear-view mirror. "You and Eddie were thick as thieves. You really like him, don't you?"

"*No way!*" Poppy laughs. "Oh, he's a cute kid but too young for you! I mean, he's twenty-four and still doesn't have a proper job! All he cares about is his music. You can't be serious, Louise!"

"I know that. She's just teasing me, Poppy." I'm longing to change the subject. "Hey, why don't we turn on the radio?" I suggest.

"Sure." Flora fiddles with the dial. I catch her eye in the mirror and she smiles.

No, I can't be serious, I think as we beetle down the motorway. Everything Poppy says is absolutely true.

So why do I feel so miserable?

Two days later, I arrive at work to find three white roses on my desk along with a note from Eddie.

You still owe me a drink.

A moment later, my phone rings. It's him.

"Hello, Louise?" There's the sound of crowds, train announcements. "Can you hear me?"

"Yes, yes where are you?"

"I'm at Waterloo. I'm about to catch the train to Paris in a few minutes. Did you get my flowers?"

"Yes, they're gorgeous! I didn't know that you were leaving today . . . Eddie . . . can you hear me?" The line fades; his voice crackling inaudibly.

"I was saying, I wanted to buy you more, a whole desk full of roses! Next time, Louise! When I get back we'll . . ." And the line goes dead.

I put the roses in a glass on my desk. When they start to wilt, I dry them upside down. And when the petals fall, I collect them and keep them in an envelope.

A month goes by.

I throw the envelope away.

After all, I can't be serious.

X

❦

Xmas

Christmas is a very special occasion. If there's one time during the year when you ought to feel good, affectionate, kind-hearted, thoughtful, and generous, it is certainly at Christmas.

It is only natural to harmonise your physical appearance with these beautiful moral qualities and this for the average woman means a new dress, a lovely hairdo, and perhaps a beauty treatment. According to the type of Christmas party you may be invited to attend, the ideal costume is a long or short evening dress, and, without going so far as trying to out-sparkle the Christmas tree, it is perfectly appropriate for you to make a special effort to create a splendid appearance.

The point to remember is that this is a very special evening, and it merits the honour of a special manner of dress.

"Are you sure you're going to be all right on your own?" Col is standing by the front door with his suitcase in one hand and his coat in the other.

"I'll be fine," I say. "It's only for a couple of days."

"But it's Christmas. It isn't just a couple of normal days. It's a couple of Christmas days!" he frets.

"I'll be all right," I assure him.

A car horn sounds outside and Ria emerges from her bedroom, dragging a bulging overnight case and two large shopping bags full of carefully wrapped presents.

"The cab's here, Col, we've got to go! Are you sure you're going to be all right, Louise? It's not too late to come to Dorset with me—my family would love to have you. Honestly, the more the merrier." Ria hates traveling and has accelerated into a total panic. I watch as she buttons her coat up wrong, puts her hat on backwards, and drops her gloves. "My keys! I can't find my keys! Damn it, Col! The meter's running! We'll miss the train and I'll be locked out of the house when I get home!"

"Have you checked your pockets?"

"Oh. Yes. Here they are. Now, the meter's running. Col!"

"Darling, it's a mini-cab. It hasn't got a meter." He gives me a hug. "Good-bye, honey, take care. Don't forget to put the alarm on and call if you get lonely. The numbers are by the phone. I still feel dreadful about leaving you but I'd better get this one to the train station before she explodes with anxiety."

I kiss Ria on the forehead and turn her hat the right way round. "Travel well, sweetheart, and Merry Christmas."

"I'm going to call you!" she shouts as she hauls her luggage and shopping bags down the steps. "I'm going to check in with you every hour on the hour to make sure you don't do anything silly!"

I watch as they pile into the cab. They wave. I wave. Even the cab driver waves. And a moment later, they pull away into the dull mist of the freezing morning air and are gone. I close the door and collapse against it. Alone at last!

Moments like these are so rare when you have flatmates. And, as much as you love them, there's still nothing like the wonderful, luxurious sense of freedom that descends when you're by yourself. I walk into the living room, switch on the Christmas tree lights and pour myself another cup of tea. Then I snuggle down on the sofa and contemplate my liberty.

It's December 23, 8:32 A.M. Very cold, but dry. Both Colin and Ria have now officially gone home for the holidays—Colin to meet Andy's parents for the first time in their home in High Wycombe and Ria to her parents' cottage in Dorset. Being recently divorced and virtually penniless, a trip to the States during peak rate time is off the cards for me. But no worries. This is my first Christmas alone and I feel oddly excited. I sip my tea and allow myself to become mesmerized by the lights on the tree. I could do anything, absolutely anything. I can listen to my own music, watch what I want to on TV, leave the dishes stewing in the sink for days. I have all the time in the world.

Three hours later I'm in the office.

"What are you doing here?" Flora demands. "You're the lucky one, remember? The one who gets to have Christmas off." She's making paper chains out of old programs and has glue in her hair.

"Oh nothing," I lie. I don't want to tell her I have nothing to do and so end up hanging out at work on my day off. "I was just passing and I thought I'd pop in and check my e-mail. Need a hand?" I can't remember the last time I made a paper chain. As a matter of fact, I don't think I've ever made a paper chain, but she looks like she's having fun and it's surprising how quickly the anticipated joys of leaving your dishes in the sink can pall.

"Sure." She passes me a pile of strips and some glue. "Wow. If I were you, I wouldn't be anywhere near this place. I'd be out doing my Christmas shopping. I haven't done any and I don't know where I'm going to find the time. I've promised to take my mother, my sister, and her two little girls to see the *Nutcracker* tonight, I've got a charity ball to go to tomorrow night . . . I might as well shoot myself!"

"But instead you're making paper chains."

She looks at me. "Louise, I take my job very seriously. God forbid I should be skiving when I have an obligation to maintain office morale and to spread goodwill via the ancient art of paper chain making. Or paper chain *fashioning*, as we skilled artisans like to call it. Do you realize how many holiday suicide attempts could be avoided by the simple addition of a paper chain to the depressed person's surroundings? At least five, I should think. Which is why I'm hanging them up around here."

"So that's you, me, Poppy, and what, two moody bystanders?"

"Face it, no one ever visits our department. We'd have to lure a couple of depressives up here."

"Or we could invite Crispin and Terrance from Finance."

We paste in silence for a moment.

"A charity ball, eh? Sounds very grand!"

She shifts uncomfortably. "Well, not really a ball . . . more like an *event*."

"Could you be more cryptic? My glue stick's dead."

She hands me hers. "The use of the glue stick marks the pro from the amateur every time."

"OK, you can stop doing that now."

"Just one more joke."

"No."

"I *sooooo* don't want to go," she moans. "I've been bullied into the whole thing by Poppy, who started on about the rampant commercialism of Christmas last February until I couldn't stand it anymore, practically forcing me, by the sheer multitude of her arguments to take rash and drastic action!"

"Calm down, girl!"

"You don't understand! She sang 'Do They Know It's Christmastime at All' to me until I snapped! She used to hobble around the office pretending to be Tiny Tim and pasted Post-its to my lunch box saying things like 'Feed me!' and 'Don't worry . . . I'll survive. . . . somehow!' "

"Flora, you're hyperventilating! What has she made you do?"

"I said I'd go with her to feed the homeless." She hangs her head in shame.

"But that's admirable," I assure her.

"It would be, except I'd give my right arm not to go. I am evil! I am!" Her lower lip trembles and she covers her face with her hands.

I eye her suspiciously. "Have you been watching reruns of *Dallas* again?"

She peers at me between two of her fingers. "Maybe just a little bit."

"Anyway, it will be fun if the two of you go," I point out, trying to paste a paper strip around my wrist as a makeshift bracelet.

"Ahh! But that's the problem! Poppy's had to go home now for the funeral."

The paper strip snaps off my wrist and flies across the room. "Funeral? My God, what happened?"

"One of her mother's dogs died at the weekend. Poppy says natural causes but her mother's convinced it was murder. You remember Albert, the terrier with the overbite and the bladder infection? Evidently the old man's been having a go at him lately because he used to pee in his slippers." She sighs. "But that's all over now."

I stare at her. "They're having a funeral for the dog?"

She nods. "Open casket. I was going to send a wreath, if you want to go halves."

The English and their dogs share a bond that foreigners like myself can only marvel at. I decide to stick to more familiar ground.

"So you have to go on your own to feed the homeless," I try to draw her back to the subject.

She glances at me sideways. "That is, unless you have any-thing better to do?"

"You are evil." I chuck a paper clip at her head.

"Come on, Louise! It will be fun, I promise! And it's only around the corner in the basement of St. Martin-in-the-Fields. We'd be the early shift, from eight till ten, and then you'd have the whole rest of the evening to yourself . . . pleeeee-eeease!"

I think about the dishes in the sink at home. What else have I got to do?

"Sure."

She squeals with delight and throws her arms around me. "You're a perfect angel! Which reminds me, every year the volunteers have a costume competition. It has to be seasonal, but I thought we could go as angels. The card shop across the road is selling little silver plastic angel wings you slip over your shoulders with matching tiaras, and I've got some old white nightgowns we can throw over our jeans."

"Perfect. Why don't you go and buy some wings. And while you're at it, make a dent in that Christmas shopping of yours. I'll hold the fort till you get back." I wave my glue stick as if it were a magic wand. "Now go and be free!"

There's nothing like a little charity to make a girl feel warm and fuzzy all over.

We meet the next evening at the Opera House and change

into our makeshift angel outfits in the loo, slipping the faded flannel nighties over our jeans and donning our plastic tiaras and wings. The mood's festive as we make our way down Long Acre towards Trafalgar Square. It's raining rather than snowing and sharing an umbrella, we shuffle in time with our arms wrapped around each other's waists. We arrive in the basement of the church to find it buzzing with activity. Elves are dishing out turkey dinners, reindeer pass out bowls of soup, partridges with or without pear trees are busy slicing up thick helpings of Christmas pudding. We're quickly assigned to coffee and tea duty by the Ghost of Christmas Present, a man named Reg, in an impressive crimson velvet robe and ginger beard.

For the next two hours we don't stop. We make countless pots of tea and coffee, refill cups, sing Christmas carols, and wash stacks of dishes. We help unload the seemingly endless supply of provisions that flood in from the local businesses; deliveries of sandwiches, fresh fruit and vegetables, whole turkeys, clothing, blankets, tinned goods, cigarettes, and shoes. Stacking them up in tall piles, they're quickly removed and reorganized by a whole other army of volunteers before being distributed, sometimes to kitchens in less central parts of London, where they're more desperately needed. People wander in off the street, curious about all the activity, and end up staying to help: groups of students, tourists, and those who aren't homeless but somehow displaced. The way I feel. And for a couple of hours we're part of something.

I'm aware of a feeling of incredible abundance—not just of supplies, but of energy, joy, and hope. As I rush to fill cup after cup, smiling and laughing with people I don't even normally make eye contact with in the street, I realize I'm happy. This is the very stuff of happiness and yet it's always eluded me in the past.

Suddenly, amidst a sea of unshaven faces, a familiar smile appears.

"So, you think you can just sleep with me and then bugger off without a trace!" Eddie grins. "Cup of tea, please while you're at it. Chop, Chop! My audience is waiting!"

He's wearing a tea towel on his head and has a large faded blue travel rug wrapped around his body.

"Eddie!" I'm conscious of the eyes upon me, especially one giggling old grandpa in the corner who's been trying unsuccessfully to seduce me all night. "Firstly, what are you doing here? I thought you were in Paris. And secondly, what are you wearing?"

"We're wearing costumes, right? Well, I'm the Baby Jesus and these are my swaddling clothes."

"You've got a tea towel on your head. Wait a minute, that's our tea towel! Eddie, you've nicked our tea towel!"

He pulls himself upright. "Someone of my class doesn't nick a tea towel, he embezzles it. But you're in luck. I'm willing to rent it out to you for a small fee. Though you may have to part with your halo."

I blush. "How long have you been back? And will that be one or two sugars?" I ask, chucking a couple of cubes at him.

"NO FOOD FIGHTS!" Reg booms across the hall.

Eddie leans across the counter and looks round furtively. "Look, I'm a Baby Jesus, you're obviously an angel, what you say we go lay down in a manger?"

"He he he!" the old grandpa giggles.

"My thoughts exactly," Eddie grins.

I look into his enormous, smiling black eyes. "Eddie!" I'm at a complete loss for words.

"Yes, my angel?" he whispers softly.

"Hey! I thought you were here to play the piano!" Reg shouts.

"As I said, my audience awaits me!" He steps aside to let the queue flow again and disappears into the crowd.

Flora leans over. "I probably shouldn't tell you this, but he was completely uninterested in volunteering tonight until he heard that you were coming along. I think he really likes you, Louise. You have been warned!"

I'm blushing again. "But Flora, when did he get back? And what could he possibly want with an old fart like me?"

"He got back yesterday, with what looks like four months of dirty laundry, and I don't even want to *think* about what he wants to do with you!"

My heart's racing. "But I'm *nine years* older than he is!"

"He likes older women, Louise."

"Gee, thanks." I've never had the dubious pleasure of thinking of myself as an older woman before. I'm not sure I like it.

"Well," she says, mopping up a warm puddle of spilt tea, "if you don't like him, fair enough. But honestly, I haven't seen him this excited since Lara."

"Lara?" An unexpected wave of jealousy overtakes me. "Who's Lara?"

She smiles slyly. "Just some cello player who broke his heart last spring."

"Oh." I imagine a beautiful, talented, Jacqueline du Pré look-alike.

"Bit of a cow, if you ask me." She squeezes her rag out into the sink.

I look across the room. Eddie's pulling a chair up to an old upright piano in the corner. Then the sound of ragtime jazz fills the hall, as infectious and buoyant as Eddie himself.

When the ten-o'clock shift arrives, Reg holds up a hand to

silence the room. "Hey! Quiet everyone! Thank you! It's around this time that we take a minute and vote on the best costume!"

There's a generous cheer.

"Now, everyone line up and when I put my hand over your head, we'll let the audience decide!"

The volunteers form a misshapen, unruly line and Reg works his way down. Eddie plays snatches of appropriate carols for each contestant and when Reg gets to Flora and me, he plays "There Must Be an Angel" by the Eurythmics.

In the end it's Reg himself who wins; with his flowing red velvet robe and booming laugh he's the perfect Ghost of Christmas Present. But we give him a good run for his money.

"Well, I guess that's it." Flora sighs, as we emerge from the basement of St. Martin's. "We're officially good people now."

"What do you say I buy you two lovely ladies a drink?" Eddie wraps an arm around each of our necks.

"Like this?" I say. "It may be Christmas Eve but not even an angel is going to get served looking like this!"

"But you forget, I *am* the Baby Jesus—I have connections! Taxi!" He hails a cab. "To the Ritz, my good man!"

"No, Eddie! We can't! Not the Ritz!" I protest. "Not like *this*!"

Flora giggles. "Chill out, Louise. It'll be fun!"

"No, no. Not for me. I think I'll just bug out and go home. To tell the truth, I'm pretty tired."

"I'll take off my swaddling clothes if you come," Eddie pulls me towards the open cab door. "As a matter of fact, I'll take off all my clothes if you come!"

Suddenly I'm nervous, out of my depth. What does this handsome, talented young man want with me anyway? Why is he so keen? I have the sudden compulsion to run away and escape before I can destroy whatever mistaken, wonderful delusions he still harbors about my character.

"Look! There's a night bus! If I run I might catch it! Good night and Merry Christmas!" I give them each a swift peck on the cheek and begin running across Trafalgar Square, my plastic wings flapping in the wind.

"Wait a minute!" Eddie runs after me, which isn't easy wrapped in a large woolly blanket. He catches my hand. "I'm having a get-together next weekend on my boat. Will you come?"

"Your *boat*?" I don't know what to say.

The bus lumbers forward, groaning under the weight of a particularly festive top deck.

He holds my hand tighter. "Please come, Louise, and don't run off now; we can drive you home if you like."

My stomach contracts with fear. I like him. I like him more than I should. That's the trouble.

The bus grinds to a halt and starts to fill up. "No, please don't worry . . . it's just here!" I look into his eyes. "Happy Christmas, Eddie, you make a wonderful Baby Jesus . . . you make a wonderful . . . anything!"

"Does that mean you'll come?" he persists.

The conductor rings the bell and the bus heaves away from the curb. I pull my hand out of his and race to jump aboard. "I'll see . . . I'll speak to Flora and let you know! Happy Christmas!" I shout.

And as the bus lurches forward down Whitehall, I turn back to see him standing forlornly in the middle of Trafalgar Square, the tea towel still on his head.

I stumble up to the top deck and find a seat next to a man wearing a red paper Christmas cracker hat, who's passed out and drooling with his head against the window. I yank the halo off my head and wriggle out of the wings. Everyone's yelling, laughing, shouting into their mobiles.

We trundle past Big Ben, the Houses of Parliament, and then the street where I lived for so many years with my ex-husband. I wonder what he's doing and if the place still looks the same. Shall I get off at the next stop and see? What would he do now if I were to show up on his doorstep dressed in an old nightgown? Would he even recognize me? Or would I be as indistinguishable to him as he had been to me that night in the theater?

The next stop comes and goes. But I don't get off. Not even for a look. The bus crosses the bridge into Lambeth and the moment is gone.

When I get home, I run a bath and put on a CD of Ria's, Chopin ballads that remind me of Eddie. I heat some soup on the stove and sit at the table, dipping water biscuits into my cream of tomato and staring at the lights on the Christmas tree.

It's a silent night.

And I think about how I'd come all this way to be sitting here, eating soup alone on Christmas Eve and how I didn't even want to get off the bus and about the people at St. Martin's and I wonder what Reg does when he isn't being the Ghost of Christmas Present and if I'd recognize him if I passed him on the street and about Flora and Eddie and if they went to the Ritz and were they there right now and then I think about Oliver Wendt and how certain I'd been that he was the man for me and about the way he looked in the back of the cab when it drove away and about my job and how frightened I'd been and how wrong I was about everyone and then about Colin and Ria, at home, celebrating Christmas with their families and about our funny little home here in London.

And an unexpected wave of happiness washes over me.

It's been worth it.

It's all been worth it. To be sitting right here, right now. Alone.

And that night, I slept in heavenly peace.

Y

∞

Yachting

The only thing that should float in the wind on board a yacht are the ship's colours. A dress or skirt that does the same would be quite out of place. Consequently, a simple, even slightly masculine style of clothing is most advisable. Adventures on the high seas only happen rarely in one's life, so seize the opportunity. Be quick to discard your evening gowns and high heeled shoes but keep your sense of humour and enter into the spirit of things by remaining, above all, a good crew member and a good sport.

Now is your chance to show everyone that you are not afraid to be seen without makeup, that you never leave a trail of disorder in your wake, that you have a wonderfully even disposition, and that your elegance is based on utter simplicity. If this is the case (and if you are not prone to seasickness and know how to swim), you will surely have the most wonderful time of your life.

The next week, when I come into work, there's a card waiting for me on my desk.

> *You are cordially invited to*
> *Edward James's Boat Christening Party*
> *2 P.M. this Saturday at the Chelsea Pier*
> *R.S.V.P. 07771283112*

Flora and Poppy giggle as I prop it up against the front of my computer.

"Are you guys going to this shindig?" I ask.

"We weren't invited," Poppy says. And they giggle again.

That night when I come home, I ring Ria, who's still in Dorset.

"What should I do?"

"What do you want to do?"

"I don't know. It's just . . . he's so young. My God! *Twenty-four!* What's he doing asking me out anyway?"

"Do you really think that's any of your business? After all, he's an adult. You've got to trust that he knows his own mind. And why do you think age matters that much anyway? Look at Colin and Andy."

I think a moment. "I guess I always imagined the man should be older . . . older and preferably not quite so attractive. If I'm honest, I want to be the young attractive one, the one in control. I mean, what future could it possibly have and why would I even bother to get involved now if I knew there couldn't be any future? Ria, when he's thirty-four, I'm going to be *forty-three!* He'll be young and lithe and I'll be fumbling about for my HRT!"

"Slow down, cowboy. You keep repeating all these numbers like they mean something. Let's start at the beginning. Do you like him?"

I smile; I can't even think about Eddie without smiling. "Oh, he's brilliant! Really bright, *so* talented and the best thing about him is his incredible enthusiasm! Everything with him is an adventure. And the way he plays the piano, Ria— you'd love him!"

I hear her laughing on the other end of the line. "Listen to yourself, Louise! Why don't you just focus on that for the time being and go along and see what happens?"

I hang up, still agitated, and decide to get a second opinion. Col is lying on the couch, flipping through a bodybuilding magazine called *Pump*. (At least, I hope it's a bodybuilding magazine.) I fling myself into an armchair.

"Col, what would you do if you were me?"

"Fuck him, of course. He sounds gorgeous!"

"Col! No, really! What would you do?"

He looks at me in all seriousness. "Fuck him. Why do you think I'm joking?"

God, gay men. Or rather, men. Period.

"But what if I get involved and then he dumps me for a younger woman?"

He raises an eyebrow "And . . . ?"

"Damn it, Col! I'd be *devastated*!"

"But that's not a reason to duck out of life, sweetie. So, you'd be hurt. Big deal. That's the chance we all take. What's the point in being alive at all if you're so afraid of pain that you can't appreciate the rare gems when they do come along?" He closes the magazine for a moment. "We all want to protect ourselves but the bottom line is: we can't. It's as simple as that. You can either enjoy this wonderful, exciting young man for who and what he is or you can hide away, waiting for some dull, average, schmuck to emerge that will make you feel safe." He starts to laugh. "Remember Oliver Wendt?"

"You are so cruel! And there's nothing wrong with wanting to feel safe . . . is there?"

"My darling, there's *nothing* safe about love!"

"Well, I don't know about love," I blush. "It's a bit early for that."

He smiles. "Yes, well, whatever. Take it from me, Ouise, if you don't take a chance, you'll regret it for the rest of your life."

I spend the rest of the week in a daze, staring at the invitation, wondering how I should respond.

A boat christening party. I don't like boats. And I've always dreaded the sea. I hate the thought of being stranded with nothing but water around me and losing sight of the shore.

Besides, what does a girl wear on a boat in the dead of winter?

"It'll be cold," Ria warns. "I'd go for something warm, like a big fisherman's type sweater and a navy pea coat."

"This is not a look I'm loving," I grimace. "You'll be telling me I need a skipper's hat any minute now."

"Well, no . . . but a cute little woolly hat and maybe a thick pair of wool trousers wouldn't go amiss."

"How am I supposed to seduce anyone looking like an extra from *Peter Grimes*?"

She shrugs her shoulders. "Out on the water, it's going to be freezing. I'd forego trying to seduce anyone and settle for being a good sport."

Being a good sport. There's that phrase again, first from Madame Dariaux and now from Ria. It echoes round my head. A good sport knows their place, accepts things at face value, loses gracefully, keeps trying, doesn't sulk or take their toys and run home. A good sport is not the same as a winner.

Do I have the courage to be a good sport in love? Or is it best just not to play at all?

On Thursday, I finally ring the number on the card.

"Hello, Eddie?"

"Hello, Louise."

"It's Louise."

"I know," he says.

"I just thought I'd ring to say I'd very much like to come to your party." My hands are shaking. Does my voice sound all right?

"Brilliant!" I can hear the smile on his face. "Oh, you've made my day! Do you want me to pick you up or anything?"

"Oh no!" Keep cool, I tell myself. "You're the host, after all, and there'll be masses to do. I'll meet you on the pier like everyone else. But how will I know which boat is yours?"

"Oh, you'll know," he laughs. "It's not terribly big, it's red and it's called the *Hammerklavier*."

I hang up. Red's an awfully strange color for a yacht.

It's Saturday, I'm bundled into a pair of black trousers and a thick cream pullover I borrowed from Colin. Incredibly chunky but also extremely warm. My hair's tied back into a long ponytail; makeup's minimal, in case the wind makes my eyes water. Hardly my idea of a woman embarking on a first date. I look completely nondescript and anonymous. I panic and am about to exit in a pair of black, kitten heel ankle boots when Ria stops me at the door.

"You can't wear heels on the deck of a boat," she explains. "They'll ruin it."

She sends me back to my room like an errant child. I emerge in a pair of old trainers, put on my woolly cap and coat, and she sends me off again looking more like the Michelin man than a chic guest at a yacht party.

It's a stunning, clear day, bright with high wind. I stop by Woolworth's and buy a copy of *Titanic* and then pick up a bottle of vintage champagne. At ten past two, I'm wandering around Chelsea Pier searching for a red yacht, hoping I'm not going to be the oldest person there.

I am.

I find the *Hammerklavier* wedged neatly between two gigantic sun cruisers and probably wouldn't notice it at all if the sound of piano music hadn't caught my attention first. I look down and there it is, all fifty feet of its slender deck, decorated with Christmas lights and tiny British flags; Eddie's canal boat. There doesn't seem to be a lot of activity. I check my watch again. Maybe I'm early. There aren't any doorbells on canal boats, or at least none that I can see, so I call out and after shouting his name at the top of my lungs for several minutes, the piano playing stops and Eddie surfaces on deck. He's wearing a beautifully tailored navy suit and a brilliant pink silk tie.

"You came! You look absolutely stunning!" he says.

All I can do is laugh. "I know for a fact that I don't. I don't know how, but I seem to have misunderstood your invitation. As you can see, I'm dressed for a voyage out on the high seas!"

"Would that please you?" He reaches out his hand.

"I'm not certain, really. I'm a little afraid of the water. And I'm sorry I'm here so early. Maybe I can help you set up for the other guests."

"Ah, well. Yes." He smiles and looks away. "That's a bit of a point. But why don't you step inside out of the cold." I take his hand, climbing down into the warm hull of the boat.

Inside it's exactly like a narrow little house. There's a galley kitchen which leads into a bright, surprisingly generous living room and a door beyond which (I assume) goes through to a bedroom at the front. The living room is charming. Its walls are lined with books and stacks upon stacks of sheet music.

Against one wall there's an upright piano, piled with even more music. The floors are layered with worn Oriental carpets. More of his vast collection of CDs are stacked against the windowsill, massed on top of books, heaped in piles on every conceivable surface. The only clear area to be found in the whole room is a small, round mahogany table. There, elegantly arranged, is a luncheon set for two.

"Oh!" I stare at the table in surprise. "Is that for me? For us, I mean."

He smiles shyly. "If you'll stay."

I can't quite get my head around what's happening. "So, no one else is coming to your party?"

"No, Louise. Just you. I hope you don't mind."

"I see." I sit down on the arm of the sofa. "Just me."

He nods.

I don't want to say it, but I feel I have to. I look down at my hands, at the space where my wedding band used to be. "Eddie, you do know how old I am, don't you? I'm thirty-three. That's nine years older than you are."

"Isn't that brilliant?" He smiles.

"But that's not all; I'm divorced. I haven't dated in years. I'm . . . I'm from Pittsburgh! I'm sorry if I in any way misled you into thinking that I was younger or . . . I don't know . . . different from how I am . . . you're an amazing person and I admire you so, so much . . ."

He stops me there. "Are you breaking up with me? We haven't even gone out yet."

In the pit of my stomach a hollow, hopeless loneliness begins to grow . . . a pounding, dull familiar feeling.

"No, I didn't mean to sound so arrogant . . . it's just that . . . I'm a little confused as to why you would even want to do a thing like this. I mean, I don't know who or what you think I am but I'm not . . . I'm . . ." My voice starts to falter. "It's just . . . I'm . . . potato."

He blinks at me. "I'm sorry, did you just say you were a potato?"

I nod. I cannot do this; suddenly I'm back in the Twentieth-Century Galleries, a bloated, sexless woman in her early thirties, dressed in a shapeless gray dress, staring longingly at a black and white world of unimaginable beauty and glamour. Eddie is more beautiful, more talented, more elegant than all the famous faces combined.

My throat is tight and my eyes stinging, suddenly welling up with tears. "Potato, Eddie, potato!"

There are no elegant potatoes.

"Take it easy, Louise." He moves closer. "What does that mean . . . what's potato?"

I stand up, desperate to leave. "Potato means I can't do this . . . potato means . . . I have to get out of here, that I'm sorry . . . I've got to go . . ."

He wraps his arms around me. "Is this a Pittsburgh thing? Come on, take it easy. There, there," he whispers.

He smells of flowers and warmth, just like he had that day we napped in each other's arms and everything inside me melts with an overwhelming longing to lose myself, to fall deeper and deeper into his embrace.

But it's too much.

You're being foolish, the voice in my head says over and over. This is wrong. And suddenly I'm drowning, from the inside out. I've lost sight of the shore and there's nothing but water on every side. I panic and push him away.

"I'm sorry Eddie, really I am." I bolt past him and clamber back to the safety of dry land.

He doesn't follow me.

And it isn't until I'm sitting in the back of the cab, crying, that I realize I'm still holding the video and the champagne.

∞

Colin and Ria are out when I get home. But a package has arrived for me from the States and is sitting on the dining room table.

It's a belated Christmas present from my mother. Neatly wrapped in gold paper and tied with a white silk bow. She's slipped a little card under the ribbon:

Hey Kiddo,

Found this in the loft the other day and thought of you. Do you remember?

You always did have a style all your own!

You have a lot of courage, Louise. I've always been proud of that.

Don't give up now. The best is yet to come.

Love you. xxxMom

I unwrap it.

And there, carefully preserved in layers of translucent tissue paper, is the cream-colored marabou jacket she bought me when I was twelve.

Z

❦

Zips

Zips are the beginning and the end. Every evening begins with a wife pleading for her husband to zip her up, which he does in a frustrated hurry. However, if she is lucky and smart, that same evening will end with him impatient to unzip her again!

"Eddie! Hello! Eddie!"

It's dark now and the wind is up, forming the water into choppy, black waves that slap against the side of the boat. A light is on inside but there's no music playing. Perhaps he's gone out, maybe even with someone else, and I'm too late.

"Eddie, are you in there? *Eddie!*"

But there's no reply. It occurs to me that he might even be in there, able to hear me, but just not willing to speak to me. Ever again.

I've ruined it.

There's nothing left for me to do. I turn and make my way back along the pier, head bent against the tremendous wind, struggling to press forward against the invisible hands that force me back. Everywhere moorings are straining, lamps and tackle swinging to and fro as if at any moment they might be whipped away into the night.

A great gust buffets me. Losing my footing, I lurch forward, stumble in the darkness, and fall. I land abruptly, as if
the ground's shot up and hit me in the face. I scrape my hands
as I throw them out to brace myself and my bag explodes as it
hits the earth, its contents rolling out in all directions.

Damn! I curse myself for changing my shoes, groping my
way like a blind man for the missing spare change, lipstick,
and keys. Stupid of me to come back in the first place. What
kind of idiot runs away from her date and then reemerges
several hours later and expects him to be at home, waiting
for her? My hair comes undone, dancing around my head,
making it almost impossible to see. Gathering what I can
find into my bag, I struggle to my feet and am brushing myself off when a man in a hooded coat walks towards me
through the gale.

"Are you all right? Have you got everything?" he calls.

I know this voice. We're standing face to face. "No, no I'm
not all right," I say. "Not at all."

He looks down at his shoes. The wind whips around us like
a thousand voices, filling the air with whispers.

"In fact, I've been extremely stupid and made a terrible
mistake," I continue.

For a long moment, he says nothing.

At last he looks up. His face is sad. "I can't be anything
other than what I am, Louise. If this is going to be a problem
for you, there's nothing I can do. It's up to you. I can't do or
say anything that will make you feel safe."

"Oh, Eddie! But I don't want to feel safe anymore! I was
wrong! Really, badly wrong!"

I reach out and bury my face into his chest, wrapping my
arms around him and holding him tight. "Please forgive me.
Even if you don't want to go out with me anymore . . . even if

you just want to be friends. I'd rather know you and have you be part of my life on any terms than none at all."

It seems I'm standing there for ages, holding him, before he wraps his arms around me too. We stand there, clinging to each other in the dark.

And then he picks me up and carries me home.

∞

"There's to be no more mention of potatoes ever again in our relationship." He kisses my shoulder, pulling me closer.

"No, never." I nuzzle my face into his chest.

"What does it mean, anyway?"

"Nothing. It's a code word. A get-out clause. It means it's time to leave." I kiss the back of his hand and his delicate, clever fingers one by one.

He withdraws them and leans back against the headboard, looking at me intently. "Parsnip," he whispers softly. "Parsnip, Louise Canova."

I laugh. "And what does that mean?"

"Stay." He kisses me softly on the lips. "Stay."

∞

Six months later, I'm unpacking my books, slipping them in beside all Eddie's CDs, when I happen upon an old friend of mine, a slim, gray volume entitled *Elegance*.

I sit down on the edge of the sofa and open it. The spine is worn, the cover frayed at the edges. The book collapses open to one of the early pages, which, perhaps fittingly enough, is headed:

Age

*There is a saying in France, "Elegance is the privilege of age" —
and, thank heaven, it is perfectly true. Between childhood, youth,
maturity, and old age, there are no particular birthdays on which
a woman automatically graduates from one to another. And she
generally retains her youth to the same degree that she retains the
same interests as young people.*

*One should, of course, defend oneself vigorously against the
attacks of extra pounds, wrinkles, and double chins, but it is a battle that should be undertaken philosophically, for even the most
skillful plastic surgery cannot recapture our youth. It is far better
to settle down without vain regrets to a life filled with the rewards
of past efforts and the joys that we at last have the means to give
to others, instead of sulking like little girls when we are far too old
to cast ourselves in such a childish role.*

*Elegance can be acquired only at the price of numerous errors
that are best remembered with good humour. And in the end, it's
in the moments when we forget ourselves entirely that we are at our
most beautiful.*

I close the book.

Here's the perfect home for it, between a biography of
Glenn Gould and a copy of Bach's *48 Preludes and Fugues.*

I like to think that Madame Dariaux would approve.

Acknowledgments

I'd like to thank my dear friends Maria and Gavin for their inspiration and encouragement, all the girls at the Tuesday night Wimpole Street Writers Workshop for teaching me how it's done, Jonny Geller, Lynne Drew, Meaghan Dowling, and the entire team at both HarperCollins/William Morrow and Curtis Brown for their support and vision. I'd also like to thank the London office of Wellington Management and Stephen McDermott in particular, who saved my manuscript from the ether more than once.

About the Author

Kathleen Tessaro is the author of *Elegance, Innocence, The Flirt, The Debutante, The Perfume Collector,* and *Rare Objects.* She lives in Pittsburgh, Pennsylvania, with her husband and son.

ALSO BY KATHLEEN TESSARO

RARE OBJECTS
Available in Paperback, E-book, and Digital Audio

"A beautifully written, thoroughly absorbing novel, full of rich
historical detail and intriguing characters."
—Hazel Gaynor, *New York Times* bestselling author
of *The Girl Who Came Home* and *A Memory of Violets*

THE PERFUME COLLECTOR
Available in Paperback, E-book, and Digital Audio

"Fragrance, fashion, and a puzzling bequest lead a 1950s British
socialite into a whirl of Parisian intrigue in Kathleen Tessaro's
The Perfume Collector." —*Good Housekeeping*

THE DEBUTANTE
Available in Paperback and E-book

"A melancholic, multigenerational romance makes the most of
a very tangled web. . . . Tessaro nudges this colorful story
of scandal, heartbreak, and second chances toward an
appropriately sweet conclusion." —*Publishers Weekly*

THE FLIRT
Available in Paperback and E-book

"Kathleen Tessaro writes beautifully and with great confidence."
—Marian Keyes

INNOCENCE
Available in Paperback

"Elegantly written and compelling."
—*Entertainment Weekly*